BRUTAL FORCE

THE APARTHEID WAR MACHINE

GAVIN CAWTHRA

INTERNATIONAL DEFENCE & AID FUND FOR SOUTHERN AFRICA
Canon Collins House, 64 Essex Road, London N1 8LR

May 1986

The International Defence and Aid Fund for Southern Africa is a humanitarian organisation which has worked consistently for peaceful and constructive solutions to the problems created by racial oppression in Southern Africa.

It sprang from Christian and humanist opposition to the evils and injustices of apartheid in South Africa. It is dedicated to the achievement of free, democratic, non-racial societies throughout Southern Africa.

The objects of the fund are:

(i) to aid, defend and rehabilitate the victims of unjust legislation and oppressive and arbitrary procedures;

(ii) to support their families and dependants;

(iii) to keep the conscience of the world alive to the issues at stake.

In accordance with these three objectives, the Fund distributes its humanitarian aid to the victims of racial injustice without any discrimination on grounds of race, colour, religious or political affiliation. The only criterion is that of genuine need.

Under its third objective, the Fund runs a comprehensive information service on affairs in Southern Africa. This includes visual documentation. It produces a regular news bulletin 'FOCUS on Political Repression in Southern Africa', and publishes pamphlets and books on all aspects of life in Southern Africa.

The Fund prides itself on the strict accuracy of all its information.

ISBN No. 0 904759 71 7 (paperback)
ISBN No. 0 904759 72 5 (hardback)

IDAF would like to thank the Committee on South African War Resistance (COSAWR) for assistance in the compilation of this book.

COSAWR (UK), B.M. Box 2190, London WC1N 3XX.

Printed by Shadowdean Ltd.

Contents

Part Two – Forces

6 STRUCTURE OF THE APARTHEID WAR MACHINE

Part Three – Operations

7 REGIONAL AGGRESSION

8 NAMIBIA: OCCUPATION AND LIBERATION WAR

9 THE BATTLE FOR SOUTH AFRICA

DIAGRAMS

MAPS

Abbreviations Used in This Book

ANC	African National Congress of South Africa
APC	Armoured Personnel Carrier
AWOL	Absent Without Leave
Armscor	Armaments Development and Production Corporation
BDF	Bophuthatswana Defence Force *or* Botswana Defence Force
BOSS	Bureau of State Security
CIA	Central Intelligence Agency (United States)
COIN	Counter-Insurgency
COIN Unit	Counter-Insurgency Unit of the South West Africa Police (*Koevoet*)
CSIR	Council for Scientific and Industrial Research
DMI	Department of Military Intelligence
DONS	Department of National Security
DTA	Democratic Turnhalle Alliance
ECC	End Conscription Campaign
Escom	Electricity Supply Commission
FAPLA	People's Armed Forces for the Liberation of Angola
FNLA	National Front for the Liberation of Angola
Frelimo	Mozambique Liberation Front
LLA	Lesotho Liberation Army
MARNET	Military Area Radio Network
MNR	Mozambique National Resistance
MPC	Multi-Party Conference
MPLA	People's Movement for the Liberation of Angola
NATO	North Atlantic Treaty Organisation
NIS	National Intelligence Service
PLAN	People's Liberation Army of Namibia
SAAF	South African Air Force
SABC	South African Broadcasting Corporation
SACC	South African Council of Churches
SADCC	Southern African Development Co-ordinating Conference
SADF	South African Defence Force
SAN	South African Navy
SAP	South African Police
SATO	South Atlantic Treaty Organisation
SIPRI	Swedish International Peace Research Institute
SRC	Space Research Corporation
SSC	State Security Council
SWANU	South West African National Union
SWAP	South West African Police
SWAPO	South West African People's Organisation
SWATF	South West African Territorial Force
TDF	Transkei Defence Force
UDF	United Democratic Front *or* Union Defence Force
UPA	Union of the Peoples of Angola
UNITA	National Union for the Total Independence of Angola
VDF	Venda Defence Force

PREFACE

This book provides a comprehensive analysis of the apartheid armed forces. It shows how they have been systematically developed for deployment against the black majority in Southern Africa, in an attempt to prevent the advance of the struggle in Namibia and South Africa and to reverse the gains made by the newly independent African states.

It explains the process of rapid militarisation over the last 25 years and shows how, at every turn, the apartheid regime has responded to growing demands for freedom by expanding the SADF and unleashing greater repression and violence against the peoples of Southern Africa.

Events during the last two years have once again demonstrated how the apartheid regime can only survive by violence.

This book is based on extensive research, drawing on a wide range of sources, and is comprehensively documented and referenced. The factual information contained in it helps unravel some of the myths peddled by Pretoria regarding the nature and strength of its military forces, and which are believed so easily in some quarters. The book shows that, despite serious limitations, the arms embargo is making an impact; that the apartheid regime is *not* self-sufficient in arms; that its military and nuclear capability is the direct result of long and extensive western collaboration; and that it constitutes a grave threat to regional and international peace.

In order to defend the apartheid system internally the regime has been forced to draw into the front line its 'last line of defence', namely the South African Defence Force (SADF). This demonstrates both the growing success of the liberation struggle and the sheer desperation of the regime. The South African and Namibian people have through their own courageous struggle – against enormous odds – effectively challenged the apartheid regime.

While it is vital not to exaggerate South Africa's military and nuclear weapons capability, it is also dangerous to under-estimate it. It is in this

1

context that this book makes a valuable contribution in enabling one to better understand the unfolding events in Southern Africa and their international implications. It contains detailed information about the apartheid armed forces and their structure, and explains the predominant role of the military in the decision-making process of the regime. It also covers the operation of the arms embargo and other measures adopted by the international community to end all external military and nuclear collaboration with South Africa.

The major Western powers have so far blocked all meaningful measures and are helping to extend the life-span of the apartheid system despite the enormous human and material costs suffered by the African people. The most shameful and criminal aspect of such collaboration is the provision of military and nuclear resources to a dangerous and desperate regime. The need for effective action has never been greater and time is short.

ABDUL S. MINTY
Director, World Campaign Against Military and Nuclear Collaboration with South Africa.

INTRODUCTION

Southern Africa has become a battleground. To maintain itself in power the apartheid regime has engaged in a massive process of militarisation. This has equipped it to continue its illegal occupation of Namibia, to extend its hold over the region by attacking other states, and to deploy military and police forces in order to suppress resistance in South Africa itself.

Tens of thousands of people in Southern Africa have been killed as a result of apartheid aggression or the deployment of surrogate military forces in campaigns of destabilisation. Newly independent Angola, Mozambique and Zimbabwe, as well as the other countries of Southern Africa, have suffered incalculable material damage, and have had to divert large proportions of their state budgets towards defending themselves from attacks.

In Namibia, the South African regime has installed an army of occupation with an estimated one hundred thousand troops under its command. It has placed much of the country under a form of martial law and subjected the Namibian people to a reign of terror.

The South African state has become militarised, with the military establishment assuming an active role in the formulation of state policy and strategy. The white population has been subjected to a wide-ranging process of militarisation. This has involved the conscription of large numbers of white men and mobilisation for a protracted war in defence of white minority rule.

The South African Defence Force (SADF), the strongest in sub-Saharan Africa, deploys nearly two hundred thousand troops on a daily basis, and can mobilise double that number through the call-up of reserves. This war machine, equipped with hundreds of armoured cars, tanks, military aircraft and troop carriers, is backed by an extensive domestic arms industry, one of the largest industrial concerns in the country.

Over the past decade the apartheid war machine has been largely directed towards the occupation of Namibia and attacks on other countries in the region. But the South African regime has increasingly concentrated on building up facilities to fight an 'area war' inside South Africa. The armed forces have been deployed in urban areas to suppress popular resistance against apartheid rule. Over the past ten years the army has been gradually moved into a front-line role against the black population of South Africa, suppressing strikes, demonstrations and boycotts, patrolling townships, and carrying out extensive urban and rural operations.

Apartheid has been recognised as a threat to peace by the United Nations (UN), which in 1977 imposed a mandatory arms embargo against Pretoria. The UN has also recognised the right of the South African and Namibian liberation movements, the African National Congress (ANC) and the South West African People's Organisation (SWAPO), to take up arms to end apartheid and white minority rule. Despite the efforts of the South African regime to destroy the liberation movements, to repress popular resistance inside South Africa and to coerce neighbouring states into acquiescence, it has faced unprecedented pressures since the uprising which began in June 1976 in Soweto.

This book examines the strength, deployment and strategies of the SADF, its war in Namibia and against neighbouring countries and its war against the people of South Africa. Part 1 deals with the strategy of the apartheid regime, tracing its historical development and analysing its present context. In Part 2, the forces at the disposal of the regime are examined and the mobilisation for war described. Part 3 details the SADF's operations and deployments in Namibia, against independent Southern African countries and inside South Africa.

PART ONE – STRATEGY

1. RULE OF THE GUN

In the history of white rule over Southern Africa, the gun has played a prominent part. In almost every struggle between white colonialism or minority rule and black resistance, armed force has figured as a decisive factor.

The Role of the Military Until the 1950s

Many of the issues dealt with in this book have their roots in the armed conflicts of Southern Africa's past. The debate amongst whites over whether to incorporate black people into the armed forces, for example, began in the eighteenth century.[1] The commando militia system, which forms the basis of Pretoria's 'Area Defence' system today, can similarly be traced back to the early days of white settlement in the Cape. The use of troops to put down resistance in black areas; the exercise of executive power by 'soldier politicians'; guerilla warfare; national service – all these issues occur and re-occur over long periods of Southern African history.

Early Conflicts

The early history of Southern Africa after the arrival of white settlers in the mid-seventeenth century was characterised by campaigns of conquest and dispossession as white rule over the sub-continent was consolidated. For two and a half centuries the settlers slowly advanced. Fragile truces between the settlers and the inhabitants of the area soon broke down as the settlers' hunger for land grew.

Resistance was fierce. African society was well organised and prosperous, but the African armies were finally overwhelmed by superior European firepower. The turning-point came in 1806, when the British captured the Cape from the Dutch and began a series of campaigns to break the back of African resistance. By the end of the nineteenth century, armed opposition to settler expansion had been virtually eliminated.

The settlers themselves were far from united. Dutch farmers – Boers – had trekked inland to establish the independent republics of the Transvaal and the Orange Free State; the British maintained colonial control over the Cape and Natal.

The discovery of diamonds and gold led to new conflicts. The British provoked a war with the Boer republics to ensure their control over the mineral wealth of Southern Africa.

The Anglo–Boer War, 1898–1902, was fought between armies representing opposing forms of military and social organisation. The Boer armies were organised into commando formations which had their roots in the early history of white settlement. Since 1659 settlers in the Cape had been expected to bear arms in support of the regular forces, and a system of civilian militias became a feature of settler society. The commandos were the cornerstone of both civil and military organisation in the Boer republics, and virtually every farmer was expected, at his own cost, to be able to turn out with his horse and gun for commando duties. No distinction was made between police and military tasks. By contrast, the British forces were organised around the model of a professional standing army, with a complex organisation and a rigid hierarchy.[2]

Unified White Rule
The British victory over the Boer republics in 1902 led to the abolition of the commandos. A police force, the South African Constabulary, was set up, and military authority passed into the hands of the Imperial Army.

The establishment of the Union of South Africa in 1910 enshrined the principle of united white rule over the entire territory. In 1912 the Union Defence Force (UDF) was formed. Just as the Union of 1910 laid the basis for the modern apartheid state on the foundation of colonial conquest, so the basic structures of the South African Defence Force as it is today were established in the UDF.

The UDF represented something of a compromise between the two opposing forms of military organisation, incorporating both a standing army and a modified commando system. British professional units like the Cape Mounted Rifles were incorporated into a small (2,500-man) Permanent Force, but the bulk of the UDF consisted of part-time volunteers or conscripts involved in Citizen Force regiments or Rifle Associations *(skietverenigings)*. These latter bodies were not unlike the old commandos in that they relied on 'the farmer with his gun' *(die boer met sy roer)*. Although their powers were substantially diminished, they were free to make their own rules and elect their own officers. As a further compromise to Afrikaner sentiment, the Defence Act specifically limited compulsory service to 'South Africa', but as this meant 'within or outside the Union' the question of the geographic limitation of the term was left open to interpretation. This clause effectively silenced Afrikaners who were raising the spectre of forcible service for the British Crown in its imperial wars in other parts of the world.[3]

Exactly why Afrikaner and English were willing to serve in the same Defence Force only a decade after a war in which they were fighting each other was made clear in an article in a British publication, *The Cavalry Journal*, at the time of the unification:

The question of defence can never become an insignificant one in South Africa, for the enormously preponderating native population forbids neglect of military forces, and there is a very considerable proportion of [white] South Africans who . . . . are absolutely convinced that a great native rising is only a matter of time.[4]

This factor apart, the British were keen to set up a South African military force that could play a role in the overall defence of the Empire, while many Afrikaners supported the establishment of a South African force in order to get rid of the Imperial troops. In fact, a British garrison remained in the country until 1921, and the Royal Navy remained solely responsible for the defence of the coast and sea routes until 1922. In general, British influence over the armed forces remained a dominant factor until 1948.[5]

The first major mobilisation of the UDF was neither to suppress an armed African uprising nor to take part in the defence of the British Empire. In 1913 Indian, African and white workers in various parts of the country initiated a number of strikes in support of various demands. In Natal 140,000 Indian workers went on strike, and on the Rand 180,000 white gold-miners struck. The government mobilised the British garrison and the police as well as sections of the new army to crush the strikes.[6]

In January 1914 the white labour federation declared a general strike in protest at wage cuts, retrenchments and working conditions. The strike was most effective amongst the Rand gold-miners. The government proclaimed martial law and mobilised tens of thousands of troops, including the Afrikaner-dominated Rifle Associations led by the Boer Generals, Beyers and de la Rey. Thousands of troops entered Johannesburg, the strike headquarters at the trades hall was surrounded and the entire executive of the labour federation arrested. The strike was swiftly crushed by this show of force.[7]

The First World War

Britain's declaration of war on Germany in 1914 included South Africa as part of the Empire. Many Afrikaners either supported Germany or wished to remain neutral. The Union government's decision to mount an immediate invasion of South West Africa, then a German colony, provoked an Afrikaner rebellion. Generals Beyers and de la Rey mustered between six and eleven thousand men for a general insurrection. The government, which was able to put some thirty thousand armed men into the field, easily crushed the Afrikaner resistance and sought to defuse the situation through a policy of immunity for the rebels. The army was then able to turn on

7

German South West Africa, which was invaded and occupied with minimum losses by July 1915. Afrikaner resentment simmered on and as the war progressed recruitment became more difficult.[8]

Many black South Africans took part in the First World War. Perceiving an opportunity for social and political progress, some thirteen thousand Coloured men volunteered for service within a month of the outbreak of hostilities. Eventually tens of thousands of African, Coloured and Indian men were recruited for the war effort. Except in the case of a limited number of Coloured men, the military and political authorities insisted on restricting blacks to non-combat roles, using them mainly as labourers and in service capacities. Nevertheless, more than five thousand blacks died serving with South African units fighting in France, East Africa and South West Africa.[9]

Suppressing Resistance

Blacks who had given their services in the war received scant reward afterwards and their participation did not lead to any significant concessions from the government.

In 1921 a heavily armed column of police carried out a massacre at Bulhoek in the Eastern Cape, when nearly two hundred members of a religious community were killed after they refused to be moved from the land they were occupying. The army was increasingly used in support of the police to put down black resistance, particularly in occupied South West Africa, where African military power had not been entirely destroyed. In 1922 the Bondelswart community in South West Africa revolted over the imposition of a dog-tax which threatened their livelihood as herders. The poorly armed Bondelswarts – only one in four of whom had a rifle – were bombed and machine-gunned into submission by the army.[10]

In the opening months of 1922 a pattern of events similar to those of 1913–14 developed on the Rand. In the midst of an economic recession, white mineworkers called a strike to protest at the mineowners' attempts to undercut their wages by employing black workers at a cheaper rate and to impose compulsory redundancies. The strike was based on a loose alliance of Afrikaner nationalists – who still dreamed of establishing an independent republic in the Transvaal – and socialists who attempted to shift the emphasis away from racist demands. The protest soon turned into an insurrection as strikers raided police stations for weapons and attacked government buildings. Once again the superior fire power of the government forces under the Prime Minister, General Smuts, won the day. The strikers were blasted out of their strongholds at Benoni, Boksburg, Brixton and Langlaagte by a combination of artillery, bombing and tank attacks. Between 230 and 250 lives were lost.[11]

During the 1920s the UDF was strengthened by the establishment of an air force and navy. In 1919, the Imperial British government made a gift of a hundred aircraft to the Smuts government, and four years later the air force was formally inaugurated as a unit of the Permanent Force. Most of the air force's time and energy was absorbed in training pilots to take over from seconded British personnel.[12]

The nucleus of the navy, a Seaward Defence Force, was set up in 1922, but before it could be properly developed the world recession set in. In 1934 it was abolished, to be re-established only in 1946. In 1921 the Royal Navy had secured the use of the Simonstown base near Cape Town and from then until 1975 the Royal Navy maintained a permanent presence on the South African coast.[13]

In the decade before the onset of the Second World War the South African armed forces declined in strength as financial cuts were made to offset the effects of the Depression. With the establishment of a Special Services Battalion in 1933 an attempt was made to use military recruitment as a means of alleviating white poverty and unemployment, but even this was not carried through to any substantial degree.

The Second World War

The outbreak of war in 1939 caught the South African government badly prepared, and the old Afrikaner–English divisions resurfaced. The cabinet and parliament split on whether to support Britain or remain neutral, but a decision to join the allies was taken by 80 votes to 67 in parliament. The Prime Minister, General Hertzog, who was in favour of neutrality, resigned and General Smuts assumed the Prime Ministership for the second time.

Afrikaners opposed to service for the allies raised the old issue of whether South African troops were legally entitled to serve outside the Union boundaries. Smuts argued that the term 'South Africa' in the Defence Act referred to all Africa south of the equator:

> The line of the Limpopo [River] cannot be held . . . . Our northern boundary cannot be held. If you want to defend this country you will have to proceed a great distance beyond it. Those who know this continent know that the proper line of defence is in the highlands of Kenya . . . .[14]

There was no conscription during the war, for fear of Afrikaner resistance, but a massive white recruiting drive took place. Those volunteering were encouraged to take an oath pledging them to bear allegiance to King George VI and to 'serve anywhere in Africa'. This oath was a source of considerable conflict in the Afrikaner community. Later, after 1943, the oath was altered to provide for service 'anywhere', enabling South African volunteers to serve in East Africa, North Africa, Madagascar and eventually in Italy.[15]

Black South Africans volunteered in their thousands. Despite an official policy that they should remain in non-combatant roles, many took an active part in the fighting. Some black political leaders were more guarded in their support, having learnt from the experiences of the First World War that participation in the conflict would not necessarily lead to any improvement in their position.[16]

The attitude of the government to the use of blacks in the war effort fluctuated with the fortunes of the allied armies. In early 1942, when it seemed that a Japanese attack on South Africa was imminent, Smuts declared that he would 'train and arm any non-European prepared to help defend South Africa'. As the situation improved, he reversed his position. Nearly 40 per cent of South African field strength during the war was black – a cumulative total of some 122,000 men. As the war progressed blacks serving in the UDF began to chafe against their inferior treatment, and mutinies were reported.[17]

The war years naturally led to a tremendous expansion of the UDF in both men and equipment, and the strengthening of relations with the British armed forces and those of other allied countries. The air force and navy were considerably expanded, and by 1946 the latter was considered strong enough to be formally constituted as a separate wing of the services.

The war period accelerated social and political changes in South Africa. Many Afrikaners – including the future Prime Minister, B J Vorster – finally broke with the Smuts government, openly supported the Nazis, and were interned. On the other hand, many white soldiers in the South African forces came to adopt more liberal attitudes as a result of their exposure to conditions in other countries and their participation in a war that was fought in the name of democracy and human equality. This liberalisation was reflected in the soldiers' and ex-service organisations, the Springbok Legion and the Torch Commando. After the war these organisations fought a rearguard action against the apartheid policies of the Nationalists and campaigned against the disenfranchisement of the Coloured community in the Cape.

The number of Africans employed in manufacturing rose by 57 per cent during the six years of war, an increase only partly attributable to the rapid establishment of an arms industry (which was almost entirely dismantled after 1945). Under the war economy the trade union movement grew tremendously among both black and white workers, but the African working class faced ruthless repression under various War Measures Acts.[18] The government did not hesitate to use force of arms to put down black resistance during the war years. On at least one occasion – during a strike by council workers in Pretoria – the army was called out. Fourteen demonstrating strikers were killed and over a hundred wounded.[19]

Apartheid and Resistance

The Nationalist government which came into power in 1948 used progressively more draconian methods to intensify the oppression of black South Africans by strengthening the pass laws, tightening residential segregation, closing the doors to African advancement on the factory floor, and suppressing the national liberation struggle. The Nationalists were also concerned with advancing the relatively disadvantaged Afrikaner workers, farmers and small businessmen. For centuries the Afrikaners felt themselves to be oppressed by the British and by English-speaking white South Africans. Afrikaners were worse off in industry and commerce, while the state remained largely a preserve of the English-speaking whites.

The Search for Alliances
The new regime soon turned its attention to the armed forces, where concerted attempts were made to replace the predominantly English speaking officers with Afrikaners.

This 'nationalisation' of the forces was not paralleled in the international arena, however. The steps taken to remove British influence over the armed forces did not imply a removal of the Union from the British sphere of influence.

The South African government had achieved a high level of integration with the Western powers during the Second World War and General Smuts played a leading role in establishing institutions like the UN. The new Nationalist regime wished to consolidate the position of South Africa in the Western world order. It was also alarmed at the accelerating drive towards national independence in the Third World, particularly on the African continent. It was determined to enter into a defence alliance and to draw the Western powers into a commitment to uphold white rule in South Africa, if not in Africa as a whole.[20]

Initially the South African regime made approaches to join the North Atlantic Treaty Organisation (NATO). As South African membership would have fundamentally altered the character of the organisation and opened up a hornet's nest of political problems, Pretoria's overtures were rebuffed, largely as a result of opposition by the United States.

The South African government then pushed for the establishment of an African defence alliance, both to check the advance of African nationalism and to uphold Smuts' strategic dictum that the best line for the defence of South Africa lay as far north as Kenya. To satisfy anti-British feeling amongst Afrikaners, this alliance was envisaged as a multilateral one between the European-controlled African countries and the various European powers. The United States would also be involved through its connections with Liberia.[21]

This idea did not get off the ground. Western policy immediately after the war was generally in favour of the process of decolonisation and newly independent countries like India put up strong resistance to international alliances with apartheid South Africa. Furthermore, Britain was reluctant to allow South Africa into multilateral arrangements which might weaken its ties to the Commonwealth.

Having failed to establish an African pact, Pretoria willingly accepted a provisional invitation by Britain to join the Middle East Defence

Organisation (MEDO), but South African participation in this alliance was prevented by the opposition of Third World countries. The regime nevertheless purchased Centurion tanks and Canberra aircraft from Britain as evidence of its willingness to support Western military campaigns. These purchases were the first major arms acquisitions by the regime for a number of years, and they marked an initial spurt in a massive military expansion that was to take place in the 1960s and 1970s.[22]

Pretoria's desire to involve itself in NATO or a similar alliance, and the West's partial acceptance of this aim, was underscored by its participation in the Berlin airlift of 1948–49 and the Korean war in the early 1950s. A squadron of South African fighters and some ground forces participated in the Korean conflict. In the last year of the war, 1952/53, South African pilots flew new American Sabre jet fighters, on loan from the US Air Force. Shortly thereafter 36 Sabres from Canada were delivered to South Africa.[23]

By the mid-1950s, it was evident that the face of the world was changing at a rate far more rapid than the South African regime had envisaged and that much of Africa would soon be independent. Internally the regime was facing the strongest challenge to white supremacy since the defeat of the African armies at the end of the nineteenth century. The ANC and its allies were engaged in a nationwide campaign of passive resistance that was being ruthlessly dealt with by the police. This conflict was fuelling growing international condemnation of apartheid, led by India and other newly independent countries.

The Simonstown agreement with Britain in 1955, which provided for joint use of the naval base at Simonstown, was the only concrete result of the apartheid regime's search for a formal defence alliance. This agreement – which was terminated only in the mid-1970s – provided the regime with something of a lifeline when international opinion against apartheid began to harden in the 1960s, legitimising the purchase from Britain of sophisticated naval and air force equipment.[24] However, South Africa's withdrawal from the British Commonwealth when it became a republic in 1961, further increased its international isolation.

1950s — Decade of Defiance
Throughout the 1950s, the Pretoria regime appeared to be confident that its external military needs would in the long run be satisfied through a multilateral defence pact with the Western powers. The expansion of the army was not a priority. Nor was it perceived to have a major internal role at the time, although it was always made clear that the threat of a 'native rising' remained, as in 1910, the primary motivation for a strong military force.

In general, the police were left to deal with internal threats to the regime during this period. Between 1952 and 1958 the government authorised a 50 per cent increase in the manpower strength of the police.[25] Police powers grew with the establishment of a pantheon of repressive laws. Most of these laws were introduced in the 1960s, but the first of them, the Suppression of Communism Act, which forced the South African Communist Party underground, was introduced in 1950.

During the Defiance Campaign of 1952–53, when the ANC led a nationwide defiance of apartheid laws, over eight thousand people were arrested. In 1956 leaders of the Congress Movement were put on trial for treason. Two years later, after the Congress Movement had organised a general strike on the eve of parliamentary elections, the army was placed on alert – an indication that if the police failed to suppress resistance, the military was ready to step in.[26]

Throughout this period the SADF was being slowly but systematically reorganised and upgraded, especially with regard to its internal role. In 1957, in response to the rising tide of black resistance, and as part of the Nationalist programme to prepare for an all-white republic, a new Defence Act was introduced. To mark the success of the 'nationalisation' process the term 'Union' was dropped and the military force was renamed the South African Defence Force. A selective ballot system of compulsory military service for white males was expanded and gymnasiums and a military academy were established to train an officer corps. The old commandos were fully incorporated into the SADF and South African decorations, uniforms and insignia were introduced.[27]

The overall structure of the SADF as it is today was thus established in 1957: a core Permanent Force, and a Citizen Force consisting of National Servicemen undergoing initial military service and part-timers called up for varying periods each year.

Sharpeville and Armed Struggle
On 21 March 1960, the day on which 69 Africans were killed by police in the Sharpeville massacre, the Minister of Defence, J J Fouche, described the changes that the Nationalist government had been bringing about in the armed forces since the mid–1950s:

It is the. . . defence policy of the Union first of all to concentrate its defence organisations upon the implementation of internal security tasks . . . The task of the Army and the Air Force is to take action for internal security as soon as disturbances have reached a degree where the Police are unable to control them. The reorganisation which was started some years ago, has been completed and the changes are starting to take shape. Greater mobility, armoured protection and increased striking power in the form of Saracens [British-supplied armoured cars], have been given to twelve of the infantry units at strategic places. These Citizen Force units, together with the two Mobile Watches which have been organised as Saracen squadrons for the maintenance of internal security, form a shock element in the Army. . . .

13

Beside these two Watches and the units of the Citizen Force, the Commandos have been reorganised over the past two years in order to ensure that they will be able to act more efficiently for internal security. . .

During the past four years internal security has received considerable attention in the curricula of the SADF. One large-scale manoeuvre, Operation Outeniqua and various small-scale manoeuvres were held. . . . The Air Force, which also has a particular task in respect of internal security, has been organised to hold on the ground support units in a continuous state of readiness. . . [28]

Whether Fouche foresaw that his warnings of army mobilisation would be implemented only a week later is not known; certainly, his words indicate that the apartheid regime was preparing for what Nelson Mandela warned was rapidly becoming a civil war.[29]

As Fouche spoke, the police were opening fire on an anti-pass demonstration at Sharpeville organised by the Pan-Africanist Congress (PAC), a breakaway from the ANC. In the following days, mass demonstrations spread through the country, and on 24 March the government banned all meetings of black people.

The ANC organised an overwhelmingly successful national strike or stayaway on 28 March, as a demonstration of protest and mourning. On the same day the government introduced a bill which would be used to ban the ANC and PAC. Hundreds of leaders of the national liberation movement were arrested.[30]

On 30 March the government declared a State of Emergency. The order was given for the partial mobilisation of the SADF. All Citizen Force and Reserve troops, as well as the Commandos, were put on stand-by.[31] In Cape Town a crowd of thirty thousand marched from the townships of Langa and Nyanga on police headquarters to demand the release of detained leaders. They were dispersed by police, and that evening thousands of troops, sailors and police cordoned off the townships, preventing all movement in and out of the area. The cordons were retained until 8 April, by which time hundreds of Africans had been arrested.[32] Troops and armoured cars were also deployed around the Houses of Parliament in Cape Town. (One of the units was led by Magnus Malan, then a captain, who was to become Minister of Defence under P W Botha.)[33]

Similar though smaller protests took place in Johannesburg, Germiston, Port Elizabeth, East London, Bloemfontein, Pietermaritzburg, Durban, and smaller centres such as Stellenbosch and Beaufort West. In Durban, army units assisted the police in surrounding and searching a hostel near Lamontville. Troops were widely deployed to protect strategic installations.[34] Several black people were killed during these operations, and over eleven thousand people arrested under emergency regulations.[35]

The rising tide of black resistance was not limited to the urban areas.

Between 1959 and 1961 serious 'disturbances' occurred in a number of rural areas, particularly in the eastern districts of the Transkei bantustan, where peasants revolted against the apartheid authorities and the land distribution system. The revolt was suppressed through the introduction of emergency legislation which extended sweeping powers to the police and local officials. In one of the most serious clashes, on 6 June 1960, eleven people were killed by the police near Lusikisiki. Aircraft and a helicopter from the South African Air Force were reported to have dropped teargas and smoke-bombs on a crowd confronting the police.[36] Later that year heavily armed Permanent Force units were moved into the Pondoland area of the Transkei to put down the simmering rebellion.[37]

On 8 April 1960 legislation banning both the ANC and PAC came into force, closing the door on fifty years of peaceful struggle by the national liberation movement. Despite the arrest of many of their colleagues, leaders such as Nelson Mandela went underground, continuing to organise mass protests and demonstrations and laying the basis for an armed struggle.

The establishment of the white republic at the end of May 1961 was preceded by a ban on meetings and a massive military mobilisation. Troops and armoured cars sealed off black townships and police carried out thousands of arrests. The country entered its 'new era' in a state of siege.

On 16 December 1961 Umkhonto we Sizwe, an underground organisation established by ANC leaders, began a campaign of sabotage. A leaflet distributed by the organisation declared:

> The time comes in the life of any nation when there remain only two choices: submit or fight. That time has now come to South Africa. We shall not submit and we have no choice but to hit back by all means within our power in defence of our people, our future and our freedom . . .
>
> We are striking out along a new road for the liberation of the people of this country. The Government policy of force, repression and violence will no longer be met with non-violent resistance only! The choice is not ours; it has been made by the Nationalist Government which has rejected every peaceable demand by the people for rights and freedom and answered every such demand with force and yet more force![38]

Over the following two years there were over two hundred sabotage operations, virtually all of them directed at strategic and economic targets. Throughout this period Umkhonto took pains to avoid loss of life – consistent with its policy of trying to force a change in government policy. No such change was forthcoming. The South African regime responded to the challenge of armed struggle by intensifying its repression, expanding the scope of the security laws and vastly increasing the powers of the police. These repressive measures were initially effective. Within a few years the

15

leadership of Umkhonto we Sizwe – Nelson Mandela, Walter Sisulu, Govan Mbeki, Ahmed Kathrada, Dennis Goldberg – was sentenced to life imprisonment, and many of the remaining members withdrew into exile to prepare for a more organised form of guerilla warfare.

The Military Strategy of the 1960s

The suppression of the armed struggle during the 1960s was handled in the main by the police Security Branch, with limited involvement by the Department of Military Intelligence. However, the regime embarked on a massive military expansion drive. Between 1960 and 1964 the Permanent Force grew from 9,000 to 15,000 and the number of National Servicemen in training increased almost tenfold to 20,000. With the police and Commandos, the regime could field a force of 120,000.[39] This expansion in manpower was matched by a boom in defence expenditure, which soared from R44 million in 1960 to R210 million in 1964.[40] The growth in military expenditure took place during an unprecedented expansion in the apartheid economy, which during the 1960s grew at a rate second only to that of Japan.

Arms for Apartheid

The expansion drive was hindered by a UN arms embargo imposed in 1963 as a result of world outrage at the Sharpeville massacre. However, the embargo was not binding on member states. Although Britain, the regime's traditional arms supplier, partially embargoed deliveries after 1964, France stepped into the breach, followed closely by Italy. By the end of the 1960s Pretoria was fielding modern French armoured cars, jet aircraft, helicopters and missile systems. British frigates and French submarines had strengthened the navy, the air force had been equipped with Italian Aermacchi 'Impalas' as well as French Mirages, and the army was resupplied with rifles, machine-guns, mortars and artillery systems, all of which were then standard equipment in many NATO armies.[41]

Much of this equipment was assembled in South Africa from imported parts and components, mainly on the basis of licensing arrangements with French, Italian and Belgian companies. The domestic manufacture of teargas, napalm and ammunition also began with the assistance of mainly British-based companies. In 1968 the South African armaments manufacturing concern, Armscor, was established to co-ordinate arms production.[42] By the time a compulsory arms embargo was imposed in 1977, the South African regime had built up the most modern and effective war machine in sub-Saharan Africa, although this had been achieved with considerably more difficulty than would have been the case had the voluntary embargo of 1963 not been imposed.

A nuclear industry was also established. The nuclear process began with the mining of uranium in the 1950s, when South Africa received considerable assistance from the USA and Britain. During the 1960s, as a result of a deal with the US, a reactor, Safari 1, was acquired. At the opening of the facility Prime Minister Vorster declared that it was the 'duty' of the regime to consider both the peaceful and the military uses of the country's large uranium reserves. These reserves could be supplemented by the mining of Namibian uranium, although this was illegal in terms of UN decisions. Another reactor, Safari 2, which was not subject to international safeguards, was opened soon afterwards and the regime began to make plans for the domestic enrichment of uranium. Within twelve years it had equipped itself with the ability to make and deliver a nuclear weapon.[43]

Southern Africa – The Wars of Liberation

In 1961 and 1964 armed struggles were launched in Portuguese-controlled Angola and Mozambique by the newly formed liberation movements, the People's Movement for the Liberation of Angola (MPLA) and the Mozambique Liberation Front (Frelimo). There was no reason for Pretoria to question the short-term survival of Portuguese colonialism, but the armed struggle was a reminder that white minority rule in Africa was not guaranteed to last forever. Military ties with the Lisbon dictatorship were strengthened and the South African regime did everything in its power to assist the Portuguese forces. A thousand South African troops were reported to have been sent to Mozambique and in 1968 a joint Portuguese–South African command centre was established in Angola to direct air strikes against guerillas.[44]

Portugal committed ever greater numbers of troops and military resources to its colonial wars – by the early 1970s one hundred thousand troops were tied down in Angola and Mozambique. By then it was clear that the liberation movements had forced the Portuguese army into a situation that could at best be regarded as a stalemate, and social and political problems in the metropolitan centre were beginning to weaken the Lisbon dictatorship.[45]

A similar military stalemate was developing in Rhodesia. The Unilateral Declaration of Independence (UDI) from Britain by the Smith regime in 1965 led newly independent Zambia to offer the British government bases for an invasion of the country. The offer was not taken up. A long series of inconclusive diplomatic initiatives followed in which South Africa became increasingly involved. UDI and the British failure to act against the Smith regime proved to be the breaking-point for Zimbabwe's national liberation movement, which began an armed struggle in 1966. This provided an opportunity for external units of Umkhonto we Sizwe to advance towards South Africa through Rhodesia.

A unit of Umkhonto guerillas began an offensive with the Zimbabwe African People's Union (ZAPU) forces in the Zambezi valley in 1967, both to strike a blow against the common enemy of white racism and to move guerillas forward to within striking distance of South Africa.

The South African government rushed troops and police to Rhodesia to assist in the campaign against the guerilla forces of ZAPU and the Zimbabwe African National Union (ZANU). Eventually up to four thousand South African troops, supported by armoured cars and helicopters, were reported to be involved in the Rhodesian war. In 1975 South African police and army units were officially withdrawn from Rhodesia, but large numbers remained secretly.[46] South African support for the Rhodesian forces included the 'loan' of aircraft which were used for cross-border bombing attacks on Zambia and, later, Mozambique and the supply of almost all its military equipment, from ammunition to major weapons systems.[47] Throughout the war Pretoria refused to admit to deploying the SADF. Military personnel were either disguised as policemen or seconded to the Rhodesian forces and dressed in their uniforms.[48]

An alliance between South Africa, Rhodesia and Portugal came to dominate regional politics. South Africa's open support for the illegal regime in Rhodesia and its blatant violation of UN sanctions, which were imposed soon after UDI, further increased its international isolation and compounded its difficulties in reaching a closer defence alliance with Western countries. At the same time considerable diplomatic pressure was being brought to bear over Namibia, where the liberation movement SWAPO began an armed struggle in 1966.

Attempts to have Namibia formally incorporated as a fifth province of South Africa after the Second World War were rebuffed by the international community. In 1950 the International Court of Justice determined that Namibia should remain an international responsibility, although South Africa's right to administer the territory was upheld. Resisting attempts by the UN to intervene, Pretoria set about systematically extending its apartheid policies to Namibia. In the early 1960s Liberia and Ethiopia took Namibia's case to the International Court of Justice seeking a ruling that the apartheid regime's mandate be terminated. The Court decided in 1966 that it was unable to make a ruling, although the UN General Assembly shortly afterwards declared South Africa's occupation of the territory to be illegal.

In 1959 South African police and military units killed 11 Namibians and wounded 54 during a demonstration in Windhoek against the forced removal of the city's black population to a new segregated township, Katutura.[49] The massacre galvanised the Namibian people into forming the national liberation movement, SWAPO, which rapidly established a network of members throughout the country. Realising that diplomatic pressure alone would be unlikely to end the South African occupation of their country, SWAPO began to make preparations for an armed struggle.[50]

The failure of the International Court of Justice to deliver a judgement on the South African occupation met with a declaration from SWAPO's external headquarters in Tanzania that Namibians had 'no alternative but to rise in arms and bring about our liberation'.[50] A month later, on 26 August 1966, SWAPO forces clashed with a South African police unit at Omgulumbashe and the following month a guerilla unit destroyed an administrative complex. Guerillas also penetrated white farming areas around Grootfontein.[52]

Like their counterparts in Umkhonto we Sizwe, the SWAPO fighters faced considerable, although not quite as severe, logistical difficulties. Portuguese-occupied Angola was of little use as a rear base and the nearest transit facilities were in Zambia. In order to get to the populated areas of the country it was necessary for the guerillas to traverse hundreds of kilometres through the Caprivi Strip.

Pretoria responded to the guerilla threat by considerably strengthening its police Counter-Insurgency forces in the Caprivi Strip and extending South African security laws to the territory. The Terrorism Act was introduced specifically to suppress the Namibian struggle and 37 Namibians were imprisoned for long periods under this act in 1968. 'Strategic' or 'security' villages were established on the Okavango River, which forms the border with Zambia, and a curfew was imposed. Reprisals against the local inhabitants were carried out and interrogation and torture became common.[53]

The South African regime was initially reluctant to commit the SADF to operations in Namibia, as it was felt that this would further harden international opposition to the occupation of the territory. Instead increased counter-insurgency training was given to the police and they were provided with military equipment.[54] With the aid of the draconian 'security' laws and with a massive show of force in the north, the police were able to put down the first wave of armed resistance. Military forces were kept in reserve but their strength was increased. The introduction in 1967 of universal conscription for white male South Africans and Namibians (to replace the ballot system) was an indication of how seriously the regime regarded SWAPO's military initiative.

In 1971 SWAPO's years of political activity, which had been conducted at great risk, bore fruit. In June the International Court of Justice finally ruled South Africa's presence in Namibia to be illegal. A wave of demonstrations spread throughout Namibia. In December of that year 13,000 Namibian contract workers went on strike and were sent to the north, where their families lived. By intimidation and coercion the police attempted to break the strike. In the Ovambo bantustan, to where most of the strikers had been returned, demonstrations and organised protests developed. The occupation authorities responded by further repression and the banning of meetings.

In January 1972 the SADF was for the first time sent into Namibia with operational instructions to assist the police in 'restoring order'. On 4 February legislation amounting to martial law was imposed on the Ovambo bantustan – this was later extended to other areas of the country. Hundreds of people were rounded up by police and soldiers, held for months without trial and tortured. On the other side of the border, in Angola, the Portuguese also sent in heavily armed troops. By 1973 the SADF had taken over control from the South African Police (SAP) of all military operations in northern Namibia.[55] Hundreds of new recruits swelled the ranks of the SWAPO guerilla force, which in 1973 was renamed the People's Liberation Army of Namibia (PLAN). Attacks on South African occupation structures and army and police units increased.

Despite widening guerilla wars in Namibia, Zimbabwe and the Portuguese colonies, the South African regime believed that it had eliminated the principal threat in South Africa, the ANC. White political confidence was high and the apartheid economy was booming. As the 1960s unfolded the regime grew increasingly confident about its long-term survival. This confidence was reflected in a growing willingness to 'go it alone', to push South Africa into a position of unchallenged regional dominance.

The 'Outward' Policy

After South Africa left the British Commonwealth following the declaration of the republic in 1961, Prime Minister Verwoerd put forward the idea of an economic community of Southern African states which would be dominated by South Africa and Rhodesia. Over the years South Africa's economic influence over the region had been extended but Verwoerd was afraid to consolidate economic influence with political links.[56] John Vorster, who succeeded him in 1966, was more pragmatic. He perceived that the key to relations with the West lay in Africa. In 1967 his government launched an 'outward policy', initiated by an exchange of ambassadors with the government of Hastings Banda in Malawi, which received a massive loan to finance the construction of a new capital at Lilongwe.[57]

The 'outward policy' was to be built on a bedrock of 'trade and aid', for the purpose of which the regime made available a low-interest loan fund and renegotiated the customs union agreement with Botswana, Lesotho and Swaziland (formerly British Protectorates or High Commission Territories), making them more dependent on South Africa. Feelers were put out to certain African governments such as Côte d'Ivoire, but in the end little came of the 'outward policy'.

The African counter-attack came in the form of the 1969 Lusaka Manifesto in which thirteen African states, including Zambia and Tanzania, committed themselves to supporting the international campaign to isolate the white minority regime and called for support for the armed struggles in South Africa, Zimbabwe and Namibia. By 1974 Pretoria was admitting that the 'outward policy' had 'gone underground'.[58]

The apartheid regime's search for allies in Africa was paralleled by initiatives taken across the Atlantic, in Latin America. Here the aim was less to ensure the regime's strategic perimeters than to pursue its long-standing interest in an international defence alliance.

In May 1968 P W Botha revealed that South Africa had taken part in a secret international conference 'at service level' with a number of countries in the southern hemisphere.[59] The South African press speculated that contacts with Latin America would lead to the formation of a South Atlantic Treaty Organisation (SATO), to supplement the role of NATO. The *Star* of 12 April 1969 commented:

> It is as well to be thinking in terms of regional links across the Atlantic. They represent another facet of South Africa's promising 'outward' foreign policies. Ultimately they may – who knows? – help us to help the free world accept our friendship without embarrassment.

The article did note however that there were considerable political difficulties involved in a formal alliance.

The projected SATO foundered on the rocks of diplomacy, in the face of increasing pressure from the African lobby in the non-aligned movement and the UN. However, the idea has been periodically dusted off.

The apartheid regime's hopes for some form of incorporation into NATO were revived in the early 1970s. In 1972 a report by a military committee of the NATO Parliamentary Assembly called for South African participation in a South Atlantic/Indian Ocean defence arrangement. P W Botha, then Minister of Defence, announced: 'There are signs – encouraging signs – in the Free World that the position of South Africa and Southern Africa is better understood.'[60]

'War of Low Intensity'

The appointment of P W Botha as Defence Minister in 1966 ushered in a period of unprecedented military expansion, in which all arms of the SADF were modernised, upgraded and reorganised. By the end of 1972 the strength of the Permanent Force was estimated to be about 18,000.[61] An even more dramatic expansion occured in the Citizen Force where over 26,000 National Servicemen were undergoing basic training. The total number of troops under arms was estimated to be in excess of 45,000, to which could be added a further 75,000 men in the Commandos and 40,000 Citizen Force reservists.[62] The growth of the Citizen Force was partly the result of an increase in the length of National Service from nine months to twelve months, followed by nineteen days' service annually for five years.[63]

In 1973 Botha announced in a parliamentary White Paper that the military expansion had only just begun. The Commandos were being improved and the country's maritime capability and air force were being strengthened as part of a comprehensive ten-year development programme for all arms of service, he revealed.[64] Command structures had been reorganised and a new defence headquarters was under construction at Voortrekkerhoogte near Pretoria.[65]

P W Botha could rightly conclude that the SADF was in a strong position to prosecute its 'main task', that of ensuring that 'the government will have the time and freedom of action to develop its internal and foreign policies'.[66] Not that the SADF was complacent. Botha and his generals were well aware that there were a number of serious threats to white minority rule.

Despite government claims, it was clear that internal opposition had not been eliminated. The ANC was continuing to organise, recruit and disseminate propaganda underground and there were growing signs of rebellion amongst the urban youth. The economic boom was slowing down, and in 1973 the first major black labour strikes for more than a decade erupted. Internationally the regime had failed to make any significant breakthroughs. On the contrary, it had become, in Botha's words, 'the whipping boy on the international scene' and faced the prospect of further isolation.[67] In Rhodesia, Mozambique and Angola the guerilla liberation struggles were continuing to make slow but sure progress, gradually weakening the economies and morale of the colonial and minority regimes. In Namibia, SWAPO was presenting increasingly strong resistance in both military and political fields.

Noting these factors P W Botha warned:

> Ideological attacks on the Republic of South Africa are progressively being converted into more tangible action in the form of sanctions, boycotts, isolation, demonstrations and the like . . . [We have not] yet eliminated the [guerilla] threat. I do not wish to spread the alarm, but I must state unambiguously that for a long time already, we have been engaged in a war of low intensity and that this situation will probably continue for some considerable time to come.[68]

2. THE APARTHEID 'SECURITY' STRATEGY

Apartheid in Crisis

In April 1974, as white South Africa went to the polls to re-elect the Vorster government, a group of young Portuguese army officers was planning a coup in Lisbon that would change the face of Southern Africa.

The overthrow of the Caetano dictatorship by the Armed Forces Movement – to a large extent precipitated by the growing successes of the liberation movements in Angola, Mozambique and Guinea Bissau – set in motion a chain of events that rapidly led to the independence of Portugal's African colonies.

The apartheid regime had hardly recovered from the shock of the collapse of Portuguese colonialism when in 1976 South Africa was convulsed by a wave of student and worker demonstrations. The uprising started in Soweto on 16 June after a peaceful student protest against the inferior African education system had been met by police bullets. It soon escalated into a nationwide confrontation between the black population and the forces of the apartheid state.

The resurgence of mass political struggle in South Africa and the fundamental shift in the regional balance of power were catalysts that led the apartheid regime to adopt a 'National Security Doctrine'. At the time, this doctrine was articulated as a 'total strategy' to deal with what was perceived to be a 'total onslaught' against the white regime.

Regional Crisis

The 1974 Lisbon coup caught Pretoria totally unprepared. Barely a few days before the event the South African Broadcasting Company had proudly described Portugal and South Africa as the only two remaining stable states in the world.[1]

It was immediately clear that the apartheid regime could no longer rely on strategic buffers around South Africa and that Pretoria's remaining regional ally, Rhodesia, would be left dangerously exposed to the guerilla armies of the Zimbabwean liberation movements. The events in Portugal also lent impetus to African demands for the full decolonisation of the continent, and international pressures on the white minority regimes in Pretoria and Salisbury were mounting.

Prime Minister Vorster responded to the regional developments by re-launching his moribund 'outward policy', dressed up in a new label, 'détente', and with a stronger regional emphasis. The essential objective of 'détente' was to consolidate the regime's strategic position and to prevent it becoming still more isolated. Contact was made with a small number of pro-Western African countries, but the main concern was to set up an 'internal settlement' in Zimbabwe that would prevent the liberation forces from coming to power.

Realising that the Smith regime had no chance of long-term survival, the South African government exerted economic and political pressure on the Rhodesian government to reach a compromise agreement with the liberation movements, or at least to forge a credible multiracial government. Simultaneously pressure was put on President Kaunda of Zambia to bring the leaders of the liberation movements to the negotiating table. This effort finally died in August 1975 when talks at Victoria Falls collapsed.[2]

The events of 1974 also prompted the South African regime to launch a five-year military modernisation and expansion programme, necessitating a drastic increase in defence expenditure.[3] A significant organisational shake-up of the South African army's combat forces was initiated with the establishment of separate conventional and 'Special Forces' formations. The establishment of the heavily armed South African Corps significantly increased the army's conventional strike capability for attacks on neighbouring countries – 'to counter-attack or to take preventive action'.[4] The Special Forces consisted of secret unconventional units, the Reconnaissance Commandos, which would have the capacity for small-unit operations in neighbouring states.

Mozambique became independent under a Frelimo government in June 1975 without South African military interference, although Pretoria provided some assistance to members of the Portuguese secret police who attempted to stage a coup in Maputo.[5]

Independence in Angola was considerably delayed, presenting the South African regime with greater opportunities for military involvement. Covert support was given to the National Union for the Total Independence of Angola (UNITA) and the National Front for the Liberation of Angola (FNLA) movements – opponents of the principal liberation movement, the MPLA. After secret consultations with the USA, the South African government apparently set itself the objective of seizing the capital Luanda before the independence date, 11 November, with the aim of installing a client UNITA/FNLA regime. In August 1975 South African troops crossed into Angola from bases in occupied Namibia. Armoured car columns made rapid northward progress but ran into stiff resistance outside Luanda. With expected US and African support failing to materialise Pretoria felt unable to strengthen its forces, and they withdrew to positions just inside the Angola border, taking with them remnants of the FNLA and UNITA.[6]

The Angola venture was a major political setback for Vorster and his lieutenant, Hendrik van den Bergh, the head of the Bureau for State Security (BOSS). Both men badly miscalculated the extent to which the US could be relied on to support the operation. Although apparently initially opposed to the invasion, the SADF, once committed, wanted to see its task through. P W Botha as Minister of Defence felt that he had been let down by the political leadership and that with proper support the SADF could have taken Luanda.[7] The simmering conflict between the military hierarchy and the Vorster/van den Bergh leadership began to intensify.

South Africa's regional position was further weakened after the Angola débâcle by an escalation of SWAPO military activity in Namibia. Many of the South African troops retreating from Angola were redeployed in northern Namibia in an effort to halt the progress of SWAPO guerillas, who had broken out of the Caprivi Strip and opened a new front in the Ovambo bantustan. The number of South African troops in Namibia swelled from some 16,000 to over 50,000 during 1975 and 1976, and strings of new bases were established in the north. In 1976 SWAPO carried out three times as many military operations in Namibia as the total for the previous ten years. SWAPO guerillas also began to extend their operations into white farming areas to the south.[8]

The changing regional situation led Pretoria into a more energetic pursuit of closer ties with NATO and individual Western powers. Within a month of the Lisbon coup top cabinet officials were in Europe and the USA seeking assurances of Western support.

These approaches were not as successful as the regime would have hoped. Independent African countries were exerting greater pressure in the UN and elsewhere for the isolation of South Africa and Rhodesia. Pretoria's traditional ally, Britain, was under the control of a Labour government which was anxious to take some steps to lessen British support for the apartheid regime. This included the termination of the Simonstown agreement in 1975. Pretoria turned its attention to the Nixon and Ford administrations in the US, with better results. In early 1976 Henry Kissinger openly sought South African involvement in his own Rhodesian settlement plan, despite tensions over the US failure to follow through its initial commitment to the invasion of Angola.

Internal Crisis
Regional issues were superseded by the internal crisis precipitated by the events of 16 June 1976. In six months an estimated one thousand black South Africans were killed, mostly by the police, and between ten and twenty thousand arrested as demonstrations, boycotts and attacks on government installations spread to every urban area in the country. During that year and the following year at least three thousand young South Africans left the country – many of them to join the guerilla forces of the liberation movement. A sharp increase in sabotage actions was registered during 1976 and 1977.[9]

The apartheid military establishment regarded the government's response to the 1976 uprising as an unmitigated disaster, believing that the level of police violence was counter-productive, and that much of the killing could have been avoided by the deployment of stronger forces. Top SADF members sent a memorandum to P W Botha, in his capacity as Minister of Defence, implying that some form of military takeover might be necessary in order to effect immediate social and political changes that would quell internal challenges to the apartheid state.[10] While such a coup was not to materialise, it was clear that in the top echelons of the military, a group of relatively young, 'modernist', technocratic officers were chafing to implement a new military and socio-economic strategy.

The concern of military commanders was matched by that of many leading business figures, who were worried about both the political stability of apartheid and the decline in the economy. The economic boom had slowed at the end of the 1960s and by 1976 recession had set in. Increasingly reliant on technology-intensive production methods, the business conglomerates urgently required semi-skilled labour from the black population. There was therefore considerable political pressure both within and outside the National Party for the restructuring of the apartheid economy to achieve a limited relaxation of controls over the mobility of black labour. The establishment of a section of the black population relatively better off than the majority would also, it was argued, have the effect of dividing black opposition to apartheid and winning new allies for the regime. This process could be assisted by the granting of limited political rights to limited sectors of the oppressed population.

Such was the *verligte* ('enlightened') argument for a shift in apartheid strategy in order to ensure the continuation of the system and its profitability, and to stabilise the political situation. On the other hand, the *verkramptes* ('narrow-minded'), representing largely the interests of white small-scale farmers and businessmen and the white working class, were bitterly opposed to any alteration of traditional apartheid, which had served them so well. This difference over strategy led to fierce conflict in both the National Party and the government.[11]

The military establishment, backed by the political forces of the large industrial and commercial conglomerates, was able to break the deadlock by advancing a doctrine which combined intensified repression with a commitment to modernising the apartheid system. Behind the 'shield' of an invigorated, aggressive defence force, it was argued, the modification of apartheid could proceed apace, supervised by a new breed of South African soldier-politicians.

'National Security Doctrine'

The basic premise of the SADF's doctrine – that there is a 'communist total onslaught' in all spheres against the security of the state – is a product of cold war thinking which gradually established itself in the minds of apartheid security planners during the 1950s and 1960s. The Suppression of

Communism Act of 1950, for example, defined 'communism' in the broadest possible terms.

The notion of a 'total onslaught' became particularly prevalent in the SADF officer corps. By the time P W Botha took up the post of Defence Minister in 1966 he was well versed in these concepts, and many of his speeches in the first few years of his ministership reflected his conviction that the state was facing a 'total onslaught'.

Towards a 'Total Strategy'

The development of a 'total response' to this perceived 'total onslaught' took somewhat longer to materialise. Probably the first concrete indication of a movement towards a unified state security doctrine was the report in 1970 of the Potgieter Commission of Inquiry which argued the case for the establishment of a centralised intelligence agency, BOSS. Noting that 'it is no secret that the enemies of the Republic are trying to attack in all fields and not only in one or another', the report listed the areas affecting state security – which included the economic, social, educational, psychological and political spheres.[12]

During the early 1970s some progress was made towards the implementation of a unified strategy, most notably by the establishment in 1972 of a State Security Council which was meant to oversee all aspects of the regime's security.[13] However, the effective implementation of a co-ordinated apartheid security policy was hindered by the divisions within the Vorster government and intense rivalry between different departments of state. Vorster's personal power base in BOSS served to pit BOSS against the military establishment under P W Botha, which in its search for 'militarily defensible policies' was increasingly becoming identified with *verligte* policies and resented the dominance of BOSS in the security field.[14] The State Security Council, like other organs of the state, became a site of struggle between the different factions and proved unable to fulfil its co-ordinating role.

The Defence White Paper which P W Botha presented to parliament in March 1975 represented the clearest exposition of the thinking in the top ranks of the SADF. 'Defence strategy embraces much more than military strategy', it asserted:

It involves economy, ideology, technology, and even social matters and can therefore only be meaningful and valid if proper account is taken of these other spheres . . . all countries must, more than ever, muster all their activities – political, economic, diplomatic and military – for their defence. This, in fact, is the meaning of 'Total Strategy'.[15]

John Sciler, a US strategic analyst whose findings are based largely on private interviews with apartheid leaders, including military commanders, has stated:

The SADF, with energy and great candour, expressed its concern about [the Vorster regime's] inertia and the need for a greater vigour in both regional and domestic politics through its close ties (via SADF Chief of Staff, General Magnus Malan) with P W Botha . . . From the SADF's perspective, urgency for change came partly from a sober and essentially rational assessment of mounting regional pressures at work on the Republic, but ever more from a peculiar preoccupation . . . that SA stood alone in a profoundly unfriendly world . . . There was another, less complicated motive. P W Botha felt comfortable with his military staff. He admired their loyalty and candour, traits often lacking in senior civilian officials who had learned to protect their domains against transitory and threatening political masters. He hoped to project these virtues onto the civilian departments of government.[16]

The most prominent of the 'Total Strategy' advocates in the SADF was General Magnus Malan, then Chief of the SADF. A son of one of the first leading Afrikaner bankers, Malan had been attached to the French forces fighting in Algeria in the 1960s, and rose rapidly through SADF ranks. He studied at the US Army Command and General Staff College, an institution which played a leading role in formulating the 'indirect' approach to counter-insurgency warfare.[17] This approach stresses the social and political methods of fighting against guerillas, placing special emphasis on a campaign to 'win hearts and minds'.[18]

Many of the counter-insurgency programmes and methods employed by the armed forces of the United States in Vietnam and Latin America were absorbed by Malan and other top officers. So too were the methods used by the British in Malaya and Greece and, in particular, the French strategies which evolved from the Algerian experience.[19]

The French theorist André Beaufre features prominently in the more intellectual of SADF training courses, particularly at the important Joint Defence College, the military staff college in Pretoria which offers courses to senior government officials and leading figures from the private sector.[20] According to Philip Frankel, who has conducted the most comprehensive study of the development of the SADF's 'Total Strategy', virtually every course at the Joint Defence College is based on one or another of Beaufre's strategic works. Frankel argues that the SADF's strategy is 'essentially Beaufre writ large in the particular counter-revolutionary context of contemporary South Africa'.[21]

A theorist of the Cold War, Beaufre devoted much of his attention to the 'indirect mode' of counter-insurgency warfare – the conflict that occurs on the broader social level rather than on the battlefield itself. His followers claim that indirect warfare, of which they say 'international terrorism' is an important component, constitutes a 'third world war' between the forces of communism and capitalism. This war is said to be 'total' in that it is fought on a global scale in every conceivable way.

28

Beaufre characterised modern warfare as all-embracing and stressed the importance of psychological as well as physical conflict. Ideas, he claimed, are more important than weapons. The object of the 'Total Strategy' is to co-ordinate policy – particularly political policy – with military, social and psychological strategy and, through careful and co-ordinated preventive planning, to select counter-insurgency tactics from the broad range of options available.[2]

In an interview in 1985 one of South Africa's leading generals and commander of the occupation forces in Namibia, Maj. Gen. G L Meiring, indicated that although Beaufre's writings were widely used on a theoretic basis in the SADF, they were too vague in details. He stated that the work used 'more than anything else' was *The Art of Counter-Revolutionary War** by Lt. Col. John J McCuen of the US army, which the SADF regarded as a good 'distillation of many other sources' that was 'more practically inclined' than Beaufre's treatises.[23]

General Malan and other military officers, influenced by their overseas training and contact, adapted the military/strategic doctrine of 'Total Strategy', particularly the Beaufre variant, and applied it to South African conditions. By 1977, under the intense pressure of the Soweto uprisings and the international isolation that followed the Angola invasion, the SADF had codified its new strategic doctrine. The Defence White Paper presented to parliament on 29 March that year for the first time spelt out the concept of a unified National Security doctrine in some detail.

In the introduction to the White Paper, P W Botha explained that Pretoria's strategic situation had to be seen in the context of a perceived global East/West conflict in which South Africa was a major battlefield. In that context, military strategy formed part of a 'broader national strategy' to ensure the survival of a society in which 'the principle of the right of self-determination of the White nation must not be regarded as being negotiable'.[24] The White Paper continued:

> The resolution of a conflict in the times in which we now live demands interdependent and co-ordinated action in all fields – military, psychological, economic, political, sociological, technological, diplomatic, ideological, cultural, etc. . . It is therefore essential that a Total National Strategy be formulated at the highest level. The Defence of the Republic of South Africa is not solely the responsibility of the Department of Defence. On the contrary, the maintenance of the sovereignty of the RSA is the combined responsibility of all government departments. This can be taken further – it is the responsibility of the entire population, the nation and every population group.[25]

According to the White Paper the establishment of the State Security Council in 1972 was a recognition of the need for a 'Total Strategy', as one of the specific functions of the council was to formulate and implement a

* Faber & Faber, London 1968.

unified security doctrine. However, this was not sufficient:

> Co-ordination between government departments is of the utmost importance. There are few, if any, government departments which are not concerned with one or the other aspect of national security, or which do not contribute to the realisation of national security.

The White Paper went on to list the aspects of 'national security' that required attention on an inter-departmental basis. The list provided a clear indication of the political ambitions of the Department of Defence. Almost every aspect of the South African state and society was viewed a legitimate concern of the SADF:

> Political action; military/para-military action; economic action; psychological action; scientific and technological action; religious-cultural action; manpower services; intelligence services; security services; national supplies, resources and production services; transport and distribution services; financial services; community services; telecommunication services.[26]

In this sweeping manner the 1977 Defence White Paper effectively broadened the concept of state security to include all aspects of society, legitimising the interest of the SADF in fields far beyond its traditional domain.

Spelling Out The Strategy
While the 1977 White Paper advanced a working framework for the implementation of a comprehensive security strategy, it did not specify the content of the social, political and organisational modifications called for. Owing to the continuing struggle in the National Party, the SADF was not yet in a position to oversee the implementation of a unified doctrine on all the necessary levels. But the military's strategy, with its promise of far-reaching reforms and increased security efficiency, was gaining powerful adherents in top industrial and financial circles and amongst strategic analysts and economic planners.

Just two days after Botha signed the White Paper, the Institute for Strategic Studies at the University of Pretoria (ISSUP) convened its first major symposium, entitled 'National Security: A Modern Approach'. The Institute, which was established in 1974 in close liaison with the SADF, assembled under one roof many of the leading South African proponents of 'Total Strategy', as well as overseas experts. Participants at the symposium included SADF officers, government economic advisers and leading Afrikaner academics.[27]

A presentation by Lt. Gen. J R Dutton of the SADF constituted the clearest description of the 'Total Strategy' concept then publicly articulated in South Africa. Assuming that any conflict was 'more or less directly related to the bi-polarised East–West conflict', Dutton explained that the Soviet Union was 'waging a total war' against South Africa which took place on military, political, economic, cultural and other levels.[28] To oppose this 'total war', the South African regime needed a 'Total Strategy'. The role of the military, he asserted, 'could no longer be confined exclusively to the employment of armed force. It is broadened to include contributory roles in virtually every other sphere of strategic action, and specifically in the psychological, economic and political spheres.'[29] Furthermore, there could be no distinction between an external and an internal, or a military and a non-military threat. Even labour strikes could be seen as 'guerilla actions'.

In order to implement this all-embracing strategy, Dutton called for co-ordinated national planning at all levels and explained in some detail the political and administrative restructuring involved. He did not seek to hide the fact that this would necessitate centralisation and the dismantling of some of the structures of government through which white – though not of course black – South Africans exercised democratic rights. He stated bluntly:

> The requirements for the application of total strategy would appear to favour a system of unified command, joint central planning, decentralised execution and sustained vertical and horizontal co-ordination. . . This would apply not only at national level but at all the different levels within all the different spheres of operation. Conventional organisations in democratic systems do not as a rule lend themselves to these procedures.[30]

The concern of the military establishment with economic and political questions was underlined at a conference organised later in 1977 by the National Management and Development Foundation which was attended by top businessmen and key SADF officers. Opened by General Malan, the conference was jointly chaired by Ian Mackenzie, chairman of the Standard Bank, and Maj. Gen. Neil Webster, the SADF Director-General of Resources.[31]

The coalescing of 'reformist' elements in the private sector with those in the Department of Defence formed the power base for the political rise of P W Botha. He already had considerable support in the National Party, for which he was for twenty years a paid organiser. After Vorster's chosen successor, Connie Mulder, was implicated in the 'Information Scandal' which revealed widespread government corruption and misuse of funds, P W Botha was able to muster sufficient support in the National Party to be elected Prime Minister on 28 September 1978.

Military and State Power

The Botha regime lost little time in implementing some of the changes

31

advocated by business and military leaders, while engaging in a wide-ranging militarisation drive. Although many of the modifications were begun under Vorster, under Botha they constituted components of an intergrated strategy designed to ensure the survival of the apartheid regime into the twenty-first century. Complex inter-relating developments in the economic, political and strategic fields have been responsible for shaping state responses as much as any consciously adopted security model. However, the all-embracing nature of the National Security doctrine has resulted in the application of its concepts to many of the modifications made to apartheid.

'Rationalisation' of State Power

The Botha government set about establishing a reliable system of policy-making and implementation which would be integrated with the military and intelligence establishments. A 'rationalisation' programme began in earnest in September 1979, entailing the strengthening of the Office of the Prime Minister and the abolition of twenty *ad hoc* cabinet committees which operated under the Vorster administration. They were replaced by five permanent committees which were later reduced to four: National Security, Constitutional Affairs, Economic Affairs and Social Affairs.[32] Of these, the Committee for National Security, better known as the State Security Council, is by far the most important.[33] (It is examined in detail in the following section.)

In April 1980 the existing 39 government departments were reduced almost by half to 22. Simultaneously the Office of the Prime Minister was further enlarged to include six planning divisions, incorporating a number of existing advisory councils. Over the following few years, functions, authority and finances within and between the different government departments were further rearranged and many of the departments renamed.[34]

This rearrangement of government and state functions served to both facilitate and disguise the establishment of a centralised and a largely secret power structure dominated by military, police and intelligence personnel and known as the National Security Management System. Conceived as an instrument for the implementation of the National Security strategy, this structure has largely taken over the formulation and execution of state policy. The rearrangement of government departments was thus accomplished as much for reasons of efficiency (the public justification of the exercise) as for the purpose of centralising decision-making under the military and security establishment.[35]

A further centralisation of state functions occurred with the implementation of the tricameral parliamentary system and an executive presidency in September 1984. Presented by the government and its supporters as a reformist move away from apartheid, the tricameral system in fact entrenched white domination and control by attempting to incorporate some of those classified as Coloured and Indian into an alliance with whites, under white control. The introduction of the executive presidency and the division and weakening of parliament also served to diminish the effective power of the legislature.[36]

'National Aims' and State Policy

According to the 1977 White Paper on Defence, 'Total Strategy' involves 'the comprehensive plan to utilise all the means of the state according to an integrated pattern in order to achieve the national aims within the framework of the specific policies'. The same White Paper pointed clearly towards the 'national aim' of the apartheid state in its declaration that 'the right of the white nation to self-determination must not be regarded as being negotiable'.[37] The 'specific policies' of the apartheid regime were spelt out by P W Botha in August 1979 in a Twelve Point Plan, which he described as 'a reaffirmation of the basic principles of the National Party'.[38]

After restating the regime's continued commitment to the maintenance of apartheid and minority rule, Botha issued a call in the Twelve Point Plan for a number of modifications to the system. He also called for the establishment of a regional 'constellation of states' involving the bantustans, and committed his regime on the international level to pursue, 'as far as possible, a policy of neutrality in the conflict between the superpowers, with priority given to Southern African interests'.[39] This latter aspect represented a desire to elevate South Africa to the status of a regional power through following a relatively independent foreign policy aimed at incorporating neighbouring states into an apartheid sphere of influence. Genuine political neutrality was clearly out of the question. Rather, in the context of the envisaged 'constellation of states', Botha was serving notice that his regime would pursue a more aggressive regional policy consistent with its view of itself as a regional power.

The Twelve Point Plan also made a clear declaration of P W Botha's intention to reorganise the process of decision-making in state structures and to integrate the armed forces into the process of administration. The eleventh point called for 'the maintenance of effective decision-making by the State, which rests on a strong Defence Force and Police Force to guarantee orderly government as well as efficient, clean administration'.[40]

The assumption that strong military and police forces are a guarantee of 'efficient adminstration' reflected the belief that the management system of the SADF could be effectively applied to the public service generally. During Botha's years as Minister of Defence the SADF became increasingly dominated by younger officers whose approach to decision-making and administration emphasised administrative efficiency and 'rational' decision-making – and it was these qualities which Botha particularly wished to establish in government and civil service.[41]

This approach to government naturally found strong support in the private sector, which regarded many of the administrative and decision-making approaches of the regime as antediluvian.

Many aspects of the Botha regime's strategy and policy were carefully tailored to ensure private sector support, and most of the changes in domestic and regional policy, as set out in the Twelve Point Plan, were conducted in close consultation with both the military establishment and business leaders. The 'constellation of states' drive, for example, was formally inaugurated at a conference at the Carlton Centre in Johannesburg in 1981 which was attended by 300 leading businessmen and the entire cabinet.[42] Business-backed organisations such as the Urban Foundation played a prominent role in the effort to 'stabilise' the black urban areas in the wake of the 1976 uprisings, and private sector organisations entered into close working relationships with the government in the manpower field. One government official declared that 'the National Party [used to] regard private enterprise as part of the onslaught, but under P W Botha, it is part of the strategy'.[43]

The modifications involved in establishing a 'militarily defensible' system of apartheid under the Botha regime were chiefly those social and economic adaptations initially called for by large business interests. These were spelt out quite clearly by the economist Jan Lombard at the 1977 Pretoria Symposium on National Security. Arguing indirectly for the legislative recognition of African trade unions, Lombard declared himself in favour of the 'decentralisation' of 'responsible participation in the processes of income production and distribution'. At the same time he made it clear that the 'order functions' of the state needed to be further centralised and that the state could not be 'subjugated' to 'the whims of simple majorities in the total population'.[44]

Furthermore, argued Lombard, it was necessary that the urban or 'permanent' African population – those with the legal right to live in the urban areas – 'be given an interest' in the 'national security of the Republic'. Discrimination, in his view, ought to revolve less around the black–white distinction and rather be aimed at drawing a firmer distinction between urban and rural blacks. 'A distinction must be drawn in our legal system between permanent residents, on the one hand, and migrant workers on the other hand, rather than a simple distinction between blacks and whites', he argued.[45] Such adaptations were necessary because

> the economic aspects of national security in the RSA very largely hinge upon domestic socio-economic policy [and] the security of the Republic demands a clear definition of the system of political economy which all its participants are asked to support in one way or another.[46]

It was this approach – particularly the attempt to deepen the cleavage between permanent urban workers and migrant workers – that characterised many of the socio-economic modifications introduced under the Botha regime.[47]

The National Security Management System
While the political attention of white South Africans was focused on splits within the National Party and on the establishment of the segregated tricameral parliament, political power was quietly shifted from parliament to new centralised state structures in which the police and military leaders played a key role. The near-invisible National Security Management System was steadily upgraded and its powers greatly extended. General Malan has described its tasks as 'the management of South Africa's four power bases (the political, economic, social/psychological and security bases) as an integrated whole'.[48]

At the pinnacle of the National Security Management System lies the **State Security Council** (SSC), technically a cabinet committee responsible for making and implementing decisions relating to state security. The other three 'power bases' referred to by General Malan are supposedly dealt with

THE NATIONAL SECURITY MANAGEMENT SYSTEM

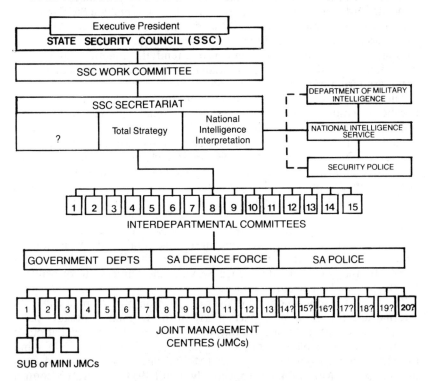

by the cabinet committees for Constitutional Affairs, Economic Affairs and Social Affairs, but the powers of the SSC far exceed those of the other committees.

Under the Vorster government the SSC met irregularly and remained politically and legally subordinate to the cabinet.[49] The cabinet and National Party remained the primary locus of political decision-making. In contrast, under Botha the Council became so powerful that it has been described as 'the focal point of all national decision-making and governmental power'.[50]

The Council differs from the other three cabinet committees in a number of ways. It is chaired by the President; it is the only cabinet committee created by law; and as a result of the exceedingly broad working definition of security, it deals with a far wider range of issues than any of the other committees.[51]

The SSC has clearly usurped many of the functions of the cabinet, which is now seen as a rubber-stamping body for strategic decisions already taken in the Council.[52] Council meetings precede those of the cabinet and also take place when the cabinet is not functioning and parliament is in recess. The Council meets in secret and its full membership is not known, but includes the Prime Minister and the Ministers of Foreign Affairs, Defence, Law and Order, and Justice. Other known members include the Directors-General of Foreign Affairs and Justice, the Chief of the SADF, the Commissioner of Police and the head of the National Intelligence Service. Military and intelligence officers also attend the meetings and other individuals – the director of the Armaments Corporation has been cited – are invited from time to time.[53] *(See Table I in Appendix)*

The armed forces play a decisive role in the Council. There are a large number of co-opted police and military personnel and there may well be others whose attendance is not divulged. Many of the cabinet ministers have themselves had experience in police, military or intelligence fields.[54]

The weight of the armed forces is even clearer on the SSC work committee and the SSC secretariat. The secretariat services the SSC and circulates its decisions to other government departments. Its composition remains secret, but one report has suggested that up to 70 per cent of its original personnel were drawn from the SADF and most of the remainder from the National Intelligence Service.[55] The secretariat consists of three branches, National Intelligence Interpretation, Total Strategy and a third which is kept secret. It is directly answerable to the Prime Minister and is served by the National Intelligence Service, the Directorate of Military Intelligence and the Security Police.[56]

The SSC is responsible for the overall direction of state policy in both internal and foreign affairs, particularly in the regional context. It is in overall control of decisions relating to the South African occupation of Namibia and the deployment of surrogate military forces like UNITA and the Mozambique National Resistance (MNR) which have devastated areas of Angola and Mozambique respectively. Until 1984 the SADF's control over these forces was never disclosed to parliament. Even the cabinet has been kept in the dark about certain major operations. A military raid on the Lesotho capital Maseru in December 1982, for instance, was approved beforehand directly by the SSC without cabinet consultation, and the SADF itself selected the time and nature of the attack.[57]

Although the SSC has masterminded Pretoria's campaign of regional aggression and internal militarisation, it would probably be a mistake to conclude that the SADF has absolute control over the body. The SADF has in fact had no need to assume such dominance. The uniform framework of values shared by both military and civilian officials on the Council has ensured that it has operated within a broad consensus over the need for military and other security action.[58] Furthermore each of the three other cabinet committees is served by a working group on which sit police and military personnel and usually a representative of the SSC. The working groups anticipate decisions by the committees, carrying out most of the analysis and debate. In this way military and police influence extends to all areas of government concern.[59]

Directly under the aegis of the SSC lie fifteen **Interdepartmental Committees** (IDCs) which together cover virtually all departments of state. They have been described by General Malan as co-ordinating 'fifteen areas of common interest in the national security field which would affect more than one government department'.[60] Little is known about these committees. Their composition, the frequency of their meetings and their exact security functions remain secret. SADF officers are believed to play a prominent role in their functioning and an SADF representative, reporting directly to the SSC secretariat, sits on every committee. The titles of the committees reveal only that they cover an extremely wide spectrum: Political Action, Economic Co-ordination, Manpower, Cultural Action, Telecommunications and Electrical Power Supply, Science and Technology, Transport, etc.[61]

Interdepartmental co-ordination and planning is also facilitated through panels of investigation and commissions of inquiry that are from time to time established by the government to investigate and recommend changes to state policy in various fields. The SADF and the SSC are usually represented on such bodies.

Interdepartmental committees are responsible for national co-ordination of the total strategy. Regional implementation is devolved to a series of **Joint Management Centres** (JMCs or, more usually, GBSs, after their Afrikaans name *Gesamentlike Bestuurssentrums*). Ten of these bodies, corresponding to the area commands of the SADF and based in a town or city in each command, cover the whole of South Africa. Separate JMCs also exist for Namibia, Walvis Bay and a number of Southern African countries – these are also based in South Africa. The functioning of the bodies is a closely guarded secret but they are believed to meet regularly and to play a vital role. According to General Malan, the JMCs are 'charged with implementing and monitoring the various strategies emanating from the

[National Security Management] system'.[62]

Each of the domestic JMCs is composed of the SADF regional commander and senior officials from government departments. In each area, so-called sub-JMCs, or mini-JMCs, operate in smaller centres under the overall control of the main committees.

The nationwide system of secret military-dominated committees is almost certainly the key to the entire national security system, ensuring that it becomes operational in all areas. However the impression given by Gen. van Deventer, the SSC secretary until 1985, is that regional implementation has been the greatest shortcoming of the National Security Management System and that bureaucratic and political resistance had been met from traditionalists. In order to facilitate the process of incorporating government employees into the SADF's ideological and organisational network, and to overcome traditionalist opposition in the National Party, senior civilian officials have been sent on five-month 'inter-agency' courses at the SADF Defence College to learn how to implement the 'Total Strategy'.[63]

The functioning of the National Security Management System is likely to have been improved by the introduction of the tricameral parliamentary system and executive presidency in 1984. Describing the proposed changes in 1982, P W Botha stated that the SSC would 'become the most important functional element of the proposed new executive presidency'.[64]

Intelligence Agencies
The restructuring of state power in South Africa has gone hand in hand with a restructuring of the intelligence organisations. Although information on apartheid intelligence bodies is severely limited, two trends are easily discernable – an effort to centralise and increase the co-ordination of intelligence activities, and the growing dominance of the military.

One of P W Botha's first moves on becoming Prime Minister was to clip the wings of BOSS, which had replaced the secret Republican Intelligence Agency in 1969. Under the leadership of General Hendrik van den Bergh – who by all accounts ran BOSS as a personal empire – the agency had doubled its size in the decade of its existence. By 1979 it employed at least a thousand operatives and other staff.

Throughout its existence BOSS had been at loggerheads with Pretoria's other two intelligence agencies, the police **Security Branch** and the Military Intelligence Section, usually known as the Directorate or **Department of Military Intelligence** (DMI).[65] The tension was heightened by the intense personal antagonism between Botha and van den Bergh, who as Vorster's right-hand man was widely regarded as 'the power behind the throne'.[66] Military Intelligence, and the Department of Defence in general, suspected that BOSS was planning to take over the military's intelligence functions entirely. Throughout Vorster's premiership the power of BOSS continued to grow at the expense of the other agencies – at one point BOSS even took over the offices of Military Intelligence.[67] Inter-agency rivalry became so intense that the departments apparently began spying on each other.[68] One report has suggested that Botha attempted to resign as Defence Minister in 1977 when he discovered that BOSS was tapping his telephone.[69]

The involvement of van den Bergh in the 'Information Scandal' was greeted with despair in BOSS circles – with good reason. Botha moved swiftly, establishing a commission of inquiry under his newly appointed Deputy Minister of Defence 'Kobie' Coetzee, which included senior military officers. A new acting BOSS director was appointed and to symbolise the break with the past the agency was renamed the Department of National Security (DONS).[70]

In January 1980 Botha strengthened military and police control over DONS by transferring to the department Rear-Admiral Willem Du Plessis, a top military intelligence officer, and Brigadier Frans Steenkamp, second-in-command of the Security Branch.[71] Lukas Daniel Barnard, a young professor from the University of the Orange Free State, was appointed to head DONS.[72]

Although a civilian, Barnard is quite explicit in his admiration of 'just force' and what he terms 'sword power sanctions', a phrase which became something of a code word for Pretoria's destabilisation campaign in Southern Africa.[73] Trained in the USA in the nuclear technology field, Barnard is also a strong advocate of a nuclear weapons programme, and once argued that Pretoria should make a clear declaration of its capability in this field.[74]

Barnard's appointment to DONS was accompanied by a further name change – the agency was renamed the **National Intelligence Service** (NIS). In May 1981 it was reported that plans had been drawn up for restructuring all three intelligence services and that a meeting between the respective agencies had been held in order to agree upon their roles. The SADF's influence over these discussions was assured by the active part played by Lt. Gen. Hein du Toit, the ex-head of Military Intelligence.[75]

The exact division of labour between the three agencies remains – like virtually everything else in this field – a closely guarded secret. NIS functions as a central intelligence 'think-tank' and is probably mostly concerned with the evaluation of intelligence gathered by its own operatives as well as by those of the other agencies.[76] The Security Branch, as the only agency (until the 1985 State of Emergency) whose operatives are invested with powers of detention and arrest, plays an important role in apprehending those suspected of activity against the apartheid state.

Military Intelligence has taken over many of the functions previously carried out by NIS when, as BOSS, it carried out covert operations all over the world. Although it remains within the SADF structure, the South African DMI is now distinguished from similar agencies in many other countries by having a 'strategic intelligence function' often handled by 'national agencies' such as the CIA in the United States.[77] DMI also has control over the surrogate military forces with which Pretoria has attempted to destabilise Southern Africa.[78]

Both NIS and DMI were implicated in a failed attempt by South African-based mercenaries to topple the government of Seychelles in November 1981. Colonel Hoare, the mercenary leader, claimed that NIS gave initial backing to the coup, but that Military Intelligence subsequently took a more active part. He said that he had received weapons as a result of discussions with the deputy head of the NIS and a brigadier in the SADF.[79] Army call-up papers were issued to some of the mercenaries and Martin Dollinchek, an NIS agent, was captured by the Seychellois during the attempted coup.[80]

The Seychelles coup attempt, which ended in ignominious disorder, led to widespread recriminations and intense speculation in the South African press as to the result of the perceived conflict between the three intelligence agencies. It was variously reported that the Special Branch was going to absorb NIS, that Professor Barnard was on the brink of resigning and that the power of NIS was in total eclipse. Prime Minister Botha intervened to halt speculation about the demise of NIS by publicly praising Barnard, and allowing the agency to stage a propaganda stunt by arranging a prisoner exchange with Angola.[81]

While there is little doubt that the DMI has grown immensely in importance under Botha, it would be a mistake to assume that the NIS is a spent force. The indications are that NIS plays a crucial role in evaluating and processing information and presenting it to the SSC. The SSC secretariat is in fact technically a sub-division of NIS and the agency must therefore exert considerable influence at that level. Professor Barnard himself has an active role on both the SSC and its secretariat and working committee.[82] It is also likely that the NIS plays an important role in the National Intelligence Interpretation section of the SSC secretariat.[83]

A committee of the SSC is responsible for the co-ordination of the activities of the three intelligence agencies, but duplication of activities and inter-agency feuding is still regarded as a major flaw in the National Security Management System. It is likely that further steps will be taken to centralise intelligence functions – in 1983, in a rare public address, Professor Barnard bluntly stated that 'the intelligence process must. . . be nationally co-ordinated and preferably be centralised'.[84] In any case the relative strength of the different agencies is probably no longer as important a factor as it was in the past, as there can be little doubt that they all share the assumptions of 'Total Strategy' and are integrated into the National Security Management System.

PART TWO – FORCES

3. MOBILISING FOR WAR

Apartheid military leaders have repeatedly claimed that warfare is 80 per cent social, psychological or political and only 20 per cent military, and the South African Defence Force has devoted considerable energies to social and political mobilisation.

Psychological warfare has played a crucial role in almost all conflicts by building the morale and unity of the troops or civilian population and undermining the fighting spirit of the enemy. In the South African situation almost all psychological operations have been aimed at the home population and very little directed at the population of neighbouring states.

Three specific aims of apartheid psychological warfare operations can be identified: maintaining the morale and loyalty of troops in the SADF itself; instilling a 'patriotic' and aggressive attitude amongst the white population; and winning the 'hearts and minds' of the black population.

In the past decade there has been a dramatic increase in the profile of the military. Soldiers are seen in uniform travelling to and from army camps, radio stations are saturated with military request programmes for 'the boys on the border', the press is full of articles and photographs glorifying troops, hundreds of thousands of schoolchildren participate in para-military cadet programmes, and images of militarism are prevalent in all walks of life.

By a concerted propaganda campaign using all the means at its disposal the South African state has instilled what can be regarded as a war psychosis in the white population. State propaganda has concentrated on persuading whites that they face a 'total onslaught' from the forces of 'world communism', necessitating a thorough-going transformation of their society into one prepared for a protracted war against neighbouring states and revolutionary forces in South Africa.

Propaganda Aimed at Troops

SADF Publications

In 1975 the SADF published a booklet called 'Citizen Training' which set out the attitude of military commanders to the psychological preparation of their troops. According to press reports, Colonel Pretorius, the author of the chapter, wrote the piece after studying the works of Mao Zedong and Beaufre and a number of other texts on modern political thought. He concluded that subversion could be defined as 'the purposive process of breaking down a nation's preparedness' with the aim of 'undermining the loyalty of a person' and the 'military, economic, political and moral strength of a nation'. To counter this onslaught, he urged troops to: 'Believe in – Your God. Your People. Yourself. Be proud of – Your People. Your Country. What You Are: a privileged citizen of the Republic of South Africa.'[1]

Since then SADF propaganda aimed at troops has increased in both quantity and sophistication, especially in *Paratus*, a magazine which is distributed to thousands of troops and sold widely at newsagents throughout South Africa. *Paratus* articles show a clear shift in recent years from generalised anti-communist propaganda to analysis of the ANC and counter-propaganda aimed at neutralising statements and positions adopted by the liberation movement. While the accuracy of the articles has not improved, the subtlety of argument and suggestion has been considerably upgraded.

Increasingly, *Paratus* propaganda has reflected the 'Total Strategy' ideology associated with P W Botha and Magnus Malan. During 1979, this ideology was for the first time clearly expounded in a number of articles analysing the 'total onslaught' against the South African state and warning that the battle for South Africa would be fought in the minds of people and not solely on the battleground. In June of that year *Paratus* melodramatically announced: 'there are some who argue that World War III has already begun, a war that is being waged for the minds of men'. Several articles focused on 'revolutionary warfare'.

The following issue of *Paratus* posed the question 'Is it worth fighting for South Africa', to which the Chaplain-General answered, 'Yes, a thousand times yes!' In November P W Botha gave a page-long answer to the rhetorical question 'Why are our men on the border?' His answer was couched in terms of 'the evils of collective socialism' and 'Marxist dictatorship from outside' against the 'fundamental rights and freedoms we all enjoy' in South Africa. Particular emphasis was given to the 'the basic right to religious worship', a theme constantly repeated in *Paratus*.

So effective is this propaganda aimed at portraying SWAPO and the ANC as 'godless communists' intent on wiping religion off the face of the continent, that in an opinion poll of soldiers engaged in operations in Namibia, 90 per cent of them said that they were fighting to defend their religion in the face of a threat by 'atheistic communism'.[2]

Since 1979, every issue of *Paratus* has contained at least one article aimed at boosting the morale and motivation of troops and discrediting the anti-apartheid cause. While for years the state largely ignored the ANC in its propaganda, preferring to identify its opponents only as 'Marxists', the upsurge in the popularity of the liberation movement and its ability to carry out dramatic sabotage attacks led to a change of direction. After 1981 the SADF went on an ideological offensive against the ANC, on the one hand identifying it as the principal source of all attempts to undermine the apartheid state, on the other labelling it as 'a very small organisation', or 'the world's least effective terrorist organisation'. In one of the longest analyses, in March 1982, the movement was throughout referred to as 'the USSR–ANC–SA Communist Party' and the thrust of the argument was that the organisation was totally under the control of 'the Kremlin'.[3]

Another consistent target of *Paratus* has been conscientious objection. For example, in an article titled 'Kremlin's guide to poverty, loneliness and heartbreak', the magazine asserted:

As Moscow's propaganda war against South Africa reaches new heights, renewed onslaughts are expected . . . Much of the Kremlin's efforts to weaken the resolve of people to resist the onslaught will be focussed on young men about to undergo, or who are at present undergoing, their military training . . .[4]

A topic often dwelt upon in *Paratus* is the role of blacks in the SADF and the supposed support for the armed forces amongst the black population of South Africa. For example, in June 1984, just prior to the elections to the segregated tricameral parliament which were widely expected to lead to the conscription of Coloured and Indian men, an article focused on the role of Coloured people in the army. It claimed that 'The Coloured men recognise that their country needs them and they are willing to serve.'[5]

More specific propaganda aimed at black troops has appeared in another SADF publication, *The Warrior*. This magazine gained public attention in March 1980 when the *Post*, a newspaper with a large black readership, complained that the previous month's issue of *The Warrior* was implying that the newspaper encouraged political violence in the townships in order to exploit the news value of the revolts.[6] It was later revealed that the same edition of *The Warrior* contained a direct attack on Bishop Desmond Tutu, then General Secretary of the South African Council of Churches, accusing him of corruption and warning against 'the religious leader in his shroud . . .leading our people not towards the love of Christ but to death and violence'. Bishop Tutu referred the publication to his lawyers.[7] *The Warrior* has been widely distributed free of charge in black schools and is handed out to the public by troops.[8]

A large number of other publications are produced by different departments of the South African armed forces, including *Servamus*, a glossy police publication, *Uniform*, the magazine of the army (as distinct from the SADF as a whole) and numerous other internal and external publications all of which glorify the role of the 'security forces' and raise the spectre of a 'Marxist threat' and 'total onslaught' against South Africa. In 1980 it was disclosed that 20 publications were being produced that year by the SADF at the cost of over a third of a million rands.[9]

Ideological Training
Propaganda directed by the SADF at its own troops is not restricted to the written word. All training involves ideological indoctrination through lectures, films and videos. The quality and content of the propaganda vary extensively. The more sophisticated indoctrination reflects the political approach adopted by leading apartheid military strategists. A conscript who had undergone training in military intelligence reported:

> We were told that the battle was 20 per cent military and 80 per cent psychological and how important it was for this reason to win over the local black population in the rural areas by not antagonising them . . . the example of Rhodesia was used to show how a war was lost for lack of local support . . .
>
> Lectures were also given on the ideological aspects of war in which the nature of the forces ranged against the South African regime was described. This included a brief history of the development of the ANC and the involvement of the liberation movements in the recent popular uprisings in South Africa.[10]

Ideological training in the SADF is usually far less sophisticated and intensive than this:

> We used to have what is known as a 'communication period' once a week. It was supposed to be an information period, but the camp chaplain always stood up and said his bit, giving his particular 'just war' line. The regimental sergeant major and the commanding officer would also give speeches – normally a sort of pep talk on the army's role and the threat of the ANC and SWAPO . . .[11]

Other deserters from the SADF have reported being exposed to pervasive racism with very little effort at ideological sophistication:

> At certain times the propaganda would be very blatant. They would just try and condition your mind that all you had to do was kill SWAPO.[12]

> The enemy is always identified as the blacks. The indoctrination is very powerful. . . they used to give examples like: 'What if a "kaffir" rapes your sister. You should be proud to kill him. You won't only be doing something for yourself, but you will be doing a duty to

your country.' Almost every day I used to end up in arguments.[13]

The wide variation in the type and sophistication of ideological motivation in the SADF is explained by the fact that the notion of indirect warfare, the 'winning hearts and minds' approach, is instilled mainly in the higher ranks and in military intelligence sections. Ideological sophistication tends to decline in lower ranks and overt racism dominates.

While the South African regime prides itself on the morale and fighting spirit of its soldiers, the evidence is less convincing. Thousands of National Servicemen have left the country rather than fight in the SADF and hundreds have deserted. There have been a number of incidents reported where conscripts have walked out en masse or mutinied. One incident which received extensive publicity was a mass walkout by over 60 soldiers from their base at Upington in 1979 in protest at their treatment.[14] Another similar incident took place in September 1985, when 45 men from 1 Parachute Battalion base near Bloemfontein went Absent Without Leave (AWOL).[15]

In May 1984, military intelligence officers met in Windhoek in occupied Namibia to discuss problems in the South African forces in the territory. The minutes of their meeting, which were leaked to SWAPO, revealed a long list of morale and security problems in the SADF. National Servicemen were reported to be carrying out acts of 'espionage and subversion' and to be sabotaging army equipment out of frustration or disaffection. Drug-taking, indiscipline and poor security were other problems, and some National Servicemen were reported to be supporting the ANC or SWAPO.[16]

Conscripts interviewed by exile sources have repeatedly told of individual and collective protests, strikes, attacks on officers and acts of sabotage by National Servicemen.[17] Most of these incidents are the result of ill-treatment and brutality. There is also a growing number of cases where conscripts have deserted or taken actions aimed at undermining the SADF as a result of their convictions. Perhaps the clearest example of this was the trial in September 1984 of Roland Hunter, a young National Serviceman accused of exposing secret South African destabilisation activities in Mozambique and passing on the information to the ANC.[18]

A further indication of low morale in the SADF is the large number of troops sentenced to army detention barracks for going AWOL, attempting to desert or refusing to undergo camps and other periods of military service. In December 1984, for example, of the 378 soldiers held in detention, 234 were detained for refusing to undergo service and 122 for being AWOL – in other words, over 90 per cent of army detentions were the result of individuals attempting to get out of military duties. The figures for other years tell a similar story.[19]

The Military and The Media

South African military commanders insist that the SADF is 'politically neutral'. In the same breath they will willingly admit that the armed forces are engaged in an extensive campaign to win the hearts and minds of the people by psychological and social campaigns.

'Nullifying' Opposition

The 'political neutrality' of the SADF in fact goes no further than an unspoken agreement with the official parliamentary opposition parties that the composition and activities of the SADF should not become a matter of controversy. At times it does not even go this far. For instance, in 1980 SADF plans for 'nullifying' opposition criticisms in parliament were leaked to the press. The subsequent scandal shed at least a few rays of light on the ideological machinations which lie behind SADF propaganda.

The plans to 'nullify' criticisms were set out in a secret document drawn up by Maj. Gen. Pretorius, then Director-General of Civic Action at SADF headquarters in Pretoria. The document, signed on behalf of General Malan, identified five targets for SADF psychological action in the month of March 1980. These included the fact that recruitment of blacks was not progressing successfully; discontent amongst white conscripts about the burden of military service; conscientious objection; and pay problems in the SADF. The SADF was instructed to ensure that suitable articles were written in national newspapers and in *Paratus* to deal with these problems. The SA Broadcasting Corporation would also be involved in the campaign.[20]

What annoyed the white parliamentary opposition and the liberal English language press was not that the SADF was engaging in psychological action of this nature, but that the programmes were directed at opposition criticism in the white parliament. The Progressive Federal Party was outraged, having taken a compliant, uncritical stance on military matters, seldom if ever disagreeing with government strategy and tactics. It did not expect to be rewarded by becoming the target of psychological action programmes.

General Malan was less perturbed. He made his position clear:

> The policy I have followed since 1966 remains unchanged, that is to keep the SADF outside the constitutional party political arena, yet positively involving the opposition as far as possible through briefings, visits etc.[21]

He subsequently accused the newspapers which published the documents of doing so in order to encourage draft resistance.[22] Under pressure, however, the SADF appointed a military commission to investigate the matter, which concluded that there had been some 'encroachment on the party-political terrain' as a result of 'serious errors of judgement'.[23]

The row would not go away, however. A few months later copies of an army pamphlet called 'The Reason Why' were shown to the press. Compiled and distributed to thousands of National Servicemen by the South African Army's Command Information Section, the pamphlet asserted that black claims to South African citizenship were 'totally absurd'. It defended detention without trial, the bantustan programme and the system of urban 'community councils' imposed on African townships outside the bantustans. At the time the Botha government was bringing in its constitutional proposals for a tricameral parliament, which were opposed by all opposition parties in parliament. The document claimed that 'extremists' were behind the rejection of the scheme.[24] Not surprisingly, the parliamentary opposition felt that the SADF had again overstepped the mark by disturbing the parliamentary political consensus on military matters.

The relatively strong response of the English-language press to the SADF's attempts to neutralise the parliamentary opposition during the constitutional debates of 1980 was accurately described by Brigadier Kobus Bosman as 'a flash in the pan'.[25] By and large the 'opposition' press has allowed itself to become a vital instrument in the military's propaganda offensive. Under the regime's security strategy, the mass media has a crucial role to play not only in mobilising the population to wage all-round war on the perceived 'Marxist enemy', but also in preparing the country for the economic and social changes involved in making the apartheid system more defensible.[26]

Seldom if ever in the South African press are reports on military matters to be seen which do not come directly from the SADF. Statements issued by Angolan, Mozambican or foreign agencies are either ignored or only cursorily referred to, usually with an immediate counter-claim by the SADF. For example, when South African troops carried out a massacre of over seven hundred Namibian refugees at the Kassinga settlement in Angola in 1978, all the South African newspapers reported a massive victory over thousands of SWAPO 'terrorists'. Some overseas newspapers available in South Africa carried radically different reports on the mass murder of hundreds of refugees. By the time the Sunday newspapers came out in South Africa, the SADF had explanations ready: 'In the trenches, alongside the guerillas, were women in terrorist uniforms. The paratroopers could not afford to take chances and the women were also killed.'[27] 'Many of our troops said afterwards that it was hell to have to shoot women. This is one of the psychological tricks being employed by SWAPO.'[28] The newspapers also spoke of 'terrorist children' as young as 14 who had to be shot. Later, when photographs of the mass graves at Kassinga became available, the SADF dismissed them as fake – they were never published in the mainstream South African press.

A similar pattern of reporting was evident when in May 1983 the South African Air Force (SAAF) bombed Maputo, killing a number of Mozambican civilians and destroying a jam factory and some residential areas. While the SAAF jets were still in the air, military headquarters released a detailed statement claiming that ANC 'bases' had been destroyed and over twenty 'terrorists' killed. This version of events was repeated word-for-word in the South African press and circulated internationally. When the truth began to emerge later as a result of journalists inspecting the bombed areas, the SADF was again ready with counter-claims.[29] An attack on Botswana in June 1985 resulted in similar attempts by the SADF to manipulate media coverage in order to disguise that the targets were civilian.

The key link in the relationship between the South African press and the SADF is provided by military correspondents attached to most of the major papers. Military correspondents who wish to preserve their sources of information naturally cannot afford to be too critical of the SADF, which can cut them off from all but official handouts simply by withdrawing their credentials. Even accredited correspondents can only visit Operational Areas – areas under SADF control – in carefully controlled groups, and reports have to be submitted to the SADF before publication.

Almost all South African military correspondents are serving or ex-members of the SADF. The most senior correspondent, Willem Steenkamp of the Cape Times, is an officer in military intelligence.[30] But even he, like some of the other military correspondents, feels that the apartheid war machine could be better served by its propagandists if they had more information at their disposal and were allowed freer rein with constructive criticism. In a rare show of solidarity in 1981 South African military correspondents lodged a joint protest about rigid censorship, the deliberate supplying of incorrect information and the censoring of questions put to the Defence Minister.[31]

Tightening the Screws on the Press
While the mainstream South African press has generally served the overall interests of the South African state and its armed forces, the relationship between the English-language press and the apartheid regime has not been an entirely smooth one. P W Botha has personally campaigned vigorously for better information control. While not hesitating to close down or ban black, radical and community papers supporting the liberation struggle, the regime has been reluctant to suppress press independence totally as this would be inconsistent with efforts to present itself as a liberalising force.

Without destroying at least the appearance of press freedom the government has for several years been engaged in tightening the leash around the media, adding new pieces of legislation to the more than one hundred laws restricting press reporting in South Africa.[32]

The bulk of these restrictions concern 'security' matters, with several broad pieces of legislation overlapping to make effective reporting on police and military issues almost impossible. The single most powerful restriction was introduced in 1975 as an amendment to the Defence Act. This empowers the regime to prohibit the publication of any information relating to the composition, movements or disposition of the SADF. The act was used to considerable effect during the 1975/76 invasion of Angola, when a complete black-out on news was imposed for several months. The clampdown was so effective that a crisis of confidence began to build up in the white community when news of South African actions leaked out through the international press and radio. As a result, the press was later given permission to record reports covered in overseas newspapers, provided the SADF was approached for comment first.[33] The regime has never again attempted a complete blackout, preferring to make arrangements with the press for the release of pre-censored information.

Strict restrictions also apply to reporting on police matters. The Police Act prohibits reporting on the composition, movement or deployment of the police without prior permission and it is an offence to report 'anything untrue' about the police; the onus is on the defendant to prove the accuracy of the report.[34]

Police and military legislation work in tandem. Under the Defence Act, reporting from Operational Areas is prohibited. Under the Police Act, any area may be declared operational. Thus, before the inhabitants of the Transvaal village of Magopa were forcibly removed by the police in February 1984, the area was first declared operational and journalists prohibited from witnessing the removal.[35]

Any loopholes in legislation are covered by the Protection of Information Act. Amongst other things this states that 'information published on security matters shall be presumed to be prejudicial to state security, unless it was received from someone acting under lawful authority'. The Act also prevents journalists from entering, reporting on or photographing a National Key Point – what constitutes a Key Point is itself, under the National Key Points Act, restricted information. It could be anything from a single factory to an entire district.[36]

Further legislation restricting media activity and information includes the Publications Act, Internal Security Act, Atomic Energy Act, Prisons Act, Mental Health Act, Petroleum Products Act, National Supplies Procurement Act, and their various amendments.[37]

During Botha's period as Prime Minister, two commissions, both under the chairmanship of an ex-administrator of Namibia, Justice M T Steyn, were appointed to look into the media's role. The first Steyn Commission, a board consisting of six men serving full time or part time in the SADF, had the specific task of tightening up on military and security coverage in the media.[38] Announcing the establishment of the commission, P W Botha declared that South Africa was 'entering a new phase in the total onslaught. . . manifested by malevolent efforts to question the very essence of military service'.[39]

The first Steyn Commission devoted considerable attention to the perceived multi-dimensional onslaught against the apartheid state, examining not only 'Russian expansionism' but also 'the American plan of action inside South Africa [for]. . . a black majority government'.[40] The commission rejected calls for a blanket ban on military reporting in favour of a system of 'voluntary' information control backed by legislative restrictions. This had the immediate result of restricting reporting on guerilla actions in South Africa. The second Steyn Commission had an even wider mandate not restricted to security matters, and recommended the further strengthening of censorship through a government-controlled licensing system for journalists.[41]

The planned licensing system was strongly opposed by both the Afrikaans and English press and a compromise was eventually worked out between the Newspaper Press Union (the proprietors' organisation) and the government. The newspapers agreed to a system of self-censorship through a Media Council which would have powers to reprimand and fine papers breaching a code of conduct. The Council has subsequently been involved in dealing with reports on military matters which have slipped through the pre-censorship system. For example, in September 1984 it upheld a complaint about an editorial in the *Pretoria News* criticising the police unit Koevoet. The newspaper based its criticisms on a report drawn up by the Bar Council of South West Africa, but the Media Council ruled that the editors had first to ascertain whether the report by the Bar Council was itself true before publishing the article.[42]

The mainstream South African press has seldom expressed strong opposition on military issues. While criticism of certain aspects of military policy is tolerated (for instance, of the massive police and army operation to surround and search Sebokeng during the uprisings of September/October 1984), there are firm limits to such criticism and even firmer restrictions on the information on which it may be based. Newspaper editors have been kept in line by threats of further curbs or prosecution under existing legislation, while police and defence liaison committees and the Media Council have ensured that the system functions smoothly. Secret guidelines are apparently issued from time to time. A four-page memorandum drawn up in August 1981 by SADF headquarters and circulated covertly to editors listed eleven 'dont's' in reporting guerilla attacks. It instructed that the press should not report on any casualties, the results of an operation or whether roadblocks had been established. It also stated bluntly: 'Say only that police are investigating. The SADF must never be mentioned.' Editors were further warned that they could be charged with treason for providing 'the enemy' with information that could be useful.[43]

The relationship between the 'opposition' press and the SADF under the Botha regime has been perhaps best summed up by Brigadier Kobus Bosman, director of the SADF public relations section:

> The media in South Africa has a very good understanding of what should not be published . . . over the years we have built up a very good relationship with our military correspondents [and through the] liaison committee of the SADF and the Newspaper Press

Union . . . problems can be raised and a compromise reached.[44]

However, relations between the media and the military were severely stretched during the State of Emergency imposed in July 1985, which led to further restrictions on the media and the arrest of journalists. In November 1985 harsh new regulations were introduced, virtually banning the reporting or photographing of resistance or unrest in emergency areas.[45]

Comics, Films and Songs
Photo-story books are widely read in South Africa. Many of these feature 'border' themes in which wholesome South African troops battle it out with 'communist terrorists', to the adoration of their girlfriends. Titles such as *Grensvegter* (Border Fighter) and *Kaptein Caprivi* (Captain Caprivi – after the Caprivi Strip in Namibia) indicate their themes. An increasing number of these books are aimed at the black population. Weekly glossy magazines, notably *Scope*, have also been regularly provided with lurid and often fanciful accounts of 'terrorist' or 'KGB' plots against South Africa and lavishly illustrated stories about SADF battlefield victories.

The South African film industry took up military themes over a decade ago with *Aanslag op Kariba* (Attack on Kariba) which focused on South African police activities during the war in Zimbabwe. Other films like *Kaptein Caprivi*, 'Terrorist', *Grensbasis 13* (Border Base 13), '40 Days' and 'April '80', have focused on the war in Namibia and in South Africa.[46]

Television has produced a series of 'anti-terrorist' programmes since its inception in 1976. In many cases this has been on the direct instructions of the government, but private companies have often taken the initiative and approached the SADF for assistance. In 1978 the English Documentaries Department of SABC-TV was ordered to stop production of current projects and prepare a military documentary to 'build up the will of the people'. When the producers refused, they were either removed to other departments or dismissed.[47]

In August 1984 the SADF revealed that it was collaborating at that stage in the production of no fewer than 21 films and TV programmes. It was especially proud of its role in *Jantjie Kom Huistoe* ('Jantjie Come Home'), billed as the first 'all-Coloured' film to be shown on 'white TV'. It told the story of a young man who joined the Cape Corps, was posted to Namibia, where he became a hero fighting SWAPO, and returned just in time to win the hand of his loved one.[48]

The music industry has also made its contribution to whipping up a war psychosis. Songs such as 'Soldier Boy' have been tailor-made for 'Forces Favourites' and other radio request programmes. Some Afrikaner balladeers have made a career out of country-and-western tunes lamenting loved ones and praising 'the boys on the border'. The tone of these songs can be assessed by the words of the Official SADF Border Song:

Dauntless our will to survive and to prosper

51

Here in our Southern land –
Free as the winds o'er our plains and our mountains
Free from oppressor's hand.
Dark are the forces that menace our country –
Frontier and city and farm.
Ours is the courage triumphant to crush them –
Ruthless the strength of our arm.[49]

'The Boys on the Border'

Civilian support groups, fundraising organisations, private companies and
voluntary organisations have been drawn into SADF schemes to build
support for the apartheid war effort and for 'the boys on the border'. These
initiatives have generated millions of rands for the SADF and relieved it of
some of its welfare responsibilities.

Support Groups

During the wars of liberation in Mozambique, Angola and Zimbabwe a
number of right-wing support groups were established in South Africa,
engaging in fundraising and publicity activities for the Portuguese and
Rhodesian armies. After the independence of these countries the groups
swung their support behind the SADF, in some cases providing the nucleus
for new support organisations.[50]

The invasion of Angola in 1975 led to an upsurge of white support for the
army. Many of the national newspapers established their own fundraising
schemes. One of the most successful funds was set up by the *Sunday Times*.
Each week it would publish a list of contributors to its Border Fund and
arrangements were made with cinemas and shops for collection boxes to be
set up.[51]

All sorts of fundraising activities were organised by the mushrooming
support organisations – from *bokjols* (barn dances) to events like the
auctioning of a cattle carcass at the Johannesburg abattoir.[52] Such was the
level of activity that the military authorities became concerned at the
administrative and financial problems involved and established a
centralised fund under SADF control, the SADF Fund.

The SADF Fund is supported by the Southern Cross Fund, one of the
agencies originally established in the late 1960s to support troops fighting in
Zimbabwe and the Portuguese colonies.[53] The organisation, which by
1982 had raised over five million rand through its 250 branches,[54] has co-
ordinated and organised a huge range of fundraising activities, most of
which have included speeches, displays and propaganda programmes by
SADF personnel. The Fund has specialised in sending gift packages to 'the
boys on the border' – usually consumer items bearing the name brand of the
supporting company and a suitable phrase indicating that the company
stands full square behind the apartheid war effort.[55]

Another Southern Cross Fund trademark has been militaristic T-shirts, for example, those bearing a picture of a soldier 'on the border' with the phrase 'I was there' (for use by troops) or 'He is there' (for loved ones).[56] The Fund has worked in extremely close liaison with the SADF and the government, and P W Botha and his wife Elize have both played an active role in promoting its work.[57] Botha once referred to the Fund as 'the Defence Force and Police Force without uniform'.[58]

In many of South Africa's towns and cities white women have been organised into groups which knit, sew and cook for 'the boys'. In towns like De Aar, a key railway junction where troop trains, including those on their way to Namibia, are regular visitors, women have provided troops with cakes and refreshments.[59] The SADF has placed considerable emphasis on the mobilisation of white women into support roles for husbands, sons or male friends in the army. The 'Women's Pages' of *Paratus* carry extensive morale-boosting reports on fundraising and other events organised by top officers' wives and offer advice to women on how to 'back up their men'. Civilian women have been offered courses at the Army College in George to learn support tasks, including how to phrase morale-boosting letters for men in the army.[60]

One of the largest support projects initiated by the SADF has been the 'Ride Safe' system introduced in 1978. Every weekend thousands of conscripts travel home on passes, clogging the country's transport systems. The Ride Safe Scheme is designed to provide lifts in private cars through a form of controlled hitchhiking. Special pick-up points have been established and advertising campaigns carried out to persuade motorists to 'Help Johnny come marching home' and 'Give your country a lift'.[61] In 1983 the scheme was expanded by 'Sleep Safe', a system whereby white householders volunteer to have their homes used as overnight accommodation for travelling soldiers.[62]

At the inception of 'Ride Safe', Maj. Gen. N Webster, then the SADF's Director-General of Resources, disclosed that the threat of oil sanctions was one of the major reasons behind the project, as rationing would prevent the SADF transporting troops to their homes. He also revealed that the scheme was being financially assisted by oil companies operating in South Africa.[63] The 'Ride Safe' and 'Sleep Safe' schemes have met with some resistance from the public, as there have been many incidents of misbehaviour, attacks on civilians and rapes by National Servicemen on weekend passes or leave.

South Africa's ex-service organisations, whose members are almost all veterans of the Second World War, have thrown their weight into supporting the SADF. They have apparently been unconcerned that the 1939–45 war was fought against a racist ideology not dissimilar to that being advanced by the South African regime today. Both of the two main ex-service organisations, the MOTHS (Memorable Order of Tin Hats) and the South African Legion, have opened their ranks to men and women who have fought in Namibia and Angola or in other SADF operations.[64] They have made their resources available for SADF welfare and support work and have utilised their international contacts for the benefit of the apartheid regime.

Representatives of British, US and other ex-service organisations have been invited to South Africa. These individuals have usually used the visits to criticise the lack of support offered by the Western powers to the Pretoria regime. Particularly important are the links that exist between South African ex-service groups and the influential American Legion. These links were exploited by Maj. Gen. Webster who, in his capacity as head of the Council of Military Veterans Associations of South Africa, was able to attend the US National Convention in 1980 and ensure that it adopted motions calling for an end to the arms embargo and other sanctions against the apartheid regime.[65] Maj. Gen. Webster – described by *Paratus* as 'the most ubiquitous military personality in South Africa'[66] – also used his post to travel to Britain, Canada, Taiwan, Korea and the Vatican (where he was received by the Pope).[67]

Private Sector Participation
The network of SADF support organisations is largely subsidised by the private sector. Through their efforts to prove themselves loyal to the apartheid military effort, businesses have made a significant contribution to the spread of a war psychosis amongst white South Africans. Companies also contribute directly to the SADF. In 1982, for instance, it was reported that a special campaign by the SADF Fund aimed at big business had raised R300,000 in just over a month – an annual target of a million rand had been set.[68]

Businesses have made regular donations of goods directly to the apartheid armed forces, often arranging for the gifts to be delivered in helicopters or military vehicles. Tons of chocolates, sweets, newspapers and other consumer items have been donated with attendant publicity campaigns. Sudsidies to the SADF have also taken less direct forms, for instance by providing cash bonuses and discounts to National Servicemen, and by paying employees while they serve in the armed forces *(see Chapter 5)*.

Major South African and multinational companies provide further subsidies to the SADF by placing suitably militaristic advertisements in the pages of official organs like *Paratus*. Some firms have sponsored *Paratus* pin-ups and special supplements on cars and motorbikes, or even entire SADF publications. Extensive advertising is also carried through the Armed Forces TV programme, a closed-circuit system showing mainly US programmes that is fed into virtually every army base.[69] Companies are encouraged by the SADF to aim job recruiting advertisments at demobilised National Servicemen, particularly in special supplements produced by the daily newspapers.[70]

Militaristic advertising in civilian journals also serves to further SADF propaganda. The range of products that can be linked to the military – from lawnmowers to shaving equipment – seems to be endless. The South African Army Foundation has raised funds for recreational facilities for troops by granting special licences to manufacturers to market products under an 'Action' label, thus indicating to consumers that one cent of every rand spent is sent to the SADF.[71]

Another important mechanism for the mobilisation of the white population is the Civil Defence structure, a government-established system which is aimed at mobilising white civilians into support and ancilliary tasks to relieve the armed forces in times of emergency. Civil Defence organisation includes a large amount of propaganda and morale-building activity, and falls under overall military command. (The system is discussed in more detail in Chapter 6.)

Education for War

In 1976, describing South Africa as 'a dynamic military society', P W Botha, then Defence Minister, declared that the regime had to 'educate for war'. The South African education system has long been an ideological battleground. One of the objectives of the National Party when it came to power was to institutionalise separate and unequal racial education systems. The black education system had the aim, in Prime Minister Verwoerd's words, of teaching the black child that 'there is no place in the European community above the level of certain forms of labour'.[72] The aim with regard to white children is best expressed in the words of a senior Nationalist MP in 1978: 'We must indoctrinate them to become true father-landers with a Christian loyalty to their people and their country.'[73]

In recent years, Christian National Education has been 'modernised'. The emphasis now is less on the 'black threat' than the 'red threat'; and the inward-looking concentration on an Afrikaner identity has shifted to the inculcation of the concepts of the National Security doctrine – 'reform' and anti-communism.

The structure and content of the education process in South Africa, particularly in subjects such as history and geography, reinforce apartheid views. Explicitly ideological indoctrination in white schools is most often carried out through the Youth Preparedness programmes. The object of Youth Preparedness, according to the Cape syllabus, is to teach the individual 'to withstand the onslaught against his spiritual and physical integrity'.[74] Weekly Youth Preparedness lectures in white high schools include films and lectures on the 'terrorist onslaught' and talks from ex-pupils who have served in the SADF. Militarism is most strongly inculcated through the cadet system, which is part of the Youth Preparedness programme.

Cadets and 'Adventure Camps'
From the time of Union, white South African schools have had cadet

training schemes, often based on the British system which flourished earlier this century. The cadet units at most schools gradually declined and by the mid-1970s many schools had abandoned them.

In 1976 the SADF reintroduced cadets as a constituent part of the armed forces themselves. The implementation of the new system was speeded up after the Soweto uprisings in June that year[75] and was made compulsory in 1977. The new programme involves ideological training, intelligence and counter-intelligence procedures, methods of warfare and instruction in fieldcraft, camouflage, tracking and marksmanship.[76]

The cadets are now controlled directly by the SADF, which provides all the equipment, finances the units, trains the officers and runs holiday camps for the 'junior leadership' element. Cadets fall under the SADF area commands, backed by a central cadet directorate at army headquarters in Pretoria.[77] By March 1985 nearly 200,000 white schoolchildren were involved in cadet training at 658 detachments throughout the country, involving almost all high schools for boys.[78]

The training itself, which usually consists of drilling and other activities one day a week (the pupils wearing their military uniforms to school on that day), is carried out by uniformed teachers who have undergone military service. At some schools curfew, ambush and 'bomb alert' procedures are practised. Elite private schools have developed more sophisticated forms of training. The Diocesan College School in Cape Town has established its own Air Section complete with aircraft, a Navy Section which receives direct instruction from the SA Navy, and a Battle School where pupils can learn martial arts techniques, strip down R1 rifles and Bren machine-guns and receive 'commando' training from the SADF.[79] The school also has an electronics section, an anti-aircraft unit and a field ambulance group. It is regarded by the SADF as 'an example to other detachments',[80] but it is surpassed in at least one respect by another Cape Town school, Rondebosch Boys' High, which can boast of an artillery section.[81]

White schoolgirls are increasingly being drawn into cadet activities and at a few schools the girls are taught shooting as well. It has been suggested that cadets will be made compulsory at white girls' schools.[82] It is also possible that attempts will be made to extend cadets to Coloured and Indian schools as preparation for introducing conscription in these communities.

P W Botha announced in February 1978 that a cadet system would be established in Coloured and Indian schools and that provision for the plan had been made in the 1978/79 state budget.[83] The announcement was initially approved by the Coloured Representative Council (CRC), a government-created advisory body with limited powers, but CRC members stressed that it would have to meet with approval from parents' and teachers' organisations.[84] News of the plan generated a storm of protest in the communities. The Cape Teachers' Professional Association, representing more than nine thousand Coloured teachers, firmly rejected the scheme.[85] The Labour Party, which controlled the CRC, was forced by public pressure to repudiate the idea.[86]

56

Faced with this opposition, the SADF dropped the cadet proposals and changed tactics, targeting Coloured and Indian school students for SADF-run 'holiday camps'. Since 1977 annual camps for 'leadership elements' amongst schoolboys have been run by the SADF in conjunction with other government departments.

The 'adventure' camps have been supplemented by regular visits by SADF recruiting personnel to Coloured and Indian schools. In 1983, in response to questioning in parliament, the Minister of Defence revealed that SADF personnel had visited more than fifty Coloured schools in July of that year alone, with the purpose of 'introducing the scholars to the SADF by means of a talk and a film show and assessing the interest in proposed youth camps and participation in rugby clinics (training sessions)'. He also revealed that the army was involved in taking Indian pupils from Natal schools to pre-arranged youth camps.[87]

Similar, but separate, camps have been organised for African children in some areas, despite strong resistance from local communities. One mother explained how the SADF organised the camps:

> We simply received a circular informing us that our children would be sent to educational camps and would be cared for. The next thing we knew, they were being taken from the school premises . . .in army trucks.

Another mother described why she opposed the scheme:

> Had I known the Defence Force had anything to do with it I would have refused to let my child go . . . it all seems so innocent which in my opinion makes it more dangerous. It is part of a slow, subtle indoctrination process.[88]

Asked how the children were selected, the army officer responsible revealed that 'leadership elements' were identified and then 'the instructors keep in personal contact with these youngsters. Usually they come back to us . . .'[89] The SADF maintains a presence in African schools by the widespread deployment of National Servicemen to make up teaching shortages. (This is discussed in detail in Chapter 10.)

Paramilitary camps have also been established for white schoolchildren, usually as an extension of the cadet system. Every summer holiday hundreds of boys in each province are creamed off for 'leadership training' camps run by the SADF – 361 camps were held in 1984 alone.[90] The programmes vary, but they usually involve intensive drilling, marching, shooting and instruction in military tactics and field craft. Children as young as 14 are armed with rifles and taught bush warfare techniques. At some camps the boys wear military or paramilitary uniforms and are subject to military discipline. According to *Paratus*, the boys learn 'almost everything a soldier gets taught during his basic training'.[91]

Special camps which have been run by the Transvaal Education Department since 1976, called Veld Schools, have come under criticism for their blatantly racist and militaristic indoctrination procedures. One report on a Veld School held in a remote camp at Schoemansdal drew an analogy between the Veld Schools and the Hitler youth.[92] Separate groups of boys and girls in Standard 5 (aged about 11) and Standard 8 (aged about 15) attended the Schoemansdal school. The camp was run along paramilitary lines similar to cadet camps, but far more emphasis was placed on ideological lectures and discussions.

Notes taken by one teacher who attended with her Standard 8 pupils record a lecture dealing with the familiar theme of a 'total onslaught from communism'. Pupils were asked to speak to their domestic servants about 'terrorism'. They were also warned about 'communist plots' including plays such as 'Jesus Christ Superstar' and badges then popular among teenagers depicting an apple with a worm in it – these were all regarded as 'communist' techniques to undermine the morality and decency of white South Africans. The lecturer added: 'Some say long haired men are communists but this is not always true – we only know when we have questioned them.'[93]

According to a report on the same Veld School drawn up by the Johannesburg College of Education, by the end of the week the children showed symptoms of physical and emotional stress.[94] Nevertheless, the pupils were assured that 'like David's victory over Goliath . . . South Africa will triumph against the Red Threat'. They were given telephone numbers of the security police and asked to report any unusual happenings.[95]

In 1985 the programme at Schoemansdal was extended to teachers, as part of their in-service training. About 300 Transvaal teachers attended an eight-day course which included lectures on revolutionary warfare and the 'total onslaught' and a course in military tactics. They were instructed to instil 'moral preparedness' in pupils by lecturing them on South African achievements in the military and nuclear fields. After completing the course, the teachers received a pay rise.[96]

The Veld Schools have spawned commercial competitors, such as an 'Adventure Camp' established by a university lecturer near Potgietersrus. Here, girls and boys as young as 11 have been trained in shooting and 'terrorist hunting' and given lectures on the 'communist threat'.[97] Another innovation has been the running of weekend camps for the children of Permanent Force soldiers. One such camp, to mark International Year of the Youth in 1985, drew together the sons of men in 44 Parachute Brigade. The boys, some of them as young as five or six, received instruction with automatic rifles, light machine-guns and mortars, and were taught bushcraft and camouflage.[98]

The SADF and the Universities

South Africa's universities have a long involvement in research and

58

development work for the military, and in recent years efforts have been made to maximise their contribution to the war effort. Through the Council for Scientific and Industrial Research (CSIR), the Human Sciences Research Council (HSRC) and other organisations which sponsor and direct research, senior students and academic staff have investigated strategic issues and developed military technology. Corporations and organisations directly involved in the arms and nuclear industries have also sponsored research.[99]

Even at the English-language campuses, which have a tradition of academic freedom and anti-government activity, extensive research into military and strategic questions is carried out and some course options have been taught by members of the Citizen Force.

On the Afrikaans campuses, military training and research have been carried out far more openly. The University of Stellenbosch is the academic home of the SADF's military academy, situated at Saldanha Bay. Pretoria University, which is closely integrated with government research priorities, houses a number of strategic and economic think-tanks. It is also possible, with appropriate security clearance, to do correspondence courses in Strategic and Security Studies through the University of South Africa (UNISA) which include subjects like 'The Advanced Study of Internal War'.[100]

One of the most obvious SADF penetrations into the tertiary education system has been the establishment of university military units at white Afrikaans campuses. All students who have received military training are compelled to join to meet their Citizen Force obligations. They are called up for training sessions during university holidays and on weekends. The units can also be used to guard university buildings and premises during times of civil emergency, and are sent to the Operational Areas for active service in the same way as other units.[101]

Since 1981 the SADF has attempted to establish military units at the white English-language campuses as well, but its approaches have been rejected by staff and students alike. Student Representative Councils have pointed out that many students do not approve of the SADF and that a military unit on campus would increase political tension, particularly if the unit were used to break up anti-apartheid meetings.[102]

Gun Mania

Beneath its brash, armoured exterior, white South Africa is beset by a deep insecurity. For white South Africans, the gun has always been the key to survival in times of crisis. The massive arming of the state in recent years has been paralleled by the arming of the civilian population. Today white South Africans possess more firearms per head of population than any other people in the world. There are at least two million privately owned firearms in circulation, almost all of them owned by whites, that is, one firearm for virtually every white adult.*

A gun boom took place in the months after the Soweto uprisings in June 1976. Gun sales increased substantially all over the country, with thousands of whites besieging gun stores and buying up stocks as soon as they arrived.[103] Whites working in black areas were particularly eager customers – staff at the University of Zululand bought 50 guns between them in a matter of a few months,[104] and the East Rand Bantu Affairs Board established a special R20,000 'gun fund' to enable its employees to borrow money to purchase personal arms.[105] The Railways adopted a different approach, selling off hundreds of .303 rifles to staff at a cost of only R7 each.[106]

The boom in gun sales led to a boom in shooting clubs and 'anti-terrorist' courses. Many white civilians have completed weekend courses run by ex-soldiers, learning a variety of skills including psychological warfare and unarmed and armed combat.[107]

Handguns are still the most popular weapons – often carried in the cubbyholes of cars – but sales of semi-automatic rifles have increased dramatically. For Christmas 1983, the state armaments corporation released for public sale a 'civilian' version of the standard-issue SADF rifle, called the LM4. With a 50-round semi-automatic capacity, the weapon was marketed as a perfect Christmas present for 'the discerning shooter'.[108] The uprisings of late 1984 led to a further rush on firearms, as did the Langa massacre in Uitenhage in March 1985 and the State of Emergency four months later.[109]

The proliferation of weapons in the hands of a predominantly racist population has led to a huge increase in violent crimes. Most of the victims are black. Incidents where blacks have been shot for trivial misdemeanours such as stealing a pack of cigarettes or bringing back the wrong change from an errand have become increasingly numerous. After a recent such incident, a judge congratulated a white man who had shot dead a black man attempting to steal some coins left out for the milk delivery.[110]

The trigger-happiness of white South Africans has also affected their own community, and the number of deaths from accidental or deliberate shootings has risen rapidly. National Servicemen returning or deserting from army service have been responsible for many of the incidents. Blacks in particular have been the victims of mindless aggression by National Servicemen. In recent years there have been several incidents where soldiers have simply opened fire on black civilians, for what they have described as 'entertainment'.[111]

Apart from the negative social effects of militarism, it is difficult to assess the effectiveness of military propaganda and training in mobilising the white community. The low level of voluntary participation in the Civil Defence structures and the rural Commando units, together with an

* In 1983 there were 1,894,333 licensed firearms in circulation (*Hansard* 18.2.83), and in 1976 it was estimated that there were at least 300,000 unlicensed firearms in circulation (*RDM* 19.10.76).

increasing incidence of conscription evasion, are indications that a proportion of the white population does not stand squarely behind the apartheid war effort. Growing support for ultra-right wing political parties in rural areas, and related resistance to Commando conscription, are also an indication that the relatively sophisticated 'Total Strategy' has been rejected or misunderstood by sections of the white rural population.

On the other hand, the huge number of guns in circulation, the high level of support for 'the boys on the border', the readiness of the white population to believe simultaneously in South Africa's vulnerability and isolation and in its overwhelming importance to 'the free world', and to attribute all black opposition to 'communism', are indications that the ideology of the 'total onslaught' has taken a firm grip.

4. CONSCRIPTION AND RECRUITMENT

No single factor indicates more vividly the process of militarisation in South Africa than the dramatic and rapid increase in the number of trained men and women under arms or available for military call-up.

The basic pattern of military service for white men has remained largely unchanged since 1957 when the present Defence Act was introduced, but there has been a massive increase in both the number of men eligible for military service and the periods for which they have to serve. Conscripts are initially liable for service in the **Citizen Force** as full-time **National Servicemen** – at present they serve for two years in this capacity. Thereafter they remain eligible for annual 'camps' – periods of further training or operational service for up to three months. Conscripts have to serve in this capacity for 12 years, during which time they should serve for a total of 720 days. After 12 years, they are then transferred to the **Active Citizen Force Reserve** for five years, and then to the **Controlled National Reserve** where they remain until the age of 55. In addition, some conscripts, and older white men who have not previously been conscripted, are called up into the **Commandos** as part of the army's Area Defence programme. The Citizen Force and Reserve units are trained and often led by members of the professional **Permanent Force**.[1]

The build-up of forces through these various structures has resulted in the SADF having at its disposal one of the largest bodies of trained men on the African continent. The standing operational force has been estimated at some 178,000 men and there are at least another 400,000 white men ready for rapid mobilisation in times of emergency. Over 90 per cent of the SADF's strength is made up of conscripts. *(See Table VI)* The increasing military pressures placed on white men have not been without their effects, both economic and political. In recent years a movement of resistance to conscription has been built up, following the lead of a number of conscientious objectors who have either gone into exile or been imprisoned. A serious political problem for the regime is the question of the conscription of sections of the black population. While the SADF has extended conscription to blacks in occupied Namibia, in South Africa the army has concentrated on recruiting relatively small numbers of blacks into Permanent Force and two-year Voluntary National Service structures. A similar strategy has been adopted with regard to white women.

COMPOSITION OF THE SA DEFENCE FORCE

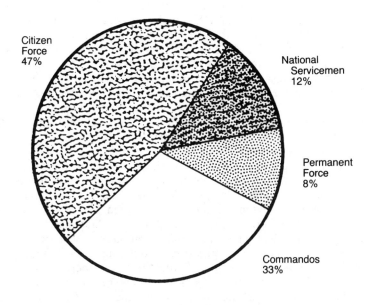

Citizen
Force
47%

National
Servicemen
12%

Permanent
Force
8%

Commandos
33%

Source: Tables V and VI (see Appendix)

White Conscription and Recruitment

Conscription of White Men

Guidelines for conscription were laid out in the 1957 Defence Amendment Act and a ballot system was implemented. By 1964 the annual intake involved 16,500, only a small proportion of eligible men.[2] In 1967, the SADF moved over to full conscription for white men in response to the launching of armed struggles in Namibia, Zimbabwe, Angola and Mozambique, and signs of renewed action from the liberation movement inside South Africa. A compulsory system of nine months' National Service was introduced for all young white men.

The initial period of military service was increased to 12 months in 1972 and a system of Citizen Force 'camps' – although only of 19 days' duration for five years – was introduced for those having completed National Service.[3] During the invasion of Angola in 1975 'emergency' three-month tours of duty were introduced for members of the Citizen Force. These three-month 'camps' have been a feature of military service ever since, and a source of considerable dissatisfaction amongst conscripts.

In 1977, ostensibly to eliminate the three-month call-ups, the SADF increased the period of initial National Service to two years, followed by eight years of annual 30-day camps. Despite the doubling of the initial period of service, the subsequent three-month tours of duty persisted, largely as a result of the SADF's escalating operations against Angola and the quickening tempo of the liberation war in Namibia.[4]

Over the past decade emphasis has been placed on expanding the Permanent Force, in part at least to provide the officers and NCOs for training the thousands of conscripts annually taken in. The total strength of the Permanent Force is estimated at 43,000 supplemented by an equal number of civilian administrative staff and labourers employed by the SADF. *(See Tables V and VI)* Despite this, shortages of technical staff and leadership elements in the SADF persist.

In 1982, a further increase in the length of military service for white males was announced. Legislation increased the period of duty in the Citizen Force to 12 years, broken into alternate annual commitments of three-month and one-month 'camps'. More significantly, conscription into the Commandos was extended to older white men who missed call-up in the 1950s and 1960s.* According to the Minister of Defence, General Malan, there were 800,000 men who could eventually be conscripted into the Commandos under this legislation.[5] Implementation is taking place in phases, with the key areas along South Africa's northern borders the first to be mobilised. By the end of 1984 some 18,000 men had been called up. As the liberation struggle intensifies, so more areas are likely to be mobilised – a strategy termed 'Area Defence' or 'Area War' by the SADF. This approach has been summed up by the Chief of the SADF, General Viljoen, in these terms:

> We are going to raise the defensibility [sic] of all the people. People living in an area must be organised [into]. . . the first line of defence. Our full time force must be a reaction force. The first line of defence will contain any terrorist attack and better equipped and trained reaction forces will deal with the insurgents.[6]

The pattern of incessant military commitments for the white male population which was so noticeable in the dying years of white minority rule in Rhodesia is already well established in South Africa. Virtually the entire white male population is being mobilised for the apartheid war effort, either as conscripts undergoing National Service, as Citizen Force members taking part in operational duties or in the Commandos as a 'first line of defence'.

---

* Under the 1982 amendment to the Defence Act, all white men who have not previously performed military service are eligible for call-up to the Commandos for an initial one-month's training after which they are required to serve for 12 days a year. In times of emergency, they can be mobilised for periods over and above the 12 days.

GROWTH OF SADF PERSONNEL STRENGTH 1960-86
(Approximate Estimates)

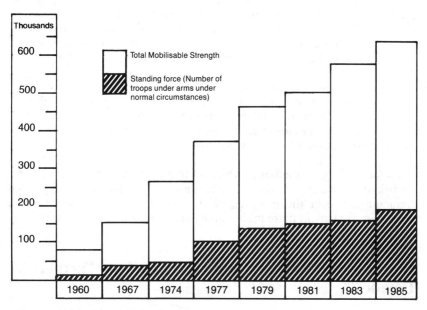

Source: Tables V and VI (see Appendix)

Sources: 1960-1977: IDAF [1980b], p41;
1979-1981: Based on IDAF [1980b], p41; *Resister*
No. 19, April/May 1982, p16; Table V (see Appendix)
1983: Table V (see Appendix)
1085: Table VI (see Appendix)

The Recruitment of White Women

The South African Army Women's College at George in the Cape Province trains white women recruits for service in the Permanent Force, Citizen Force and Commandos.[7] The women undergo a year of Voluntary National Service at the College, after which they are encouraged to join the Permanent Force.

Women were first trained at George in 1970. After a slow start, the number of women in the SADF increased rapidly.[8] Today there are an estimated 3,500 white women serving in the Permanent Force,[9] constituting nine per cent of its total strength.[10] Thousands of women, both black and white, are also employed in the state armaments manufacturing complex, Armscor.

Most of the SADF women are engaged in traditional tasks, such as administration, catering and nursing, but increasingly white women are being trained for jobs in more technical fields, including communication and intelligence. The women are given training in the use of side arms for self-defence purposes, but it is not policy to deploy them in combat roles.[11]

In casting around for greater numbers of conscripts, the regime has naturally had to consider calling up white women. There have at various times been suggestions from apartheid politicians that white women should be conscripted – if not into the SADF itself, then into an auxiliary service such as nursing. The 1982 Defence White Paper made it clear that:

> The SADF will be more and more dependent on other sources of manpower, such as white females and members of other population groups, and to involve these people in a meaningful manner, their utilisation is already being based on programmed manpower development plans which extend to 1990.[12]

By far the largest number of white women in the SADF are serving in a part-time capacity in the Commandos. Numbers have expanded tremendously over the past decade. Of the 26,000 whites serving in a volunteer capacity in these militia units, about 10,000 are women.[13]

Blacks in the SADF: 'Cannon Fodder' or 'Partners in Defence'?

The thorniest issue in the SADF's personnel expansion drive over the past twenty years has been the question of how to make use of black manpower. The idea of arming and training the black population has naturally been regarded with some trepidation by white racists, who fear that the guns might be turned against them.

Throughout the 1950s and 1960s the notion of Africans in the SADF – save as labourers and unarmed auxiliaries – was anathema to the National Party, although Coloured men were recruited in an armed but non-combatant capacity into the Cape Corps.[14] P W Botha went on record in 1970 saying that Africans would never be employed as soldiers in the SADF. 'If the bantu wants to build up a Defence Force, he could do so in his own eventually independent homeland', he stated.[15]

Two years later, however, African members of the South African Police were deployed in combat roles in the Caprivi Strip and in Rhodesia.[16] By 1979 an estimated 7,000 black South Africans and 5,000 Namibians were serving in a variety of different units, some in bantustan units but others in regular segregated SADF units.[17] The apartheid regime is now firmly in favour of black incorporation into the SADF and the compulsory conscription of Coloured and Indian men has been placed on the agenda.

The shift in policy is a reflection both of the priorities of the National Security doctrine, and of the growing manpower, economic and political pressures on the Pretoria regime.

Targeting Coloured and Indian Men

The 1957 Defence Act excluded blacks from conscription, but provided that the government could by proclamation extend the act to cover 'persons who are not white persons'.[18] In 1963 the old **Cape Corps** was revived as a non-combatant volunteer formation.[19] This was the opening salvo in what was to turn into a long battle for the 'hearts and minds' of the Coloured community in the Cape, as the apartheid regime attempted to utilise sections of the community as junior political and military allies.

The Cape Corps was not initially a success. By 1965, when its strength was supposed to be over 500, fewer than 100 had volunteered.[20] The annual intake remained at fewer than 100 until 1968, when the regime introduced far-reaching legislation to force Coloured youth in the Western Cape to register for paramilitary **cadet training** at a labour camp established at Faure near Eersterivier.[21]

As of January 1968, all Coloured males between the ages of 18 and 24 were obliged by law to register for cadet training at police stations, and subsequently all those turning 18 had to register within three months. Depending on their circumstances, youths were eligible for compulsory training of one year's duration, the first three of four months of which would be spent under semi-military conditions at the Faure base. They would then be allocated to various employers to complete their 'service'.

The cadet system had three aims – to prepare for military conscription; to develop the 'preferential labour system' in the Western Cape whereby Coloureds had preference over Africans for jobs; and to exercise political and ideological control over the youth. These motivations were clearly expressed at the time by the Minister of Labour and Coloured Affairs, Marais Viljoen:

> The Coloured is going to be taught to work. . . He is going to protect and secure the Western Cape for the Coloureds and the whites with his labour. As far as whites are concerned, military service was expanded. . . something similar is now envisaged for the young Coloured adults in order to lend some direction to their lives and to train them for some kind of work.[22]

Interviews conducted with inmates of the Faure camp revealed that very little work experience was gained and that training consisted mainly of paramilitary drilling. After completing their four months' 'training', they would be sent back to their employers, but for a further eight months would be subject to camp discipline. At least one case was reported in the press of an apprentice being fired by his employer and ordered to report to Faure the following day while other young men were taken out of productive employment and sent to the camp.[23] The trainees were also used as forced labour on farms.[24] Hundreds of youths escaped from the camp – if they were recaptured they faced prison sentences of up to three years.[25]

The drive to register youths for the scheme ran into strong opposition. Of the 15,000 expected to register each year, never more than 9,300 and usually fewer than 5,000 registered annually.[26] All in all, fewer than 40 per cent of eligible youth registered during the 11 years that the scheme was in operation, despite risking penalties of up to six months' imprisonment and being required to produce a registration certificate within seven days when demanded by a policeman. At one stage the Minister of Coloured Affairs threatened to authorise police raids to obtain recruits for the camp unless registration improved.[27] The cadet scheme was abolished in 1979. There were plans to replace it with a schools-based system of cadet training, but they were abandoned in the face of community protests.[28]

In 1972 structural changes were made to the Cape Corps when a **Voluntary National Service** scheme was introduced through a Special Service battalion. As service in the battalion was only of one year's duration (increased to two in 1980), it was expected that this would improve the recruiting situation – there is also some evidence that 'graduates' from the Faure camp were placed in the unit.[29] A concerted propaganda drive took place, emphasising the First World World record of the Corps, and recruiting became more successful.

The 1975 White Paper on Defence announced that 'as soon as suitable terrain is obtained, the training of Coloured members as infantrymen will begin. . . [and] the first Coloured officers will be appointed this year'. In September the following year, in a blaze of publicity, a unit of the Cape Corps was sent to Namibia for operational service.[30] The Corps has since played an active role in the Namibian war. The total number of Coloured men in the SADF service is now estimated to be over 5,000, approximately one-fifth of whom serve in the navy and air force as Permanent Force members. Most of the men have joined for economic reasons as a result of unemployment.[31]

A small number of Indian men have also been incorporated into the SADF. A naval unit – now called **SAS Jalsena** – was established in Durban in January 1975, training about 200 men annually.[32] The scheme involves a system of Voluntary National Service of 22 months' duration, after which the trainees are encouraged to join the navy Permanent Force.[33] There have been no reports of the Indian corps being sent to Namibia, but in October 1984 a group of 20 Indian members of a part-time Commando in Durban volunteered for active service.[34]

Despite the small numbers involved, SAS Jalsena has received extensive publicity. Its aim is cleary expressed as an attempt at political incorporation, 'to show the Indian community of the RSA that there is a useful place for them in the SADF where they can contribute to the defence of the RSA'.[35] From the outset the unit has been closely tied to the regime's constitutional plans through its links with the South African Indian Council, the precursor of the Indian chamber in the segregated tricameral parliament.[36] Soon after the inauguration of the tricameral parliament, a group of Indian MPs was taken on a military tour of Namibia.[37]

The SAS Jalsena programme received a setback in 1980 when the first Indian to become a commissioned officer resigned and accused the SADF of discrimination. He said that he was 'forced to lie' when he was paraded to overseas visitors and sent on recruiting trips into the community. 'I found I wasn't helping my community at all,' he concluded.[38]

In 1985 nearly 1000 Indian men served in the Commando militia system in a part-time volunteer capacity. Over 1,700 Coloured men and 431 Africans were also involved in the Commandos.[39] The participation of blacks in the Commandos has been a source of friction as white parties to the right of the ruling Nationalists have viewed their participation as a betrayal of the principles of apartheid. In general, however, blacks are recruited into separate Commando units or kept separate in black platoons.

Since 1982 there have been repeated indications that the regime intends introducing conscription for Coloured and Indian youth. The Minister of Internal Affairs, F W de Klerk, declared in that year:

> You can't ask a man to fight for his country if he can't vote. Among the terms of the new dispensation [the tricameral parliament] is the guarantee that Coloureds and Indians will get full voting rights. It follows that their responsibilities will increase accordingly, which means they will hold obligations to defend these rights.[40]

The threat of conscription was one of the major issues raised by the United Democratic Front and other organisations campaigning for a boycott of the first elections to the Coloured and Indian houses of the segregated parliament in August 1984. The success of the boycott clearly set back the SADF's plans to introduce conscription. Furthermore, the Coloured and Indian parties which participated in the parliament did not seek to add to their unpopularity by coming out in support of conscription.

The regime has a difficult decision to make over Coloured and Indian conscription. It fears resistance on a massive scale and a further radicalisation of the community; on the other hand conscription is an integral aspect of its co-option strategy and essential to its National Security objectives. However, any attempt at conscription would have to be preceded by military registration and, judging by the experience of the Cadet scheme, this would be strongly resisted.

Africans in the Apartheid Army

The SADF's approach to the Indian and Coloured communities has hinged on the state's overall strategy of co-opting sections of communities as junior partners in the defence of apartheid South Africa. The approach to the role of Africans in the armed forces has been substantially different, reflecting the regime's attempts to impose the bantustan system on the African population.

A centralised 'multi-ethnic' unit designated **21 Battalion** has been established at the Lenz base near Bloemfontein as a training school for bantustan military units. The Battalion, initially called the Bantu Army Training Centre, was established in 1974 with a mere 16 recruits. For the first few years of its operation the SADF's intentions with regard to the unit were not clear. In 1974 General Dutton described the unit in terms of reconstituting the Bantu Labour Service, through which tens of thousands of Africans were employed in menial tasks in the SADF:

> For many years a Bantu Labour Service has existed in the Defence Force. It included labourers, drivers and firemen, and a long time ago, guards. But over the years it ran down and became dormant. A nucleus of it is left. . . and we will develop our new South African Guard Unit on this nucleus.

He added, though, that the 'guards' would be armed and that this 'could be described as a step towards the military training of Bantu in South Africa and also towards assisting homeland governments to train troops'.[41]

P W Botha indicated at the time that the SADF would offer the 'Coloured people a share in the maintenance of the military security of South Africa. . . [and could] give the Indian population an opportunity', but that Africans could only be incorporated in **bantustan forces**.[42] It was made absolutely clear that African troops would not be used for operational duties. In General Dutton's words: 'These men have no connection with the Caprivi Strip. They will not be sent there.'[43] By 1976, 21 Battalion was training the nucleus of a Transkei bantustan military unit and a number of Namibian bantustan recruits although it had only 83 members.[44]

In January 1978 it was announced that Africans would be recruited into the Commandos. P W Botha did not explain if 'citizens' of the nominally 'independent' bantustans would be eligible, nor would he disclose under what conditions blacks would be accommodated.[45]

Despite General Dutton's categorical assurance to the contrary, it was disclosed in May 1978 that members of 21 Battalion had been serving in the Namibian war zone for some months and had engaged in clashes with guerillas.[46] In the same month, a black journalist was recruited to write an article in *Paratus* arguing that the SADF was 'fostering harmonious race relations. . . [as] one of the first government departments to welcome blacks in its ranks without considering race, colour or creed. . .' Describing the SADF as 'a willing friend, an educationalist and a defender of the interests of the black people' and 'a great friend of the various homelands in South Africa', the article concluded that 'the welfare of the blacks is top priority within the defence force'.[47] The SADF had clearly moved on to the ideological offensive with regard to the military recruitment of Africans, albeit largely into bantustan structures rather than the SADF itself.

By this stage recruits for the forces of the Transkei, Venda, Ciskei and Bophuthatswana bantustans had already passed through 21 Battalion and been assigned to their respective units *(see Chapter 6.)* In January 1979 it was announced that other **'regional' units** would be established in areas where bantustans had not been made 'independent'. At least some of the men for the new units were expected to be trained at 21 Battalion, the strength of which was revealed as 400.[48] The character of the battalion, as a kind of African military academy training troops mainly for bantustan units, was becoming clear. According to an article in the SADF journal *Paratus* in 1985, 'The prime function of 21 Battalion is to train black soldiers for the South African Defence Force and for the National States.'[49] Part of this training can involve active service in the Namibian war zones.[50]

In recent years the SADF has concentrated on building the regional units and integrating the bantustan forces into its overall operations. When a bantustan becomes nominally 'independent', the troops of that particular regional unit are transferred to the bantustan force.[51] The regional units – 121 Battalion in northern Natal and 111, 113 and 115 Battalions in the Northern Transvaal – act as front-line counter-insurgency units and have regularly been sent for active service in Namibia.[52]

Segregation

The incorporation of black South Africans into the apartheid armed forces is closely bound up with the respective political roles the regime has allocated to each of the groups into which apartheid divides the population. At all stages the SADF has attempted to maintain that those it calls 'community leaders' had 'requested the opportunity' to 'assist in the defence of South Africa'. Those who have done so represent discredited groups such as the SA Indian Council, the Coloured Labour Party and bantustan leaders who have little popular support. The endorsement by this small minority has been used by the regime to push ahead with its 'new dispensation', and has also been the basis on which the SADF has recruited blacks into its ranks. The South African regime's military and political objectives are inextricably intertwined. In this sense, blacks are seen as 'partners in defence' – but junior partners, segregated and hierarchically divided according to the ideology of apartheid.

In the operational context there is considerable evidence that blacks are deployed in front-line combat roles to a much greater extent than whites. A widely accepted estimate for the proportion of blacks in the front ranks engaged in operational duty in the Namibian and Angolan war zones is between 35 and 40 per cent, the majority of these troops being drawn from the population of Namibia.[53]

This is far higher than the overall percentage of black troops in the SADF's standing operational force. The total number of blacks serving in the SADF is in the region of to 14,000, to which could be added perhaps another 10,000 black Namibian troops. *(See Table VIII)* This constitutes less than ten per cent of the standing operational force of the SADF and the South West Africa Territory Force, and less than two per cent of the total strength of the apartheid military forces. The conclusion drawn in a study by Kenneth Grundy is that blacks in the SADF 'bear a disproportionate burden of combat' and can be regarded as 'a form of cannon fodder'.[54]

South African propaganda projects the SADF as 'multi-racial' and claims that there is no racial discrimination in its ranks. This is taken further – it is asserted that the army is a modernising force and the standard-bearer of a new 'multi-racial' state. This view was expressed in the words of one journalist:

> The army. . . has become the outstanding institutional model for the kind of multi-racial society South Africa could one day become. And it has happened under the personal supervision of the Prime Minister, when Mr. Botha was still Minister of Defence. . . From the moment a civilian enters the army he leaves behind the racially segregated life he knows at home.[55]

As has been shown, the 'institutional model' on which the army structure is based is that of apartheid, in which people deemed to be Coloured and Indian are targeted for incorporation as junior 'partners in defence', and Africans divided into 'ethnic groups' and allocated to bantustan forces. Furthermore, except to some extent in the Operational Areas, segregation is clearly enforced. There is pay parity between White, Coloured and Indian only amongst officers, and none at all with Africans,[56] and black units remain almost entirely officered by whites.

Why, then, do blacks join the apartheid army? The most obvious answer is probably the most relevant – for employment. With three million out of work, poverty rife and prospects of jobs for those without the necessary papers minimal, the SADF provides one of the few employment opportunities.

Conscription in Namibia

As a result of the illegal South African occupation of Namibia, which Pretoria for many years ruled virtually as a fifth province of the republic, white Namibian men have been conscripted into the apartheid forces in the same way as white South African men. At the end of 1980, conscription was extended to black Namibians, although the bantustan areas in the northern war zones, where the majority of the black population lives, were excluded.

The call-up was met with considerable resistance and thousands of people were reported to have left Namibia as refugees in order to avoid conscription. Despite strong protests from a wide variety of Namibian organisations, especially the churches, limited numbers of black Namibians have been conscripted every six months since 1981. The total call-up is, however, small compared to that in South Africa – the January 1985 mobilisation amounted to little over 2,000. A relatively large proportion of these men were likely to have been white.[57]

In 1984, the SADF began to apply the Area Defence legislation, with its provision for the conscription of older men, to Namibia, but without limiting it to whites. Registration took place in some districts, but was suspended during 1985.[58]

The conscription of black Namibians has reached a far more advanced level than in South Africa. It is a key aspect of Pretoria's attempts to establish a compliant pseudo-independent administration in the territory in order to circumvent the UN plan for full independence, and to devolve as much responsibility for the war as possible on to Namibian troops. The issue is discussed in more detail in Chapter 8.

Resistance to Conscription

The extension of the call-up in 1967 to all young white men led to the imprisonment of a number of pacifist objectors, mainly members of the Jehovah's Witness sect.[59]

In 1974 a new dimension was added to the issue of objection when the annual congress of the South African Council of Churches (SACC) adopted an outspoken motion questioning the validity of military service under apartheid. The motion argued that South African society was fundamentally unjust and discriminatory and that the armed forces were being used to defend an unjust system. Pointing out that it was hypocrisy to 'deplore the violence of terrorists or freedom fighters while we ourselves prepare to defend our society with its primary institutionalised violence by means of yet more violence', the motion went on to call on member churches to reconsider the provision of chaplains to the SADF and 'to challenge their members to consider whether Christ's call to take up the cross and follow him in identifying with the oppressed does not, in our situation, involve becoming conscientious objectors'.[60]

By invoking this argument, the SACC both established the parameters for debate around the question of conscientious objection for the next decade or more, and provoked a strong reaction from the apartheid state and its ideological allies. The motion was seen as an attack on the legitimacy of the apartheid regime and a call to civil disobedience. The South African churches themselves split on the issue, and outside the religious community the only significant support forthcoming in the white sector was from the National Union of South African Students (NUSAS). The government responded swiftly by introducing legislation making it an offence punishable by up to six years' imprisonment to 'recommend to, encourage, aid, incite, instigate, suggest to or otherwise cause any person or any category of persons or persons in general to refuse or fail to render [military] service'.[61]

This legislation effectively silenced church and other opposition on the issue for some years – even though no prosecutions were brought. It did not stop conscientious objectors themselves. Hundreds of young men left the country to avoid military service, many of them applying for political asylum in countries as far afield as Great Britain, the USA and the Netherlands, and others settling in the Front Line states and countries neighbouring South Africa. Support organisations such as the Committee on South African War Resistance (COSAWR) were established in exile and the numbers leaving increased steadily.

In 1978 it was revealed in parliament that more than 3,000 conscripts had failed to turn up for military duties annually during the previous three years. Between 500 and 1,000 of these defaulters were convicted each year and, presumably, in most case imprisoned.[62] What happened to the remaining 2,000–2,500 young men each year is not clear. In this period perhaps 200 war resisters applied for asylum overseas and in Southern African countries – the remainder must either have emigrated, gone 'on the run' inside South Africa or accounted for their default to the satisfaction of the SADF.

Hundreds of objectors from the Jehovah's Witnesses and other pacifist churches were imprisoned over this period, but it was only in 1979 that a member of a mainstream church confronted the SADF on the issue of the justice of the apartheid war. In October of that year a young Baptist, Peter Moll, who had previously completed his initial period of military service, wrote to his commanding officer informing him that he was not prepared to attend an army 'camp'. He put forward three reasons: South African society was fundamentally unjust; he was called upon to fight fellow South Africans with legitimate grievances; and he was not prepared to fight or die for apartheid.[63] Moll's court martial attracted considerable interest, for it was seen as a test case for the churches' 'just war' position. He was sentenced to 18 months' imprisonment, later reduced to one year.

But the issue did not end there. Moll, like most other objectors, was expected to serve his sentence in the SADF's detention barracks where he had to undergo military drill and wear a brown military-style overall. He refused, on the grounds that he could not in any way identify with the apartheid military. At the end of February 1980 Moll was joined by another objector, Richard Steele, a pacifist who also had explicit objections to fighting for apartheid, and together they faced a series of punishments for refusing to don military overalls. Their stand galvanised many individuals in the mainstream churches into action, and the debate around conscientious objection was considerably sharpened.[64] The SADF eventually backed down and granted the two men concessionary rights to wear the blue non-military uniforms worn by Jehovah's Witnesses.

In the following three years a number of other selective objectors followed Moll and Steele into detention barracks, in some cases taking strong political stands not necessarily based on religious convictions. They were supported by small but influential support groups which sprang up in the major cities, and by international campaigns co-ordinated by exiled war resisters. On the white university campuses it was clear that a movement against the apartheid war, similar to, if much smaller in scale than the anti-war movement in the USA during the Vietnam period, was beginning to take root.[65]

Church pressure on the state was continuing to grow, and in response the government set up a commission of inquiry headed by an ex-SADF Chaplain General, Naude. At the beginning of 1982 this commission recommended the establishment of a system of alternative non-military National Service for religious pacifists. The proposals were rejected by the mainstream English-language churches, which were increasingly concerned with the issue of resistance to apartheid militarism rather than universal pacifism. The alternative service scheme was widely condemned as repressive as it excluded selective objectors and moral and political resisters. Furthermore, the scheme called for an alternative service system of six years' duration, which was clearly punitive, and it drastically increased penalties for non-pacifist resisters from two years' imprisonment to six. Despite widespread protest, the proposals passed through parliament in March 1983.[66]

If the Botha regime hoped that the new legislation would put paid to criticism of apartheid militarism and stem the tide of conscientious objection, it was mistaken. The new legislation came at a time when information on SADF destabilisation campaigns against neighbouring states and atrocities in Namibia, although rigorously suppressed, was gradually filtering through to the public. The army was increasingly being seen in high-profile roles in support of the police in internal suppression, and the evidence of creeping militarism in the state bureaucracy was becoming a source of fairly widespread concern. In 1983 and 1984 a new factor became of overriding concern: it was evident that the regime would use the new constitutional system as a pretext for the conscription of Coloured and Indian men.

Groups concerned with supporting conscientious objectors coalesced with church organisations, student groups and organisations associated with the United Democratic Front (UDF) to launch a campaign against conscription itself.[67] This call was both an affirmation of the right of individuals to object conscientiously as well as an attack on the legitimacy of the state and its military policies. It constituted a rejection of the civil war strategies pursued by the Botha regime in its efforts to dragoon sections of the black population in both Namibia and South Africa into the apartheid armed forces.[68]

Launched in late 1983, the End Conscription Campaign (ECC) was put on to a national footing in October 1984, coincidentally at the same time as several thousand troops were used in the suppression of protest activities in townships in the Vaal Triangle and the Cape. The deployment of troops in these circumstances – an event widely regarded in the black community as an 'act of war'[69] – underlined the importance of the anti-conscription campaign, which was adopted by the UDF as one of its campaigning priorities. Co-ordinating committees were established in the major centres to mobilise in both black and white communities against the SADF, to publicise the illegal occupation of Namibia and to support those resisting military service. Protests were mounted against SADF and police actions, and at the time of military call-ups. In June 1985 a 'Peace Festival' was organised to popularise a call to 'Cancel the Call-Up', and after the imposition of the State of Emergency, the ECC mounted a 'Troops Out of the Townships' campaign. As the crisis deepened, the ECC became a focus for many people opposed to what was perceived as a growing war situation, and it gained fairly wide support amongst white youth.[70]

Immigrants and Mercenaries

Casting around for ever larger numbers of conscripts, the SADF has had to face the problem of whether to conscript the tens of thousands of white foreign nationals enticed to 'sunny South Africa' by the prospects of a high standard of living at the expense of the oppressed black majority.

The South African regime has been reluctant to take any measures which could discourage immigration. The racist structures of education, training and employment in the country have created a huge shortage of skilled and managerial personnel which the regime has alleviated by overseas recruiting rather than by training black South Africans. On the other hand, there has been intense political pressure from white South Africans for the conscription of immigrants, who became something of a scapegoat for those chafing under the yoke of military service. Throughout the 1970s there were repeated calls from all the white political parties for immigrant conscription, and the SADF itself made clear its desire for increased manpower.

In 1984, after years of hedging on the issue, the government finally responded to the pressure by introducing legislation making it compulsory for immigrants between the ages of 15½ and 25 to take out South African citizenship after five years' residence, thus becoming liable for military call-up.[71] The measures led to an immediate fall-off in the rate of immigration to South Africa and widespread protests from the immigrant community, but the SADF stood to gain an estimated 45,000 potential new members.[72]

The immigrants conscripted into the SADF added to the 2,000 foreign nationals already serving in its ranks – some of whom volunteered to do National Service, others who signed up for the SADF as mercenaries. Most of the mercenaries in the SADF are black Angolans, Mozambicans, Zimbabweans and citizens of other neighbouring countries who have been recruited into surrogate forces such as UNITA and the MNR, trained at South African or Namibian military bases and deployed in their home countries for destabilisation activities. Some black mercenaries have also been recruited into the SADF units themselves – notably 32 Battalion, which has at least 1,000 ex-Angolans in its ranks, and 201 Battalion, both of which are based in northern Namibia. Units like 32 Battalion are officered by white South African soldiers and white mercenaries recruited from a number of different overseas and Southern African countries. White mercenaries are also found in significant numbers in the Reconnaissance Commandos.[73] *(See Chapter 6)*

Concrete information on mercenaries in the SADF first came to light in January 1981 when a British mercenary who had signed up to 32 Battalion defected and told his story in the British press.[74] He disclosed that he had commanded Angolan mercenaries on raids of destruction and indiscriminate killing in southern Angola. The mercenary, Trevor Edwards, described operations of 32 Battalion in these terms:

> Our main job is to take an area and clear it. We sweep through everything in front of us, cattle, goats, people everything. We are out to stop SWAPO and so we stop them getting into the villages for food and water.
>
> But half the time the locals don't know what's going on. We're just fucking them up and it gets a bit out of hand. Some of the guys get a bit carried away. . .[75]

He went on to describe how his colleagues had tortured Angolan civilians and murdered children. He also revealed that the unit worked closely with UNITA and sometimes disguised itself as UNITA or even SWAPO.

As a result of this publicity, the SADF was forced for the first time to admit that 32 Battalion did in fact exist, but it strongly denied that the unit was composed of mercenaries. The Angolans, they claimed, were 'South West African citizens' as they had been settled in occupied Namibia, and the white officers where simply members of the Permanent Force.[76] An SADF spokesman explained that 'they receive the same basic pay and are employed under the same conditions as any other South African Permanent Force member', but he admitted that at the end of their contract the foreign soldiers received a cash bonus of R1,000.[77] He did not mention the fact that troops in units like 32 Battalion wore irregular, unmarked uniforms, used non-SADF equipment (including Warsaw Pact weapons), could choose their own 'personal weapons', were given generous leave and other benefits and were rewarded with cash 'bounties' for every killing they perpetrated.

Edwards' confessions were soon followed by those of two other defectors from 32 Battalion, one an Angolan and the other an Australian. Both confirmed Edwards' evidence.[78]

Another mercenary who served in the SADF's HQ 44 Brigade Pathfinder Company, which was constituted as an all-mercenary unit between November 1980 and January 1982, disclosed further details of mercenary activities in the SADF. Writing under a pseudonym in the magazine *Soldier of Fortune* (which claims a world-wide circulation of 200,000),[79] he disclosed that the Pathfinder Company was formed on the instructions of the commander of 44 Parachute Brigade 'to provide him with an independent force capable of carrying out clandestine and unconventional operations in the border areas of South West Africa'.[80]

The Pathfinder Company mounted so-called 'tackie' (gym shoe) patrols in the war zones of northern Namibia. These patrols – which have been independently reported by SWAPO – used 'turned' guerillas who had been kept in a cage at the Oshakati military base. Forced to pose as genuine SWAPO guerillas, they would be sent into settlements to request food and assistance or ask about the movement of SWAPO members. If help was received, the Pathfinder Company would move in to round up or kill the inhabitants. The Company was also deployed on operations in Angola, mainly in support of 32 Battalion.[81]

Mercenaries from Western countries – and there are reportedly also Chilean and Israeli mercenaries[81] – are recruited through international networks and mercenary magazines like *Soldier of Fortune*. The SADF does not advertise openly in these magazines, preferring to recruit by discreet small advertisements | and | editorial comments ' and through frequent lavishly illustrated articles detailing successful South African military operations. Many of the articles in mercenary magazines have been written by Al J Venter, who specialises in producing television propaganda films for the South African Broadcasting Corporation (SABC). South African military intelligence operations and military attachés overseas are also alleged to have been involved in mercenary recruitment.[82]

In recent years the SADF appears to have cut down on the number of mercenaries it has been recruiting overseas. In December 1982 *Soldier of Fortune* reported that the SADF had halted all mercenary recruitment. Six months later the magazine corrected itself, saying that the SADF was 'still accepting foreign volunteers on a very limited scale [but] is interested only in people with military experience and some specialised skills'.[83]

There are two likely reasons for the reduction in mercenary recruitment. Firstly, the SADF has had a number of experiences with mercenaries defecting and telling their stories, and there have also been reports of disciplinary problems. Secondly, with the independence of Zimbabwe, hundreds of troops and officers in the Rhodesian forces crossed the Limpopo and signed up with the SADF.[84] Some of them were mercenaries of long standing – at least 1,500 foreigners were employed in the Rhodesian armed forces[85] – and almost all of them were experienced, professional bush fighters. This influx made it unnecessary for the SADF to recruit overseas.

An army spokesman admitted: 'We would surely be stupid not to have accepted professional soldiers with the qualifications of some of the Rhodesians who came south and offered their services.'[86] The Rhodesians, many of them ex-members of the notorious Selous Scouts and the Special Air Services (SAS), were assigned to 32 Battalion, the Pathfinder Company of 44 Battalion and the élite and secret Reconnaissance Commandos. Others were employed in training and leadership roles in new camps set up along the Zimbabwean border, where a force was being trained for destablisation activities in Zimbabwe.[87] Virtually the entire white membership of the SAS was reported to have crossed to South Africa with their weapons and equipment,[88] and so many members of the all-white Rhodesian Light Infantry (RLI) moved to South Africa that the Regimental Association was able to hold its annual general meeting in Johannesburg a year and a half after Zimbabwean independence.[89]

Rhodesian soldiers who were rejected by the SADF set themselves up as security experts or joined up as mercenaries with bantustan military units. In 1981 the Selous Scouts commander, Colonel Ron Reid-Daly, obtained the lucrative post of the commander-in-chief of the Transkei Defence Force.[90]

The recruitment of large numbers of Rhodesians was preceded some years earlier by an influx of ex-members of the Portuguese armed forces as Portuguese rule in Angola and Mozambique came to an end. With their extensive experience and knowledge of neighbouring countries, these men played an important role in South Africa's campaign of regional aggression and destabilisation.

It was this ready availability of mercenary manpower from the collapsing 'bastions' of white rule to the north that enabled the SADF to limit the number of mercenaries recruited from overseas and to disguise the presence of large numbers of mercenaries in its armed forces.

In 1983, in a propaganda exercise to demonstrate its ostensible opposition to mercenaries the South African government introduced legislation making it an offence punishable by up to five years' imprisonment to recruit mercenaries in the country.[91] The legislation was largely a response to the international embarrassment resulting from an abortive coup attempted in the Seychelles by the SADF and the National Intelligence Service. The mercenaries flew to the Seychelles capital Victoria on a scheduled flight, uncovered hidden weapons on landing and seized the airport. After running into stiff resistance, they hijacked an Air India jet and forced the pilot to fly them to Durban.[92] They were arrested and some of them received light prison sentences.[93]

The 1983 'anti-mercenary' legislation did not prevent the SADF from allowing some of the Seychelles mercenaries to remain in its ranks – and it certainly did not lead to the prosecution of military officers for recruiting hundreds of mercenaries into various units of the SADF. In 1982 the Minister of Defence himself admitted that of the over 2,000 foreigners serving in the SADF, 672 of them were career soldiers in the Permanent Force.[94]

It may be asked why, with a large, fairly well-trained and well-equipped army, the SADF needs the services of mercenaries at all. The answer is mainly to be found in the tremendously rapid expansion of the National Service and Citizen Force component of the SADF over the past twenty years. Most Permanent Force members have been needed for training and leading conscript units, and the situation has been exacerbated by the failure of the SADF to compete successfully with the private sector for skilled technical personnel. The training requirements of the Citizen Force are considerable. As a part-time soldier each Citizen Force member is in effect only in uniform for one out of every ten days. Ten thousand trained Citizen Force members are therefore needed to maintain a permanent operational presence of 1,000 troops. The flexibility provided by the Citizen Force structure thus becomes a cumbersome burden when deployments reach a high level over a relatively long period of time, as they have in recent years.

The training strain on the Permanent Force has resulted in a situation where only a few hundred South African troops have been spared for allocation to units like the Reconnaissance Commandos and 32 Battalion. Their ranks and command structures have thus been filled by mercenaries.[95]

5. ARMING APARTHEID:
TOWARDS A WAR ECONOMY

To supply its war machine, the South African regime has established an extensive network of strategic industries and arms manufacturing concerns. It has spent billions of rands on efforts to protect itself from international sanctions, and has taken political, economic and legislative steps to ensure that private companies have been integrated into the war effort.

The Booming Military Budget

The enormous increase in South African military expenditure over the past twenty years is something which the regime attempts to disguise and minimise. It claims that military expenditure accounts for about 15 per cent of the total state budget, which is not high by world standards. Furthermore, it argues that once inflation is taken into account only slight increases in military expenditure in real terms are registered, alleging that the price of military hardware increases at a faster rate than that of normal consumer prices.[1]

Research by the Stockholm International Peace Research Institute has countered the myth that military inflation runs at a higher rate than inflation as a whole.[2] When SADF expenditure increases are compared against the national inflation rate, it becomes clear that the 500 per cent increase in the military budget during the 1975–85 period far outstrips the estimated 380 per cent increase in prices caused by inflation, during the same decade.[3]

Furthermore, since 1974 at least half of all military funds have been allocated to capital development programmes – a total over the ten years to 1984/85 of some R13,000 million. Most of these funds have been earmarked for the purchase of new and better equipment or the establishment of manufacturing facilities for military hardware. This spending alone has led to a very significant expansion in the facilities at the SADF's disposal.[4]

The assertion that military expenditure accounts for only 15 per cent of the state budget is also untrue. The sum of R4,274 million allocated to defence in the 1985/86 budget represents only a portion of overall military expenditure.[5] The SADF has admitted that 'the cash budget has become obsolete'.[6] A more relevant figure is the so-called 'Committal Authority' for the Department of Defence, which is about R4 million higher than the actual budget allocation.

In addition, vast resources earmarked for military purposes are hidden in the budgets of state departments other than the Department of Defence. Funds for Military Intelligence are channelled through the Secret Services Account; the Department of Public Works pays for the construction of military bases; the Department of Community Development is responsible for housing military personnel; the Health Department underwrites a proportion of military medical expenditure; and military research is carried out under the auspices of the Council for Scientific and Industrial Research and various university institutes and departments.

Furthermore, some SADF expenditure can be reclaimed from the Commission for Administration and extra funds have also been transferred to the SADF through the sale of Defence Bonds and Bonus Bonds.[7] Defence Bonds are bought by private businesses and local authorities, and until their abolition at the end of 1984, Bonus Bonds were sold to the public as a lottery. The schemes have raised hundreds of millions of rands for the SADF.[8] If all this funding is still insufficient, extra money can be made over at the end of the year through the Additional Appropriation Act.[9] It is impossible to put a figure to the additional military expenditure incurred in these ways, but it clearly adds several hundred million rands to the defence budget, pushing direct military expenditure probably to beyond 20 per cent of overall state spending.

Apart from the 20 per cent of the state budget directly and indirectly allocated to the military, further large sums are allocated to the police (about three per cent of the total budget) and for other aspects of state security. Under the National Security system implemented by P W Botha, it is virtually impossible to distinguish military and non-military expenditure, as all departments of state are integrated into the overall system. The expense involved in the centralisation of state power under the National Security Management System, the monies consumed by state propaganda organs, the rapidly increasing expenditure on the judicial and prisons system are all vital to the regime's military and strategic objectives. Expenditure in all these areas has risen sharply in recent years. For example, police spending increased by 44 per cent in 1984/85.[10]

Securing Strategic Industries and Energy Supplies

Between 1983/84 and 1984/85 the defence cash vote rose by over R600 million. Total defence expenditure undoubtedly rose by much more – an estimated R900 million. The situation is rapidly approaching the scenario described by Professor Jan Lombard, one of the apartheid regime's leading economists, in 1977 at the symposium on national security held at the University of Pretoria. According to Lombard:

> When the defence budget begins to rise by amounts of R1,000 million per annum and begins to absorb significantly large proportions of the gross domestic product, the need to interface defence expenditure with the matrix of industrial processes in the economy becomes real . . . it may be necessary to resort to more direct controls over private expenditures. At that stage the national security strategist assumes control over the economy as a whole.[11]

It is clearly not the case that the government and its 'national security strategists' have sought direct control over the private sector. The regime has repeatedly stressed its commitment to the maintenance of 'private enterprise' in South Africa and has taken some steps towards loosening government control over the economy – for example, by lifting restrictions on the repatriation of capital. But the 'national security strategists' mentioned by Lombard have been hard at work to ensure that key sectors of the apartheid economy are interfaced with the military and security systems. There are a number of aspects to this process. The development of strategic industries, including a local armaments manufacturing capability, and the establishment of an integrated state/private sector security system for 'National Key Points', are the most visible effects.

Manpower: Military and Private Sector in Competition
Some sectors of South African industry have benefited tremendously from the strategic and military initiatives taken by the regime over the past twenty years. The close working relationship between the state and the private sector in the economic field is symbolised by the participation of leading businessmen in key policy-making bodies falling under the State President's Office – the Economic Advisory Council, Scientific Advisory Council and so on. State intervention in the economic sector has not been entirely without its critics, however, and certain issues have involved a short-term conflict of interests between the two sectors.

The greatest source of friction between the military establishment and the business sector has been in the manpower field. White men between the ages of 18 and 55 are expected both to bear the burden of conscription and to fill key managerial, supervisory and skilled labouring positions in the economy. The discriminatory character of education and training prohibits the rapid incorporation of blacks into these positions and even the modest training initiatives taken recently have failed to dent the skills shortage in South African industry. Competition for scarce labour resources has led to periodic conflicts between business and military interests. The introduction of highly disruptive three-month 'camps' at the end of 1975, for example, led to criticism, and when conscription was drastically extended in 1981, there were strong protests from business circles.[12]

On the whole, however, business representatives have accepted that the survival of the apartheid system demands that white men spend long periods fighting to preserve it. Almost all companies make up the difference between army salaries and company salaries while their employees are undergoing military service. A fifth of all companies continue to pay full salaries. This amounts to an incalculably large subsidy to the SADF, which can thus get away with paying very low wages to National Servicemen. Some companies have agreed to pay employees who volunteer for extra military duties, as well as those who are conscripted.[13] In at least one case a firm which refused to pay up was threatened with legal action by the SADF.[14] Smaller firms, which cannot afford to pay non-productive labour costs for long periods of time, have often defaulted, however, and there is no legal obligation on their part.[15]

Competition for manpower between the SADF and the private sector was resolved through the Defence Advisory Council established by P W Botha in 1973 when he was Minister of Defence. With Botha as chairman, the Council brought together the Head of the Defence Force (then General Malan), the president of the Armaments Board and a small number of businessmen and military officers.[16] When Botha became Prime Minister in 1977, 13 prominent businessmen were co-opted to the Council, including the chairmen of some of the largest corporations in South Africa.[17] Influential businessmen were also brought on to the Public Service Commission, which is responsible for overseeing state expenditure.[18]

In the first five years of P W Botha's premiership, the Defence Advisory Council played an important role in integrating state security planning with economic objectives, as well as gaining business support for the regime's political initiatives. In 1982 the Council was disbanded and some of its functions – specifically manpower planning – were transferred to the Defence Manpower Liaison Committee which was first established on a smaller scale as the Defence Liaison Committee in 1978. According to the 1982 White Paper on Defence the Manpower Liaison Committee

> meets regularly and consists of the Chief of Staff Personnel, the chiefs of staff personnel of the four Arms of the Service and representatives of 21 employer organisations, and its aim is to promote communication and mutual understanding between the South African Defence Force and Commerce and Industry with regard to a common source of manpower.

The Committee sets overall policy, and 'practical matters' are decided by regional committees established under the chairmanship of local military commanders.[19]

In January 1984 the SADF publication *Paratus* carried an in-depth article on the progress of the Manpower Liaison Committee and its regional committees, making it clear that 'liaison does not have to deal with manpower issues alone', as 'opportunities must be created to project the image of the SADF on a variety of levels'. It disclosed that the committees had been involved in planning the massive increase in conscription that was embodied in the Defence Amendment Act of 1982. The Liaison Committee had also compiled 'guidelines' for private companies to make up the pay of their employees undergoing military service. The formation of regional committees, it was said, had been 'enthusiastically received by both military and civilian organisations'. The regional committees, which met in secret, had dealt with a variety of issues and received 'intelligence briefing sessions . . . to place controversial subjects into the correct perspectives'.[20]

Although clearly a very influential body, the Liaison Committee was presumably thought not capable of dealing with the increasingly severe manpower and economic problems which beset the apartheid regime after 1983. In May 1984 the Minister of Defence announced the establishment of a Committee of Inquiry to look into 'adaptations that might become necessary to meet future demands on the SADF', as a result of 'challenges arising from the Republic's difficult economic realities, changes in the security situation, the new constitutional dispensation and so forth'. The committee, which was chaired by General Geldenhuys, the Chief of the Army, included the Armscor chairman, Commandant Marais, and the ex-chairman of the General Mining Group, Wim de Villiers.[21]

As an interim measure, to reduce economic pressure on both the SADF and the private sector, changes were announced in September 1984 to the call-up system. Periods of 'border duty' (service in the war zones) were increased from three months to six months at a stretch for National Servicemen, thus reducing the need to call up Citizen Force and Commando units. The saving in transport costs to the SADF was put at R180 million and businesses were reported to be expecting to save 'millions of rand in productivity and a more stable workforce'.[22] Such expectations disappeared in the face of the growing upsurge of township rebellion which led to a State of Emergency in July 1985 and the mobilisation of thousands of white conscripts for the 'pacification' of the townships.

Key Points

As early as 1965 the South African government began to identify industrial plants and installations deemed to have strategic value, with the aim of protecting them against sabotage and other acts of resistance.[23] The following year legislation was introduced to accord protection by Commando units to identified National Key Points.[24] The number of sabotage incidents declined after the intense repression of the early 1960s and for the following ten years security at industrial installations was not seen as a priority. Even after the 1976 uprisings few industrialists were prepared to implement more than rudimentary security precautions.

Within a few years the situation had changed. This was dramatically confirmed on 1 June 1980, when Umkhonto we Sizwe guerillas carried out a highly damaging sabotage attack on the regime's showpiece Sasol oil-from-coal plants, the most vital strategic industrial installations in the country. The Sasol plants were regarded as the best protected in the land, and in the six months preceding the ANC operation the regime had invested R4 million in upgrading security there.[25] The multi-million rand sabotage operation coincided with the passage through parliament of far-reaching legislation obliging companies to implement rigorous security procedures.

The National Key Points Act of 1980 empowered the Minister of Defence to declare any place or area a Key Point; compel its owners to implement, at their expense, security precautions as laid down by a government committee; and prohibit publication of any information regarding security measures at the Key Point. Owners who failed to comply with the regulations faced prison sentences of up to five years and fines of up to R20,000.[26]

There was some resistance to the Key Points Act from companies which baulked at being forced to pay for 'services' they regarded as the responsibility of the government. Some companies also feared that their increasing involvement with the SADF would lead to political accusations that they were openly collaborating with the apartheid war effort.[27] This opposition soon waned and within a few months it was reported that 85 per cent of the 633 identified Key Points were 'fully co-operating' with the government.[28]

The Key Points measures went some way towards meeting the security fears of private companies. In a memorandum leaked from the General Motors Corporation in 1978, the company complained that South African industry was 'poorly prepared to handle industrial disruption and civil unrest'. It noted, however, that 'almost 100 per cent of white employment at General Motors South Africa would not be party to creating or stimulating civil unrest . . . and could be relied on to take action to contain it'. The memo set out an 'Action Plan' in the case of civil unrest or industrial disruption, which included arming security staff and maintaining contact with the police and Civil Defence authorities.[29]

The Key Points Act set South African security firms on course for what one journal headlined as 'A Multi-Million Rand Bonanza'. According to the *Financial Mail*, by 1983 the security industry in South Africa had an annual turnover perhaps as high as a R1,000 million, spread among 500 companies with over a quarter of a million employees. Business had increased by over 500 per cent in a decade, and was still booming.[30]

White Rhodesians fleeing from independent Zimbabwe were responsible for many small, short-lived security firms that sprang up to fulfil the growing needs of an increasingly concerned private sector. Cashing in on their military experience, ex-Rhodesian soldiers appointed themselves directors of new security firms or joined existing ones. They were largely responsible for stamping a paramilitary character on to security firms.[31] Retired SADF and police personnel also took up executive posts in security firms. Lt. Gen. Dutton, formerly Chief of Staff

Operations in the SADF and ambassador to Chile, was put in charge of the exports division of one of the largest firms.[32]

Security companies in South Africa today have the appearance of private militias. The guards are often armed with automatic rifles and drilled in military fashion. A recent innovation has been a 'Rapid Deployment Force', a highly trained, heavily armed security unit that can be deployed by helicopter to any company willing to pay the price.[33] Security firms liaise closely with the SADF. At the end of 1985 links between the firms and the military establishment were cemented at a conference 'aimed at realising a uniform security strategy' and attended by top SADF officers and leading businessmen.[34]

Industrial security is further strengthened by the Commando system. White employees at Key Points who have received military training are organised into Industrial Commandos attached to industrial plants, groups of factories or industrial areas. At some installations platoons of 'reliable' black workers have also been recruited. Contingency planning and other aspects of Industrial Commando training and deployment are jointly worked out by SADF commanders and the management of the factories concerned.[35]

Despite these massive security precautions, the South African regime has not been very successful in protecting industrial facilities and Umkhonto we Sizwe guerillas have attacked many installations. In order to function all South African industries have to employ hundreds of black workers – and any one of these workers could become an 'enemy within', assisting guerillas or taking on sabotage operations. It is highly unlikely that the ANC could have carried out its more dramatic sabotage operations without inside assistance – and it is equally unlikely that a stronger Industrial Commando or an upgraded security corps would have saved the installations from attack.

Oil – 'A Munition of War'

The apartheid regime has moved to secure its strategic industrial interests in a number of areas. The most important of these is in the provision of energy resources, particularly oil, as this is one of South Africa's most vulnerable points of dependence on the outside world. As the mechanised nature of the SADF makes it absolutely dependent on a supply of oil and other petroleum products, oil has been designated 'a munition of war'. The regime has full powers over the industry in times of emergency.

Despite the discovery of a large natural gas field off the coast of Namibia and a smaller gas and oil field off Mossel Bay in the Cape, the results of more than a decade of intensive exploration, no oil or gas has been pumped from South African or Namibian territory. There are political problems for the regime attached to the exploitation of the Namibian resources and major economic questions need to be answered about the Mossel Bay field. As an alternative strategy, the South African regime has established three plants to convert its abundant coal resources into oil – known as Sasol.

These have been established at immense cost and together are one of the largest single industrial projects in the world.[36]

The first Sasol plant was built in 1955, long before there was any threat of political oil sanctions against the regime.[37] This plant now only accounts for about one per cent of the country's oil requirements. The international oil crisis in 1973 coincided with the first moves by the international community to use the 'oil weapon' against the apartheid regime, when the Arab summit conference meeting in Algiers called for 'a complete Arab oil embargo' against South Africa, Rhodesia and Portugal. As a result, Pretoria lost half its supplies. Iran, then South Africa's principal supplier, stepped into the breach and until the overthrow of the Shah provided over 90 per cent of South Africa's imported oil.[38]

In 1974 the South African regime drew up plans to construct a further Sasol plant at Secunda in the northern Transvaal, with a capacity about ten times that of Sasol I. This was completed in 1980. In February 1979, after the termination of Iranian oil supplies, a third plant was announced, to be constructed adjacent to Sasol II. The projected cost of the two plants was in excess of half the South African government's total annual budget.[39]

Even at full production, the combined capacity of the Sasol plants has been variously estimated to meet only between 22 and 40 per cent of South Africa's oil requirements.[40] Efforts have been made to establish other alternative fuel supplies, such as the production of ethanol and methanol, but these are expensive and can only offset a small proportion of energy needs.[41]

South Africa thus remains vulnerable to an oil cut-off from the outside world. The cancellation of the Iranian contracts in 1979 led to an immediate 40 per cent drop in oil imports[42] and it has been estimated that Pretoria's oil import bill doubled between 1979 and 1980, even after the reduction in import levels. This was partly because the regime was forced to obtain secret supplies of oil on the spot market at premiums sometimes 60–80 per cent above the OPEC listed price.[43]

All OPEC countries have embargoed oil sales to South Africa and embargoes have been imposed by other oil-producing nations. Since December 1979 the UN General Assembly has called for a total embargo, although mandatory restrictions have been imposed. In the absence of effective international enforcement of the embargo, South Africa has been able to obtain adequate supplies of oil (estimated at 300,000 barrels a day), albeit at a considerable premium.[44]

Oil has been obtained from a handful of small oil-exporting countries which chose to ignore the embargo, and through intermediaries – other countries and commercial companies which have disguised the source and destination of the oil.[45] The expense involved in procuring oil by these methods has been immense. To the cost of embargo-breaking operations and the establishment of oil-from-coal and oil-substitution technology must be added the cost of stockpiling.[46] In 1983 a Pretoria Cabinet Minister admitted that 'the acquisition of oil was more difficult than arms' and that the oil embargo 'could have destroyed' the apartheid regime.[47] The ANC and SWAPO have calculated that the total annual cost to the South African regime of overcoming the oil embargo has been nearly US $2 billion.[48]

The South African regime has tightened its control over oil supplies by a series of regulations governing the conduct of oil companies in South Africa. Companies are obliged by law to stockpile reserves, to sell a certain percentage of their products to the state (including the SADF), to produce specified products regardless of commercial considerations and to liaise closely with the regime in the expansion of plant facilities.[49]

A blanket of secrecy has been thrown over the oil industry, both to provide a cover for those involved in procuring oil for South Africa and to disguise Pretoria's strategic vulnerabilities in this field. Since the 1973 oil crisis no statistics on oil imports have been published, and the Protection of Information Act further restricts the supply of information on the oil industry. In June 1979 an amendment to the Petroleum Products Act was introduced making it a criminal offence to publish information on 'the source, manufacture, transportation, destination, storage, quality or stock levels of any petroleum acquired or manufactured for or in the Republic'.[50]

The regime's continuing concern at its vulnerability to oil boycotts was underlined by a government report drawn up in August 1985, which called for a 'national energy strategy' and investment of billions of rand in further oil-from-coal facilities and to exploit the Mossel Bay field.[51]

Imported Arms and the Arms Embargo

As a result of far-reaching developments which have been instituted to protect the apartheid regime from arms embargoes, South Africa now claims to have the largest military-industrial complex in the southern hemisphere, manufacturing and assembling a wide variety of arms and components, from rifles to jet aircraft.[52]

Until the imposition of the UN arms embargo in 1963, South Africa obtained most of its armaments from Britain. After 1963, Pretoria turned to other Western countries, especially France and Italy, and devoted considerable resources to developing a domestic arms industry. Since 1977, when the arms embargo was made mandatory, the SADF has had to rely on expensive domestically produced weaponry and on companies and individuals willing to circumvent the mandatory embargo. It now faces serious equipment shortages, especially aircraft.

The Arming of Apartheid
A domestic arms industry was first established in South Africa with British aid during the Second World War. Most of the facilities were dismantled after cessation of hostilities. Thereafter, South Africa armed itself almost entirely with British imports, some of which are still in service today – for example, Canberra bombers. Even the Saracen armoured cars, the

mainstay of the SADF during the early 1960s and much in evidence during the 1961 State of Emergency, were resurrected in 1984 for township patrols.

In terms of the 1955 Simonstown Agreement Britain undertook to supply Pretoria with a small modern naval fleet and a number of patrol aircraft. The agreement also provided for joint defence of the Cape sea route and for Britain to use the Simonstown base in times of war. Pretoria expected the Simonstown Agreement to lead to a wider bilateral defence treaty, but the process of decolonisation, and rising international concern about apartheid, prevented this. Nevertheless, the weapons involved in the deal were duly delivered, forming the backbone of the apartheid navy for many years, and the Simonstown Agreement itself was cancelled only in 1975.

The events of 1960–61, culminating in the banning of the ANC and the PAC and the declaration of an all-white republic, set Pretoria on a political road that would lead both to increasing international isolation and internal resistance. Preparations were made for the development of a domestic arms industry. Prime Minister Verwoerd announced: 'We want to enlist the assistance of the industries in this country for the manufacture of armaments so that we shall not be solely dependent on countries abroad.'[53] As a first step, the South African government began to manufacture ammunition.

On 7 August 1963, after considerable lobbying by African and other third world countries, the UN Security Council recognised South Africa as 'a threat to the maintenance of international peace and security' and called on all states 'to cease forthwith the sale and shipment of arms, ammunition and all types of military vehicles to South Africa'.[54] A further resolution passed a few months later additionally prohibited 'the sale and shipment of equipment and materials for the manufacture and maintenance of arms and ammunition in South Africa'.[55]

The 1963 embargo 'called on countries' to abide by its provisions – it was not mandatory. Both the UK (after 1964) and the USA, until then South Africa's major arms suppliers, indicated that they would obey the embargo, but continued to allow the supplies of spare parts, radar and electronic equipment. Furthermore, in terms of 'firm contracts' entered into before 1964, the transfer of British Buccaneer and Canberra jet bombers, Wasp helicopters, naval shells and chassis for armoured cars and military trucks was allowed. Prohibitions were not enforced on the transfer of technology and weapons through third parties – amongst other things permitting Pretoria to acquire Rolls Royce jet engines through Italy for its Impala aircraft.[56]

The British firms Marconi and EMI established electronic component subsidiaries in South Africa which went into the production of military goods. Other British firms circumvented the arms embargo through their South African subsidiaries. British Leyland (SA) provided vehicles to the SADF, and ICI South Africa, wholly-owned by its parent company in the UK, helped establish an explosives factory.[57] When the Conservative Party came to power in Britain in 1970, it announced that it would re-open direct armament transfers to South Africa, but domestic and international opposition was such that only six Westland Wasp helicopters were supplied.[58]

France and Italy filled the gaps left by the US and Britain. The strike capability of the SAAF relies on French aircraft supplied or assembled in South Africa under licence during the 1960s and 1970s. These include a variety of helicopters, transport aircraft, and Mirage Fls and Mirage IIIs, at the time amongst the most modern and sophisticated military jets available.[59] French companies also supplied the apartheid regime with a variety of modern missiles, entering into an agreement for the joint production of Cactus ground-to-air missiles. French armoured cars became the mainstay of the SADF's armour and South Africa also obtained its first submarines from France.[60]

Between 1960 and 1983 French companies were by far the largest suppliers of weapons to the apartheid regime. According to the Swedish International Peace Research Institute (SIPRI), 44 per cent of South African weapons imports came from France in the 1960s, and between 1970 and 1974 this percentage increased to over half. Even in 1980–83, France was estimated to be the source of nearly 30 per cent of Pretoria's arms acquisitions.[61]

Italian and Belgian firms also became important arms suppliers to South Africa. Between 1970 and 1976, SIPRI estimates that Italy accounted for 19 per cent of South African arms imports.[62]

Increasingly, the SADF obtained its arms through locally assembled weapons produced in South Africa under licensing and co-production agreements. French Mirage and Italian Aermacchi jets, Belgian FN rifles, French Panhard armoured cars and other weapons were assembled in South Africa. South Africa also obtained arms by deception through third parties.

One of Pretoria's most successful embargo-breaking exercises was 'Project Advokaat' – the establishment of a sophisticated underground electronic surveillance centre at Silvermine near Cape Town. Opened in 1973, the Silvermine centre is reported to be able to monitor shipping and air traffic from North Africa to the Antarctic, and from South America across the Atlantic and Indian Oceans to Bangladesh.[63] Silvermine was equipped with modern computer, radar, and communications equipment supplied by companies in a number of countries, including the Federal Republic of Germany, Britain, France, the Netherlands, Denmark and the USA.[64]

Silvermine was linked with the Royal Navy in Simonstown and London, the US naval base in San Juan, Puerto Rico, and also to Argentina, Portugal and the French naval bases at Dakar and Madagascar.[65]

The SADF has made no secret of the fact that it has passed on information from Silvermine to the Western powers, and that it has expected to receive information, technology and military and political support in return. For example, Admiral Biermann, ex-commander of the

SA Navy, has stated:

> Information gained by Shackleton and Albatross aircraft operating in the 50 mile range is passed to the United States and the United Kingdom through the Joint Maritime Headquarters Communications Centre at Silvermine. This surveillance operation is very expensive and it is one in which NATO countries should assist.[66]

In April 1976, the British Ministry of Defence admitted that it was in constant direct contact with Silvermine.[67]

The facilities at Silvermine were used by Pretoria in its efforts to integrate itself with NATO, and thereby to place itself under the West's nuclear and conventional military umbrellas and to internationalise the conflict in Southern Africa. Documents presented to the UN Security Council in 1975 revealed that South Africa had been given access to NATO codification forms and to the system used to order NATO military communications equipment and spare parts, specifically for the monitoring equipment at Silvermine.[68] Subsequently, in 1976, the British government admitted that it had allowed the transfer of NATO military catalogues to the apartheid regime. The codifying and cataloguing system used by the SADF for all its equipment subsequently employed the NATO register.[69]

In 1972, a subcommittee of the North Atlantic Assembly drew up a report recommending South African participation in an extended NATO arrangement for the surveillance and protection of shipping lanes in the South Atlantic and Indian oceans.[70] Two years later a secret NATO contigency plan drawn up by the Supreme Allied Commander Atlantic for air and naval operations around Southern Africa was revealed.[71]

In November 1980, the NATO Secretary-General, Joseph Luns, met 'privately' with the South African Foreign Minister, Pik Botha, at his residence in Brussels.[72] Further reports of co-operation between NATO and South African military authorities appeared in the British press following the arrest of South African Navy Commodore Dieter Gerhardt and his wife Ruth Gerhardt in 1983, both of whom were found guilty of spying for the Soviet Union. Details were given of the access which Gerhardt, as a senior South African naval officer, had to NATO information. According to the *Mail on Sunday*, this pointed to a regular exchange of information on weapons and intelligence matters between South Africa and the Western powers.[73]

South African links with the military establishments in Western countries have been further strengthened by the posting of South African military attachés at embassies overseas, and the presence of Western military attachés in South Africa. In Britain, the South African military attaché was implicated in illegal arms deals, while attachés from the NATO countries in South Africa have attended SADF military exercises.[74] Most Western military attachés were withdrawn from South Africa following the 1985

State of Emergency, but in most cases the South African attachés remained at their overseas posts.

Many of South Africa's present generation of weapons have been acquired as a result of collaboration with Israel. In the 1960s, as the regime cast around in search of alliances outside NATO, Pretoria began to cement economic, military and political relationships with the government of Israel.

South Africa strongly supported Israel in the 1967 Middle East war. A flurry of military and political exchange visits followed the war, culminating in a visit to Israel in 1976 by Prime Minister Vorster. This visit was reported to have put the official seal of approval on growing covert links between the two countries in the field of arms production, intelligence and nuclear technology.[75]

The fruits of South African–Israeli collaboration have been extensive. The SADF's acquisitions from Israel include a wide range of weapons and armaments, and Israeli Reshef and Aliyah class fast attack boats have been assembled in South Africa.[76]* A number of Israeli military specialists have visited South Africa in unofficial capacities and close military links have been established between Israel and the Ciskei bantustan. Twenty-three pilots for the fledgling Ciskei 'Air Force' were trained in Israel in 1983, and Israeli mercenaries have been hired as personal bodyguards for Ciskei cabinet ministers and as advisers to the Ciskei 'Defence Force'.[88]

Violating the Arms Embargo

By 1977 international pressure on South Africa had reached a new level following the invasion of Angola, the Soweto uprising, the death of black consciousness leader Steve Biko, and the banning of nearly twenty anti-apartheid organisations in South Africa. On 4 November 1977 the UN Security Council adopted Resolution 418, declaring that 'the acquisition by South Africa of arms and related material constitutes a threat to the maintenance of international peace and security'. The Security Council instructed all states 'to cease forthwith any provision to South Africa of arms and related material', to review licences granted for the manufacture and maintenance of arms and to 'refrain from any co-operation . . . in the manufacture and development of nuclear weapons'.[126] There were a number of weaknesses in the resolution: it merely called for the 'review of existing licensing arrangements; it left it up to member countries to decide what exactly constituted 'arms and related material'; it did not call for a total ban on nuclear collaboration; and the committee set up to monitor

---

* Israeli weapons in SADF service include a 105mm gun and modification package for Centurion tanks,[77] Gabriel anti-ship missiles,[78] Shafir air-to-air missiles (unconfirmed),[79] Barak point-defence missile systems (unconfirmed),[80] anti-personnel mines,[81] Mooney TX-1 military training craft for the Ciskei Air Force,[82] RPV pilotless reconnaissance aircraft,[83] naval attack and patrol craft,[84] fire control systems for the SADF's 155mm nuclear-capable artillery,[85] and a variety of military electronic components and goods.[86] There are also unconfirmed reports that the SADF has acquired 36 Kfir fighter aircraft (which are virtually identical to the Mirages) and Arava tactical troop transport aircraft.[87]

and enforce the embargo had limited powers. Nevertheless, the mandatory arms embargo was a severe blow to the apartheid regime.

Three principal methods have been used to circumvent the mandatory arms embargo. Firstly, covert deals have been conducted, usually arranged through third parties and involving false shipping papers, bribes and the establishment of front companies. Secondly, the South African regime has acquired military equipment such as computers, radar and aircraft on the grounds that these could be considered to be civilian items. Thirdly, components, technology and industrial assembly lines have been transferred to South Africa, often disguised as civilian materials, enabling the regime to establish new military manufacturing facilities.

Some clear violations of the arms embargo have been detected, and some prosecutions have been brought, but in the majority of cases those involved have been able to argue that the equipment has fallen into a 'grey area' not explicitly covered by the embargo.

Perhaps the most spectacular, and certainly one of the best documented violations of the embargo concerns the acquisition by the SADF of US/Canadian 155mm artillery, and the subsequent manufacture of a variation of this weapon in South Africa.

In the mid-1970s the SADF made contact with the US/Canadian firm, Space Research Corporation (SRC), which had developed an advanced 155mm artillery system with an extended range shell capable of being modified to take nuclear warheads. Through a highly complicated series of transactions, in which a number of front companies were established and millions of dollars changed hands, at least four of the 155mm guns, 60,000 shells and a number of accessories were provided to Armscor. Patents (including the technology to convert the shells to nuclear use) were also acquired.[89]

SRC personnel went to South Africa to assist in the establishment of a machine line to manufacture the weapons and special manufacturing equipment was imported from France and West Germany. A few years later Armscor announced the 'indigenous development' of an advanced 155mm artillery system called the G5, which was quite obviously a modification of the SRC weapon.[90]

As well as entering into commercial production of the G5, Armscor has developed a mobile version called the G6, which, although only in prototype, is regarded as one of the most advanced weapons of its kind. To offset the huge costs involved in producing the weapons, Armscor has been desperately attempting to find an export market, describing them as 'world beaters'.[91]

Other less spectacular breaches of the arms embargo have led to the continued upgrading of South Africa's military strength. South African arms agents have been particularly active in the United States and Britain. As much of the equipment, components and spare parts required by the SADF are British in origin, the United Kingdom has naturally been a focus for Armscor agents.

In October 1982, three British citizens were imprisoned after being found guilty of smuggling arms and arms components to South Africa. The goods, described as hydraulic equipment, were exported without licences to an Armscor front company. In 1984 four top Armscor officials were arrested in Britain together with three Britons and charged with acquiring missile components, spare parts for Buccaneer bombers and other military equipment. The South African officials were bailed and returned to South Africa, where they admitted to their embargo-breaking activities, declared that they would do the same again, and refused to return to Britain to stand trial. The Britons were found guilty and fined or imprisoned. Also in 1984, it was revealed that British customs officials had uncovered a series of arms smuggling deals worth over £2 million by the firm Redman Heenan International, which paid a penalty to customs to avoid publicity.[92] A report by the Anti-Apartheid Movement in 1985 on the arms embargo noted that the cases of arms smuggling brought before the courts in Britain 'only reflect the tip of the iceberg as there continues to be a massive clandestine trade in armaments to South Africa, in total violation of the arms embargo'.[93]

One of the most serious circumventions of the arms embargo has been the acquisition of advanced radar systems from the British companies Plessey and Marconi. This has enabled the SADF to modernise both its static and mobile military radar facilities, a crucial factor in its war against the Front Line States.

A sophisticated radar system was acquired from Marconi in the 1960s, and this was supplemented in the late 1970s by mobile radar units obtained secretly from Plessey. SADF personnel were sent to Britain for training on the Plessey equipment, which is described by the firm as a military radar system. When the deal was exposed, the UK government retorted that the equipment was civilian in nature and was being supplied to the civilian air traffic control body in South Africa. Some years later exactly the same equipment was installed at the British military airbase in the Falkland Islands.[94]

By the end of the 1970s the SADF's original Marconi static radar systems were in need of modernisation and expansion to co-ordinate the increased level of aggression against neighbouring states. A decision to allow Marconi to update the system was taken by the UK government in 1981. On 24 April that year the *Observer* newspaper broke the news that the first consignment of Marconi equipment, worth £5 million, was about to be delivered to South Africa. The system, the S247, is described in *Jane's Weapons Systems* as 'a high-powered static radar system used for defence purposes'. The British Foreign Office indicated that, as it believed the radar was 'predominantly for civil purposes', it could be supplied to South Africa without violating the arms embargo.[95] The supply of this equipment led the retiring Chief of the SAAF, Lt. Gen. Muller, to announce in 1984 that good progress had been made with 'a modern automatic command and control system for communication and information during operations with fighter aircraft' which were thus 'more effective in the operational area'.[96]

A further area in which the SADF has benefitted from the transfer of 'dual purpose' or 'grey area' technology is in the field of computers and electronics, which are essential to a modern army. British and US firms in particular have supplied sophisticated computers to Armscor, the Council for Scientific and Industrial Research, the police and the SADF itself.[97]

The USA has been a vital source of technology and equipment, especially since 1981 when the Reagan administration relaxed export controls to South Africa. A detailed study by a group convened by the American Friends Service Committee revealed that, in the fiscal years 1981–83, the US State Department authorised commercial sales of more than US$ 28.3 million-worth of military-related equipment to South Africa – the highest level on record.[98] In addition, US$ 556 million-worth of aircraft not on the munitions list, but in many cases suitable for adaptation to military use, was sold during 1980-82.[99] Tracing a series of visits by South African military officials to the US, and technology and other sales to the apartheid regime and private companies in the South African military-industrial complex, the authors concluded that the arms embargo was being seriously eroded.[100] The same report also listed a number of military patents deposited with the South African patents office by weapons and munitions concerns in the USA, Britain, the Federal Republic of Germany, Belgium, France, Israel, Switzerland and Italy.[101]

South African arms buyers have been active in many countries. Between 1978 and 1980 a Danish company, Trigon, illegally shipped 6,000 tons of arms and ammunition to South Africa. One of the individuals involved was prosecuted in 1984 and given a fine and a suspended prison sentence. Spain, Switzerland and Austria have also been used as trans-shipment points for illegal arms and components supplies to South Africa.[102]

South African arms purchases overseas, particularly illegal deals, have been facilitated by an act of parliament introduced in 1974. The Defence Special Account Act (No. 6 of 1974) established an account for finances 'to be utilised to defray the expenditure incurred in connection with such special defence activities and purchases . . .as the Minister of Defence may from time to time approve'. The bulk of the funds in the Defence Special Account has been used for the purchase of arms and the development of the South African military-industrial complex. The advantage of the Special Account is that it is not liable to state audit and expenditure. It can thus be kept secret both from the general public and from other government departments.[103]

Over R10 billion has passed through the Defence Special Account over the past decade. In 1977, 60 per cent of the defence budget went through the special account.[104] The percentage declined slightly to about 50 per cent in 1984, representing the sum of R2.224 million.[105] *(See Table III)*

The secrecy surrounding arms and components purchasing is further enhanced by legislation which prohibits:

96

the disclosure of any information in relation to the acquisition, supply, marketing, importation, export, development, manufacture, maintenance or repair of, or research in connection with armaments.[106]

Furthermore, 150 companies have been exempted by ministerial decree from disclosing details of their operations, including most of the firms involved in arms, petroleum and strategic minerals.[107] Many of these firms are the South African subsidiaries of overseas companies. These multinational subsidiaries have played a vital role in enabling the SADF to circumvent the arms embargo by manufacturing military goods and components under licence, transferring technology, patents and technical information to South Africa and recruiting skilled personnel from the holding companies overseas. (One out of ten Armscor employees is an immigrant or foreigner.)[108] The contibution made by these companies is illustrated by advertisments for military-related goods in South African military magazines.

Apartheid's War Economy

Armscor
As explained above, during the 1960s the South African regime began to build up its military manufacturing ability, initially on the basis mainly of French, Belgian and Italian licences, and making extensive use of private sector links with Western countries. By the end of the decade the SADF was being locally supplied with rifles, mortars, ammunition, bombs, grenades, mines and napalm.[109]

In 1968 two state organisations were established: the Armaments Board, for purchasing arms and maintaining quality and cost control in arms production, and Armscor, which was responsible for controlling arms manufacture.[110] The Armaments Board was subsequently amalgamated into Armscor. The approach adopted by Armscor in the manufacture of arms has been clearly spelt out by its chairman, Commandant Piet Marais:

> Armscor is part of and exists only to render a service to the SADF. The aim of course is to procure and manufacture arms at the lowest possible cost . . . The Defence Force is responsible for determining new types of weapons that it requires to defend South Africa, and expansion of existing lines. After these have been defined, we come into the picture. Through a joint committee, they state their needs relative to the external threat, then we state our capabilities of meeting those needs within cost and time limits.[111]

From the outset, it was made clear that Armscor would not undertake the development or production of armaments in its own name. This would be done either through subsidiary companies or through companies in which the corporation would 'participate by way of shareholdings and/or financial assistance'.[112]

Private sector involvement in the provision of materials to the SADF was further strengthened by the introduction in 1970 of the National Supplies Procurement Act, which gave the Minister of Defence the power 'when necessary for the security of South Africa' to order any individual or company to 'manufacture, produce, process or treat and to supply or deliver or sell' any goods or services to the SADF.[113] These sweeping powers were first used in 1975 to meet a shortage of tents required for troops invading Angola.[114]

The development of a domestic military-industrial complex has been expedited by a policy of import substitution for the economy as a whole and for strategic industries in particular. Over the past two decades heavy import tariffs have been imposed on a wide range of selected imported goods to protect fledgling domestic industries. This highly expensive process became almost an obsession in the 1970s, although domestic goods could in many cases only be produced at much higher cost than imported goods due to the small scale of production.

Armscor was supplied by the government with an initial share capital of R100 million, with which it gradually set about establishing or taking over subsidiary companies and distributing military contracts to the private sector.[115] One of the first companies to be taken over as an Armscor subsidiary was Atlas Aircraft Corporation, established in 1965 by government initiative. With assistance from the French company Sud Aviation, the firm acquired licences from Italy to produce the Aermacchi jet trainers and light attack planes, which were renamed Impalas to give the impression of local production. Later Atlas also produced the Bosbok light military aircraft, a slightly modified version of a Lockheed model produced under Aermacchi licence, and a similar aircraft named Kudu.[116]

In 1971 Atlas announced that it intended assembling French Mirage fighter interceptors and ground attack jet aircraft which had been imported since 1963. Two years later an agreement was reached for the local assembly of Mirage IIIs, and in the following years more advanced Mirage F1s were assembled under licence. Despite South African claims that the aircraft were manufactured largely from local components, the planes were assembled almost entirely from imported kits.[117]

Missile research was started in South Africa in the 1950s, and in 1968 a test range was established in northern Natal.[118] A new Armscor subsidiary, Kentron, was set up to work on the development of missile technology.

In 1968 the first contract for the construction of a naval craft – a torpedo recovery vessel – was awarded to a Durban company.[119] In the following year the firm of Musgrave and Sons was incorporated into Armscor and charged with the production of rifles and high-precision arms components.[120] In 1970 Armscor took over the African Explosives and Chemical Industries plant at Somerset West for the manufacture of a variety of propellants and explosives.[121] Progress was also made in the assembly of military vehicles, initially Panhard cars and later Ratel armoured personnel carriers.[122] In the early 1960s small arms and artillery production was stepped up and the standard NATO rifle, the Belgium FN 7.62mm, was manufactured under licence.[123] This was replaced in the 1970s by production of the Israeli Galil, designated the R4.[124] *(See Table IX)*

The 1977 White Paper on Defence reported:

> The manufacture of small arms and heavy ordinance artillery showed an increase varying from 300 per cent to 500 per cent over the past period . . . important progress has been made with the establishment of ship-building facilities . . . the infantry combat vehicle 'Ratel' has been successfully industrialised and is already being manufactured at required rates . . .the successful development of a locally designed missile is being followed up by serial manufacture . . . telecommunication requirements are being met locally to the greatest possible extent . . . large scale utilisation of the private sector for the maintenance, upgrading and modernisation of existing armaments of the SADF has been undertaken.[125]

Despite this apparently impressive list, South Africa was nowhere self-sufficient in arms at that stage and, with the possible exception of ammunition, still relied on overseas imports and components.

Only a few months after the publication of the 1977 White Paper, the arms supply situation was dramatically changed when the mandatory arms embargo was imposed.

Because of the weaknesses in the implementation of the embargo, Pretoria was able to continue the build-up of its domestic arms industry, although at a slower pace and with considerably more difficulty.

Today Armscor is one of the third largest industrial concerns in South Africa, with assets of over R1,400 million.[127] It owns 15 factories and wholly controls eight major subsidiaries employing 23,000–33,000 staff.[128] *(See Table XIII)* Fifty main private sector contractors are engaged in producing components and military materials for Armscor, and 400 sub-contractors service the Armscor subsidiaries. Armscor's managing director claims that a further 1,500 firms are engaged in supplying 'nuts and bolts' for the military industry, but this may well be an exaggeration. According to the 1982 White Paper on Defence, nearly 100,000 private sector employees are kept in work by Armscor contracts.[129]

The eleven-member board of directors of Armscor consists of the Chief of the SADF, the SADF Director-General Finance, the chairman and managing director of Armscor, the president of the Atomic Energy Corporation and six leading industrialists and financiers.[130] The chairman of the board, Commandant Piet Marais, worked his way up through one of Armscor's major subsidiaries, Pretoria Metal Pressings, and via the De Aar

Commando, of which he was commanding officer in the 1960s. In 1979 Johan Maree was transferred from South Africa's largest industrial corporation, Barlow Rand, to serve as Armscor's chief executive for four years.[131] Maree's appointment underscored the close working relationship between the private sector and the government in the military field – at least 60 per cent of the armaments industry is contracted out to the private sector.[132]

Self-sufficiency?

In the mid-1970s, when Armscor was still in its infancy, the South African regime claimed that about a third of its arms and ammunition requirements were being met locally. This rose to three-quarters in 1977, and it is now claimed that the regime is 95 percent self-sufficient.[133]

Closer analysis of the apartheid military–industrial complex disproves these claims and reveals serious equipment shortages in all arms of the SADF. With regard to the air force, Atlas Aircraft has been scaled down since the delivery of Mirage kits was halted, and Armscor admits that it cannot make jet engines.[134] In effect, without access to imported kits, Atlas has been reduced to assembling light aircraft like the Bosbok and Kudu.

Atlas has also been unable to re-supply the air force with long-range patrol aircraft. The aging Shackletons were kept flying for 25 years with painstaking care and refitting but they had to be grounded at the end of 1984. To pressurise Britain or the USA into supplying replacements – Lockheed Orions or BAE Nomads – Pretoria announced that as a result of its inability to patrol the coasts, it would no longer pass on to Washington and London information from its Silvermine facility.[135] P W Botha was believed to have had the acquisition of new long-range patrol aircraft high on his list of priorities during his European tour in May and June 1984.

Air force commanders are also seriously concerned about the decline of their first strike capability, and their inability to upgrade the jet strike force. The British Canberras are nearing the end of their useful life and there are only six Buccaneers left in service as a result of crashes. Even the French Mirages, of which there is an abundance, are aging and will certainly need to be replaced before the end of the century.[136] Another serious deficiency in the air force's armoury is its shortage of helicopters and in particular the lack of armoured attack helicopters. Armscor is planning to build helicopters, but local production will not start until well into the 1990s.[137]

The South African Navy faces similar equipment problems, exacerbated by the accidental sinking of its flagship, the President Kruger, in 1982. Since 1978, the navy has largely abandoned its deep-sea role due to a shortage of appropriate craft. Its strike power is today built largely around eight small Israeli Reshef-class missile strike craft, five of which were built in Durban under licence. *(See Table X)* A further four of these craft are being constructed with Israeli assistance. The 'Skerpion' anti-ship missiles with which the craft are armed are claimed to be a South African development, but are in fact simply copies – if not direct imports – of Israeli Gabriel missiles.[138]

The army is somewhat better off than the navy and air force, as most of the basic armaments have a relatively high local production (but not design) content. The Centurion tanks, which have been modified by an Israeli package and redubbed 'Olifant' (and yet again claimed to be an indigenous development), are not up to world standards but are probably adequate for the SADF's needs. In any case, the South African army is not built around the tank, but the armoured car. The Ratel armoured personnel carrier (APC), reportedly developed by the Belgian company Sibmas, whose own APC is virtually identical to the Ratel, is manufactured in large numbers and in different configurations, as is the modified French Panhard called 'Eland'.[139]

South African standard-issue infantry weapons are readily available – but these are licensed productions of foreign models. The standard assault rifle, the R4, is an Israeli Galil, the MAG light machine-gun is Belgian, the heavy machine- guns are US/Belgian Brownings, and pistols and other light arms have been imported directly from Italy and the Federal Republic of Germany. *(See Table IX)*

The manufacture of the SADF's 155mm artillery system, the G5, is dependent on imported machine lines and technology, and the same applies to its mortars and other equipment. South African claims to have made major breakthroughs in the fields of missile research and development appear on the surface to be impressive, but in every case the missiles turn out to be modifications of equipment obtained from other countries.

In 1980 the SADF unveiled the Valkiri multiple rocket artillery system, claimed to have been locally produced. *Jane's Weapons Systems* (1982/83) strongly suggests that this is almost identical to a Taiwanese system and that the weapon is the result of co-production. The Kukri air-to-air missile, claimed to be a weapon 'the superpowers have spent years trying to perfect'[140] is in fact an amalgam of the US Sidewinder and French Matra X Magic systems with South African modifications and a largely South African-developed aiming system. South African claims to have developed an anti-aircraft missile, Cactus, are blatantly false – Pretoria simply put up 70 per cent of the finance for the French firm which developed the system, which is called Crotale in France.[141]

In a recent study issued by the Institute for the Study of Conflict in London, it was concluded that the SADF was in need of more modern radar and night fighting equipment, sophisticated communications equipment, up-to-date anti-tank weapons and modern surface-to-air guided missiles in addition to its shortages of air and naval craft.[142]

Electronics Industry

No modern army can function without sophisticated electronic command and control and communications facilities, and the development of a domestic electronics industry has thus been one of the South African regime's priorities. It is in this field that Armscor has claimed to have provided the 'most dramatic boost to local manufacturing capability'.[143] Considerable efforts have been made on the part of the SADF and the state to promote the local industry, including facilitating the takeover by local firms of overseas subsidiaries operating in the country and imposing protectionist import tariffs.[144]

Three main South African electronics companies, Altech, Reutech (Barlow Rand) and Grinaker Electronics, have all established themselves by taking over the assets of overseas subsidiaries and have drawn heavily on military contracts.[145] At least ten per cent of the South African electronics market is accounted for by military contracts – mostly at the high-technology end of the scale.[146] The SADF has also acted as a test bed and captive market for local products and, in turn, manufacturers have undertaken small and expensive production runs of equipment required by the SADF.[147]

Claims by Armscor officials that the military electronics industry is self-sufficient do not stand up to analysis. In 1982 it was estimated that more than 80 per cent of the industry's annual turnover of R2,000 million was controlled by foreign companies[148] and, in 1981, over 95 per cent of the computer industry remained foreign controlled.[149] A confidential government report has admitted that 'any move towards disinvestment from South Africa would have a particularly severe effect on the electronics industry'.[150] Disinvestment moves in the United States in 1985 led to renewed calls for direct government subsidies to underwrite the development of a South African computer industry.[151]

The head of the Department of Electrical Engineering at the University of Pretoria, Professor Louis Biljoen, declared in 1980:

> In spite of talk of high local content and other red herrings that are drawn across the trail from time to time, the horrible truth is that if we are not able to buy components such as diodes, integrated circuits and transistors, we cannot make anything.[152]

The situation has altered somewhat since 1980 but the 'horrible truth' of dependence on component imports remains. Armscor has tried to disguise this dependence by advertising 'locally developed' military communications equipment, especially frequency-hopping radios, which it has attempted to export to underwrite some of the huge sums invested in the industry.[153] In a review of one of these frequency-hopping radios, the Erinel TR178, the authoritative *International Defence Review* stated that 'most of the components used in the TR178 are of foreign origin and easily obtainable on the world market'.[154]

Motor Industry
A similar picture of dependence on imported components and technology

102

emerges in the motor industry, which has also been strongly promoted by the government and operates under strict local content rules. Since 1980, 66 per cent local content (by weight) for cars and 50 per cent for light trucks has been mandatory.[155]

The SADF's trucks and lorries, known as the Samil range, are assembled at a plant near Pretoria. It is claimed that they have a minimum 55 per cent local content, and that the range has been 'developed and manufactured in South Africa'. A new range launched in November 1984 was claimed to have a local content of 80 per cent.[156] But the company itself, Magnis, which draws its name from the FRG Magirus-Deutz and the Japanese Nissan group, advertises itself in South Africa as 'created to give the South African trucker the best of both worlds, Nissan Diesel value engineering and German technology'.[157] The trucks are based on vehicles which have previously been imported[158] and press reports have indicated that 'considerable international expertise' has been needed for the development of the range.[159]

Magnis vehicles are supplied with diesel engines manufactured at the Atlantis plant near Cape Town. This is a state-owned company which began production in 1981, using imported Perkins and Daimler-Benz production lines. To cover the immense cost of establishing the plant, the government raised import tariffs on diesel engines to a prohibitive level despite strong protests from the private sector. The *Financial Mail* complained that 'the local content programme being forced on the entire truck industry neither solves the military need, nor is good for the country's transport industry'.[160]

It is evident that in many key areas the apartheid regime remains extremely vulnerable to a strictly enforced arms embargo and to international sanctions, and that its military and economic capabilities have been substantially reduced by the existing arms and oil embargoes. The arms manufacturing and assembly facilities which have been established in South Africa have been built up at tremendous cost. A South African study group on industrial development strategy has concluded that 'the establishment of some so-called strategic industries definitely had the economic effect of raising the cost structure in industry and some other sectors'. In July 1982 General Viljoen, then head of the SADF, remarked:

> The [cost] escalation figures for military equipment can be as much as 30 per cent per annum . . . We have less equipment because we have to maintain a war and also pay more for the equipment we get.[161]

Despite the immense investment in domestic strategic industries, the SADF's requirements cannot be met domestically. According to evidence presented in 1984 to the committee of the UN Security Council responsible for monitoring and enforcing the arms embargo, the South African regime spent R900 million out of its total arms procurement budget of R1,620 million on arms purchases from overseas during that year. In another study carried out in July 1982, the Johannesburg *Sunday Times* concluded that imports from overseas accounted for 15 per cent of annual defence spending, which stood at over R3,329 million for that year.[162]

Arms Exports

Armscor's economic problems have been compounded by the recession in South Africa and by the small production runs – and thus high unit costs – forced upon it by the relatively small size of the domestic arms market. The size of the corporation's market diminished considerably after the end of the Zimbabwean war of independence – the Rhodesian regime was Armscor's only significant customer apart from the SADF.[163] To save money, cutbacks have been ordered in the Armscor programme. Between 1981 and 1984, staffing levels were reduced by a third and some 800 private sector companies faced reductions or cancellations in arms contracts.[164] It has been reported that since 1983 many Armscor plants have been running at less than half their capacity.[165]

Armscor has also attempted to increase its production runs and offset costs by finding new markets overseas. In 1981, Armscor's exports, by the company's own admission, amounted to only R10 million. Towards the end of 1982 Armscor executives launched a large international publicity drive and predicted exports of more than R150 million a year.[166] International military magazines were inundated with Armscor advertisements, claiming that its products were 'Born of necessity, tested under fire'.[167] In October 1982 Armscor exhibited its G5 gun and other equipment at an international arms fair in the Greek port of Piraeus – until the Greek government intervened and closed the stand.[168] In March 1984 Armscor products were again on display at an international air show in Chile.[169]

The corporation is most anxious to find a market for its G5 and G6 155mm artillery systems, and it is also looking for customers for Ratel armoured vehicles and the Samil truck range, the Valkiri and Kukri rocket systems, and its frequency-hopping military radios.[170] According to the South African *Financial Mail*, it is likely that Armscor is attempting to market these weapons in conjunction with Israel and Taiwan, with which it has developed many of the systems.[171]

The *International Defence Review* has reported:

> A number of successes have been chalked up, notably in Latin America. Because of political sensitivities, however, several South African firms prefer to market their products under different designations via companies in Western Europe and elsewhere.[172]

Overseas subsidiaries of South African companies involved in arms production have been used to sell South African-manufactured military equipment so that its origin is disguised. For example, a British subsidiary of Plessey South African holdings, Tellurometer, has marketed a South African- manufactured military range-finding device, claiming that the equipment originated in Britain.[173]

In December 1984 the UN Security Council adopted a resolution which noted that 'South Africa's intensified efforts to build up its capacity to manufacture armaments undermines the effectiveness of the mandatory arms embargo' and requested 'all States to refrain from importing arms, ammunition of all types and military vehicles produced in South Africa'. Although this resolution was non-mandatory and did not embrace a prohibition on the sale of 'related material', which would have strengthened its provisions, it clearly constituted a severe blow to Armscor's export drive which was already considerably constrained by political resistance to apartheid.[174] At the time the UN restrictions were imposed, a senior Armscor official admitted, 'to be frank, our export efforts have had limited results'.[175]

Nuclear Weapons and Chemical Weapons

On 22 September 1979 a US Air Force Vela surveillance satellite registered a double flash of light consistent with that which would have been caused by a nuclear explosion in the South Atlantic–Indian Ocean area. The South African Navy was conducting exercises in the region at the time. Three days later Prime Minister Botha announced that South Africa was in possession of 'military weapons they [the world] do not know about'.[176]

On the basis of information provided by the Vela satellite and other evidence, the US Defence Intelligence Agency and Central Intelligence Agency (CIA) as well as the Los Alamos Nuclear Laboratory and the Naval Research Laboratory concluded that a nuclear weapon had been tested on 22 September. The CIA reported to the US National Security Council that the explosion was probably a tactical two or three kiloton weapon detonated by South Africa with Israeli and possibly Taiwanese participation.[177]

Despite the conclusions of intelligence and scientific agencies, a scientific panel appointed by the Carter administration to investigate the event decided that the evidence was inconclusive. However, in 1985 the Washington Office on Africa, which conducted its own research into the 1979 event, obtained fresh evidence supporting the conclusion that a nuclear test took place in the South Atlantic–Indian Ocean region on the night of 22 September, and it is now generally accepted that the South African regime was responsible. Some analysts believe that the most likely delivery system would have been the G5 nuclear-capable artillery system. The G5 could easily be mounted on a South African warship, and the pattern of the explosion was consistent with that of a nuclear shell fired from such a weapon.[178]

The 1979 test was a sequel to another incident which occurred two years previously. In August 1977 a Soviet surveillance satellite detected South African nuclear test preparations in the Kalahari desert. US, British, West

German and French intelligence rapidly confirmed the information, and strong international protests were made to the South African Prime Minister. The suspected test facilities were dismantled and the South African regime claimed that it had had no intention of exploding a nuclear device.[179] Later Donald Sole, former South African ambassador to the USA admitted: 'We were going to test something, but not a weapon.'[180]

South Africa's Nuclear Industry

The apartheid regime clearly has at its disposal all the elements necessary for the manufacture of nuclear weapons. South Africa possesses more than sufficient quantities of uranium and the facilities to have enriched enough of the material to manufacture a number of nuclear weapons; its scientists and weapons specialists have the necessary technical skill; and the SADF possesses a variety of nuclear-capable delivery systems. Furthermore, South African military and government leaders have made oblique references to the fact that they could be developing nuclear weapons. The regime has refused to allow its most sensitive nuclear facilities to be opened to international inspection and has declined to sign the Nuclear Non-Proliferation Treaty.[181]

South Africa's nuclear programme began in the closing days of the Second World War, when, at the request of the USA and Britain, a secret study of the country's uranium resources was commissioned. Production of uranium began in 1952, and by 1955 19 mines were in operation under the control of the South African Atomic Energy Board. South Africa rapidly became one of the largest producers of uranium in the world, a fact it utilised in negotiations with Western countries for the provision of nuclear technology.

The South African regime began to develop a nuclear research capability in the mid-1950s, making use of international contacts through the newly-formed International Atomic Energy Agency (IAEA).[182] In 1957 the regime signed a fifty-year agreement on nuclear co-operation with the USA under Washington's 'Atoms for Peace' programme, and the following year a South African team was invited to observe US nuclear weapons tests.[183] The USA supplied Pretoria with its first nuclear reactor, Safari-I, which was put into operation at the National Nuclear Research Centre at Pelindaba in 1965. Enriched uranium for use in the reactor was supplied and South African scientists were trained to run the plant. With further US assistance Pretoria was able to establish another research reactor, Safari-II, which was also supplied with enriched uranium. South African nuclear engineers trained in Britain, the FRG, France and the USA were able to run Safari-II unaided.[184]

Close links were by this stage being forged with companies in the FRG, partly as a result of extensive South African supplies of uranium to that country. As a result of collaboration with the Steag firm, South African scientists were able to develop a uranium enrichment technique which was eventually incorporated into a pilot enrichment plant set up at Valindaba in 1975.

The pilot plant was conceived as a forerunner for a commercial enrichment plant capable of producing 5,000 tonnes of enriched uranium annually for export. For financial reasons the commercial plant was shelved, but construction began on a smaller enrichment plant in 1978. This facility, which was scheduled to come on stream in 1987, was reported to be capable of producing about 300 tonnes of enriched uranium annually, enough to meet the needs of South Africa's entire nuclear programme and with the possibility of a relatively small excess for export.[185]

The South African authorities have refused to allow international inspection of the Valindaba plants on the grounds that the process employed there is 'revolutionary' – although there is little evidence to support this claim. For the same reason, Pretoria has also refused to sign the Nuclear Non-Proliferation Treaty. As a result of this refusal to open its facilities to international inspection, the USA terminated supplies of enriched uranium for the Safari reactors in 1975. This had little effect as the South African authorities were able to replace the US supplies with uranium enriched at the Valindaba pilot plant.[186]

In 1976 the South African Electricity Supply Commission (ESCOM) entered into a contract with a French consortium headed by Framatome for the construction of a nuclear power station at Koeberg near Cape Town. A deal for the supply of enriched uranium for the two Koeberg reactors was reached with the USA in 1974 – the Valindaba plant could not supply sufficient enriched uranium to fuel Koeberg. However, South Africa's continued refusal to sign the Non-Proliferation Treaty obliged the US administration, in terms of an act of congress introduced in 1978, to refuse to honour the Koeberg deal. This raised the problem that the Koeberg reactors, then under construction, could not be commissioned due to a lack of fuel.[187]

Periodic high-level consultations were held between US and South African officials in an effort to break the deadlock over uranium supplies. Relations between the apartheid regime and the USA improved dramatically after the Reagan administration took office in 1981, and this was reflected in increasing nuclear collaboration. The administration did not interfere when, later in the year, two US companies worked out an elaborate arrangement to supply enriched uranium for the Koeberg reactors by obtaining uranium in France that had been prepared for a cancelled Swiss plant.[188]

The Reagan administration made a number of other concessions to Pretoria's nuclear programme, authorising the export of nuclear-related materials and research equipment. In the year starting 1 July 1981, South Africa became the third largest recipient of US nuclear exports.[189]

During 1983 South African expenditure on nuclear research was increased by 55 per cent and in June of that year it was announced that a new nuclear research establishment was to be established on the Cape coast. A thorough shake-up of the nuclear industry had been instituted in the previous year with the creation of a new body, the Atomic Energy Corporation, to replace the Atomic Energy Board. Recruiting of overseas personnel particularly in Britain and the USA was also stepped up, and a new uranium mine – the first to produce uranium as a main product in South Africa – was established at Beisa in the Orange Free State.[190]

On the basis of decades of nuclear assistance from the USA, Britain, France, the FRG and other countries the South African regime has acquired a civilian nuclear industry providing all the components necessary for the manufacture of nuclear weapons. There are a number of different ways in which highly enriched uranium or plutonium could have been diverted from the 'civilian' nuclear process into a weapons programme. The most likely source of weapons-grade uranium is through the enrichment facility at Valindaba, which is both capable of enriching uranium up to weapons-grade and free from international monitoring agreements. An expert report commissioned by the UN has estimated that by diverting uranium from Valindaba, Pretoria's nuclear scientists would have had sufficient material to make one or two fission bombs by August 1977, the date of the preparations for a test in the Kalahari, and seven or eight bombs by the time of the explosion over the South Atlantic, September 1979.[191]

South Africa is well provided with potential nuclear delivery systems. Its Mirages, Buccaneers and even Canberras are all capable of carrying a first generation fission weapon, and its 155mm artillery is adaptable for use with nuclear warheads. Larger bombs could be delivered by military transport or civilian aircraft.[192]

There have been persistent reports that South Africa and Israel have collaborated in the field of nuclear weapons and delivery systems, and further allegations have been made regarding collaboration with Taiwan, with which the South African regime maintains close military ties. An expert report presented to the UN General Assembly in 1981 noted:

> . . . There has been growing concern about possible nuclear co-operation between South Africa and Israel. Such speculations grew particularly persistent after Prime Minister John Vorster visited Israel in 1976 and signed various agreements of co-operation. However, there have been no official statements to confirm such co-operation in the nuclear field.[193]

Despite the lack of official confirmation, as has been noted, the CIA concluded that the 22 September 1979 event was a joint Israeli–South African nuclear test with possible Taiwanese participation.[194]

South Africa's approach to nuclear weapons has been described by the UN as most likely to be one of 'latent proliferation'. While letting the world know that it probably has a nuclear weapons ability and thus increasing its status as a regional power, Pretoria has avoided taking steps which would have absolutely confirmed its nuclear capability. This approach leaves the regime with bargaining space for preserving ties with the West, and lessens the possibility of international sanctions and extra-regional military intervention.[195] The director of Pretoria's Institute of Strategic Studies has made this point forcefully:

> Rumours that South Africa is already in possession of nuclear weapons may . . . provide a measure of deterrence, albeit limited, without the political disadvantage of open possession of these weapons.[196]

Nevertheless, voices have been raised in Pretoria in favour of an open declaration of the regime's nuclear strength. One of the strongest has been that of the head of the National Intelligence Service, L D Barnard, who has argued that: 'The acquisition of nuclear weapons will not necessarily isolate South Africa any further . . . Without a strong power base all modern diplomacy is doomed to failure.'[197]

As far as Pretoria is concerned, and as was stated in the 1977 White Paper on Defence, 'the right of the white nation to self-determination is not subject to discussion'. In terms of this perspective, the Deputy Minister of Defence, H J Coetsee, has made it clear that the regime would regard it as legitimate to use nuclear weapons if its back was against the wall: 'As a country with a nuclear capability, it would be very stupid not to use it if nuclear weapons were needed as a last resort to defend oneself.'[198]

Chemical Weapons

The SADF has been using, and there is some evidence that it has been developing, chemical weapons and other weapons banned by international conventions.

In 1968 the regime announced that it had started the domestic manufacture of napalm, which has subsequently been used extensively in Angola and Namibia.[199] In 1963 the Council for Scientific and Industrial Research (CSIR) said that South African scientists were 'working on deadly gases known to be capable of massive destruction comparable with the nuclear bomb'.[200]

A number of reports on the use of demobilising gases have been received from Angola. An investigation by the UN High Commissioner for Refugees and the World Health Organisation into the Kassinga massacre in 1978 noted that a paralysing gas had been used to incapacitate some of the victims before they were shot.[201] In 1981 the Angolan authorities reported that poison gas had been used during South African attacks on the village of Techipa[202] and in 1984 they reported that the SADF had been dropping 'bombs containing toxic substances on our troops and on the civilian population'.[203]

Evidence has also come to light pointing to the use of poison gases by the South African-supplied MNR force in Mozambique. When the Mozambique army captured an MNR base at Tome in Ihambane province at the end of 1983, they found 40mm shells containing an unidentified toxic substance. A public hearing on South African aggression, held in Amsterdam in early 1984, concluded that 'the use of chemical warfare in Mozambique was established to our satisfaction'.[204] The use of 'asphyxiating, poisonous or other gases' is outlawed by the 1925 Geneva Protocol, to which South Africa is a signatory, while international law prohibits the use of napalm against civilians.[205]

There is also extensive evidence of SADF use of chemical defoliants in Namibia and Angola, and the authorities have admitted to using defoliants in Namibia in order to establish cleared 'free-fire zones'.[206]

6. STRUCTURE OF THE APARTHEID WAR MACHINE

The structure and composition of the SADF and the South African Police have evolved since the Second World War in response to the changing regional and internal situation and in accordance with the minority regime's determination to preserve and retain domination of the South African region.

Until the consolidation of political power by the Afrikaner Nationalist Party in the 1950s, the SADF remained modelled on the British armed forces. This is still reflected in some of the Citizen Force units which retain British traditions, dress and designations.[1] During the 1950s the Nationalists began promoting Afrikaners preferentially at the expense of English-speaking officers. By 1975, 75 per cent of the SADF Permanent Force was made up by Afrikaans-speakers. Today, although official policy is one of bilingualism, Afrikaans is the *lingua franca* in the Permanent Force and the dominant language in most military structures.

At the same time that the Nationalist government began to replace English speaking permanent staff with Afrikaners, it laid plans to restructure the SADF – a reorganisation reflected in the 1957 Defence Act. As explained earlier, this established four categories of service in the SADF: a full-time Permanent Force of career soldiers; a Citizen Force of part-time conscripts, including those undergoing two-year periods of full-time National Service; and a Commando system of localised militia groups consisting of part-time volunteers and conscripts.

Command Structures

The SADF is divided into the traditional three arms – **army, navy,** and **air force**, and in 1980 the **Medical Services** were constituted as a fourth arm for administration. Since the mid-1970s, and the collapse of the colonial and minority rule 'buffer states' around South Africa, a shadowy 'fifth arm' has been developed under a separate command structure, **Special Forces** (*Spesmag* in Afrikaans). The past decade has also seen the establishment of

THE STRUCTURE OF THE SA DEFENCE FORCE

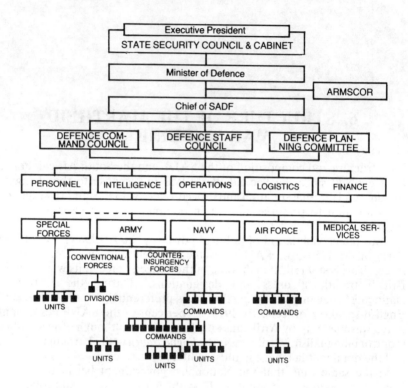

four small forces to serve the Transkei, Ciskei, Bophuthatswana and Venda bantustans.

The army is broken into a **Conventional Force** and a **Territorial Force**, which is primarily equipped for counter-insurgency warfare. The Territorial Force is divided into eleven separate **commands**, one of which, Namibia, is now nominally an 'independent' structure called the South West Africa Territory Force (SWATF). Until the end of 1983 there were nine commands but at that stage Northern Transvaal was split into three in order to facilitate operational deployment along the Botswana, Zimbabwe and Mozambique–Swaziland borders.[2] Joint operations involving other arms of the SADF – usually the air force – are co-ordinated through these army command structures.

The SADF's operations fall under the overall guidance of the **State Security Council** and its related structures. The highest body in the SADF itself is the **Command Council**, on which sit the Chief of the SADF, the Chiefs of the army, navy and air force, the Chief of Staff Operations, the

112

four other SADF Chiefs of Staff (Personnel, Intelligence, Logistics and Finance), and the Quartermaster-General and Surgeon-General.[3]

Financial management and arms production handled by the **Defence Planning Committee** composed of officers, representatives from the private sector and the chairman of Armscor. Overall SADF management is in the hands of another top committee, the **Defence Staff Council.**[4]

All five arms of the SADF have their headquarters in Pretoria, South Africa's 'military capital'. Each significant command structure within the various arms, at both national and regional level, is serviced by five **staff divisions**: personnel, intelligence, operations, logistics and finance, each headed by a Chief of Staff or Senior Staff Officer.

The Air Force

With about 250 combat aircraft the SAAF forms a reasonably modern strike force which is unequalled in sub-Saharan Africa. *(See Tables XI and XII)* With Headquarters in Pretoria, the SAAF operates through a number of commands: Main Threat Area, Southern (Maritime), Western (Namibia), Airspace Control, Tactical Support, and Logistics and Training Command.[5]

Main Threat Area Command operates the bulk of combat and transport aircraft. Spearheaded by three air superiority/fighter-bomber squadrons of French Mirages and six ground attack squadrons of Impala Mk2s, it also commands a squadron of medium bombers (Canberras) and long-range strike aircraft (Buccaneers). The Canberras double up in carrying out high-altitude reconnaissance – the SADF possesses up-to-date photo-reconnaissance facilities that are vital for cross-border strikes. Five squadrons of Impalas back up the Mirages, Buccaneers and Canberras in ground attack roles.[6] The combat aircraft are mainly based at Pretoria (Waterkloof), and in the Northern Transvaal at Hoedspruit and Louis Trichardt.[7]

For **transport** the air force relies on over forty Douglas C-47s, as well as Transall C-160s. For heavy lifts, Lockheed Hercules are used. These can be supplemented by 'civilian' variants of the Hercules run by the Safair air-freight company, which operates as a front for the SAAF.[8]

Southern Command (previously known as Maritime Command) lacks long-range patrol aircraft since the retirement of the old Shackletons, and is now restricted to coastal patrolling using a squadron of Piaggio Albatrosses. The naval replenishment ship, Tafelberg, has been refurbished with a helicopter deck, enabling it to carry large helicopters for deep-water patrolling and anti-submarine warfare – a flight of Westland Wasp anti-submarine helicopters is available. Buccaneer jets can also be used in a naval strike capacity although most are equipped for ground attack.

Although primarily concerned with maritime reconnaissance, Southern Command is also responsible for operations over the mainland, especially in the Cape Province.[9]

The air force makes extensive use of four squadrons of Bosboks, Kudus, Cessnas and other **light aircraft**, which are responsible for low-level tactical reconnaissance, forward air control, casualty evacuation and light transport. It also maintains seven squadrons of French **helicopters** which perform a number of vital tasks. Pumas and Super Frelons, the largest of the air force's helicopters, are used for transport and dropping and retrieving infantry patrols. Pumas and Alouettes are employed as gunships, providing air cover and following up guerilla contacts, and for casualty evacuation. They are also used for reconnaissance roles in urban areas.

Vital for counter-insurgency operations, helicopters are in short supply in the SADF, partly as a result of operational losses, and military commanders have often expressed a need for armoured helicopter gunships.[10]

Training Command controls six flying schools which use a variety of aircraft from Mirages to ancient propeller-driven Harvards – all of which can be diverted for operational duties in an emergency.

Aircraft are flown almost entirely by Permanent Force personnel, with National Service and Citizen Force members employed mainly in back-up ground roles. The permanent component is supplemented by a smaller number of voluntary Citizen Force members flying part-time in the six Impala squadrons. Thirteen **Air Commando** squadrons, one an all-women unit, consist of civilian light aircraft owners who volunteer for part-time duties under SAAF control. These can be mobilised in an emergency.[11]

The air force operates from eleven major air bases in South Africa, concentrated in the strategic area of the Northern Transvaal, and at five major bases in Namibia. These are supplemented by a network of tactical airfields, initially established mainly in Namibia, but now extended to the Northern Transvaal and northern Natal. As an economy measure, some country roads have been reinforced to double as runways.[12] It is the responsibility of **Tactical Support Command** to be able to establish a fully operational airfield at any location in South Africa in less than 48 hours.[13]

Over the past five years the SADF has been engaged in an extensive overhaul of the military radar system. The aim of this modernisation programme, involving the installation of Plessey and Marconi mobile and static systems, has been to co-ordinate fighter control more effectively in cross-border strikes and to monitor air traffic over countries to the north. The 1984 Defence White Paper announced:

> A start was made some years ago with the establishment of centralised command and control system for the air battle in the RSA in areas with a high threat potential. Since 1982 good progress has been made with the expansion of the communication network between bases and command posts and hence in the establishment of central control.[14]

The chain of fixed and mobile radar stations along the borders and in Namibia is controlled by **Air Space Control Command**, which also looks after the deployment of Cactus missiles and other anti-aircraft facilities.[15]

The Navy

As discussed in Chapter 1, the South African Navy (SAN) was formed only in 1946. Before that South African waters were patrolled by the British Royal Navy, which developed the Simonstown base.[16]

During the 1960s, South African strategists apparently failed to foresee that the future would bring not more but less Western support and that the arms embargo would severely undermine the strength of the fleet. Rear-Admiral A P Putter, the Chief of the SAN, has admitted that failure to take steps towards naval self-sufficiency during the Simonstown period 'was in part caused by the spurious shelter the Simonstown Agreement appeared to offer together with the belief that South Africa formed part of a military alliance with the West'.[17]

The Simonstown Agreement of 1955 called for the considerable expansion of the navy, which was accomplished through the purchase from Britain over the following twenty years of ten coastal minesweepers, four frigates, four seaward defence boats, and Buccaneer, Albatross and Wasp naval aircraft and helicopters. Regular exercises continued to be held with the Royal Navy.[18]

The SAN was further strengthened by the acquisition of three French Daphne-class submarines in the early 1970s, the establishment of the Silvermine surveillance and command centre, and the upgrading of the naval dockyard and other facilities at Simonstown which doubled its capacity.[19]

The termination of the Simonstown Agreement by the British Labour government in 1975 cut off the supply of British ships and equipment. The navy placed orders with France for the provision of two Agosta-class submarines and two corvettes. They were never delivered, as a result of the mandatory arms embargo imposed by the UN in 1977.[20]

The arms embargo put paid both to the navy's expansion plans and to the strategic objective of integration with Western powers. A change in strategy was clearly called for. The navy, declared the SAN Chief in 1978, would no longer 'look to its voluntary duty to care for the security of the Cape route' and would in future 'concentrate on our primary task of defending our own coast and harbours and patrolling our traditional fishing waters'.[21]

At the time, military spokesmen tried to present the post-1977 strategic shift as a positive, logical development. They now admit that it was very much second best. In the words of the navy Chief, Admiral Putter:

> South Africa has been forced to abandon its previous commitment to share in the defence of the wider Cape Sea Route in favour of a policy of concentrating on the defence of its own narrow interests –

this is not a situation which arose from South Africa's own making. It was not a policy which South Africa deliberately chose – it was a policy forced upon her because all other policy options were closed to her. It resulted from the abandonment by Western navies of their joint responsibilities in defending the Cape Sea Route. . . It resulted from the arms embargo.[22]

As a consequence of these developments the SAN now has virtually no deep-water capability. Its strength has been reduced to one frigate, three submarines and 11 fast attack craft, supported by five nearly obsolete British patrol boats, eight minesweepers and 30 small harbour patrol vessels.[23] Four more Reshef-class and three Dvora-class fast attack craft are on order, at least some of them being manufactured in South Africa.[24] The regime has also indicated that before the end of the decade it intends acquiring a small fleet of Israeli-model corvettes, which will probably be built in South Africa. However, no firm orders appear to have been placed for such craft.[25]

With its small fleet, the SAN has concentrated on coastal patrol duties and harbour protection. At least one South African naval strategist has recently suggested that the SAN should adopt a more aggressive regional role and expand its resources accordingly – the acquisition of corvettes would facilitate this process. For the present, the navy is concerned mainly with supporting destabilisation campaigns against neighbouring countries (supplying MNR and UNITA forces and landing SADF sabotage groups) and counter-insurgency tasks (harbour protection, coastal patrolling). According to the 1984 White Paper on Defence:

> The SA Navy is responsible for the protection of 42 national key points. . . for conducting sea and land patrols, manning check points, providing reaction forces and for explosive ordnance disposal.[26]

The counter-insurgency role of the navy has been expanded by the establishment of Marine units, which are basically specialised infantry units deployed around harbours and at SADF bases. Some of these bases are hundreds of miles from the sea – for instance, a unit is based in the Caprivi Strip in north-eastern Namibia. The 1984 White Paper states:

> For its counter-insurgency the SA Navy is compelled to train marines in urban, rural and maritime counter-insurgency operations. The marines are therefore capable of being deployed on a routine basis on land, and at sea both on the surface and under water. The SA Navy also provides a company of marines on an ongoing basis for operational service in Namibia. At present the SA Navy is devoting some 4,500 man-hours per year to support the SA Police/SA Railways Police in respect of road blocks. In addition, some 140,000

man-hours are devoted to the protection of national key points and naval installations.[27]

The Army

The army is by far the largest section of the SADF, taking up over half its budget and employing over 80 per cent of its manpower.[28] Like most armies it is divided for training purposes into **corps**, including infantry, armour, artillery, signals, personnel services, engineers, ordnance, military police, catering and intelligence.[29] Units falling under the various corps are administered through the territorial command system. For operational purposes formations are drawn from units of the various corps regardless of their original location.

The **infantry** is the backbone of the army. It consists of some 16 Permanent Force and full-time National Service units, 45 part-time Citizen Force units and over 200 Commando units. All the infantry units are trained in both rural and urban County-Insurgency (COIN) warfare techniques. Most of the Citizen Force units are based at training camps near the major cities, and are available to back up the police in joint urban operations. Over a third of the Citizen Force and two of the National Service infantry units are also trained in conventional warfare.[30]

Three National Service and 15 Citizen Force units constitute the SADF's **armour** force. These units rely mainly on modified Panhard AML 60 and AML 90 armoured cars, renamed 'Eland'. Tanks are in service in five units, but the difficult terrain and the shifting nature of the conflict lends itself to the more mobile armoured cars.[31]

The **artillery** consists of 16 field artillery units and 11 anti-aircraft units, all but two of which are Citizen Force formations.

As in any army, a large proportion of the SADF's troops are tied up with **logistics, support and administration** – Supply and Transport Depots, Maintenance Units, Technical Stores Depots, Field Workshop Squadrons, Engineers and the like. In 1979 the Minister of Defence reckoned that for every combat soldier 3.5 men and women were needed in support roles – in 1982 General Malan doubled that figure to seven.[32]

While most of the SADF's resources are tied up in COIN formations based on the infantry, a large proportion of the Citizen Force – an estimated 40,000 men – is trained and equipped for conventional as well as COIN warfare. This formation, **1 SA Corps** is broken into the 7th Infantry and 8th Armoured Divisions, each with three brigades.[33]

The Corps was established as a conventional force in 1974, when Pretoria's military strategists realised that they were losing the 'buffer states' to the north. According to the 1975 White Paper on Defence:

> Recent events in Southern Africa. . . accentuated the need for adjustment. . . The most obvious need was that the composition of

the South African Army should be brought closer into line with its two main tasks. These two main tasks, viz. countering all forms of insurgency and maintaining a credible and balanced conventional force, demand, because of their different natures, two separate organisations, each with its own command and control structure. This resulted in the subdivision of the land forces into a Counter-Insurgency force and a conventional force[34]

Each of the units involved in 1 SA Corps is regularly mobilised for training at a huge battle school which has been established in the north-west Cape at Lohatla. The largest-ever exercise, involving some 11,000 troops, was held there in September 1984.[35] Training call-ups are co-ordinated so that the SADF always has at its disposal a large force ready for instant deployment in conventional operations.[36]

The two conventional divisions constitute a formidable force which is not suited for use in anti-guerilla operations in South Africa or Namibia. The alleged justification for such a force is the 'communist onslaught', described in successive White Papers as: 'Marxist militarism. . . casting a shadow over Southern Africa' (1977); 'the military threat against the RSA. . . intensifying at an alarming rate' (1979); 'the presence of Soviet armaments in neighbouring countries. . . [increasing] the possibility of a conventional threat to the RSA and SWA even in the short and medium terms' (1982); and 'the USSR's pursuit of world domination. . . [and] the consolidation and expansion of Soviet influence in certain states in Southern Africa. . . [creating] an increased threat potential' (1984).

This type of propaganda reached a peak in 1982, when the SADF journal *Paratus* carried a number of articles warning that the Soviet Union was preparing a conventional onslaught against South Africa 'within the next five years'.[37] The following year General Viljoen, the SADF Chief, published an article in which he warned that the 'growing build-up of conventional weapons and surrogate forces in the RSA's neighbouring states' was part of the Soviet Union's 'global strategy', which Pretoria had to counter by a further arms build-up.[38] But a comparison between the SADF and the combined strengths of all the Front Line States shows quite clearly that there is no conventional threat against the apartheid regime.[39] Futhermore, none of South Africa's neighbours has attacked it or indicated a desire to do so. It is evident that the build-up of conventional forces has the aim of maintaining the SADF's ability to strike at neighbouring countries and to launch invasions aimed at devastating Southern African states or occupying their territory.

The massive build-up in conventional strength over the past ten years has been equalled if not exceeded by the training and equipping of vast numbers of COIN troops who are deployed in a variety of different units. All members of the army, whatever their mustering, are now trained in counter-insurgency. Tank and artillery regiments, for example, have been deployed as infantry in COIN operations at times when their conventional capacity has not been required.

Commandos
COIN forces are organised under the **Area Defence** system which covers the whole of South Africa. Citizen Force and National Service units (mostly infantry battalions) provide a reaction force in each territorial command while the Commandos – the localised militias – play an increasingly important role as the Area Protection element.

OFFICIAL SADF BREAKDOWN OF THE COMPOSITION AND ROLE OF THE COMMANDO FORCE

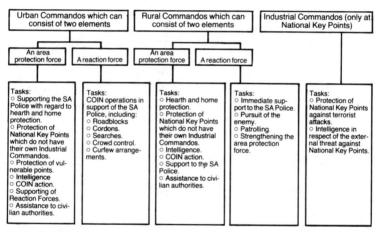

Source: *Star* 8.11.82

The role of the Commandos was described in the 1983 White Paper as: 'to act immediately in support of the SAP. . . to defend the territorial area allocated to them against insurgency and to assist the force deployed within those areas in a conventional battle'.[40]

Since 1979 an increasing number of conscripts have been allotted to the Commandos, to bolster the previously largely volunteer force. In 1982 legislation was introduced providing for the mass conscription of older white men into Commando structures *(See Chapter 4).*[41]

Commandos are divided into three distinct types: Rural or Country Commandos, Urban Commandos and Industrial Commandos. According to the South African Army publication *Uniform,* **Rural Commandos** are responsible for: '[protection of] their own districts [and] national key points, collecting information and area studies, anti-terrorist action and the

119

promotion of Civic Service'. It was further stressed that: 'These Commandos will give immediate support to the SAP. They will also help to track down the enemy until Reaction Forces arrive and will be responsible for the constant patrolling of their area.'

The main task of **Urban Commandos** was described as: 'to assist the SAP with crowd control, cordons, road blocks and curfews' and that of **Industrial Commandos** to 'collect information on the external onslaught against national key points and. . . assist with their protection'.[42]

All three types of Commando have a crucial front-line role in the regime's efforts to suppress the liberation struggle. Commando activity is not restricted to military actions but includes police work, intelligence gathering and participation in schemes to 'win the hearts and minds' of the black population. Most Commando units have sent detachments to the war zones of Namibia and Angola to gain additional battle experience, but this has become unusual since the inauguration of the Area Defence system (*See Chapter 4*).

Rural Commandos are the most common type of Commando. There are over 150 of these spread around the country. Each Territorial Command is divided into between three and six Commando Group Areas, with each Group in turn responsible for between five and nine Commandos.[43]*

Older white men are being mobilised for service in Rural Commandos as the Area Defence system is gradually activated in different parts of the country. The 1984 White Paper on Defence explained how this process is being implemented:

> The Defence Amendment Act, 1982 enables the South African Army to utilise additional manpower on a selective basis in the Commando Force. . . As implementation is closely related to the security requirements in Commando areas the new system is being applied in stages. When the system is implemented in a Commando Area the Minister orders a registration of citizens in the magisterial district concerned. . .

By the end of 1985, the areas in which this system had been activated included the Northern Transvaal and northern Natal, the area around East London bordering on the Ciskei and Traskei bantustans, and some areas around Lesotho. (*See Map and Table XVII*)

The Commandos are only part of 'the first line' in the Area Defence system, which includes the police, Civil Defence and local government structures, school cadets and a variety of state, private sector and voluntary bodies, all of which are integrated with the Commandos. Local police, railways police, education and administrative officials, town council heads, magistrates and Civil Defence chiefs meet regularly.[44] It is the task of these

---

* In conventional terms the Territorial Commands correspond to infantry divisions and the groups to brigades.

'first line' organisations to engage in intelligence gathering and 'preventative counter-insurgency' (including civic action, or 'winning hearts and minds') and to hold off a guerilla force in a combat situation or contain civilian 'unrest' until the 'offensive reaction force' can be brought in. This consists of Citizen Force and National Service units mustered under Territorial Command HQs and spearheaded if necessary by 'rapid deployment' police units or Special Forces.

Specialist Units

Reconnaissance Commandos
In the mid-1970s, the SADF established the **Reconnaissance ('Recce')**
Commandos, secretive, highly trained units which specialise in unconventional, covert operations.[45] The Reconnaissance Commandos fall under their own command system – Special Forces – and are answerable only to the head of the SADF.

Before the formation of the Reconnaissance Commandos, the **Parachute Battalions** constituted the elite reaction force. National Servicemen and Permanent Force members were recruited into the parachute (or 'parabat') units and subjected to rigorous training. Later a Citizen Force (part-time) parachute unit was also established. There are four Parachute Battalions, organised into 44 Parachute Brigade and based at various points around South Africa and Namibia.[46] The 'parabats' still play an important reaction role, but the more demanding tasks are reserved for the Reconnaissance Commandos and other specialised units.

The first of the 'Recce' Commandos – number 1 – was established in Durban towards the end of 1972. Since then further units have been established – 2 'Recce' in Pretoria, which is a Citizen Force part-time unit, 3 and 5 'Recce' at Phalaborwa in the northern Transvaal and 4 'Recce' at Langebaan in the Cape Province, which specialises in water-borne operations.[47]

The 'Recces' are extensively involved in the training and deployment of surrogate forces, including the MNR, which has been responsible for destabilising Mozambique and UNITA, which operates in Angola. They have also trained other specialist units and have engaged in 'pseudo operations' in the Namibian and Angolan war zones, disguising themselves, or black troops under their command, as SWAPO guerillas and then carrying out retributive attacks against civilians who have assisted them.[48]

Although large numbers of ex-Rhodesian troops, notably from the Selous Scouts, and white mercenaries (many of them also Rhodesian war veterans) are incorporated into the five regiments, the bulk of the 'Recce' force is made up of white South African troops. Before being called up for their National Service, conscripts are required to fill in a questionnaire in which they can indicate whether they wish to serve in the Special Forces.

Volunteers are subjected to a rigorous physical, psychological and medical pre-selection examination. Those chosen are then put through an intensive eight months' training course, including parachute training, instruction in the use of small boats and canoes, advanced weapons and explosive training, navigation, diving and exhausting physical endurance tests. Only about 45 out of 700 annual applicants finally qualify, after which they are despatched to the various 'Recce' units.[49]

The SADF journal *Paratus* has described the 'Recce' members as:

> particularly well trained in waging unconventional warfare. . . [including] the reconnaissance of the enemy's territory and the destruction of strategic targets, which are reached on foot, in vehicles, helicopters, across water or by parachute.[50]

The units are believed to have been responsible for some of the bloodiest massacres carried out by the SADF – the attacks on South African refugees and citizens of neighbouring countries in Maseru and Maputo, the capitals of Lesotho and Mozambique respectively. (Responsibility for the Kassinga massacre in Angola in 1978 rests with the paratroop units.)[51]

The 'Recce' Commandos operated in almost total secrecy until May 1985, when a member of 1 Commando was captured and two of his colleagues killed on a raid to sabotage an oil refinery in the northern Angolan enclave of Cabinda. The captured man, Captain Wynand du Toit, revealed that he had been transported with a nine-man sabotage team by a navy fast attack craft from a base at Saldanha Bay to a drop-off point off the Cabinda coast. The team had been landed by inflatable rubber boats with instructions to attack oil storage depots at the Gulf Oil installation. After completing the operations, they were to daub 'Viva UNITA' slogans on the road and distribute pamphlets to give the impression that the operation had been carried out by UNITA. Du Toit also admitted that he had participated in other sabotage operations in Angola, some of which had been claimed as UNITA actions, and in Mozambique.[52]

Further confirmation of the 'Recces' role in carrying out sabotage operations in neighbouring countries which have been claimed by surrogate forces such as UNITA and the MNR was provided by the South African army magazine *Uniform*. In 1985 it published details of an operation carried out by frogmen from 4 Commando who swam underwater at night to plant limpet mines on oil installations. The time and place of the action was not mentioned, but it could refer only to the destruction of oil storage facilities in the Angolan port of Lobito in August 1980 – an operation claimed by UNITA.[53]

It has been alleged that 4 'Recce' have been engaged in the supply from the sea of surrogate groups operating in Angola and Mozambique. The 3 and 5 Commandos are also involved in activities with surrogate forces. They operate largely from a purpose-built base established in the Northern Transvaal at Phalaborwa capable of housing 3,000 troops. A large number of MNR members have been trained at this base and it is believed that command and control of the destabilisation force has been exercised through this facility.[54]

Other Specialist Units
A number of specialist police and military units have been established in addition to the 'Recces' of Special Forces.

The **Headquarters Pathfinder Company of 44 Brigade** existed as an all-mercenary unit engaged in Namibian 'pseudo-operations' and other covert activities during 1981, and appears to have been reconstituted as a largely South African-manned unit thereafter.[55]

The **Police Special Task Force** was established at the beginning of 1976 after senior police officers had visited various European countries to examine potential models for an urban counter-insurgency unit. The two hundred members of the Task Force are trained in a variety of skills, especially as marksmen and explosives experts, and are permanently on standby in Pretoria for airlift for deployment anywhere in South Africa. The unit was responsible for killing three ANC guerillas and a number of hostages they had taken in a bank in Pretoria in 1980, but since then its operations have not been publicly reported.[56]

Two similar units have been modelled on the original Task Force – the **Railways Police Special Task Force**, which is responsible for quick-reaction specialist COIN operations related to the country's transport network, and the **SWA Police Special Task Force**, which is based in Windhoek and operates in Namibia.[57]

This unit was trained for 'anti-riot' work in urban areas and has been deployed in the white farming areas north of Windhoek every year since 1975 to counter SWAPO guerilla activities during the rainy season.[58]

The nature of the training received by members of the Task Forces was revealed when a white member of the SWA unit, Louis Nagel, was sentenced to an effective three years in prison for murdering a black man in Windhoek. For no apparent reason, Nagel opened fire on the man while walking down the street. In his defence, it was stated that members of the Task Force were expected to react with 'lethal efficiency' to suspected SWAPO supporters. Nagel was described as having the 'qualities of a good soldier', namely 'psychopathic and sociopathic tendencies'.[59]

The most active and notorious of the special units operating in Namibia is undoubtedly the South African Police unit, Koevoet (Afrikaans for 'crowbar') sometimes referred to as 'Operation K'. Since the middle of 1985 it has been officially known as the **SWA Police Counter-Insurgency Unit** (COIN Unit). Although it is only about a thousand strong, it is reported to account for 80 per cent of 'kills' in the Operational Area.[60]

In 1980, SWAPO published a secret SADF death list containing some fifty names of people to be assassinated by Koevoet. A number of prominent Namibians, believed to be supporters of SWAPO, were subsequently murdered – their deaths being blamed by the SADF on guerillas.[61] It was also widely believed that Koevoet was responsible for blowing up an Anglican seminary at Oniipa and the printing press of the Evangelical Ovambo-Kavango Church, which produced one of the few indigenous-language newspapers in Namibia. Although both institutions were sympathetic to SWAPO, and there were a number of factors pointing to the involvement of Koevoet, the actions were blamed by the SADF on the liberation movement.[62]

In 1983 a number of Koevoet members were put on trial in Windhoek, charged with murder and other serious offences. These trials provided the first official confirmation of the existence of the unit. Victims of Koevoet atrocities gave evidence of the extreme brutality of the unit and its commanding officers were obliged to speak out in its defence.[63] Four other court hearings in the closing months of 1983 led to further exposure of Koevoet and its unrestrained cruelty.[64]

As a result of this publicity, and other charges levelled by church delegations and political groups, the police lifted the veil of secrecy over Koevoet in January 1984. While admitting that the unit was 'cold, calculating. . . and very ruthless', the police insisted that it was well disciplined and enjoyed 'the complete co-operation of the local population'.[65] Over the following year, more details of the unit and its methods of operation became known.

Koevoet was established in 1979 by Brigadier Hans Dreyer, a commander of the Security Branch in Natal. He had served with the Rhodesian Special Branch at a time when that unit was working in close co-operation with the infamous Selous Scouts, and was thus personally acquainted with irregular operations and the ruthless tactics of the Scouts. He had also made a study of the *Flechas*, or Arrows, a special unit established by the Portuguese intelligence service during the liberation wars in Mozambique and Angola.[66] With assistance from the Reconnaissance Commandos Dreyer spent some months in Namibia studying the situation and making preparations on the basis of information extracted from captured SWAPO fighters.[67]

The initial recruits for the COIN Unit were obtained mainly from the ranks of the Special Constables, black policemen who were then being trained for auxiliary roles. Later recruits were also drawn from ex-members of the Angolan groups working with the SADF – UNITA and the FNLA – and from 'captured' former SWAPO guerillas coerced into joining. The white officer element was provided by experienced SAP members and by former Selous Scouts and other ex-Rhodesian mercenaries.[68]

Until May 1985, Koevoet fell under the overall command of the South African Commissioner of Police, the former Security Police Chief, General Johan Coetzee, who took a personal interest in the unit.[69] In May 1985 nominal control of the unit was passed to the SWA Police and the unit became known officially as the Counter-Insurgency Unit.[70]

COIN Units are established at the garrison towns of Opuwa, Oshakati and Rundu, but can operate anywhere in Namibia. Mechanised groups, normally composed of four Casspir armoured personnel carriers, a supply truck and a fuel bowser, set off on week-long patrols, or are directed on 'hunts' for guerillas once they have been detected. Combat is usually conducted from the Casspirs rather than on foot, relying on the protection provided by the vehicles and the concentrated firepower that can be mustered.[71] Koevoet units also engage in 'pseudo- operations'.[72]

The conflict in Namibia has spawned a further specialist unit which is one of the most unusual units in the apartheid machine. Called the **SWA Specialists** (SWASpes for short), it combines highly trained infantry and trackers with mounted groups, 'scrambler' motorcycles and both tracker dogs and pack hounds. Formed in 1978, the unit is composed of 'psychologically and physcially handpicked' South African Permanent Force members and National Servicemen, who are trained either at the SADF Equestrian Centre at Potchefstroom or at the dog handling centre at Bourke's Luck base. The unit relies primarily on surprise and speed of pursuit in its operations and is deployed almost entirely in a follow-up capacity once the presence of SWAPO guerillas has been detected. The use of motorcycles and horses is reported to give the unit a greater mobility in the bush-covered terrain of northern Namibia.[73]

Bantustan Forces

The apartheid policy of territorial and political segregation of the African population has involved the creation of nominally independent military units. In the case of each bantustan which has been made nominally 'independent', a core group of recruits has been trained by the SADF – usually at 21 Battalion in Lenz. A base has then been established in the bantustan and the core group has trained a second intake of recruits, some of whom have been sent for more advanced training at 21 Battalion or other SADF units.[74]

All these units are funded, supplied, trained and in most cases led by the SADF. Nevertheless, each has a separate uniform, structure and identity. The bantustan forces serve a dual task: to protect the repressive bantustan authorities, and to carry out local and regional military operations as dictated by the strategic priorities of the central government in Pretoria.

The protection of the bantustan authorities is essential to apartheid rule. In the words of Professor Gerrit Viljoen, a leading figure in the National Party:

> Effective and continuous implementation of our homeland policy. . . [will establish] political homes for the majority of black people in their own homelands or states in order to form the basis of the maintenance of political power by whites in the so-called white country.[75]

The bantustans remain under the South African regime's economic, political and military control. Those which have become nominally 'independent' are bound in the security field by ties of dependence on the SADF and by formal 'non-aggression treaties' with Pretoria. At the same time, the establishment of structures with inadequate resources responsible for ruling over pockets of often widely dispersed land has inevitably created further security problems for the SADF. However false the territorial segregation of the bantustans, the fact remains that Pretoria has created several thousand miles of new 'borders' and a string of client regimes whose stability and ability to rule must constantly be open to question.

In 1974 P W Botha announced that the SADF 'had been approached by some of the homeland leaders and governments, who said they would like to have a greater part in the combatting of terrorism and promotion of security in their part of the country'.[76] In August 1975 70 carefully selected volunteers from the **Transkei** bantustan began infantry training at the Cape Corps base at Eesrsterivier – they were later transferred to 21 Battalion at Lenz. By the time of 'independence', October 1976, Transkei Battalion had been established with a strength of about 250 men, under the control of white SADF officers.[77]

A new base was constructed to house the Battalion near the 'capital', Umtata, and the unit was handed over to the Transkei administration as the 'Transkei Defence Force' (TDF). To assure Pretoria's control, a 'non-aggression treaty' was signed and Brigadier Pretorious, the SADF commander of the battalion, was named as 'Secretary of Defence for the Transkei Government'. Kaiser Matanzima, the 'Prime Minister' (and an honorary colonel in the SADF), announced that a system of 'voluntary national service' would begin.[78] An intelligence agency and a State Security Council were also established.[79]

By the end of 1977 relations between Umtata and Pretoria had deteriorated, largely as a result of Pretoria's unwillingness to allocate any further land to the bantustan. Matanzima adopted a tactic of 'brinkmanship' to try to force concessions and to increase his international credibility. He suspended 'diplomatic relations' with Pretoria in April 1978 and the following month announced that the 'non-aggression pact' was no longer in force.[80] The SADF retaliated by cancelling arrangements for the training of personnel from the bantustan unit and withdrawing its seconded instructors. Nevertheless, supplies and arms for the TDF continued to arrive in Umtata.

In 1980, 'diplomatic relations' were re-established and the 'non-aggression pact' restored.[81] However, the withdrawal of the SADF for over two years had left the TDF in a weak position, as it did not have enough trained officers to run the unit. A solution was found – presumably with Pretoria's tacit agreement – through links with the minority regime in Rhodesia, and a number of trainee officers were sent to Salisbury on various courses. But the TDF experienced a rapid collapse of discipline and efficiency. Fearing that the force would be used to carry out a coup on behalf of one of the feuding factions in Umtata, Matanzima appointed a

Commission of Inquiry into the unit. As a result of this inquiry, in May 1981 Lt. Col. Ron Reid-Daly, the founder of the Selous Scouts, was hired with 35 of his ex-Rhodesian colleagues to 'reconstruct' the TDF. [82]

Col. Reid-Daly was promoted to Major General, appointed Commander-in-Chief and given a vastly increased budget. With assistance from the SADF, which agreed to reopen training facilities, Reid-Daly expanded the TDF into a full-strength infantry battalion (1 Transkei Battalion) and established a Special Forces Regiment, an Infantry School and the core of a mounted regiment. [83]

The infantry battalion is organised along the same lines as a motorised SADF COIN unit, with three rifle companies and a support weapons company. The Special Forces group, reflecting Reid-Daly's experience in the Selous Scouts, is a specialised group responsible for covert and irregular operations and intelligence gathering. The SADF has assisted in the unit's training, which includes paratroop training. [84]

Legislation for male conscription in the Transkei was enacted in 1977, but according to a recent report, 'this is more or less in a state of suspended animation. . . . and is used more as an additional means of selection rather than to increase the size of the force or to create a reserve'. [85]

A Transkei Police Force, modelled on the SAP, with an active security section, has also been instructed and equipped by the SAP and ex-Rhodesians. [86]

Attempts have been made to establish a 'navy' and 'air force', based on rubber dinghies and light aircraft respectively. The 'navy' suffered a setback when its first Commanding Officer, 'Captain' J Fourie, fled the territory after a drugs incident and turned out to have had only the rank of Able Seaman, Second Class, in the SAN. [87]

Pretoria has kept a close grip over the 'Defence Force' of the **Bophuthatswana** bantustan, the second to be given nominally 'independent' status. With its headquarters at Mmabatho, the BDF controls two major infantry bases, and a third is under construction. It is organised into a conventional infantry battalion and two self-contained infantry company groups, supported by a maintenance unit and a technical service unit. There is also a small military school. [88] Personnel are trained at SADF bases, and supplies and equipment come from the SADF.

The BDF has been provided with an air wing operating Alouette helicopters 'on loan' from the SADF and Helo-Courier and Partenovia light aircraft. The air wing is vital as the bantustan is composed of ten widely dispersed parcels of land. Since 1978 the military unit has been supported by a police force, including a security section. An intelligence agency, termed the Bophuthatswana Internal Intelligence Service, has also been established. [89]

A SADF officer is in charge of the BDF and another officer, Brigadier Hennie Riekert, holds the post of 'Minister of Defence' in the Bophuthatswana cabinet – although he has reportedly refused to take out bantustan 'citizenship'. [90] The BDF works in very close conjunction with

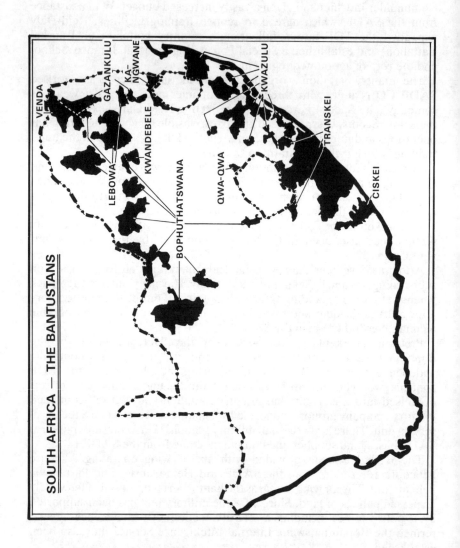

SOUTH AFRICA — THE BANTUSTANS

VENDA

GAZANKULU

KA-
NGWANE

KWAZULU

KWANDEBELE

LEBOWA

QWA-QWA

TRANSKEI

BOPHUTHATSWANA

CISKEI

the SADF, a working relationship formalised by the obligatory 'non-aggression pact'.

It is likely that the Bophuthatswana military unit will continue to expand under close SADF direction, as it is responsible for strategically vulnerable territory along the Botswana border, a zone described in BDF communiques as 'the Operational Area'.[91] The unit has received lavish praise in the SADF journal *Paratus* as a 'perfect example' of 'the new armies of the developing states of Southern Africa'.[92]

A 'National Force' has been in existence since the 'independence' of the **Venda** bantustan in September 1979. The VNF was initially structured differently to the Transkei and Bophuthatswana units in that it was a combined force consisting of army, police, traffic police and prison service personnel.[93] The force was the joint creation of the SAP, the SADF, the Department of Prisons and the Department of Co-operation and Development, which decided that a combined force would be more appropriate given the size of the territory and the high costs of establishing so many different structures.[94]

In 1980 and 1982 separate military (Venda Defence Force) and police structures were established.[95] Personnel for the VDF were drawn from the SADF's 112 Battalion. Commanded by an SADF officer, Colonel Faure, the unit has undertaken operational duty with the SADF in Namibia.[96] It has also been involved in joint operations with the SADF and SAP against ANC guerillas operating in the area.[97] According to Col. Faure, by 1992 the strength of the VDF should be some 2,500, consisting of infantry units and mobile reaction units.[98]

As the Venda bantustan borders on Zimbabwe, a corridor five kilometres wide has been left between the bantustan boundary and the Zimbabwe border, a zone which is patrolled by the SADF itself.[99] The SAAF continues to operate a military airfield at Madimbo, a border base in the SADF controlled corridor. The Madimbo base is also used for the training of VNF troops.

While not strategically situated near South Africa's borders, the **Ciskei** bantustan covers an area in which the liberation movement has always had a strong presence. Since 'independence' in December 1981, the Ciskei bantustan's military and police forces have been locked in an escalating battle to suppress popular resistance and guerilla activity.

Before 1983 the Ciskei police, military and intelligence service were organised into a combined force headed by the 'President's' brother, General Charles Sebe, an ex-South African security policeman and BOSS operative. In 1983 General Sebe and his white deputy seconded by Pretoria, General Minaar, were arrested under the National Security Act and accused of attempting to stage a coup. The Central Intelligence Service, which had become Charles Sebe's personal militia, was dissolved and the military and police forces put under the control of hastily established 'ministries' of Defence and Justice.[100] An SADF officer, Brigadier V Nel, became commander of the military component of the

Ciskei Security Force.[101]

As in the Transkei bantustan, a crack Special Force unit has been established with assistance from ex-members of the Rhodesian army. Codenamed 'Sword of the Nation', the unit initially involved 50 men who were given advanced training, including training in parachute operations from two Skyvan aircraft.[102] Its commander in 1983 was a South African former member of the Selous Scouts.[103]

The Ciskei military unit operates from a headquarters and three major bases, as well as a Special Warfare Centre at which the Sword of the Nation is trained.[104] Since 1980 Ciskei bantustan troops have regularly been sent to Namibia.[105]

'President' Sebe has also established a powerful militia referred to as the 'Green Berets' – an unofficial police reserve which has repeatedly been mobilised in attempts to crush resistance. During August and September 1983 Green Beret 'vigilantes' supported the police and army in a campaign of terror against the inhabitants of Mdantsane township, indiscriminately beating, shooting, rounding up and torturing people in a vain effort to break a bus boycott.[106]

A youth organisation called 'Pillar of the Nation' is run along military lines and trained under SADF guidance. It is officially part of the Ciskei Security Force.[107]

The possibility of conscription into Ciskei military units, should the political and economic situation allow, is provided for by legislation which makes it compulsory for all males between the ages of 18 and 65 to undergo military service.[108]

In January 1985 Brig. Nel was suspended from his post following an investigation into 13 incidents of violence in the military unit and the deaths of two soldiers. Two other top SADF officers were also suspended.[109] Pretoria retaliated by withdrawing 44 SADF personnel occupying key posts in the bantustan. However, the apartheid regime's continued backing for the bantustan authorities was underlined some months later by the appointment of Lt. Gen. van Deventer, the powerful ex-Secretary of the State Security Council, as 'ambassador' to the bantustan.[110]

The six bantustans which do not have nominally 'independent' status have not been allocated separate military forces. Instead, as has been mentioned, regional units have been established in, or just outside the bantustan areas under direct SADF command. In bantustans with 'self-governing' status, however, some control over the police has been passed over to the bantustan authorities. In the **KwaZulu** bantustan, for example, police in some areas have been designated a KwaZulu Police Force, nominally under the control of a Department of Police which is answerable to Gatsha Buthelezi in his capacity as Acting Minister of Police. The KwaZulu Police enjoys similar powers to the SAP, with the authorisation to enforce bannings, restrictions, banishments and arrests. Parts of the KwaZulu and other bantustans have at various times been placed under emergency regulations which have further strengthened police and military powers.[111] In May 1985 Buthelezi announced that the KwaZulu Police would be establishing a 'para-military wing' in order to 'hit back with devastating force' at ANC guerillas.[112]

In 1984, after the **KwaNdebele** bantustan authorities indicated their acceptance of nominal 'independence', the SADF established 115 Battalion for the training of recruits. In January 1985 the trainees were moved to a base which was built within the bantustan boundaries. Uniforms and insignia were also designed.[113]

The Occupation Army in Namibia

The structure of the South African-controlled occupation army in Namibia is more complex than in South Africa itself, and, owing to strict censorship and deliberate misinformation, it is difficult to develop a detailed picture of how the bewildering variety of police and military units interact. *(See Table XV)*. The situation has been further complicated by the establishment in 1980 of the **SWA Territory Force** (SWATF), which entailed the renaming of units and the development of parallel command structures. Furthermore, many of the units operate under conditions of absolute secrecy. For example, the press was prohibited from even mentioning the name 'Koevoet' for some years after this police unit was formed, even though it was responsible for most of the deaths inflicted by the occupation forces.[114]

The forces occupying Namibia are composed of full-time and part-time troops recruited and conscripted into the SADF and SWATF. Units manned mainly by Namibian troops work in conjunction with South African National Service and Citizen Force troops, posted to Namibia for three to six month 'tours' of operational duty. Contingents of conscripts are drawn from their SADF units and allocated to specific bases where they fall under the headquarters designation at that base (for example, 518 Battalion at Ruacana refers to all the troops there at the time, regardless of which unit they have been drawn from). In addition, large numbers of Citizen Force troops from 1 SA Corps, the SADF's conventional formation, are stationed at bases in nothern Namibia. These forces are not usually engaged in COIN activity, but are used for operations on Angola.

Increasingly, the conduct of the Namibian war has been devolved to Namibian-manned units. The Namibian units are not capable of independently fighting the war, however, and large numbers of South African troops are deployed in patrolling and follow-up operations.[115]

The backbone of the COIN fighting force is made up of specialist units composed of Permanent Force members, mostly black Namibian or Angolan troops led by white South African officers and ex-Rhodesian mercenaries (discussed in the section on Specialist Forces). These units are supported by other segregated black professional units in the SWATF, notably **201 Battalion**, which is composed of individuals categorised as 'Bushmen', **101 Battalion** based in the Ovambo bantustan, **202 Battalion** in the Kavango bantustan, and a number of other units – **203, 701 and 102 Battalions**. Most of these units include men who have signed up for Voluntary National Service for two years, rather than the minimum six years involved in joining the Permanent Force itself. All the units are under the control of white SADF and SWATF officers. While Koevoet and 201 Battalion operate throughout the Operational Area, the other units are usually restricted to the bantustan area from which they are drawn. Elements of 201 Battalion are integrated with other units and deployed as trackers.[116]

The core of the SWA Territory Force is provided by one large unit, **911 Battalion**, which is headquartered at Windhoek but based at a number of small centres south of the war zones. Although technically 'multi-racial', almost all the companies of 911 Battalion are segregated.

Professional troops in the SWATF are supplemented by conscripted black and white Namibians. White Namibian men have been called up for military service in the same way as white South African males since the 1960s. In 1981 smaller numbers of black Namibians began to be conscripted, but the process has met with strong resistance. Many white farmers – and some blacks – are also mobilised into the **Area Force Units,** the equivalent to the Commandos in South Africa, which are responsible for first-line operations outside the bantustan boundaries which mark the southern limit of the Operational Area.

In addition to the specialist units, the regular SADF and SWATF units and the Area Force units, an array of paramilitary and pseudo-police militias has been established in the bantustan areas. Loosely referred to as '**Special Police**' or '**home guards**' (a designation which may also be applied to the SWATF units) these groups carry out first-line defence roles in the bantustan areas and protect bantustan leaders participating in the South African occupation structures.

Police

Apartheid military strategists make no secret of the fact that they regard the South African police and military forces as integrally linked components of a common 'security force'. Thousands of troops have been deployed in the suppression of resistance in the townships, assisting the police, while police have served in the war zones of Namibia and assisted the SADF in operations in rural areas of South Africa. The two forces share much of the same or very similar equipment and all members of the **South African Police** (SAP) and the **SWA Police** undergo COIN training that is indistinguishable from that of the SADF.[117]

During the first two decades of National Party rule in South Africa, the regime used the police as its principal security force. The authorised strength of the force was more than doubled between 1945 and 1960.[118] Tremendous increases in the defence budget between 1960 and 1979 led to

132

rapid expansion in the strength of the SADF at the expense of the SAP. Since 1980, however, the increase in police spending has far outstripped that of the SADF, reflecting the regime's renewed interest in building up the SAP as a frontline force. *(See Table IV)*

Between 1981 and 1983, the actual strength of the SAP increased by more than 8,000 members, equivalent to the total increase for the previous 21 years. In 1984 its strength again increased by 3,000, bringing the total to some 45,000, slightly less than half of whom were black.[119] There are concrete plans to increase police strength to 68,000 by the middle of the 1990s.[120]

Despite the rapid increase over the past few years, the overall strength of the SAP remains only a fraction of that of the SADF – but its importance as a professional frontline force in the suppression of resistance to apartheid cannot be overestimated. Furthermore, the strength of the SAP can be doubled by the call-up of available reservist formations, and there are a number of Development Board, bantustan and municipal police forces, most of which are armed.[121]

There are two SAP reserves, confusingly named the Police Reserve and the Reserve Police. The **Police Reserve**, which was established in 1973, consists only of ex-full-time members of the SAP who have left the force. An Active Group draws on men who served for less than five years – all these men are required to render 30 days' service each year for five years after their retirement from the police. There are currently about 4,000 men involved. The inactive Group involves other ex-police members who are mobilised in times of emergency.[122]

The **Reserve Police**, established in 1961, is a part-time force of white volunteers, currently involving 16,000 civilians who undertake police duties at weekends, during the evenings after work and at times of emergency when they may be mobilised for full-time duty. There are four distinct groups of volunteers – Group A, who are allocated to police stations, freeing the full-time police for other duties; Group B, who patrol white residential areas; Group C, who consist of white employees at industrial key points and stand in for Industrial Commandos where these do not exist; and Group D, who are based in rural areas. There is also a force of 200 volunteer divers and a Radio Reserve which assists in communications. White teenagers have been incorporated into a junior reserve which mobilises schoolboy volunteers for police duties during their holidays.[123] One thousand four hundred youths were involved in this unit in 1985. A white women's reserve (800-strong in 1985) and a small black reserve have also been established.[124]

Outside of the SAP, the **Railways Police** functions as a separate force responsible for policing railways, airports and harbours. It is administered by the SA Transport Services (SATS) and has a strength of about 6,000, almost all of whom are armed.[125] Members of this force, who have powers of search and arrest, play an active role in manning roadblocks and suppressing popular resistance to apartheid. Their activities are not restricted to property controlled by SATS. For example, during 1984 the Railways Police manned 388 roadblocks in the Port Elizabeth area alone, all of which were outside SATS property.[126] The force has its own security branch.[127]

Provincial Administration and city municipalities control separate forces of **Traffic Police**, most of whom are armed and also play a part in the suppression of protests and resistance. The **Development Boards**, which are responsible for the control of Africans living outside the bantustans, maintain a police force colloquially referred to as 'blackjacks'. They are responsible for enforcing the pass laws, rent collection and so on. Since October 1984 the **Black Local Authorities** (Town/Village or City Councils, replacing Community Councils in these areas), which were the target for much of the militant anger that swept black townships from the last few months of 1984, have been authorised to establish their own police force.

Sixteen town councils, including many of those in the Eastern Cape and East Rand where anti-apartheid resistance has been at its most intense, took up the government's offer immediately and began training forces.[128] The first batch of 'community police', as they were referred to, finished their training in May 1985.[129] The units were condemned by the United Democratic Front and other opposition groups as political police forces responsible for protecting the institutions of apartheid rule in black areas.[130] It is expected that the Town Council forces will gradually replace those controlled by Development Boards.

Private forces of **Mine Police**, paid and controlled by the mining companies, are deployed on the major mines for labour control. In addition, all the **bantustans**, whether 'independent' or not, have their own police forces which are closely integrated with the SAP.

The total number of police and para-police mustered into these various forces in South Africa is probably in the region of 100,000, making South Africa one of the more intensively policed countries in the world. Despite this, the country has one of the world's worst records for serious crime and crime solution rates are low and declining.[131] The reason for this is that the police are engaged primarily in paramilitary activities, suppressing popular resistance, and administering the apartheid system and influx control (pass) laws.

At the forefront of the political activities of the police is the SAP's **Security Branch** (SB), originally known as the Special Branch.[132] Engaged in the systematic infiltration and destruction of organisations deemed to be hostile to the apartheid state, the Security Branch is involved in both covert and open operations. In the war zones of Namibia and in border areas of South Africa it engages in military intelligence tasks. Containing a mixture of uniformed and undercover plainclothes operatives, the Security Branch operates separately from the SAP with its parallel command structures, and has personnel based at all SAP divisional and district headquarters.[133] Members of the Security Branch are also deployed at police and military bases in Namibia.

For the suppression of demonstrations, breaking of strikes, manning of roadblocks and assault-type operations, the police make extensive use of specially trained 'anti-riot' units based at divisional headquarters. Known as **Riot Squads**, these units vary in strength from 20 or so men to more than 200 and are fully equipped with their own armoured vehicles and specialised weapons.[134] Riot Squads from different areas can be brought together to deal with resistance at a specific point. During uprisings in the Vaal Triangle townships towards the end of 1984, for example, more than 400 Riot Squad personnel from outside divisions were brought in to strengthen the local unit.[135] Some sections of the Reserve Police have also been organised into 'anti-riot' units.[136] Small ' **Reaction Units'** which are outgrowths of the Special Task Force, are attached to Riot Squads. These units, usually 12 to 18-men strong, are deployed locally to contain situations until the Task Force itself arrives.[137]

In addition to the Riot Squads, ordinary police are regularly drafted for spells of duty in **Counter-Insurgency Units** which are deployed in Namibia and, until the end of 1985, patrolled South Africa's northern borders.

Riot Squads based in large black townships have been expanded in recent years. Nearly R3 million has recently been spent on improving facilities for the Riot Squad and SB in Soweto. During the State of Emergency in 1985 and 1986, the Riot Squads were further strengthened by the transfer of hundreds of ordinary policemen into their ranks.

A massive increase in strength has also been authorised for the **Police Special Guard Unit** which in 1983 had a membership of about 300 and was primarily responsible for guarding the property and persons of government ministers.[138] The strength of the unit more than tripled in 1984, and it is planned to increase its membership to more than 10,000 before the end of the decade. The function of the unit will be expanded to make it responsible for the security of 'every government building in South Africa'.[139]

The Civil Defence Network

The Civil Defence structure, while not officially part of the SADF or SAP, is an important mechanism for mobilisation of the white population in both South Africa and Namibia. A civilian system aimed at co-ordinating and maintaining essential services in times of emergency, Civil Defence is a vital component of the state's military strategy. The system both relieves the armed forces and the police of responsibility for maintaining emergency services, and provides the regime with a hierarchical structure under overall military control in which the entire white population can be organised. In the words of the Director of Civil Defence, the system 'is needed to maintain the national morale in war' as it strengthens the 'ability of the nation to resist any form of external or internal attack'.[140]

In 1963 a Directorate of Civil Defence was established in Pretoria under the Ministry of Justice – six years later it was transferred to the Ministry of

Defence. By 1974 most local authorities in South Africa and Namibia had established basic Civil Defence structures, but it was only after the crisis of 1975–76 that a co-ordinated system was introduced.[141]

At a conference in 1979, the Director of Civil Defence, Brigadier C J Muller stated:

THE SOUTH AFRICAN CIVIL DEFENCE STRUCTURE

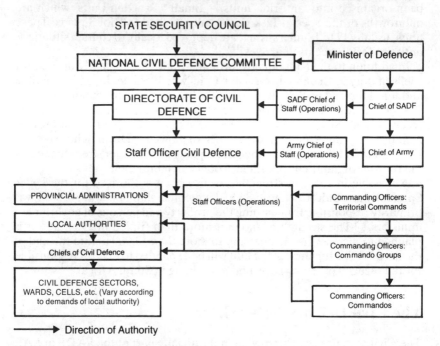

Source: *Resister* No. 27, Aug/Sept 1983

The SADF's increasing operational commitments, as a result of the present threat in the form of a total onslaught on the RSA, means that in future help may not be as readily available as it was in the past [from the SADF for the maintenance of essential services]. . . as a result we investigated and identified all sources and capabilities in other state departments with an eye to making use of them in support of Civil Defence.[142]

The military objective of Civil Defence, in the context of the 'total

136

onslaught' ideology, was thus clearly spelt out.

The Civil Defence command structure in Pretoria is answerable to the Minister of Defence and is co-ordinated by one of the 15 interdepartmental committees under the State Security Council. It is supervised at a provincial level by army Territorial Commands. Local authorities in turn have directors of Civil Defence who liaise with local military commanders, drawing up plans for the management of essential services and the mobilisation of the population into support tasks. Most white local authority employees are drawn into the scheme, supplemented by volunteers from the community, who have to sign contracts binding them to a number of hours of 'voluntary' service. As a result of the binding contracts, few whites have been prepared to volunteer, and the authorities have often complained about the poor state of Civil Defence structures.[143]

In recent years the situation has altered somewhat. According to the 1984 Defence White Paper, at the end of 1983, out of the 646 Civil Defence organisations, 86 had achieved the highest preparedness rating – compared to only 33 at the end of 1981.[144]

Civil Defence structures have been most comprehensively implemented in Pretoria.[145] The city is divided into seven regions, each divided into main cells, cells, sectors and streets or blocks. The organisation is run from a special control centre with access to all strategic information about the city. The construction of a new semi-underground control complex was announced at the end of 1985.[146] In times of 'riots, strikes and rebellion' or natural disaster, warnings would be sounded amd a range or emergency services brought into operation. Exercises are regularly carried out to test the efficiency of the arrangements. For example, at the end of 1982 the system dealt simultaneously with simulations of a sabotage attack on oil installations, a 'terrorist occupation' of a nursery school, a bomb in the high street and a 'seizure of hostages' in an office block. All the emergency services, the police, the army and even the air force were mobilised.[147]

Black urban areas are also expected to develop Civil Defence structures but these are at best paper arrangements. According to the SABC, Civil Defence structures are also being established in 'almost all the self-governing black national states' – the KwaZula, QwaQwa, Gazankulu and KwaNdebele bantustans.[148]

Part III — Operations

7. REGIONAL AGGRESSION

South Africa was developed historically as the centre of a regional economic sub-system in which neighbouring territories played a subordinate role. These countries supplied labour, raw materials and transport services for South Africa's industrial growth, which was focused around the Witwatersrand and its mineral wealth.

The white minority rulers of South Africa regarded themselves as the natural inheritors of the British Empire in the region, and pressed for the incorporation of Botswana, Lesotho, Swaziland and Zimbabwe, as well as Namibia, into South Africa. Namibia was ruled virtually as a fifth province of South Africa after the Second World War. However, Pretoria was restrained from formally incorporating Namibia and the white settlers in Rhodesia refused incorporation. In the face of the growing anti-colonial movement, resistance from the territories themselves and South Africa's departure from the Commonwealth, the High Commission Territories – Botswana, Lesotho and Swaziland – became independent in the 1960s.[1]

Regional Strategy

With the failure to establish formal political control over neighbouring countries, during the 1960s the apartheid regime put forward the concept of a Southern African economic community based on the white-ruled states of South Africa and Rhodesia.[2] The strategy was to cement South African regional domination primarily through economic structures and by establishing a 'free trade zone'. It was calculated that the strength of these economic links would soon lead to the formation of a regional political structure centred on Pretoria.[3]

Pending the establishment of the economic 'commonwealth', Pretoria maintained its regional hegemony by strengthening its alliance with white-ruled Rhodesia and the Portuguese colonial rulers of Mozambique and Angola. In the late 1960s South Africa felt confident enough to attempt to consolidate its growing economic penetration of independent Africa by establishing ties with member countries of the OAU. This 'outward' policy achieved some initial success, but it was vigorously countered by the adoption by the OAU of the Lusaka Manifesto. Drawn up in 1969 by Presidents Kaunda and Nyerere, this declaration committed independent Africa to supporting the armed struggle against the white minority regimes in the south. *(See Chapter 1)*[4]

The disintegration of Portuguese colonial rule in the mid-1970s threw the South African regime's regional strategy into disarray. As discussed earlier, its response was twofold. On the one hand, it drastically increased its defence budget and invaded Angola in an effort to prevent the MPLA becoming the government there. It also relaunched the 'outward' initiative under the banner of 'détente'. The failure of these military and political initiatives was followed shortly afterwards by the Soweto uprisings which directed the regime's attention to internal matters.

By 1979, with international financial confidence in South Africa largely restored and the independence of Zimbabwe imminent, the regime again turned its attention outwards, dusting off the old plan for a regional economic 'common market'.

'Constellation of States'

The regional plan was first announced by Foreign Minister 'Pik' Botha, who declared that Pretoria would concentrate on 'the advancement of our own Southern African region through the establishment of a "sub-continental solidarity"'.[5] It was reported that the planned scheme would 'draw into South Africa's orbit all Southern African states up to and including Zaire'.[6]

The details of the scheme were made public in November 1979 at a conference which drew together top government and private sector figures. Named after the hotel in Johannesburg in which it was held, the Carlton Conference was described by the South African press as a 'watershed' in that it laid the basis for close collaboration in both national and regional initiatives between the Botha regime and South African-based multinational companies. Participants committed themselves to maintaining and developing the South African economic system not only in South Africa itself, but throughout the region. The aim was a 'Constellation of States' centred on Pretoria.

The Carlton plan called for the private sector to play a leading role in re-establishing South African dominance over the region. There appeared to be overwhelming confidence that this would succeed. In the words of an Anglo–American director:

Whether the states of the region like it or not, they have no choice but to accept Mr P W Botha's proposals if they want Southern Africa to have some possibility of advancing into the future on a reasonably stable social and economic basis.[7]

But the independence of Angola and Mozambique, followed by the independence of Zimbabwe in 1980 after the decisive electoral victory of ZANU (PF), had altered the balance of regional forces to a greater extent than South Africa had anticipated.

Two months later neighbouring countries signalled their rejection of the constellation plans and their determination to turn their backs on the apartheid economy by establishing the Southern African Development Co-ordination Conference (SADCC). Angola, Botswana, Mozambique, Tanzania, Zambia, Swaziland, Zimbabwe, Lesotho and Malawi adopted a joint declaration committing themselves to a multifaceted development programme. Designed to break apartheid's stranglehold over the region and increase co-operation between the independent countries, SADCC set itself the priority of establishing a transport infrastructure which would reduce member countries' dependence on the South African network.

The South African regime was thus faced with the prospect of its planned 'Constellation of States' being reduced to a constellation of bantustans. None of the states in SADCC were showing any signs of reducing their opposition to apartheid. The government of newly independent Zimbabwe, while making it clear that it would not allow the ANC to establish military facilities, joined the Front Line States grouping and subscribed to the Lusaka Manifesto. Mozambique and Angola were continuing their efforts to build socialist economies and follow non-aligned foreign policies. More importantly, inside South Africa and Namibia SWAPO and the ANC were carrying out more widespread and effective military actions than ever before, and it was evident that the suppression of the 1976 uprising had granted the regime only a temporary respite from mass resistance.

Destablisation
The response to these challenges was the launching of an aggressive campaign by South Africa of military attacks, economic sabotage and attempted political destablisation against virtually all the SADCC countries.

The objectives of this campaign were spelt out at the beginning of 1981 by Deon Geldenhuys, a prominent South African foreign policy analyst. According to Geldenhuys the first and most important aim of South African regional policy was to force neighbouring countries to prevent the ANC or SWAPO establishing military or political facilities. The second objective reflecting the 'total onslaught' ideology, was to make sure that, in his words, 'Soviet bloc powers do not gain a political and least of all a military foothold in Southern African states'. A further aim was to ensure that 'existing economic ties with the states in the region are maintained and indeed strengthened'. This would ensure the political acquiescence of these states to apartheid and prevent them from supporting moves to impose sanctions against South Africa. Finally, the Botha regime wished to ensure that Southern African countries 'moderated' their political criticism of apartheid.[8]

To achieve these objectives Pretoria strengthened its military instruments of destabilisation. The secret Reconnaissance Commandos were expanded by the recruitment of ex-Rhodesian mercenaries, and the armoured and mechanised units were considerably strengthened. The SADF began to arm and train surrogate forces such as UNITA and the MNR.

UNITA which fought unsuccessfully with South African forces to prevent the MPLA leading an independent Angola, was re-established at bases in northern Namibia. By 1980 it was carrying out widespread destabilisation operations in Angola. After Zimbabwean independence, the MNR a small, covert military group established by the Rhodesian intelligence services, was taken to South Africa where it was set up at bases in the Transvaal. Thousands of troops from the Rhodesian army were also removed to South Africa after Zimbabwean independence, and camps were established to train them for infiltration back into Zimbabwe. The SADF also established a surrogate force to destabilise Lesotho, the Lesotho Liberation Army (LLA).

Despite the huge expenditure and logistical outlay in establishing these forces the projects were carried out in secret. Even as late as February 1983, when the MNR was causing widespread destruction in Mozambique and large numbers of UNITA members were being deployed in SADF-occupied areas of Southern Angola, P W Botha refused to admit to his own parliament that the army was involved in the deployment of surrogate forces.[9] The Botha regime has never admitted that it has engaged in any form of destabilisation in Southern Africa. It has contrived to argue that South Africa itself has been the target of destabilisation and that its activities in the region have been limited to operations against SWAPO and the ANC.

From the middle of 1980 – when the phase of more generalised aggression was signalled by a massive invasion of Angola – to the end of 1981, destabilisation tactics were applied in fairly indiscriminate ways. The SADF mounted large-scale conventional attacks on Angola, stepped up the deployment of the MNR in Mozambique and the LLA in Lesotho and began the infiltration of trained men into Zimbabwe. A number of attacks were carried out against South African and Namibian refugees in Angola, Mozambique, Zimbabwe, Botswana, Lesotho and Swaziland. The first large-scale efforts to apply pressure through economic coercion were also made during this period.

From the beginning of 1982 the South African regime became more selective both in the targets it attacked and in the methods it employed, although there was no overall reduction in destabilisation activities. More sophisticated use was made of 'carrot and stick' techniques – offering 'concessions' for co-operation as well as threatening further attacks if this was not forthcoming.

Four basic methods of destabilisation have been used against Southern African countries. Firstly, direct attacks have been made on the liberation movements. A number of members of the ANC, the South African Congress of Trade Unions (SACTU) and SWAPO have been assassinated; ANC and SWAPO residences and offices have been attacked in Mozambique, Angola, Botswana, Lesotho, Zimbabwe and Swaziland. Secondly, the South African regime has attempted to undermine the governments of Southern African states through deploying surrogate armed forces and mounting propaganda offensives. Thirdly, economic pressures have been brought to bear. Trade has been deflected from neighbouring states to South African ports, rail and other facilities denied, supplies held up and borders blockaded, economic agreements manipulated or terminated, labour contracts restricted, import and export curbs imposed, and communications and economic installations in neighbouring countries sabotaged. Lastly, open military aggression has taken place, with attacks on the capitals of Lesotho, Botswana and Mozambique, violations of the airspace and territories of all the Southern African states and major invasions of Angola.[10]

In many cases the objective of this pressure has been to force Southern African countries into entering into bilateral 'security' pacts with the apartheid regime.

The government of Swaziland entered into such an agreement in 1982, undertaking to remove and restrict ANC refugees in return for a South African commitment not to destabilise the country. This agreement was kept secret. In the first few months of 1984 Pretoria concluded a public agreement with Mozambique apparently laying the basis for an end to hostilities, and undertook to withdraw from Angola. These undertakings were made in a climate of growing international condemnation of the destabilisation policy and after the SADF had failed to expand the area of southern Angola under its military occupation. To a lesser extent objections were also being raised within South Africa, where concern was growing about the war drain on the apartheid economy and information on the SADF's operations was beginning to filter out.

The Nkomati Accord signed with Mozambique in March 1984 committed the Mozambican government to preventing the ANC from making any military use of its territory. In return Pretoria undertook to stop the deployment of the MNR and to cease its campaign of destabilisation. The undertaking with Angola provided only for the withdrawal of South African troops and the joint monitoring of the process. The Angolan government agreed to ensure that no SWAPO forces would move into the area concerned while the SADF withdrew.

The South African regime presented the two undertakings as both a victory for the SADF and an indication of its desire for regional peace. Official propaganda suggested that in future Pretoria's regional strategy would rest on economic rather than military domination. But by the end of 1984 it was clear that the agreement with Mozambique and the undertaking to withdraw from Angola had been honoured by the apartheid regime more in the breach than the observance. South African troops remained in Angola in considerable numbers and were continuing their aggression, and there had been no move by Pretoria to implement UN Resolution 435 on Namibia. In Mozambique, thousands of MNR members had been deployed in a clear violation of the Nkomati Accord and in some areas the security situation had significantly deteriorated.

A further escalation in South Africa regional aggression took place in 1985 with a failed attack on oil installations in the Angolan enclave of Cabinda, further operations in southern Angola, attacks on the capitals of Botswana and Lesotho, and a blockade of Lesotho's borders aimed at forcing the government into signing a security pact with Pretoria. Partly as a consequence of this blockade, which led to serious shortages in Lesotho, the government of Leabua Jonathan was replaced by a military council headed by General Justin Lekhanya. The new government agreed to remove some South African refugees from Lesotho.[11]

The cost to neighbouring states of South Africa's destabilisation campaign, particularly to Mozambique and Angola, has been immense. It has been calculated that Angola has suffered material damage in excess of US$ 12 billion as a result of South African aggression, and well over ten thousand Angolan citizens have been killed.[12] MNR attacks on Mozambique have resulted in direct losses estimated at over US$ 300 million, while the indirect cost of the war to the economy has been estimated at nearly US$ 4 billion.[13]

Despite the battering they have taken from years of attempted destabilisation by the apartheid regime, the Front Line States have continued to adhere to the Lusaka Manifesto, and maintained their commitment to the liberation struggle in South Africa. Pretoria has also largely failed to replace the governments of Southern Africa with ones sympathetic to itself, or to get its surrogate forces incorporated into 'power-sharing' agreements with the national governments. Nor can the destabilisation campaign claim much success as a strategy to push the conflict over apartheid outside South Africa's borders. The uprisings which began at the end of 1984 were an indication that the South African regime could not halt the struggle for liberation by attempting to regionalise the conflict.

While the destabilisation campaign has been multi-faceted, involving economic, political and military pressure, this book focuses on military aspects. As Mozambique and Angola have been subjected to continuous military attack over the past decade, the SADF's operations against the two ex-Portuguese colonies are examined in detail. Thereafter, the pattern of military operations against other states in the region is dealt with.

Angola

The principal Angolan liberation movement, the MPLA, was established in 1956. Committed to end five centuries of Portuguese colonial exploitation of the country, it began an armed struggle in 1961. A rival movement, the Union of the Peoples of Angola (UPA), which played on regional differences, was established in 1958 by Holden Roberto. A few years later the UPA was reconstituted as the FNLA, and in 1966 a breakaway faction led by Jonas Savimbi established a new group, UNITA.

Holden Roberto was reportedly on the United States CIA payroll from 1962. Savimbi, on the other hand, made contact with his supposed enemies and by 1972 had established a working relationship with the Portuguese secret police, PIDE. The relationship revolved around UNITA undertaking to fight the MPLA, in return for which the Portuguese forces would turn a blind eye to UNITA activities.[14] The conditions for a South African-UNITA-FNLA alliance against the MPLA were thus established some years before the SADF invasion in 1975.

Pretoria actively entered the Angolan war in 1966 when helicopter squadrons began cross-border patrols from bases in occupied Namibia. Two years later the SADF established an air base at Kuito Kuanavale in south-eastern Angola, from where reconnaissance and transport operations were carried out against both Namibian and Angolan guerilla forces.[15]

By the early 1970s the tide of the liberation war in Angola was turning against Portugal. In Mozambique FRELIMO was making similar gains, and armed liberation struggle was also under way in Guinea Bissau. The colonial wars proved an intolerable burden on the Portuguese dictatorship. Under the burden of war and considerable domestic pressure, the dictatorship was overthrown in the military officers' coup of April 1974.

South Africa Invades

After the April coup UNITA and FNLA almost immediately signed a ceasefire with the new Portuguese government. The MPLA agreed to a ceasefire in November after the Portuguese government finally recognised the right of the colonies to independence. Portuguese forces withdrew from the northern borders, allowing FNLA troops to enter the country. The FNLA forces, being based in Zaire and supported by its government, were backed by Zairean army units. The FNLA launched an attack on MPLA supporters in the capital Luanda, shelling the shantytowns. UNITA took steps to consolidate its positions in the central provinces around Haumbo, while the MPLA expelled the FNLA from Luanda, and held on to its positions in the far south and east. According to John Stockwell, then head of the CIA's Angolan operation and responsible for a large CIA supply operation in support of the FNLA, 'each major escalation was initiated by our side, by the United States and our allies'.[16]

The United States government was naturally keen to ensure that Angola

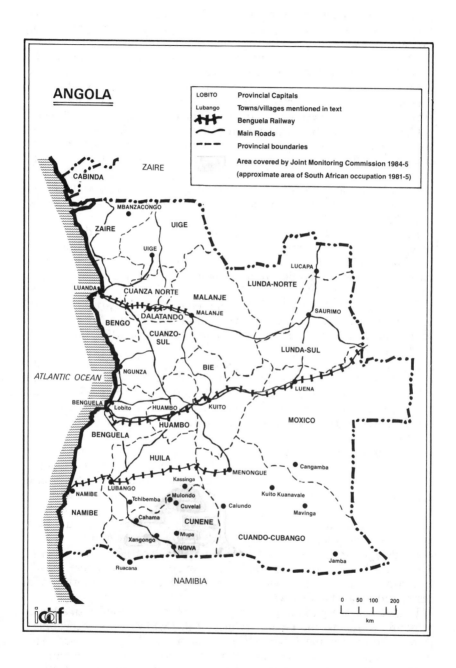

ANGOLA

Legend:
- LOBITO — Provincial Capitals
- Lubango — Towns/villages mentioned in text
- Benguela Railway
- Main Roads
- Provincial boundaries
- Area covered by Joint Monitoring Commission 1984-5 (approximate area of South African occupation 1981-5)

ZAIRE

CABINDA

MBANZACONGO

ZAIRE

UIGE

UIGE

LUCAPA

LUNDA-NORTE

LUANDA

CUANZA NORTE

MALANJE

BENGO

DALATANDO

MALANJE

SAURIMO

CUANZO-SUL

LUNDA-SUL

ATLANTIC OCEAN

NGUNZA

BIE

BENGUELA

Lobito

HUAMBO

KUITO

LUENA

MOXICO

HUAMBO

BENGUELA

HUILA

MENONGUE

Cangamba

NAMIBE

LUBANGO

Kassinga

Tchibemba

Mulondo

Cuvelai

Caiundo

Kuito Kuanavale

NAMIBE

Cahama

CUNENE

Mavinga

Xangongo

Mupa

NGIVA

CUANDO-CUBANGO

Ruacana

Jamba

NAMIBIA

0   50   100   200
km

idaf

passed to a pro-Western government, but in the immediate aftermath of the Vietnam war public feeling in the US was strongly against any new foreign military intervention. Pretoria was equally concerned to keep the MPLA from power. Angola was of vital strategic importance, not only for the struggle in Namibia but for the whole of Southern and Central Africa. The MPLA made no secret of its support for the ANC and SWAPO and its socialist orientation. From Pretoria's point of view, MPLA control over Angola, with its vast economic potential, had to be prevented at all costs.

General van den Bergh, the head of BOSS, maintained close contact with the CIA over the Angolan situation and twice went to Washington to confer with the chief of the agency's Africa Division.[17] According to Senator Barry Goldwater: 'There is no question but that the CIA told South Africans to move into Angola and that we would help with military equipment.'[18] P W Botha has stated that the BOSS-CIA link was 'not the only channel' used for co-ordination.

In preparation for an intervention in Angola before the date set for independence, 11 November 1975, Pretoria began to establish links with the FNLA and UNITA.[20] In the second week of August 1975 SADF troops crossed the Angolan border from Namibia and took up positions around the South African-Portuguese-financed hydroelectric installation at Ruacana. On 21 August UNITA, confident of South African support, formally declared war on the MPLA, and the following day an SADF armoured car column entered Angola and attacked the MPLA-held town of Ngiva.[21]

During September about a thousand South African troops were despatched to Angola, including a team of instructors which was sent to UNITA headquarters at Kuito (Silva Porto).[22] A number of Zairean battalions simultaneously crossed into Angola from the north in support of the FNLA. At this stage the MPLA controlled 11 of the 16 provincial capitals, as well as Luanda.[23]

The fighting began in earnest in October. In the north, over six thousand Zairean and FNLA troops, aided by a few hundred mainly Portuguese mercenaries and an SADF artillery battery, began an offensive to capture Luanda.[24] A South African column of about fifty Panhard armoured cars supported by ground troops, including a thousand UNITA men, crossed from the Namibian border and advanced with considerable speed up the coast. Another force cut through the centre of Angola from the south, eventually joining up with the first column at the coastal town of Lobito. The SADF operation was conducted covertly – the troops, mostly conscripts, were issued with green Portuguese-style uniforms and instructed to say that they were mercenaries.[25]

Unable to face up to the vastly superior firepower of the South African armoured columns, the defensive lines of the MPLA army, the People's Armed Forces for the Liberation of Angola (FAPLA), collapsed. The major centres of Lubango and Namibe (Mocamedes) were quickly captured and within a week the SADF column had joined up with UNITA forces in the central provinces around Huambo. Despite a spirited defence, the MPLA stronghold of Benguela fell on 5 November, while an SADF force advanced eastwards along the Benguela railroad.[26]

On the eve of independence, the invading South Africans controlled the vast part of Angolan territory, holding a front some 400 km south of the capital, but they were unable to advance beyond the Queve river. The day before independence, the FNLA forces to the north of Luanda, then only 20 km from the capital, launched a final infantry offensive under the cover of a South African artillery bombardment. After ten hours of fierce fighting, FAPLA, reinforced by a Cuban contingent and equipped with a Katyusha rocket launcher that had been secretly installed the previous night, emerged the decisive victors.[27] The MPLA was thus able to hoist the flag of independent Angola when the Portuguese departed on schedule on 11 November 1975.

The failure to install the FNLA and UNITA in power before 11 November left the South African regime with a serious dilemma. The SADF columns had outrun their supply lines while the MPLA forces were rapidly reinforcing themselves with heavy arms. On 5 November the Cuban government had responded to an Angolan request for military aid, and increasing numbers of Cuban combat troops were beginning to arrive in Luanda.[28]

If the SADF was to make any headway, it would have needed substantial reinforcement. This would have generated serious diplomatic consequences, given that Angola was by then formally independent. The political difficulty was compounded by the fact that expected international support for the venture had failed to materialise as few countries wished to be seen to be backing racist South Africa in an attack on another African country. Furthermore, information on the supposedly covert South African operation had leaked out in the international press and white public opinion in South Africa was alarmed.

A 'high level emissary' was despatched to Washington to clarify whether the US would back a South African escalation of the war, and Savimbi was called to Pretoria for consultations.[29] In the meantime the South African forces continued to attempt to advance. Despite considerable reinforcement – at least three thousand more troops were committed to the Angola campaign in November and December[30] – the SADF was unable to make further headway northwards. Instead, the South African units concentrated on consolidating their control over the Benguela railway and installing UNITA and FNLA administrations in captured towns. UNITA and FNLA troops carried out a reign of terror against those suspected of supporting the MPLA. A new 'Republic' was declared in Huambo in the South African occupied zone, but the administration was in disarray.

FAPLA began a counter-offensive in the north, re-establishing its control up to the border of Zaire by the middle of February 1976. The counter-attack against SADF positions began in the third week of January. The South Africans offered little resistance and withdrew, swiftly abandoning the key city of Huambo. The UNITA forces, most of which withdrew with the SADF, spread panic amongst the population in the Huambo area, telling people that the MPLA would massacre them. Thousands of civilians took to the bush, as did small bands of UNITA fighters, who turned to banditry. Savimbi himself flew to Namibia, where the SADF was already attempting to reconstitute his force.[31] A new front line was established about eighty kilometres from the Namibian border, where South African troops remained until the final withdrawal at the end of March 1976.[32]

The South African Defence Minister, P W Botha, concerned to protect the image of the SADF, argued that the Angolan war had been lost by the politicians. Other apartheid leaders blamed the United States for failing to deliver the promised support.[33] Whatever the political miscalculations involved, it is clear that the SADF made a number of serious tactical and strategic errors and that its offensive was mistimed. Inside South Africa the black population saw the Angolan débâcle as a defeat for the regime.[34]

Destabilising Independent Angola

After the withdrawal from Angola, the SADF established a string of new bases along the Namibia-Angola border and began to re-equip and reorganise the remnants of the UNITA and FNLA groups that it had taken with it in its retreat. Most of the FNLA members were incorporated directly into the SADF, mainly into 32 Battalion, a mercenary-led unit which was established near Rundu in northern Namibia. Large numbers of Portuguese mercenaries were also signed up for SADF service. UNITA was retained as an 'independent' force, and efforts were made to make contact with the UNITA bands roving the bush in central Angola. UNITA groups, usually acting directly on SADF instructions, were soon at work sabotaging the Benguela railroad and attempting to destabilise areas near the Namibian border.[35]

South African objectives with regard to the destabilisation of Angola were summed up by Deon Geldenhuys, when he described the outlook of the 'hawks' on the State Security Council:

> Pretoria's primary objective would be to force the MPLA into a fundamental policy shift on Namibia. Ideally, the Luanda regime should deny SWAPO bases and protection on Angolan soil. Alternatively, South Africa would want Angola to exert pressure on SWAPO to support an international settlement in Namibia on terms which South Africa would regard as favourable to its own interests. The way to achieve either objective, is to punish Angola militarily in much the same way as Israel reacts against Arab hosts of the PLO. South Africa would furthermore like to see structural change in Angola, by getting UNITA at least into a government of national unity with the MPLA; ideally, UNITA should replace the MPLA in power. Should one or the other happen, South Africa believes it would bring an end to the Cuban presence in Angola and produce a

148

government in Luanda which is amicably disposed towards South Africa (and to a non-SWAPO government in an independent Namibia).[36]

In the decade after Angolan independence Pretoria's tactics and strategies regarding Angola underwent various changes, but its objectives – to end Angolan support for the liberation struggle and to weaken the MPLA government or replace it with UNITA – remained consistent.

Unlike Mozambique, Zimbabwe, Botswana, Swaziland and Lesotho, Angola is not linked economically to South Africa, and the apartheid regime has been unable to exert economic pressure. Angola, potentially one of the richest countries in Southern Africa, therefore also poses one of the greatest potential threats to the apartheid regime. Partly for these reasons, it has borne the brunt of South African military activities in the region.

The resuscitation of UNITA as a destabilisation force in 1976 was accompanied by a number of small-scale South African operations, mainly landmining operations carried out in southern Angola to impede the movement of FAPLA. A number of economic and civilian targets were bombed. On 4 May 1978 the first major operation since the 1975 invasion was launched, against the SWAPO refugee camp at Kassinga. After an air force rocket and bomb attack, 200 paratroopers assaulted the camp, killing men, women and children indiscriminately. The small SWAPO self-defence unit was completely overwhelmed in the first few minutes, but the South African troops continued the hunting and killing of unarmed refugees for over six hours. By the end they had killed 147 unarmed men, 167 women, 298 children and 12 soldiers. A further 611 Namibian refugees were wounded. Many of those killed died from single shots through the back of the neck.[37]

In February 1979, another attack was carried out on a refugee settlement – on this occasion, a school for Zimbabwean refugees. A combined force of Rhodesian Air Force Canberras and South African Mirages dropped 30 tons of anti-personnel and fragmentation bombs on the school in the small town of Boma, killing 198 people and wounding 600.[38] The Rhodesian regime described the school as a training base for ZAPU guerillas.[39]

From the middle of 1979, South African bombing raids on Angola were stepped up. The town of Xangongo and a furniture factory at Lubango were amongst the targets.[40] Heliborne troops carried out sabotage attacks hundreds of kilometres into Angolan territory and UNITA operations were increased. In April and May 1980 there was a further significant increase in operations, and in June the first major invasion since 1975 was launched. 'Operation Smokeshell' involved more than two thousand troops, backed by the air force and armoured cars. The force advanced about 140 km into Cunene Province, attacking villages, shops and schools, destroying crops and driving cattle across the border into Namibia.[41]

In the eighteen months leading up to December 1980, 400 Angolan

149

civilians and 85 military personnel were killed.[42]

The SADF maintained that its operations in Angola were directed solely against SWAPO targets and that it was engaged in 'hot pursuit' of SWAPO guerillas. It disclaimed any responsibility for UNITA, which it presented as an independent force.

Early in 1981 a British mercenary serving with 32 Battalion in Angola exposed details of the SADF's Angolan operations in the international press *(See Chapter 4)*. Trevor Edwards disclosed that the battalion, which was composed entirely of Angolans recruited from the FNLA and UNITA, and officered mainly by white mercenaries, carried out extensive operations in southern Angola which were then claimed by UNITA. He pointed to the capture of the village of Savate, which was claimed as a UNITA victory, as an example. According to Edwards, the town was seized by 32 Battalion after heavy fighting. Afterwards two UNITA representatives who had been waiting 'down the road', came to hoist the UNITA flag. Edwards' information was subsequently confirmed from other sources.[43]

In addition to these revelations, the Angolan government delivered detailed reports on the effects of South African aggression to the UN Security Council.

The South African regime's concern at the growing international condemnation of its 'secret war' against Angola was alleviated by the stance of the Reagan administration in the United States. The Reagan administration shared Pretoria's objective of securing a UNITA presence in the Angolan government, and US and South African officials secretly discussed the best way of bringing this about.[44] One of the first moves of the new administration was to seek the repeal of the Clark Amendment, legislation which was introduced in the US Congress in 1976 to prohibit US military aid to UNITA or FNLA.[45] The move was defeated in Congress, but the administration nevertheless invited Savimbi to Washington for top-level consultations at the end of the year.[46] (The Clark Amendment was eventually repealed in July 1985.)

Occupation of the South
With new confidence resulting from the sympathetic stance of the Reagan administration, Pretoria scuttled UN efforts to bring about a settlement in Namibia and launched a new wave of aggression against Angola. Throughout the first half of 1981 South African aircraft carried out systematic reconnaissance, strafing and bombing raids, while ground forces infiltrated large areas of the south, mining roads and intimidating the local population. In July the Angolan authorities detected a huge troop build-up along the Namibian border and warned that a major invasion was being planned. An SADF brigade commenced operations in Cunene province, encircling the town of Ngiva, and during August more forces were deployed. By 23 August 11,000 troops were stationed along the Angola–

Namibia border, and 'Operation Protea' – the occupation of southern Angola – commenced.[47]

The towns of Cahama and Chibemba were flattened by repeated bombing attacks, and three heavily armed motorised infantry columns attacked and occupied Xangongo and Namacunde. The SADF's immediate objective was to seize Ngiva, the provincial capital. The town was subjected to a massive air and artillery bombardment and attacked on the morning of 27 August. A force of almost 6,000 men advanced from the north, while an armoured car and tank column struck from the south and the west. Fierce fighting took place all day, the SADF offensive being repulsed three times. Unable to achieve a victory by a ground attack, the South African commanders ordered another massive bombing raid, causing further civilian suffering. FAPLA withdrew from Ngiva the following day, leaving the SADF in control of about 40,000 sq. km of Cunene Province.[48]

With Ngiva secured, the SADF turned its attention to the road leading north to the strategically important town of Lubango. The South African column was stopped by FAPLA about 20 km south of Cahama where another fierce battle ensued. The invaders failed to break through Angolan lines and later in September began to withdraw their heavy armour and artillery. Another unsuccessful attempt to take Cahama was made a month later by a force of heliborne troops.[49]

After 'Operation Protea' the SADF set about consolidating its occupation of Cunene Province and establishing a *cordon sanitaire* in the area, ostensibly to prevent SWAPO operation in Namibia. Roads were mined, crops and villages destroyed and livestock and agricultural equipment impounded or destroyed.[50]

Towards the end of 1981, the Angolans launched a counter-offensive, recapturing Ngiva and other small settlements, but FAPLA was soon driven out again by South African air and ground attacks which included the use of poison gas.[51]

Throughout 'Operation Protea', which resulted in the largest battles ever fought on Southern African soil, and the subsequent occupation of Cunene, the SADF claimed that it was carrying out only 'limited operations' directed solely at 'SWAPO bases'.[52] The authorities also stated that South African troops were 'under orders' not to engage FAPLA or attack Angolans.[53] In fact SWAPO was not involved in the fighting in Cunene Province: the battles were fought between FAPLA and the SADF for the control of Angolan territory. The occupation of Cunene was only partly an attempt to hamper SWAPO activities in Namibia. The more important objective was to strengthen the strategic position of UNITA. South African propaganda presented the occupied zone as 'UNITA liberated territory',[54] but UNITA operations were mainly restricted to the remote and underpopulated Kaundo Kubango region to the east and in the central highlands.

To build up UNITA's international prestige the SADF carried out high-profile sabotage attacks which were claimed by UNITA. Just prior to

Savimbi's visit to Washington at the beginning of December 1981, a South African commando unit carried out a spectacular but not entirely successful sabotage attack on the oil refinery at Luanda. Although UNITA claimed responsibility documents, weapons and corpses left at the site of the attack pointed clearly to the SADF.[55]

At the end of 1981 the Angolan authorities counted their losses for the year at at least 350 dead, nearly half of them civilians. A further 1,000 soldiers were missing in action. As Cunene remained under SADF occupation, the authorities were unable to make a proper assessment of damage and the actual total of dead was likely to have been higher. As a result of SADF devastation, 160,000 Angolans had been forced to flee nothwards, establishing huge refugee settlements around Lubango and other centres.[56]

Unable to reoccupy Cunene because of the large numbers of South African troops stationed there and, most decisively, South African air superiority, FAPLA concentrated on building up its defences to the north of the South African-occupied zone, paying particular attention to strengthening its anti-aircraft defences. These developments were seized upon by apartheid military propagandists as the justification for a further build-up in the SADF's conventional strength.[57] Pretoria also stepped up its propaganda operations in support of UNITA and, in conjunction with the Reagan administration, attempted to pressurise the Angolan government to accept a linkage between the presence of Cuban troops in Angola and a settlement in Namibia. The South African strategy was becoming clear: it would only accept Namibian independence if it could first weaken Angola by destroying large areas of the country, undermining the economy, forcing the termination of Cuban assistance and securing a place in the government for its protégé, UNITA.

From 1982 UNITA gained international media attention by kidnapping Red Cross officials, Angolan church leaders and a number of foreign aid and development personnel. Many of these prisoners were released at media events at UNITA headquarters established at Jamba, just across the border from Namibia in Kuando Kubango province.[58] Reports appeared in the Western press claiming that UNITA controlled up to two-thirds of the country and was on the brink of seizing power. Often these articles were written by journalists taken to Jamba from South African-occupied Namibia.[59]

UNITA operations were extended north of Kuando Kubango and into Moxico province, and persistent sabotage attacks on the Benguela railway continued. To finance UNITA operations, South African commanders arranged for the smuggling of large quantities of Angolan diamonds and ivory across the border into Namibia, where they were traded by Portuguese businessmen with South African military and intelligence connections.[60]

Throughout 1982 the SADF attempted to extend the 50,000 sq. km area under its occupation to facilitate UNITA's northward thrust. No attempt

152

Volunteers during World War II – the government refused to arm black troops.

Black soldiers and white officers in the Namibian Occupation Forces.

Weapons demonstrated at a South African army base for children aged between three and six.

Two hundred thousand white schoolboys are involved in cadet training.

Army conscript on township patrol – Westbury, 1981.

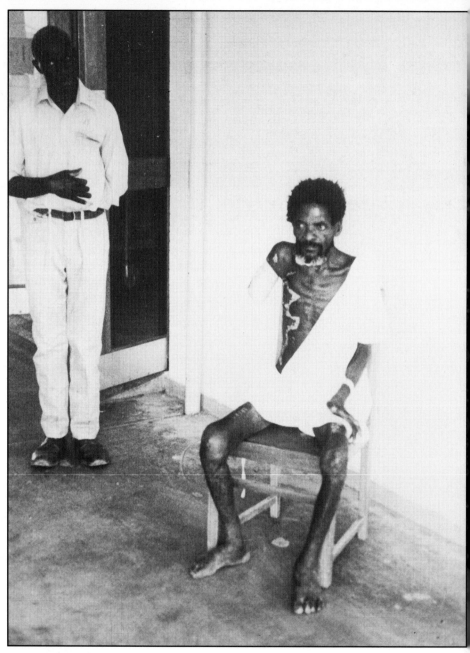

Victim of torture – Ndara Kapitango was roasted alive by two members of Police Counter-Insurgency Unit in Namibia. His persecutors were each fined R50 as punishment.

Umkhonto we Sizwe guerillas under training.

PLAN guerillas – supported by the Namibian people.

South African aggression: **Top left:** *Victims of SADF raid on Maputo, January, 1981.* **Top right:** *South African Special Force member 'blacked up' for raid.* **Bottom:** *Furniture factory in Lubango, Angola after South African bombing attack, 1979.*

Police and soldiers on joint patrol during the 1985-6 State of Emergency.

Residents defy township patrol.

A common demand at township meetings.

was made to establish any form of administration in the occupied zone, which remained devastated and depopulated, although a force of about 5,000 occupation troops was kept permanently based in Cunene. In March 32 Battalion carried out a strike at Cambeno, to the west of the occupied area, in which it was claimed over 200 SWAPO guerillas were killed.[61] The Angolan authorities accused the SADF of carrying out an attack on a Namibian refugee transit centre and said that unarmed women and children had been amongst those killed.[62]

Another South African offensive began at the end of July 1982, with a bombing attack on FAPLA's forward defence lines.[63] The main attack, involving four SADF regular brigades, one 'independent regiment' (UNITA) and a number of combat vehicles and helicopters, was launched on 2 August.[64] By the middle of the month the South African troops had penetrated more than 200 km into Angola, reaching north of Cuvelai, but avoiding FAPLA positions around Cahama. Later, further bombing attacks took place.[65]

These offensives were followed by an increase in South African activities in relation to UNITA. Savimbi, who made at least one secret visit to South Africa during 1982, was given extensive publicity in the South African and Western press. For the first time he openly admitted that he received supplies through occupied Namibia and described himself as an 'ally' of Pretoria.[66]

At the end of January 1983 a South African Commando group sabotaged the Lomaum Dam, cutting electricity supplies to the cities of Lobito and Benguela,[67] and in March UNITA attempted unsuccessfully to attack a hydroelectric installation in Central Angola.[68] UNITA operations were stepped up – dozens of villages were attacked and temporarily occupied. On many occasions massacres were carried out as UNITA attempted to intimidate the population.[69]

The 1983 dry season, around March, saw a further infiltration of UNITA and SADF forces from Namibia. These units surreptitiously made their way through the vast spaces of Kuando Kubango province skirting the Zambain border and established themselves in Moxico province. At the same time UNITA groups already established in the Central Highlands, which had been extensively resupplied by SADF airdrops, fanned out into the provinces of Bie, Huambo and Benguela. The strategy was to establish large permanent bases in remote areas in order to extend the campaign of destabilisation.[70]

These offensives were coupled with propaganda to the effect that UNITA had surrounded Huambo and was on the brink of seizing Luanda. With the majority of its forces committed to holding back the South African invaders in Cunene, FAPLA was not fully prepared for the UNITA offensive in the central provinces and was to some extent caught off guard. To counter the threat the government mobilised militias – People's Vigilance Brigades – and brought the local People's Defence Organisation directly under military command. Regional Military Councils were also established and élite commando units trained. With the mobilisation of the population FAPLA was able to move on to the offensive against UNITA, whose terror tactics left it with little support.[71]

FAPLA Turns the Tide of War

To divert FAPLA and to shore up UNITA a huge force of South African and UNITA troops launched an attack on the town of Cangamba, in the centre of Moxico province, early in August 1983. Although vastly outnumbered, the Angolans were well dug in and the attackers had to advance across a minefield. The UNITA force suffered a defeat, leaving a thousand dead on the battlefield, and the South African commanders ordered a withdrawal. However, the international press had already been alerted to the forthcoming 'UNITA victory', so twelve days later the SADF launched another attack on the town. After extensive bombing, which reduced Cangamba to rubble, an armoured car column advanced and captured the centre.[72]

FAPLA continued its counter-offensive in the Central Highlands and for the following six months hardly a day passed without the Angolans scoring a victory over UNITA. Numerous UNITA bands were destroyed and thousands of civilians who had been kept by UNITA as concubines and labourers were freed. The released civilians told harrowing tales of the physical hardships they had been subjected to and explained how the UNITA bands had been supplied by South African planes and helicopters.[73]

Faced with these battlefield setbacks UNITA resorted to propaganda, claiming responsiblity on different occasions for the accidental crash of a Boeing jet at Lubango airport and a fire that destroyed an apartment block in Luanda.[74] It was becoming increasingly clear, however, that the long-promised UNITA offensive would not be coming.

In December 1983 the SADF launched a major attack (named 'Operation Askari') aimed at restoring UNITA's fortunes. A heavily armed mechanised force advanced from Xangongo on Angolan positions, and a few days later attacks began against Caiunda and Cahama. After a flanking monoeuvre involving the temporary capture of Kassinga, Cuvelai was attacked. By late December the apartheid forces were engaged in fighting at four major points across a 400 km front.[75]

As in previous invasions SADF strategy depended on air superiority. Caiundo suffered a twelve-hour bombing attack in which the town's hospital and school were destroyed and many civilians killed. Chemical bombs were also used. The Angolan anti-aircraft defences were far more effective than before, however, and the SAAF lost an unprecendented number of aircraft – at least ten, according to Angolan figures, including four Mirages.[76]

Without air support the SADF ground forces were unable to break through FAPLA lines at any of the four points attacked, and neither Cahama, Mulondo, Cuvelai nor Caiundo fell into South African hands.

The decisive battle was fought at Cuvelai from 4–7 January 1984, after which General Malan announced that the SADF would be withdrawing to its previously held positions. The pull-back was also prompted by a unanimous vote in the UN Security Council on a motion demanding an immediate withdrawal of South African troops from Angola – previously, the US had protected Pretoria in the Security Council by exercising its veto.[77] The South African forces withdrew in some disorder, struggling against the muddy conditions of the rainy season.

The setbacks of Operation Askari underlined the limitations of the apartheid regime's strategy regarding the destabilisation of Angola. UNITA had failed to mount its long-promised offensive on Luanda, and it was evident that if the SADF wished to extend the area under its occupation in the south it would have to risk a serious escalation of the war, in the face of hardening international protest. Furthermore, although the occupation of Cunene had the claimed objective of halting SWAPO military activities in Namibia, SWAPO launched its largest-ever guerilla operation soon after Operation Protea and maintained a high level of operations thereafter. Pretoria's attitude to Angola was also influenced by the overall regional situation. Under Western pressure P W Botha was on the brink of signing the Nkomati Accord with President Machel of Mozambique, an act which the apartheid regime intended exploiting to end its international isolation. If this strategy was to work it was essential that similar diplomatic progress was seen to be being made with regard to Angola

The Lusaka Undertaking

For four years President Reagan's envoy, Chester Crocker, had been hard at work in Southern Africa implementing the policy of 'constructive engagement' with Pretoria. The Nkomati Accord was the first concrete indication of progress in the US approach. For its part, the Angolan government had already stated its readiness 'to take part in all initiatives capable of leading to the solution of the conflict in Southern Africa'.[78] The Angolans insisted, however, that such negotiations should not be used to undercut the UN plan for a settlement in Namibia (Resolution 435), and stressed that a solution to the Namibian conflict was the responsibility of SWAPO and the South African regime. The Angolan government made it clear that the only negotiated regional peace would be one

> based on the unconditional and immediate withdrawal of the South African army from the part of Angolan territory it occupies. . ., the implementation without delay of United Nations Security Council resolution 435 on Namibia's independence, the cessation of the white minority Pretoria regime's aggression against Angola, and the cessation of all logistical and military support by that regime for the puppet bands terrorising the Angolan population.[79]

Only once these four conditions had been met would Angola effect the withdrawal of Cuban troops from its territory, the issue which Pretoria had been attempting to establish as a precondition for Namibian independence.[80]

Despite the gulf between the Angolan government and the South African regime over the Namibian issue, the two sides reached an understanding in Lusaka at the end of February 1984 which specified the conditions under which a South African withdrawal from Angola would take place. Pretoria committed itself to withdrawing all its forces from Angola by the end of March. In return, the Angolan government undertook to ensure that SWAPO forces did not move into the areas being vacated by the SADF.[81]

Although limited to the issue of South African withdrawal from Angola, the Angolans hoped that the agreement would pave the way for the implementation of the UN plan for Namibian independence.[82] The South African regime put a different slant on the undertaking, arguing that it had been made on the basis of unspecified 'assurances' from the US, and presenting it as a breakthrough for P W Botha's 'peace initiatives' and a major setback for SWAPO.[83]

In terms of the Lusaka arrangement, a Joint Monitoring Commission (JMC) of Angolan and SADF officers and troops was established to oversee the South African withdrawal. The JMC was expected to convene in a number of towns in Cunene province, moving steadily closer to the Namibian border until the last of the SADF troops had withdrawn at the end of March 1984. A month later the JMC would be disbanded.[84] However, it soon became apparent that the South African regime had no intention of withdrawing its forces from Angola until it had secured key political concessions from the Angolans. The withdrawal process fell behind schedule, with Pretoria raising repeated objections about continuing SWAPO activity. At the same time the SADF continued to deploy UNITA, moving it into the areas the SADF had vacated.[85]

Pressure was put on Angola to force it into negotiations with UNITA, and to concede that an end to Cuban assistance was a precondition for the continuation of the 'peace process'. When the Cuban and Angolan governments reiterated their position on the conditions for a Cuban withdrawal, the South African Foreign Minister, Pik Botha, threatened to cancel the Lusaka undertakings – despite the fact that the arrangements had made no mention of the Cuban issue.[86] A high profile was maintained for UNITA by the tactic of kidnapping overseas aid workers in Angola and holding them to political ransom. This included a party of 16 Britons who were eventually handed over to a representative of the British government in a blaze of publicity.[87]

The South African regime continued to promote the idea of round-table talks between 'all parties' in the region – which would have brought UNITA into the negotiations as a separate force.[88] South African negotiators also attempted to get the JMC established as a permanent body, hoping that it could replace the proposed UN force whose task would be to monitor a Namibian settlement and thus to ensure South African control over the Namibian independence process.[89] Later the regime demanded that the Angolan government end its support for the ANC before the SADF withdrew.[90]

By June 1984 it was clear that the South Africans had halted their withdrawal about 40 km from the Namibian border and had dug in while their negotiators attempted to wrest concessions from the Angolan government, in particular to force it to end its support for the Namibian struggle.

UNITA, having failed to re-establish itself in the central areas, was deployed northwards along the Zambian border and infiltrated northwards to Lunda, the diamond-producing region.[91] UNITA bands attacked towns in the Lunda region and captured a number of foreign development workers. Regular ambushes were mounted on the important road links, but in general the Angolan army retained the initiative. In October the commander of the region covering the two Lunda provinces, Major Keba, announced that UNITA had failed in its objective of gaining control over the major highways or 'economically strategic areas'.[92]

In the north the struggles against remnants of the FNLA was nearing an end. The group was thrown into internal chaos as a result of leadership disputes and factionalism. At the beginning of 1984 the FNLA Chief of Staff, top military commanders and hundreds of men handed themselves over to the MPLA authorities and began a process of reintegration into Angolan society.[93]

Throughout 1984 the Angolan press reported victories against UNITA and growing numbers of defections to the government. In January 1985 ANGOP reported that the UNITA Chief of Staff had been removed from his post as a result of military setbacks and factional struggles.[94] The news agency also noted that

massive desertions are making the process of disintegration in the counter-revolutionary ranks an irreversible fact. . . even in the far south of Angola where the presence of racist South African troops should guarantee their cohesion. . . large numbers of Kwachas [a derogatory term for UNITA members] are giving themselves up and there is every reason to believe that the numbers of those who do so will continue to increase in geometric proportion.[95]

UNITA desertions were the result of military setbacks and a policy of clemency towards those who gave themselves up, which was introduced in 1978. In the central provinces of Huambo, Bie and Benguela over 4,000 UNITA members were confirmed killed during 1984; 594 were killed in Huila Province; and in Moxico, where UNITA made its push north towards the diamond area, over 600 members were killed in the second half of the year.[96] Defectors from UNITA reported the hardships suffered by members and their civilian captives, tyranny and factionalism of UNITA commanders and hunger suffered by the civilians.[97] The UNITA bands turned increasingly to random massacres, rampaging through villages and carrying out widely dispersed but poorly co-ordinated acts of sabotage and destruction. Typical of these attacks was that on a village in the municipality of Longonjo in Huambo Province, which took place in December 1984. After destroying a power station and a liquor factory, the UNITA troops turned on the civilian population, massacaring about 140 peasants.[98]

In its annual report for 1984 the International Committee of the Red Cross stated that it was working with the Angolan government on aid and resettlement projects affecting 200,000 people displaced by the combined effects of drought and UNITA activities. It noted:

> The presence of mines, ambushes and the destruction of transport and communications infrastructure in many areas of the country have virtually paralysed supplies of essential goods, especially seeds, agricultural implements, clothing, soap, salt and foodstuffs.[99]

South African destruction was most severe in Cunene Province. In October 1984, when the Angolan authorities entered the Cunene capital Ngiva for the first time since its occupation three years previously, they reported that they 'had to walk over the ruins of what were yesterday schools, health post [and] commercial establishments'. Water and electricity facilities had been destroyed and the wells and surrounding land poisoned. All the livestock had either been removed to Namibia or destroyed. The remaining inhabitants of Ngiva were driven to eating dogs and cats. They reported that South African aircraft had flown into the town daily, bringing food and weapons, but that none of the food had been distributed to the local population.[100]

In an interview published at the beginning of 1985 the Angolan Defence Minister, Pedro Maria Tonho, made it clear that the Angolan government was under no illusions as to the likelihood of South Africa ending its ten-year war against the People's Republic:

> We have been at war since independence. . . During their last invasion [in December 1984] the South Africans were surprised to find us so well defended. Our soldiers resisted for days and sometimes weeks against land and air attacks of extreme violence. . .
>
> For some time [the South Africans] have been talking of 'regional peace', but for us these words have no meaning as long as there is apartheid in South Africa. As far as we are concerned, even if they stop attacking us directly, as long as they aid UNITA, or more precisely, as long as they train and equip it, we will consider that they have not stopped their aggression against us.[101]

In April 1985, well over a year after they had undertaken to do so, the South African forces finally withdrew from Angola, but tens of thousands of South African troops remained massed on the Angolan border and support for UNITA continued. Only six weeks after the SADF withdrawal, a South African commando group was intercepted in the northern FAPLA enclave of Cabinda on a raid to sabotage oil installations. The leader of the group, Captian Wynand du Toit, who was captured, made it clear that UNITA would have claimed responsibility for the sabotage[102] *(See Chapter 6)*. In June, SADF troops launched a ground attack which penetrated 40 km into Angolan territory, the most serious violation of Angolan territory since the Lusaka undertaking.[103]

Angolan government forces began a major offensive against UNITA's remaining postions in the east and south-east of the country in July 1985, recapturing the town of Cazombo in Moxico Province, which had been destroyed and occupied by UNITA, and advancing on UNITA positions around Mavinga in Kuando Kubango Province. This advance threatened the main UNITA base at Jamba, near the Namibian border.[104]

Realising that the fall of Jamba would be a probably irreversible setback for UNITA, the SADF deployed a mechanised unit backed by heavy artillery at Mavinga, and carried out two devastating bombing attacks on Angolan forward positions, halting the FAPLA advance. As on previous occasions UNITA claimed responsiblity for this action which resulted in considerable human and material losses.[105] By the end of 1985 four battalions of SADF troops were again occupying Cunene province and attacks were taking place over a wide front hundreds of kilometres into Angolan territory.[106]

The resumption of large-scale military operations in Angola was accompanied by an increase in South African propaganda in support of UNITA, especially after the repeal by the US Congress of the Clark Amendment, the legislation prohibiting direct US support for UNITA. After the battle of Mavinga the South African Foreign Ministry reportedly sought the support of the United States for a further escalation of the war. Two bills were introduced in the US Congress to authorise logistical and military assistance for UNITA. President Reagan indicated in November that he was in favour of covert support.[107]

The situation at the end of 1985, with a large-scale South African intervention in Angola in support of UNITA potentially backed by the US, was similar in a number of respects to the situation ten years previously, when South African armoured car columns were advancing towards Luanda. However, after more than a decade of experience at repelling South African attacks, the MPLA government and FAPLA constituted a far more formidable opposition than in 1975.

Mozambique

Today's government of Mozambique, Frelimo, was founded in 1962 as a national liberation movement to end Portuguese colonialism in the territory. In the face of Portugal's determination to maintain its African colonies, Frelimo took up an armed struggle in 1964 and gradually established 'liberated areas' in the north of Mozambique. Portugal committed thousands of conscript soldiers to the war, doubled the number of colonists in the territory, and strengthened its military, economic and political ties with Rhodesia and South Africa. But by January 1974, when Frelimo for the first time began military operations in white farming areas, Mozambique was virtually bankrupt and it was evident that the guerilla forces were gaining the upper hand.[108]

Independence and the Establishment of the MNR

The coup in Lisbon on 25 April 1974 did not end the war in Mozambique, but by July, with widespread mutinies in the Portuguese army, Frelimo was meeting with little resistance as it extended its operations into the centre of the country. An agreement with Portugal was signed in September providing for a ceasefire, a transitional government and full independence under a Frelimo government nine months later. The transitional government was inaugurated in September 1974, and the Frelimo flag was hoisted over independent Mozambique in June 1975.[109]

Although alarmed at these developments, the South African regime did not intervene militarily in Mozambique. The reasons for this are not difficult to ascertain. While it would have been relatively easy for the SADF to have seized Maputo, this would have been seen by the outside world as an act of blatant aggression. Pretoria could not have hoped to have disguised its intervention as it attempted to do in Angola, nor did it have the pretext that it was simply assisting one side in a 'civil war'. In any case, a Frelimo-controlled Mozambique did not appear to constitute the same threat as an MPLA-controlled Angola. The Mozambic economy remained dependent on South Africa and Rhodesia, and the country itself was in a situation of administrative and economic crisis.

Mozambique's economy deteriorated rapidly after independence. Half the whites – who occupied virtually all the key economic and administrative posts – had left the country by 1975. In the following year, when Frelimo nationalised the land, the social services and rented accommodation, most of the remaining whites left, taking with them large sums of money, destroying records, and wrecking equipment. These economic problems were greatly exacerbated after 1976 when the South African regime cut the number of Mozambicans working on the Witwatersrand gold mines from over 100,000 to less than 40,000, sharply reducing one of the country's principal sources of foreign exchange.[110]

Despite huge social and economic problems, Frelimo was confident that

160

it could build a non-racial and socialist system in Mozambique. Its third party congress at the beginning of 1977 drew up a blueprint for such a transformation. Substantial gains had already been made in the fields of health and education and the economy was beginning to recover. But the recovery was to be short-lived and Mozambique was soon to face the devastating effects of a South African destabilisation campaign.

The principal vehicle for this destabilisation was the MNR. During the independence process a number of members of the Portuguese secret police, PIDE, fled to Rhodesia and South Africa where they made contact with intelligence services of the two regimes. After Mozambique's independence, and using PIDE contacts, the Rhodesian Central Intelligence Organisation began to recruit the nucleus of the MNR from amongst PIDE agents, ex-members of the Portuguese forces in Mozambique and deserters from Frelimo.[111]

In March 1976 Mozambique stepped up its support for the Zimbabwean liberation movement and closed its border with Rhodesia to conform with international sanctions against the illegal Rhodesian regime. The Rhodesians responded by establishing a radio station, *Voz da Africa Livre* (Voice of Free Africa), which broadcast anti-Frelimo propaganda. They also began to deploy the MNR, infiltrating small groups of armed men into Mozambique. The MNR groups carried out sabotage attacks and disrupted communications, but their main role was to gather intelligence for the Rhodesian forces, especially to locate Zimbabwean guerilla bases and refugee camps.[112]

The MNR was closely controlled by the Rhodesians and had no independent political existence. To establish its credentials as an independent organisation, the Rhodesians appointed an ex- Frelimo member, André Matsangaiza, as president of the organisation. He was killed at the end of 1979 in an attempt to establish bases inside Mozambique. After a bitter leadership dispute, he was succeeded by Alfonso Dhlakama who, like Matsangaiza, had defected from Frelimo after being exposed for corruption and criminal activities. Orlando Christina, an ex-PIDE agent, was appointed general secretary. By the time the leadership crisis was resolved the MNR had been all but destroyed inside Mozambique, and when ZANU (PF) swept to victory in the Zimbabwean elections a few months later, the organisation faced the prospect of annihilation.[113]

The Rhodesian commanders of the MNR approached the SADF for assistance and the force was evacuated and re-established at new bases in the Northern Transvaal. Hundreds of MNR men were infiltrated into Mozambique from their new bases and they in turn forced others to join the bands inside Mozambique. To facilitate SADF logistical support, the MNR made a drive for the coast, opening up new seaborne supply routes from South Africa. With this support, the MNR was able to consolidate its operations in the central provinces and expand its operation northwards and southwards.[114]

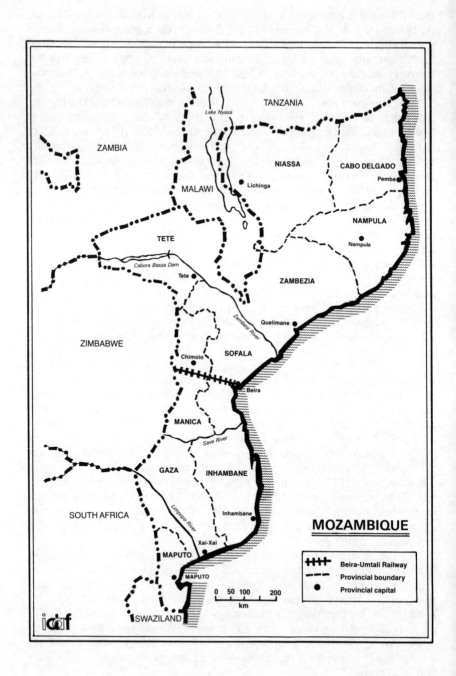

MOZAMBIQUE

	Beira-Umtali Railway
	Provincial boundary
●	Provincial capital

0 50 100   200
km

TANZANIA

ZAMBIA

Lake Nyasa

NIASSA

CABO DELGADO

Pemba

MALAWI

Lichinga

NAMPULA

TETE

Nampula

Cabora Bassa Dam

Tete

ZAMBEZIA

ZIMBABWE

Zambesi River

Quelimane

Chimoio

SOFALA

Beira

MANICA

Save River

GAZA

INHAMBANE

SOUTH AFRICA

Limpopo River

Inhambane

Xai-Xai

MAPUTO

MAPUTO

SWAZILAND

idaf

162

MNR activities involved both sabotage attacks on key targets identified by South African military officers – mainly railways, roads, the oil pipeline to Zimbabwe, factories and development projects – and random attacks on villages. Health posts, schools, shops and other facilities were razed, crops and equipment destroyed, and the population terrorised. Despite its lack of any political programme, and its complete reliance on SADF support, the MNR attempted to establish itself internationally as a viable alternative to the Mozambican government. Making use of South African communications facilities, the group was able to generate a considerable amount of sympathetic coverage in the Western press.[115]

Direct Aggression

While the SADF relied mainly on the MNR for its destabilisation campaign, it showed an increasing willingness to engage in direct attacks against Mozambique.

The first – and most devastating – SADF raid took place on 30 January 1981 when a South African Reconnaissance Commando team crossed the border in trucks disguised as Mozambican army vehicles and attacked residences occupied by South African refugees in Matola, a suburb of Maputo. Thirteen refugees – all members of the ANC including some members of the SACTU – and one Portuguese worker were killed before the raiders withdrew across the border. Two months later an SADF group was intercepted crossing into Mozambique along the beach from Natal. In the ensuing gunfight, two of the troops were killed.[116]

In 1982 and 1983 a number of SADF sabotage squads were intercepted while on covert operations in Mozambique. In August 1982 a heliborne commando unit attacked three houses in the town of Namaacha, on the Swaziland border. Three people were killed and three kidnapped.[117] An SADF sabotage squad was intercepted a few miles inside the Mozambique border in April 1983. After a brief firefight, the group fled, abandoning equipment including explosives and forged identity documents.[118] Later in the year two South African undercover agents were captured in separate incidents. One of them was carrying a time-bomb. The other admitted to being a member of Military Intelligence and claimed that he was on a mission to assassinate President Machel.[119] Pretoria's readiness to engage in political assassination was demonstrated in 1982 when the exiled South African writer, Ruth First, was killed by a parcel bomb in Maputo.[120]

Direct aggression took a new form in May 1983 when the SADF responded to a devastating ANC car bomb attack on air force headquarters in Pretoria by launching an air strike against Maputo. The attack appears to have been carried out largely for propaganda purposes and to bolster the morale of white South Africans. The SADF claimed that 41 ANC 'terrorists' and 20 Mozambican troops had been killed and that ANC 'bases' had been destroyed. In fact the air force had attacked two residential areas, a bridge, a jam factory and the Maputo oil refinery. Five Mozambicans and one South African refugee were killed in the bombing. The ANC President, Oliver Tambo, issued a statement making it clear that the ANC had no bases in Mozambique.[121]

Its inability to locate the claimed ANC bases in Maputo did not deter the SADF from attacking ANC residences and offices in the Mozambican capital. In October 1983 the ANC's office and library in a Maputo apartment block was sabotaged by three bombs planted on the roof. Despite extensive damage to the buildings there were no serious casualties. Later in the year another ANC residence was blown up, again without loss of life.[122]

The escalation of direct South African aggression during 1982 and 1983 was accompanied by a significant increase in MNR deployment. In early 1982 the provinces of Inhambane and Gaza were attacked in force. In August a new front was opened to the north in Zambezia province. The Zambezia offensive was an unexpected blow to Frelimo. By the end of the year the MNR bandits had overrun parts of the province, destroying many centres of development.[123]

The MNR drive towards Maputo was halted in the Limpopo valley in mid-1982. In December, hundreds of MNR members poured across the border from the Kruger National Park in South Africa, and another push towards Maputo and the coast began. After heavy fighting, this offensive was also repulsed. In Zambezia too, the tide turned against the MNR bandits at the end of 1982, and the MNR's main base in that province was captured.[124]

In 1983 the Mozambican army began a counter-offensive. In a process similar to that which occurred in Angola, the government activated a system of local militias, armed peasants and workers in affected areas and despatched experienced ex-guerilla commanders to the provinces. By the end of 1983 large areas of the south had been cleared of MNR activity. Although the MNR mounted a new push in Zambezia province, most of the group's major bases had been destroyed.[125]

Despite its ability to operate over large areas and disrupt travel and communications, even at the height of its activity in 1982 and 1983 the MNR did not gain long-term control over any substantial areas or win the support of the population. MNR attacks were characterised by extreme brutality and an unwillingness to draw a distinction between military and civilian targets. Trains and buses carrying civilians were raked with machine-gun fire; suspected Frelimo supporters had their eyes, ears, noses, breasts and limbs hacked off; travellers in cars were roasted alive in their vehicles; crops were burned and bodies stuffed down wells to destroy water supplies. Countless other atrocities were perpetrated in the campaign to terrorise the population, undermine the economy and remove areas from Frelimo control.[126]

Over 800 schools, 900 village shops, 200 health posts and at least 200 villages were destroyed by the MNR during 1982 and 1983. The situation was further exacerbated by a devastating drought. By the end of 1983, tens of thousands of people faced starvation in Gaza and Inhambane provinces, and thousands of refugees were flooding into the towns and villages. MNR activity prevented the government from taking effective emergency measures as it had done under similar circumstances in 1979/80.[127]

The Nkomati Accord

During 1982 and 1983 the Mozambican government was extremely active on the diplomatic level, aiming to bring pressure on the South African regime to end its destabilisation activities. Part of this process involved making closer contacts with the Western powers, which were pressed to exert their influence over Pretoria. The South African regime refused to negotiate, instead increasing its support for the MNR. However by the end of 1983 the pressures on Pretoria to secure a diplomatic settlement with Mozambique had become intense.

Between December 1983 and February 1984 a number of bilateral meetings were held at ministerial level between South Africa and Mozambique, as a result of which the Accord of Nkomati was signed on the banks of the Nkomati River on 16 March. The accord was the fruit of over eighteen months of Mozambican diplomatic activity and marked the first tacit admission by Pretoria that it had been destabilising Mozambique.

The accord pledged both Mozambique and South Africa to 'refrain from interfering in the internal affairs of the other'. This included preventing the use of their respective territories by armed groups, the closure of radio stations used by such groups and an undertaking not to carry out any acts of aggression. A joint security commission would be established to monitor implementation of the agreement. Many of the provisions of the accord applied only to Pretoria, as Mozambique had never carried out any acts of aggression against South Africa or even allowed the ANC to establish military bases.[128]

The South African regime perceived in Nkomati the long-awaited international breakthrough to bring itself out of the cold, and an opportunity to present P W Botha as a peacemaker and statesman. It regarded it as a blow against the ANC and a step towards undermining the support of the Front Line States for the liberation movement and its armed struggle.

To indicate its commitment to the accord the Mozambican government removed almost all ANC members and South African refugees from its territory and strictly limited the ANC's activities. The South African regime mounted a huge propaganda offensive around Nkomati, and P W Botha undertook a tour of a number of European capitals in the following months. The ANC stated that Pretoria's objective in signing the Nkomati Accord was not regional peace but the isolation of the ANC, the 'liquidation of the armed struggle for the liberation of Southern Africa', the destruction of the SADCC and the removal of the threat of international sanctions.[129]

The South African attempt to undermine the authority and resistance of

165

the Front Line states grouping through the Nkomati process misfired. Meeting at the end of April, the heads of the Front Line states – together with the presidents of the ANC and SWAPO – reaffirmed their commitment to the armed liberation struggle. They called for intensified political, moral, material and diplomatic support to be given to the liberation movements and stressed that regional peace was impossible while apartheid existed.[130]

Mozambique's willingness to implement the Nkomati Accord was not matched by South Africa. Even while the agreement was being signed, the SADF was infiltrating hundreds of freshly trained MNR members into Mozambique. MNR documents captured by the Mozambicans in 1985 revealed that the SADF provided the MNR with a six-month supply of arms and ammunition immediately prior to the signing of Nkomati. Arrangements were made for the continued re-supply of the MNR, and the SADF assured MNR commanders of their ongoing support. Within weeks of the accord there was a noticeable increase in MNR activity, especially in Maputo province, close to the South African borders. Attacks on aid workers, food relief lorries and Red Cross officials took place in drought-stricken areas.[131]

A number of emergency meetings were held between Mozambican and South African authorities where Pretoria was pressed to stick to the accord.[132] Mozambican demands for the demobilisation of the MNR were met with counter-demands, not laid out in the Nkomati document, which indicated that the South Africans wished to extract further, more far-reaching concessions from Maputo. In particular, Foreign Minister 'Pik' Botha demanded the installation of MNR members in civil and government positions and negotiations between the government and the MNR.

On 3 October a new agreement was signed between Mozambique and South Africa after talks in Pretoria. It was announced at a press conference at which the MNR was present. The agreement called for the termination of all acts of violence and the establishment of another joint commission, this time with a tripartite composition (including the MNR) to oversee technical aspects of the agreement.[134] The agreement included a statement 'acknowledging' Samora Machel as President of Mozambique – and by implication establishing the authority of the Frelimo government. The Mozambique Information Agency stated that the agreement 'should put an end to all speculation about a possible political accommodation between Mozambique and the MNR bandits'.[135] The apartheid regime put an entirely different gloss on the agreement. The South African press immediately presented the declaration as the start of negotiations between the MNR and the Mozambique government and an open invitation for South African troops to move into Mozambique on the pretext of monitoring the accord – an event predicted by the South African press since the signing of Nkomati.[136]

Nothing came of the 3 October agreement. The MNR representative at the talks announced almost immediately that the MNR was withdrawing from the monitoring commission. The South African authorities blamed the MNR's failure to stick to the 3 October agreement on internal strife within the organisation. It is evident, however, that Pretoria was unwilling to hold the MNR to the agreement when the Mozambique government did not accept its interpretation of the implications of the arrangement. In the last quarter of 1984, the MNR intensified its destructive activities, using arms and ammunition provided by the SADF in an extensive re-supply operation carried out between July and October.[137]

The breakdown of the 3 October agreement was followed by further warnings from the Mozambican authorities that the Nkomati Accord was in danger of collapsing as a result of Pretoria's refusal to implement its conditions. P W Botha responded by issuing a number of public 'appeals' to the MNR to cease its operations, and by ordering a purge from SADF ranks of individuals supposedly supporting the MNR against the instructions of senior commanders.[138] Commentators in Maputo dismissed these moves as window-dressing, pointing out that hundreds of MNR members remained under South African training in the northern Transvaal.

On the first anniversary of the Nkomati Accord, in March 1985, the Mozambique Information Agency noted that there was little to celebrate:

> Workers and peasants are still being killed and maimed, foreign citizens working on development projects are gunned down or kidnapped, vehicles are still ambushed and burnt, economic installations destroyed. . . Sabotage of the transmission lines carrying electricity from South Africa to Maputo is carried out by gangs who operate from the South African side of the border. . . Unidentified planes and helicopters have violated Mozambican airspace and flown over Maputo province. . . Inside Mozambique the belief is growing. . . that South Africa has not respected the Nkomati Accord, because it saw the agreement as a mere tactic, a first step in a master plan, the goal of which was to force Mozambique to accept sharing power with the bandits.[139]

The struggle against the MNR intensified in the middle of 1985. Between July and September the Mozambican army, aided by Zimbabwean troops initially deployed to guard road, rail and other links to Zimbabwe, captured most of the MNR's major bases in central Mozambique. At the MNR headquarters, known as Casa Banana and situated in the remote Gorongoza game reserve, the Mozambicans captured two years' supply of arms as well as hundreds of documents. These included a diary and notebooks belonging to a personal secretary to the MNR leader, Dhlakama. The documents provided incontrovertible proof of continued South African support for the MNR, recording in detail deliveries of supplies from South Africa including AK47 rifles, fuel, bazookas and radio equipment. The diary revealed that the South African Deputy Minister of

Foreign Affairs, Louis Nel, had visited Casa Banana on three occasions, and that MNR members had been taken to South Africa by a submarine which picked them up on the coast. It also noted that the SADF assisted the MNR in constructing an airstrip at Casa Banana to facilitate the delivery of supplies and personnel.[140]

Despite this evidence, President Botha refused to admit violating the Nkomati accord, although 'Pik' Botha conceded that there had been 'technical' violations. In response, Frelimo withdrew from the joint security commission, thus finalising the collapse in all but name of the Nkomati process.[141] Shortly afterwards, renewed threats were made against Mozambique, and Mozambican leaders warned that a wave of regional aggression was being planned in Pretoria.[142]

Patterns of Military Aggression

Although direct military aggression and the deployment of surrogate forces has been most marked in Angola and Mozambique, all the countries of Southern Africa have been subjected to apartheid destabilisation campaigns. Depending on the extent of economic links and geographic and political factors, the Pretoria regime has employed varying degrees of force and varying combinations of pressure.

This section focuses on just one element of a strategy which has also included economic and political measures. Military aggression against the SADCC states, other than major conventional military operation of the kind directed at Angola, has taken five principal forms: raids; assassinations; sabotage actions; violations of borders and airspace; and the deployment of surrogate forces.

Surrogate Forces and Sabotage
The SADF has made extensive use of surrogate forces in its campaign of destabilisation against neighbouring states. These forces have carried out a variety of operations and attacks. On many occasions South African troops have used them as a cover to carry out sabotage attacks.

SADF attacks against Lesotho were preceded by the establishment in 1979 of the LLA. From the middle of 1979 the LLA carried out a spate of bombings in Lesotho, mainly directed at government offices and economic installations.[143] Although Pretoria disclaimed responsibility for the LLA, the Lesotho government pointed out that the weapons and explosives used by the group were of South African origin and that it operated from South African territory.[144] On one occasion when two LLA members were arrested in South Africa for illegal possession of arms, they were released on bail and nothing further was heard of them.[145] Otherwise the LLA operated with impunity from South African territory. Of the twenty or so LLA attacks carried out in 1982, almost all occurred in north-western Lesotho within two kilometres of the South African border.[146]

Further sabotage and mortar attacks – including one on a Catholic mission – took place during 1983.[147] On the eve of a high-level meeting of SADCC and donor countries in Maseru, a Danish-funded abbatoir was sabotaged, and an attempt was made to destroy the water supply to the capital.

In March 1983 a group of 50 LLA raiders, led by an SADF officer, Major Mackenzie, and a number of other whites, attacked a base of the Lesotho Para-Military Force at Ongeluk's Nek. After a fierce battle the invaders were driven back into South Africa. The Lesotho authorities reported that 20 of the invading force had been killed or wounded. Subsequently some members of the LLA were captured, and admitted to having been trained in South Africa.[148]

Later in the year a number of attacks were launched from the Transkei and QwaQwa bantustans, including attempts to assassinate leading government officials.[149] Some of the attacks involved large numbers of LLA members – on 26 June, for instance, 100–200 armed men attacked the village of Taung, retreating into South Africa.[150]

LLA operations declined during 1984 following the Nkomati Accord, but strong economic pressure was put on Lesotho to sign a 'non-aggression pact' with Pretoria. During 1985, LLA operations continued, especially after August. Pretoria continued to issue thinly veiled threats against Lesotho, and threatened reprisals when the Maseru government supported the call for international sanctions against the apartheid regime.[151]

The destabilisation of Zambia has also involved the training and deployment of surrogate forces. In 1981 President Kaunda estimated the number of Zambian nationals being trained by the SADF at 500–600.[152] Banditry and indiscriminate destruction have characterised the operations of the destabilisation groups, the most notorious of which was that led by Adamson Mushala, who was trained at South African bases in Namibia. He was captured and killed by the Zambian army towards the end of 1982.

In 1980 Pretoria was implicated in an attempt to stage a mercenary coup in Lusaka. A gang of fifty well-armed mercenaries and Zambians was discovered on a farm some 15 km from the Zambian capital and rounded up by the Zambian security forces.[153] At the same time, South African forces in the Caprivi were reported to be making preparations for an attack. President Kaunda issued a statement linking the two events as part of a South African plan to overthrow the government and install a compliant regime.[154]

No identifiable surrogate force has been established to destabilise Botswana, but agents of the apartheid regime posing as refugees have infiltrated into the country and engaged in disruptive activities.[155]

A potential surrogate force to destabilise Zimbabwe became available to the SADF after independence when thousands of 'auxilliaries' in the Rhodesian army and hundreds of members of the Selous Scouts, Special Air Services and other units fled to South Africa. Apart from white Rhodesian troops who were signed up as mercenaries by the SADF, the

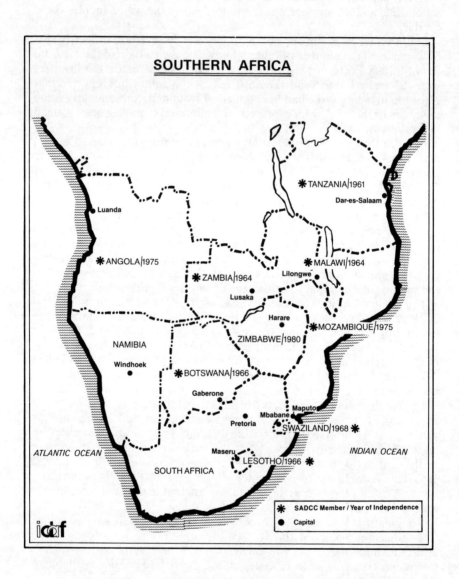

SOUTHERN AFRICA

Luanda

✳ TANZANIA/1961

Dar-es-Salaam

✳ ANGOLA/1975

✳ MALAWI/1964

✳ ZAMBIA/1964

Lilongwe

Lusaka

Harare

✳ MOZAMBIQUE/1975

ZIMBABWE/1980

NAMIBIA

Windhoek

✳ BOTSWANA/1966

Gaberone

Maputo

Mbabane

Pretoria

✳ SWAZILAND/1968 ✳

ATLANTIC OCEAN

Maseru

INDIAN OCEAN

LESOTHO/1966 ✳

SOUTH AFRICA

✳ SADCC Member / Year of Independence

● Capital

idaf

Zimbabwean government estimated that 5,000 auxilliaries were put into training at specially established bases in the Northern Transvaal.[156] Furthermore the SADF had at its disposal a huge amount of intelligence information. Many Rhodesian Military Intelligence and Central Intelligence Organisation operatives defected to South Africa, taking with them large quantities of materials. [157] Others continued working in Zimbabwe but became double agents for Pretoria.[158]

Soon after independence groups of armed men were infiltrated into Zimbabwe to carry out sabotage and other operations.[159] The groups made no attempt to win political support, instead carrying out numerous apparently random attacks in which villagers were killed or mutilated. At the same time a radio station, Radio Truth, was established in the Transvaal to broadcast into Zimbabwe.[160]

In early 1984 the Zimbabwean government estimated that there were about 100 South African-trained armed men operating in Zimbabwe.[161] During 1983 the government detected evidence of South African involvement in almost 50 attacks, including ambushes of government troops, the killing of farmers and overseas visitors and attacks on a bridge and a mine.[162] By August 1984 over 200 armed men who had undergone training in South Africa had been captured by the Zimbabwean authorities.[163] On one occasion ex-Rhodesian mercenaries carrying SADF equipment were intercepted on a mission to sabotage an important railway depot at Nyala.[164]

The first in a series of major sabotage attacks in Zimbabwe which were blamed on the apartheid regime took place at the end of 1981 when an explosion destroyed the Harare headquarters of the ZANU-PF party.[165] The most devastating of these sabotage attacks was at the Thornhill air base in July 1982, when almost a quarter of the combat strength of the Zimbabwean Air Force was destroyed.[166]

The South Africa regime has also attempted to destabilise Zimbabwe by using the MNR and the Reconnaissance Commandos to sabotage Zimbabwean transport links through Mozambique. The oil pipeline between Mutare and the Mozambican port of Beira has been a particular target. At the end of 1982, seaborne South African commandos blew up tanks storing Zimbabwean oil in Beira, and MNR groups have made repeated attacks on the pipeline, causing fuel shortages in Zimbabwe.[167] Convoys travelling through the Beira–Tete corridor have also been attacked.[168]

Raids and Assassinations
Ostensibly aimed at eliminating ANC personnel and facilities, military raids have led to the deaths of citizens of neighbouring states as well as South African refugees. They have caused extensive damage and destruction and have been aimed at intimidating the people and governments of neighbouring countries.

The first of these raids was the attack on Maputo, in January 1981. (Dealt with in the section on Mozambique.) In December 1982 a similar raid was launched on the Lesotho capital Maseru, and in June 1985 Gaborone, capital of Botswana, was attacked.

On the night of 9 December 1982 a 100-strong heliborne Commando force landed in Maseru. Powerful searchlights set up across the Caledon River border on South African territory lit up the town as the Commandos spread out to different residential areas, opening fire with grenades, incendiary devices and machine-guns on houses which they subsequently said they believed to be occupied by ANC refugees. By the end of the night, 30 South African refugees and 12 Lesotho nationals had been killed, many of them gunned down in their beds. Five women and two children were amongst the dead.[169] Sixty SADF troops remained behind for several hours – South African commanders warned Lesotho forces through radio contact that any attempt to interfere with them would lead to bombing attacks on Maseru.[170]

In June 1985 the SADF launched a similar raid on Gaborone which left 12 people dead. Units of the SADF surreptitiously crossed into Botswana and simultaneously attacked several houses which they thought were occupied by South African refugees. The raiders burst into bedrooms and sprayed the occupants with automatic fire, killing children and adults who attempted to hide in cupboards or under beds. Some of the houses were also mortared or bombed.[171]

The South African government claimed that it had destroyed an ANC guerilla 'nerve centre' in Gaborone, but all those killed were civilans, some of them South African refugees and others citizens of Botswana or other countries. The President of Botswana, Quett Masire, called the attack 'a blood-curdling act of murder'. He issued a statement noting that:

> The stated objective of South African strategy is expressly to cower [neighbouring countries] into submission to its will as a regional power. The purpose is to convince themselves that the wrongs they are perpetrating in their own country and Namibia are made right by the innocent blood they spill to justify them.[172]

In addition to commando-type raids a number of assassinations of South African refugees have been carried out. Attempts have also been made to assassinate leading members of the governments of neighbouring states.

The ANC's chief representative in Zimbabwe, Joe Gqabi, was assassinated in 1981 and attempts have been made on the lives of other South African refugees in Zimbabwe.[173] In June 1982, the ANC's deputy representive in Swaziland, Petrus Nzima, and his wife Jabu, both of whom were also active SACTU members, were killed by a car bomb in the Swaziland capital, Mbabane.[174] In 1983 another two South African refugees were killed in Swaziland when their house was attacked with grenades and machine-guns.[175] A number of other assassination and bomb attacks were carried out on ANC members in Swaziland during 1982 and 1983.[176]

Assassination attempts have been made on South African refugees in Lesotho through parcel bombs and other methods. This policy was extended to leading Lesotho political figures in 1982. Amongst those killed was the Lesotho Minister of Works, Jobo Rampeta.[177] Attempts were made on the lives of the Minister of Agriculture and on Prime Minister Jonathan, whose house came under attack by a group of armed men who fled across the South African border.[178] In December 1985, six South African refugees and three Lesotho nationals were killed in a night raid by a South African assassination squad on Maseru. The SADF denied responsibility but eyewitnesses reported that the assassins, who carried out the killings with silenced handguns, were white and spoke in Afrikaans.[179]

South African refugees in Botswana have also been killed, and during 1982 at least two bomb attacks on ANC and SWAPO members were attempted.[180] In February 1985 a house in Gaborone occupied by two South African refugees was destroyed by a bomb and in May a car bomb killed Vernon Nkadimeng, a leading SACTU activist living in Botswana.[181]

Attempts have been made to kidnap South African refugees in neighbouring states and take them back to South Africa. During 1982 the Botswana government protested strongly to Pretoria about one such case in which a refugee, Peter Lengene, was kidnapped and taken to South Africa for interrogation.[182] Three South African security policeman subsequently arrested in Botswana were jailed for six years after being found guilty of carrying out the kidnapping.[183]

South Africans in Angola and Mozambique have also been assassinated. In a parcel bomb attack similar to the one which killed Ruth First in Maputo, an ANC member, Jeanette Schoon and her six-year-old daughter were killed in Lubango, Angola in June 1984.[184]

Border Incidents and Airspace Violations
Apart from commando-style raids, the SADF has persistently violated the borders and airspace of neighbouring countries.

Before the independence of Zimbabwe in 1980, South African forces regularly supported the Rhodesian army and air force in attacks on Zambia.[185] In 1978 South African troops crossed into Zambia's South Western province from the Caprivi Strip in Namibia, occupying a village. The following year they carried out a similar operation, which was described as an anti-SWAPO action. Border incursions continued to increase throughout 1979. In October a force of 600 South African troops invaded Zambia from the Caprivi Strip, while 400 Rhodesian troops struck from the south.[186]

The end of the Zimbabwean war of liberation did not mark the end of South African aggression against Zambia. In 1980 the SADF launched attacks on Zambia in support of its offensive against Angola. In February and March, South African aircraft bombed villages in the South Western province, killing a number of civilians.[187] The following month two battalions of South African troops equipped with armoured cars and tanks crossed into Zambia. They broke up into groups and were active in the remote south-western areas for most of the rest of the year, burning crops, attacking villages and mining roads. Road blocks were set up and government vehicles seized, and health and other facilities attacked.[188] The South African attacks were unanimously condemned by the UN Security Council, which demanded that Pretoria withdraw from the area.[189]

Apartheid aggression against Zambia continued into 1981, particularly during August, when the SADF carried out a massive invasion of neighbouring Angola. The Zambian Red Cross reported that 'constant attacks' by South African troops had 'led to famine and outbreaks of various diseases' in the south-west.[190] Extensive landmining of roads made relief work difficult. Further SADF incursions took place in 1982, including attacks by armoured car columns and airspace violations.[191]

A further dimension to South African aggression against Zambia became apparent in August 1985, when the authorities revealed that they had been under attack from joint UNITA/SADF forces based in southern Angola and the Caprivi Strip in Namibia. They said that 18 Zambians were abducted between January and August 1985, and there had been five territorial violations, 43 border movements and 26 instances of small-arms and artillery fire.[192]

South African forces have repeatedly violated the border with Zimbabwe since that country's independence, and more extreme actions have been threatened. Prior to independence the SADF was actively involved in Zimbabwe, fighting with the illegal Salisbury regime against the liberation movements. *(See Chapter 1)*

The South African military build-up in Rhodesia continued during the Lancaster House independence negotiations at the end of 1979. Even after the signing of the ceasefire on 5 December 1979, there were reports that truckloads of South African troops were arriving in Zimbabwe to reinforce the thousands of troops already in the country.[193] Most of those troops were withdrawn prior to the elections of March 1980, which ended minority rule in Rhodesia. During the election period the conventional strike force of the SADF, the 8th Armoured Division, was put on 24-hour standby. South African newspaper reports openly speculated on the possibility of an invasion while SADF journals carried numerous articles evidently preparing troops for action in Zimbabwe.[194]

Persistent border violations took place after independence. During 1983, the Zimbabwean Security Minister, Emmerson Munangagwa, reported that South African forces were 'violating the border day in and day out' and that the South Africans 'wanted to do the same thing here in Zimbabwe as they do in Mozambique and Angola'.[195]

In December 1985 Pretoria issued explicit threats to attack Zimbabwe following ANC guerilla actions in the northern Transvaal. A large-scale build-up of military forces took place along the Zimbabwe border, and the Zimbabwean army was put on alert.[196]

From the middle of 1979, Lesotho, which is entirely surrounded by South

African territory, was subjected to a number of border attacks. In August 1981 a mortar barrage was launched from South African soil on Lesotho's only petrol depot[197] and in March 1982 the headquarters of the Lesotho Para-Military Force near Maseru were attacked twice, on both occasions from South African territory.[198] Many other attacks were carried out across the border, all of them being passed off as actions of a surrogate force, the LLA. (These incidents have been dealt with in the section on Surrogate Forces.)

South African agents and police have violated Botswana's borders for many years, and during 1981 and 1982 tension increased considerably as a result of SADF aggression. In January 1981 South African soldiers based in Namibia opened fire on Botswana Defence Force (BDF) positions 'without any provocation'.[199] In March that year the Botswana government lodged an official complaint to Pretoria about a number of SADF border violations, including one incident involving an armoured car and two troop carriers. The government also revealed that a South African helicopter had flown over BDF positions warning that the country would be invaded. Border incidents increased during the following few months. A night raid was made on a BDF unit across the Chobe river frontier, a fisherman was kidnapped, and an SADF helicopter carried out strafing operation against Botswana soldiers in a game camp.[200]

At the end of 1981 President Masire warned that South Africa was fabricating reports of aggression by Botswana in order to justify a 'counter-attack', and in the first few months of 1982 South African troops based in the Caprivi Strip made a number of incursions into northern Botswana, firing on BDF patrols.[201] Also during 1982 the Botswana authorities registered complaints about repeated ivory poaching by South African troops, who slaughtered dozens of elephants on Botswana territory, sometimes firing on them from helicopters.[202]

South African border violations, including incidents in which BDF patrols came under fire, continued during 1983 and 1984. At the end of 1985 the BDF was put on full alert in response to a South African troop concentration along its border. This followed a number of landmine explosions in the northern Transvaal which the SADF blamed on guerillas operating from Zimbabwe and Botswana. Both governments strongly denied any responsibility.[203]

South African police and military personnel have also violated the Swaziland border. Violations continued even after the Swaziland government signed a bilateral security pact with the apartheid regime in 1982. In December 1985, SADF troops were reported to have crossed into Swaziland and threatened villagers.[204]

8. NAMIBIA:
OCCUPATION AND LIBERATION WAR

For almost two decades the illegal South African occupation of Namibia has been challenged by a sustained armed struggle waged by the liberation movement SWAPO. The war has been fought with particular bitterness since the independence of Angola more than a decade ago, and the number of South African troops occupying Namibia has increased more than tenfold in this period. Thousands of Namibians have also been drawn into the occupation army.

Military and political moves have been closely interrelated as Pretoria has sought various ways of perpetuating its occupation of Namibia. South African strategy has increasingly reflected the regime's interest in destabilising the MPLA government in Angola and the war in northern Namibia has spread into southern Angola.

The Liberation War

The occupation of Namibia is estimated to absorb nearly ten per cent of South African government spending and has become a considerable drain on the apartheid economy. The official figure for the cost of the occupation in 1984/5 was given as R1,143 million – over three million rand a day. The actual figure could be double that.[1] Direct military expenditure, according to official figures, accounts for about half the total cost of the occupation.

Up to half the total mobilised strength of the apartheid armed forces have been committed to the war in Namibia and attacks on neighbouring Angola. Despite this huge military effort, the SADF has not succeeded in destroying the liberation movement. Even if SWAPO could be militarily defeated – and there is little indication that this would be possible without a prohibitively expensive escalation of the war – it is unlikely that the movement would lose its position as the force which has the allegiance of the vast majority of Namibians. According to a defector from the South African National Intelligence Service (NIS) in 1980 a detailed study by the NIS calculated that SWAPO would take over 80 per cent of the vote in a free election in Namibia.[2]

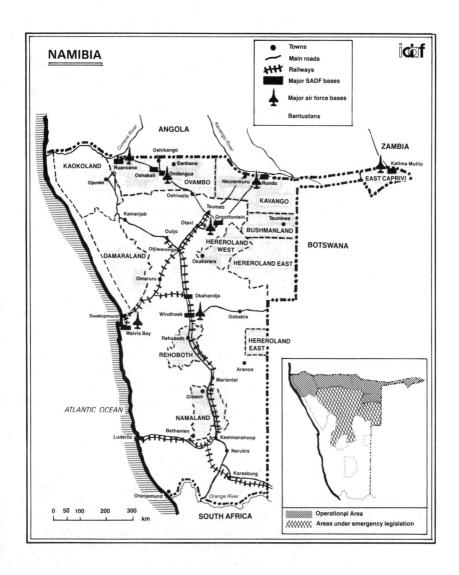

NAMIBIA

Towns
Main roads
Railways
Major SADF bases
Major air force bases
Bantustans

ANGOLA

Cunene River

Kavango River

ZAMBIA

Oshikango
KAOKOLAND   Ruancana   Eenhana
Opuwo   Oshakati   Ondangua
                OVAMBO   Nkurenkuru   Rundu   Katima Mulilo
        Oshivello   EAST CAPRIVI
                Tsumeb   KAVANGO
        Kamanjab   Grootfontein   Tsumkwe
            Otavi   BUSHMANLAND
            Outjo
        Otjiwarongo   HEREROLAND   BOTSWANA
                        WEST
DAMARALAND   Okakarara   HEREROLAND EAST
        Omaruru

            Okahandja

Swakopmund   Windhoek   Gobabis
    Walvis Bay
        Rehoboth   HEREROLAND
        REHOBOTH   EAST

                Aranos
            Mariental
        Gibeon
ATLANTIC OCEAN   NAMALAND
        Bethanien
Luderitz   Keetmanshoop
                Narubis
            Karasburg
    Oranjemund   *Orange River*

0 50 100 200 300
              km

SOUTH AFRICA

Operational Area
Areas under emergency legislation

icaf

177

The South African regime's failure to establish a viable political 'alternative' to SWAPO in Namibia, and the collapse of successive bantustan and surrogate administrations, is testimony to the political strength of SWAPO. With regard to the military aspect, the South African authorities claim that the war in Namibia is one of low intensity, that there is no significant military pressure on the occupation forces. In fact, Namibia is in the grip of one of the most intense and sustained military occupations in modern history.

The exact number of South African-controlled troops in the territory is unknown. The SADF does not provide any detailed breakdowns of its troop strengths. One concrete figure that has been given is that of 20,000 SADF troops.[3] To this must be added at least another 20,000 troops in the South West African Territory Force (SWATF), which is nominally independent of the SADF, and a fluctuating number of SADF troops engaged in Angolan operations but based in northern Namibia. Some ten thousand militarised police need also to be added. It is likely also that the figure of 20,000 SADF troops refers only to combat forces and excludes logistic and support personnel. This is borne out by a statement in June 1985 by the commander of the occupation forces, General Meiring, in which he said that there were 40,000 SADF and SWATF troops 'on the Angolan border' – implying that his figure excluded troops engaged in support roles outside the Operational Areas.[4]

SWAPO has estimated that there are around 100,000 troops under South African control in Namibia – that is, including the SWATF and police units. This figure has been corroborated by many researchers and journalists and accepted by the United Nations Council for Namibia (the legal administering authority over the territory).[5] If, according to SADF figures, there are 40,000 combat troops, an overall total of 100,000 would be a very conservative figure. It can therefore be regarded as an acceptable working estimate, subject to fluctuations depending largely on Angolan operations.

The population of Namibia has been estimated at 1.4 million, giving a ratio of one soldier to every fourteen Namibians – men, women and children.[6] Such a situation can hardly be characterised as a conflict of 'low intensity'. An examination of casualty figures also indicates that this characterisation is inappropriate. In 1984, for example, the SADF admitted 26 combat deaths amongst its troops and claimed to have killed or captured 584 SWAPO combatants.[7] SWAPO stated that it had killed 71 SADF and SWATF troops in May, June and July alone and in previous years its figures had been far higher than those admitted to by the SADF.[8] Such disparities are not unusual in war, and can be ascribed to a number of factors. It is obvious, however, that South African casualty figures are grossly understated. The deaths of black troops, who now carry the brunt of the fighting, are hardly ever reported – since 1976 it has been official SADF policy not to reveal their names or provide statistics.[9] There is also evidence that white deaths are covered up in various ways.[10]

In January 1985 an academic expert on Namibia, Professor Reginald

Green, calculated on the basis of official South African figures that white casualties in Namibia since the onset of the armed struggle in 1966 could have been as high as 2,500. As a proportion of the white South African population this death rate would have been three times that of the American forces in Vietnam. Professor Green based his calculations on the fact that annual tallies released by military headquarters have excluded deaths related indirectly to military operations or incurred on specific raids.[11] His figures are still lower than those provided by SWAPO, but SWAPO makes no racial distinction in its casualty statistics, and in recent years the majority of SADF and SWATF members killed by SWAPO have been black, as a result of the South African policy of deploying a disproportionately high proportion of black troops in front-line roles.

Other statistics go some way to reveal the extent of the war and the suffering endured by the Namibian people under the South African occupation. An estimated six to ten per cent of the population have gone into exile to escape persecution, terrorisation and economic devastation.[12] At least ten thousand Namibians have been killed.[13] There are no statistics, however, which can quantify the suffering caused by forcible population removal, the ripping apart of families, the assault on social structures, the destruction of agriculture and the many other devastating social and economic effects of war and military occupation. Church leaders who have visited Namibia have described the South African occupation as a 'reign of terror' in which the only law is the law of the gunman and torturer.[14]

Apartheid and Colonialism

The Namibian people have suffered some of the worst excesses of colonial rule. During their conquest of the territory in the last decade of the nineteenth and the first decade of the twentieth centuries, German colonists ruthlessly exterminated seventy per cent of the Namibian population in the south and centre of the territory. They nevertheless failed to establish complete control, leaving the populous northern areas unpoliced.[15]

After the South African regime displaced the German colonial administration during the First World War, Pretoria moved to extend its control up to the border of Angola. The pass laws and other aspects of apartheid policies were extended to the territory, as the regime intended incorporating Namibia into South Africa. In the 1950s, as independence swept down the African continent, Pretoria began to regard Namibia as a strategic buffer between the white heartland and independent Africa. The onset of the armed liberation struggle in neighbouring Angola saw the establishment of modern airfields and military bases in northern Namibia, both to assist the Portuguese and to prepare for possible guerilla activity in Namibia itself.[16]

As has been documented in Chapter 1, the first guerilla activities after the launching of the Namibian armed struggle in 1966 were dealt with by the South African Police, who were equipped and trained for counter-insurgency warfare. The general strike of 1971/72 led to the deployment of SADF units. By 1973 the army had taken over responsibility for counter-insurgency operations and the first large contingents of National Service troops were brought into the territory.[17]

The South African regime attempted to fragment Namibia by establishing bantustans. Thousands of troops were deployed to assist in the implementation of the bantustan programme, but the scheme was strongly rejected by the Namibian population. Elections in the Ovambo bantustan, the most populous of all, resulted in a poll of only 2.5 per cent.[18]

Angolan Independence and the Turnhalle Conference

The events in Portugal in April 1974 and the prospect of Angolan independence opened a new chapter in the Namibian conflict. The SADF ordered more troops to the north of Namibia and increased the pace of its military construction programme there, building strategic roads and establishing military bases. In the face of growing international demands for an end to its occupation of Namibia, the regime revised its bantustan strategy and devised a scheme to establish nominal 'independence' for Namibia. This would be achieved on the basis of the existing bantustans and other segregated authorities, thereby ensuring a fragmented, politically weak country in which SWAPO could be excluded from power.

A number of carefully nurtured political groups working within the bantustans or other segregated systems were brought around a conference table to draw up a constitution for a nominally independent Namibia. The Turnhalle Conference, as it was called, opened in September 1975 and continued to meet until early in 1978. During this period the South African occupation authorities engaged in a wide-ranging drive of repression and militarisation designed to halt the growing military and political strength of SWAPO.[19] Two hundred leading SWAPO members were arrested, emergency legislation amounting to martial law was extended to cover most of the northern areas of Namibia and thousands of people were rounded up by the army. Many of those detained were tortured in makeshift corrugated iron and barbed wire detention centres attached to military and police bases.[20]

International pressure on the regime to abandon the Turnhalle programme grew. In January 1976 the UN Security Council unanimously condemned the South African occupation of Namibia, denounced its brutal oppression and military build-up in the territory and demanded free elections under United Nations supervision. Faced with the prospect of having to repeatedly exercise vetoes in the Security Council over demands for sanctions against the South African regime, the United States, Britain, France, the FRG and Canada formed a Contact Group to negotiate with Pretoria over the issues of Namibian independence.[21]

As a result of negotiations, a compromise was reached whereby the South African regime agreed to install an Administrator-General to administer the territory and to prepare for UN-supervised elections. After further negotiations, the Contact Group put forward detailed proposals for a settlement in Namibia, calling for a phased withdrawal of South African troops, a ceasefire between SWAPO and the SADF and the holding of elections under the supervision of a UN Transition Assistance Group (UNTAG). These provisions were incorporated into UN Security Council Resolution 435 adopted in September 1978.[22]

In August 1977 Pretoria issued a Proclamation providing for Walvis Bay, Namibia's only deep-water port, to be administered as part of the Cape Province, thereby effectively annexing the town and surrounding areas.[23] Parallel with the negotiations, the South African occupation authorities strengthened the bantustan system and intensified their repression, especially in the north of Namibia, and soon began to raise objections to details of the UN Plan. The day before the adoption of Resolution 435, Pretoria announced that it would unilaterally hold elections in Namibia for the Constituent Assembly. This move was condemned by the United Nations, which declared the elections to be null and void.[24] The South African regime nevertheless went ahead with its sham elections in December 1978.

The parties in the Turnhalle Conference were incorporated into the Democratic Turnhalle Alliance (DTA) for electoral purposes. Through intimidation, bribery, and extensive propaganda, the occupation authorities attempted to establish the DTA as the major political party in Namibia. In an atmosphere of intensified repression, with SWAPO virtually driven underground and thousands of troop reinforcements brought into the territory, the DTA won an overwhelming majority in the elections to the Constituent Assembly which were boycotted by SWAPO.[25]

The War 1975–80

The settlement negotiations and related political developments in Namibia took place in the context of intensified military conflict. After the MPLA victory in Angola, SWAPO guerilla forces, the People's Liberation Army of Namibia (PLAN), began to operate over a broad front extending from the plains of the western part of the Ovambo bantustan through the scrub and dense bush of eastern Ovambo, the Kavango bantustan and the Caprivi Strip.

By August 1976 the number of troops based in Namibia had swollen from 16,000 to an estimated 50,000. White Citizen Force and Commando units in Namibia were activated, and northern towns such as Grootfontein, Ondangua and Ruacana were transformed into sprawling fortified garrisons. Small, operational size bases were established and squadrons of helicopters and Mirage attack aircraft were moved in from South Africa.[26]

A 'free-fire' zone one kilometer wide was cleared along 2,000 km of the Angolan border, entailing the forced removal of villages, homesteads and shops. In 1976 the UN Commissioner for Namibia estimated that in three months between forty and fifty thousand villagers had been forcibly evicted from their properties and homes.[27] Army and police forces were instructed to shoot and kill anyone found in the cleared zone.[28] Villagers removed from the border area were resettled in 'protected villages' under SADF control. Some white areas of towns were fenced off and surrounded by watchtowers. Boreholes and water supplies in the north were destroyed, and the cleared zone was defoliated.[29]

These efforts to 'sanitise' the border failed. During 1976 the number of guerilla attacks and skirmishes reported by the SADF was more than three times the total for the previous ten years. By the middle of the year PLAN guerillas were operating in strength in the white farming areas to the South of the bantustan. Farmers were reported to be 'panic stricken' and the press was ordered not to publish information on guerilla contacts in the white areas in order to maintain morale.[30]

Throughout 1976 PLAN kept up a constant barrage of attacks on SADF units and bases, both in the northern areas and to the south. The occupation regime launched a major drive to recruit Namibians into bantustan military units, and by the end of the year some five hundred men had been incorporated into such battalions.[31] In May 1977 the SADF announced that the period of National Service for white South African and Namibian conscripts would be doubled to two years, allowing for the deployment of much larger numbers of National Servicemen. Information on incidents in the war zones was more rigorously suppressed.

For most of 1977 the SADF claimed that PLAN was 'avoiding contact' and concentrating on political mobilisation. In October, however, the SADF Director-General of Operations divulged that the army had been involved in over one hundred engagements with PLAN every month.[32] There were also occasional reports of large-scale guerilla attacks on major army and air force bases in the north. Towards the end of the year new emergency legislation, allowing for wider powers of detention, was introduced in the northern areas.[33]

The Kassinga massacre of May 1978 and an intensification of police and army repression prior to the elections for the 'Constituent Assembly' did not prevent a further escalation of guerilla activity. During this period PLAN concentrated on attacks on major military bases such as Katima Mulilo and on sabotage operations. According to the SADF sabotage increased ten-fold during 1978.[34]

PLAN units also began to attack the bantustan forces which were being deployed to back up the DTA campaign of intimidation during the election. The election itself was accompanied by a huge show of force involving the mobilisation of 2,500 Citizen Force and Commando troops.[35]

According to the SADF, the opening months of 1979 saw a 'dramatic increase in SWAPO activities', including a number of sabotage operations. Power supplies from the Ruacana hydroelectric power station on the Angolan border, which was being commissioned for the first time, were sabotaged, blacking out the whole of Namibia.[36] PLAN was able to repeat this blow on a number of occasions during the following years.

On 10 May 1979 emergency legislation was extended to cover the central areas of Namibia. Over half the country and 80 per cent of the population was thus placed under a form of martial law. Troop strengths in the new 'security districts' were substantially increased and SADF personnel were posted permanently to a number of white farms. Bantustan officials and other apartheid functionaries were given personal bodyguards, kraals were fenced and white farmers integrated with military structures. These moves were in response to growing and widespread support for SWAPO and its armed struggle. According to official figures, military 'incidents' of all types doubled during 1979 compared to the previous year.[37]

A similar pattern of attacks on army patrols and bases persisted into 1980 when the SADF conceded a 50 per cent increase in casualties.[38] In May PLAN guerillas attacked the air force base at Ondangua, causing serious damage.[39] Transport in the north became an increasing problem for the occupation army, with vehicles having to travel in convoy and rail routes being periodically sabotaged. By September 1980 it was estimated that PLAN was tying down about 75,000 troops in Namibia. In areas of the north where the SADF was hard pressed to retain control it was falling back on terrorist tactics. Evidence of indiscriminate brutality, including barbarous torture and mutilation, was coming to light.[40]

Any illusions the South African regime harboured about preventing a SWAPO victory in UN-supervised elections were undermined by the overwhelming victory for the liberation movement in independence elections in Zimbabwe. New attempts were made to prevent the implementation of the UN plan for elections and to steer Namibia to a nominal independence under South African control. An executive 'Council of Ministers' and a 'National Assembly' was established, the bantustans were provided with 'Representative Authorities', and an 'independent' civil service was set up.[41]

As part of this process, in August 1980 a separate defence department was created in Windhoek and all the Namibian-manned SADF units were transferred to the newly-formed SWA Territory Force (SWATF). Eight months later a similar process took place in the police force when the SWA Police (SWAP) was created.[42]

Angolan 'Linkage'
A new stage in the Namibian conflict was opened after the collapse of the second major round of talks on a settlement, the Pre-Implementation meeting held in January 1981. These talks were deliberately sabotaged by Pretoria on the grounds that the DTA had no confidence in the United Nations.[43] The day the talks broke down, South African forces attacked and briefly occupied the town of Cuamato in southern Angola.[44] In August 'Operation Protea' was launched against Angola leading to the occupation of Cunene province. The SADF presented the operation as the death blow against PLAN, which, it claimed, relied entirely on rear bases in southern Angola.[45]

The objectives of 'Operation Protea' were not in fact limited to cutting off SWAPO's alleged rear bases. The SADF wished to intensify its campaign of destabilisation against Angola, especially with regard to extending the influence of its surrogate UNITA group. The wider implications of Operation Protea have been discussed in the previous chapter, but it is evident that the occupation of southern Angola did not have any immediately significant effect on PLAN's operations in Namibia. Although SWAPO has support facilities in Angola, where tens of thousands of refugees have settled, it has always insisted that its operational bases are in Namibia itself. Newspaper reports have revealed that some guerillas hold down ordinary jobs during the day and then at night rendezvous at secret places, pick up uniforms and arms and carry out operations.[46]

The invasion of Angola was a manifestation of Pretoria's new strategy with regard to the settlement negotiations – from then on, a solution to the Namibian issue would be tied to the regime's designs on Angola. In 1982 South African diplomats, taking their cue from the United States, began to raise the demand that Cuban troops brought into Angola by the MPLA government during the 1975 war should be removed before a settlement in Namibia could be implemented.

This became one of the principal themes of South African military and political strategy with regard to Namibia. The 'linkage' of Angolan to Namibian issues also involved South Africa's aim of bringing UNITA into the Angolan government. Pretoria wished to play for time to ensure that conditions for a Namibian election – whether carried out under UN or South African auspices – would be such that SWAPO would be prevented from gaining an outright victory. The regime calculated that further delay in the Namibian settlement proceedings would give it an opportunity to strengthen the political and military capability of the 'internal parties' collaborating with its occupation.

Throughout 1981 and 1982 the Western Contact Group engaged in negotiations aimed at satisfying South African demands for the modification of the UN plan set out in Resolution 435. These modifications chiefly involved a provision for drawing up a constitution prior to elections and a complex electoral arrangement which was calculated to make the prospect of an outright SWAPO victory less likely. At the end of 1983, the UN Secretary General, Perez de Cuellar announced that 'virtually all outstanding issues' in the plan had been resolved to the satisfaction of all parties. However South Africa and the United States continued to insist on 'linkage' with the Angolan situation. By this stage the idea had been firmly rejected as an extraneous and irrelevant issue by the UN and the international community as a whole.[47]

Pretoria's intransigence was to a large extent prompted by its failure to establish a credible alternative to SWAPO inside Namibia. Rent by defections, disagreements, financial mismanagement and corruption, the DTA proved itself incapable of managing the complex three-tier system of eleven different 'ethnic' authorities Pretoria had imposed on the territory.

South African authorities, especially military officers, were increasingly concerned at the DTA's weakening position. Military commanders complained that what they were gaining by military action and police repression was being lost by the politicians.[48]

Towards the end of 1982 the occupation authorities entered into secret talks with bantustan leaders and other small groups outside the DTA. In January 1983 the DTA was abandoned. The Council of Ministers and National Assembly were allowed to collapse in disarray and the South African Administrator-General resumed direct control. In July a new body, called the State Council, was established but this too collapsed soon afterwards. In September a Multi-Party Conference (MPC) was launched. Despite defections and disagreements this body was eventually installed in Windhoek in 1985 as a replacement administration for the DTA-dominated National Assembly.

The War 1981-82

Despite the commitment of more troops to Namibia the SADF did not make any discernible military progress between 1981 and 1984, while SWAPO opened up a new front in the west, in the arid Kaokoveld. In April 1981 a newspaper report commented:

> The Ovambo-speaking region is progressively sliding deeper and deeper into a state of war . . . the number of guerillas present in the region has sharply escalated . . . The endless procession of armoured cars, the troop carriers, the men in their serge uniforms will remain a feature of life here for years to come . . .'[49]

It was disclosed that Ondangua and other towns were virtually surrounded by guerillas, who were reported to be 'walking around by night, passing the airbase at 200 metres'. Dressed as civilians, the guerillas were carrying out reconnaissance in the towns and gaining information on the movements of army units.[50]

PLAN fighters were reported to be handing out leaflets, copies of the PLAN journal and other information. Rail tracks, road bridges, telephones and power lines were being sabotaged. On 4 May 1981, the third anniversary of the Kassinga massacre, the SADF bases at Okalongo and Ogongo were mortared.[51] In July – after Operation Protea had supposedly destroyed SWAPO's military capability – the major air base at Ruacana was attacked. SWAPO claimed to have wounded or killed more than a hundred soldiers and to have inflicted serious damage.[52] By September, the death toll in the war had officially risen to over 2,000 that year – the highest ever.[53]

To increase the power of the bantustan leaders, the SADF intensified its drive to establish Namibian-manned military units. Thousands of 'home guards' or 'special police' were given rudimentary training and deployed as the personal militia of bantustan chiefs.[54]

The occupation forces also stepped up their drive to 'win the hearts and minds' of the Namibian population by establishing development projects, stationing National Servicemen at schools and medical institutions and creating a dependence on the SADF in some communities. In the Ovambo bantustan, where SWAPO already had a strong presence amongst the local communities, these projects largely failed to gain support. Bantustan leaders had to be removed from their home villages and installed in heavily guarded compounds to isolate them from attacks by the people they were supposed to be representing.[55]

As PLAN operations spread west into the Koakoland bantustan, new South African military bases and air facilities were constructed there and white settlements took on the fortified garrison appearance of the Ovamboland towns. Opuwa, the administrative centre of the region, was described as 'an armed camp' from which whites would only venture by aircraft or in armoured convoys.[56]

Further south, the escalation of the war could be seen in the rapid expansion of military facilities at major towns. A huge new base was planned south of Windhoek, and a large warehouse purchased in the industrial area. A new training centre was established at Okahandja, mainly to accommodate the expansion of SWATF.[57]

Namibia's tiny white population (less than 100,000), was reduced even further as farmers abandoned the countryside and resettled in South Africa. By September 1981 a third of farms in the strategically important Kamanjab-Outjo area were reported to be unoccupied. To stem the tide, loans and other financial facilities were made available to farmers who were prepared to guarantee occupancy and join part-time police or army units. Despite state aid, the exodus continued.[58]

PLAN operations were again stepped up in January and February 1982 but by March, the SADF claimed to have severely reduced the strength of the liberation army as a result of further attacks on Angola.[59] It was argued that the destruction of SWAPO 'bases' in Angola had crippled the movement and that it was unable to launch any significant military offensives.

Only a few weeks later, the SADF had to deal with a force of between three hundred and five hundred heavily armed guerillas who had quietly slipped into the white farming areas south of the Ovambo bantustan. Taking advantage of the vegetation cover provided by the annual rains, the guerillas attacked SADF and police bases and patrols and destroyed a number of armoured troop carriers. A major mobilisation was ordered to deal with the incursion. Roadblocks were set up around towns, including Windhoek, and the part-time Commandos were called up. Farmers in the Tsumeb and Otavi areas were placed on 'full alert'.

Over the following few weeks several clashes took place as thousands of troops scoured the bush in search of the guerillas. Despite the massive hunt, and heavy casualties taken by the South African forces, some of the guerillas were believed to have infiltrated the urban areas, and blended in with the local population. It was assumed that they would establish bases and carry out clandestine political work – many of them had distributed pamphlets addressed to the local population and members of the police and army.[60]

Operations then shifted to the Koakoveld area where guerilla incidents were reported to be 'sky-rocketing', and to the Kamanjab area where other guerilla groups were operating. Power supplies were sabotaged and the rail lines near Windhoek blown up, derailing a train carrying military equipment to the north.[61]

After a brief lull, the activities of the liberation army were again stepped up in August 1982 when a base at Omahenene was attacked and a number of helicopters shot down.[62] The SADF admitted that 15 troops had been killed in one of the helicopters in an accident, but denied that any helicopters had been shot down.[63] It also denied that the Omahenene base had been attacked, labelling the SWAPO claim as 'blatant propoganda . . . so futile that not even SWAPO's own supporters will be impressed'. Three days later an army spokesman admitted that the attack had in fact taken place, but denied any casualties – SWAPO claimed 30 dead.[64]

Despite these widespread PLAN actions military headquarters in Windhoek continued to claim that the tide had been turned against SWAPO as a result of the occupation of Angola. These claims were backed by increasingly strong control over media reporting and vague official communiques in which the number of 'terrorists' shot dead in single operations often reached into the hundreds. For example, during 'Operation Super' early in 1982 the SADF claimed to have killed 200 heavily armed PLAN guerillas, without incurring a single casualty on their side.[65]

The War 1983-84

Accurate information on the Namibian war became extremely difficult to obtain after February 1983, when the SADF imposed a blanket ban on all but officially-sanctioned military reports. To prevent 'a false image of the war' being portrayed in the press, all press reports on military matters had to be submitted to the military authorities for censorship before publication.[66] This move was described by one South African newspaper, the *Star*, as 'a complete blackout on all but authorised (or officially tailored) news'. The newspaper remarked; 'Henceforward, compulsive secrecy will call the tune. 'The public will have to judge the value of what it reads about Namibia in this light.'[67]

The press clampdown was imposed to stifle information on a large SWAPO military operation, the biggest single offensive yet carried out during the war. The PLAN operation, dubbed 'Volcano' by the SADF, was preceded by a sabotage attack on the heavily fortified post office in the garrison town of Oshakati, and the destruction of a road bridge outside the town.[68] A few days later, the telephone lines to the north were brought down, and most of Namibia was plunged into darkness as a result of the sabotage of power lines.[69]

A force of PLAN guerillas between six hundred and eight hundred strong was reported to be heading towards the white farming areas, operating over a wide area from the Kaokoveld to the western part of the Kavango bantustan. The media clampdown prevented any information on contacts being disclosed, but by the 4 March the SADF claimed to have killed 129 guerillas. Instructions had been issued to farmers to regard the Tsumeb, Otavi, Grootfontein, Kamanjab and Outjo areas as 'infested' with guerillas.[70] A SWAPO War Communique of 9 March disclosed that PLAN had 'broken through enemy defence lines' and that white farmers in the affected areas were fleeing to the south for safety.[71] The SADF remained silent, apart from raising the figure of SWAPO deaths that year to over two hundred by the 19 March.[72] One of few press reports dealing with the operation reported: 'The war is now being fought over virtually the whole of Ovambo and western Kavango, while insurgents have succeeded in penetrating the "white" farming areas in the Tsumeb and Outjo districts'.[73]

The official silence was finally broken only at the end of April, when an SADF briefing was arranged. An army spokesman claimed that about six hundred and fifty guerillas had launched a multi-pronged offensive in the Kaokoland, Ovambo and Kavango bantustans to break through into the 'white areas'. Simultaneously, a further nine hundred and fifty guerillas had launched operations in the northern border areas to tie down the occupation forces. He claimed that the offensive had been a total failure, and that over three hundred guerillas had been killed for the loss of less than thirty police and army personnel. He did not, however, say what had happened to the other 1,200 guerillas involved in the operation.[74]

An indication of continuing PLAN activities was provided during a number of 'security sweeps' carried out in the western Kavango bantustan. Mass arrests and forced removals, which began in November 1982, were still reported to be in operation in April 1983. The operations were described in the press as part of an 'anti-insurgency drive'.[75] Thousands of people were reported to have been forced to move from their homes and resettle along the Kavango River next to military bases, as the SADF attempted to establish a free-fire zone in which 'anyone who moved must be shot.'[76] Military authorities denied reports of forced removals, but visitors to the region reported seeing several totally depopulated settlements. The SADF was also engaged in an extensive bush-clearing and defoliation operation in the Ovambo bantustan, clearing and poisoning areas around the major strategic roads.[77]

In May 1983 the SADF tersely disclosed that it had 'stopped a second large incursion of more than 100 SWAPO terrorists'.[78] Two months later it dismissed press reports of another major PLAN operation in the north.[79] However, in September military and police units were reported to be engaged in 'follow-up operations' against a group of about 100 guerillas which had been intercepted carrying explosives and other military supplies to combatants permanently based in the Kavango area. Military spokesmen estimated that there were about 800 guerillas active in the region.[80] In the same month, the SADF transferred to Namibia the deputy head of the army, Major-General George Meiring, underlining the high priority placed on the Namibian war.[81]

By the end of 1983 it was clear that the SADF's occupation of southern Angola had failed in its claimed objective of destroying SWAPO's military capability by cutting off its support and logistic facilities. The black-out on news reports could not suppress the fact that the year had been one of the busiest for the occupation forces since the onset of the liberation struggle. P W Botha later revealed in parliament that on average more than 43 incidents a month had been recorded.[82]

Effects of the Lusaka Undertaking

Towards the end of 1983, the Namibian situation was once again affected by wider regional developments. In December the SADF launched Operation Askari against Angola in order to shore up its protégé UNITA force and to secure further leverage over the Angolan government. This proved a costly failure, and for reasons explained in the previous chapter, the regime was obliged to halt its military drive in Angola and enter into an agreement with the Angolan government for the withdrawal of South African troops.[83]

SWAPO shared the Angolan government's view that the undertaking should be viewed as a step towards securing South African agreement on the implementation of Resolution 435. The South African regime regarded the matter in an entirely different light. It used the Angolan government's agreement to prevent SWAPO moving into the vacated areas during the withdrawal process as the basis for an entirely unfounded propaganda campaign. This campaign tried to create the impression that SWAPO would be forced to give up the armed struggle and join forces with the Multi-Party conference in a South African-arranged 'internal settlement'.[84] False stories were planted in the South African press reporting clashes between Angolan and SWAPO forces and warning of hundreds of 'out of control' guerillas 'fleeing' towards Namibia.

Operations by SWAPO in Namibia were seized upon as pretexts for delaying the South African troop withdrawal, which soon ground to a halt. The demand for a Cuban withdrawal became a condition for the implementation of the Lusaka Undertaking. As an alternative to the implementation of Resolution 435, Pretoria proposed that a 'regional peace conference' be called, involving the MPC, SWAPO, the Angolan government and UNITA. This represented a more extreme form of 'linkage' between the Angolan and Namibian issues and was naturally rejected by the Angolan government and SWAPO.[85]

With the withdrawal from Angola stalled, arrangements were made for another attempt to get South Africa to agree to the UN plan for Namibia. Talks were convened in Lusaka in May by President Kaunda, but they rapidly broke down. The South African representatives made it obvious that they had gone not to discuss Resolution 435, but to promote the image of the MPC and restate their position on 'linkage'. By insisting on an MPC presence at the conference, Pretoria hoped to weaken SWAPO's position and give the impression that the liberation movement was talking to the so-called 'internal parties'. This tactic backfired when a number of the 'internal parties' crossed the floor and joined the SWAPO delegation. They included the Damara Council and a section of SWANU, thus denuding the MPC of two of its main constituents.[86]

Operation Askari at the end of 1983 had as little success in stemming PLAN activities as the earlier Operation Protea and other invasions of Angola. A strong force of guerillas was operating in Namibia at exactly the time the SADF claimed to be attacking SWAPO positions some three hundred kilometres to the north near the Angola towns of Lubango and Cuvelai. The news black-out prevented any comprehensive reports from being published, but small units of guerillas were intermittently reported to be operating south of the Ovambo bantustan.[87] The SADF admitted to 34 guerilla incidents in January 1984 and 58 in February – a steep rise, contradicting claims that SWAPO had been weakened by Askari.[88]

Shortly after the withdrawal agreement with Angola came into operation, the South African authorities released details of 'a massive force of 800 SWAPO terrorists' moving south through the Kaokoveld. This information appears to have been released mainly to undermine the disengagement process in Angola, as little follow-up was reported, although Opuwo came under mortar attack, and an attack was launched on the main air force base in Ondangua.[89] A small group of SWAPO guerillas were reported to be operating in the Rietfontein area to the south-west – the first time since 1979 that guerillas had been reported that far south.[90] Sabotage attacks on communications and strategic facilities in various parts of Namibia were also reported.[91]

To counter 'subversion' the army rounded up an estimated 1,000 people in the Ovambo bantustan in March and transported them to a spot near the Ondangua military base. Each person was asked whether they would support 'SWAPO or South Africa' in an election and their names and photographs were taken.[92] Reports were also received of an intensified campaign of intimidation and repression in the Kavango bantustan.[93]

Under internal and international pressure, during 1984 the authorities released most of the SWAPO refugees captured at Kassinga in May 1978, who had been held without trial at a detention camp in Mariental.[94] Also released, apparently in the vain hope that he would split SWAPO or prove a 'moderating' force, was Andimba Toivo ya Toivo, one of the original SWAPO leaders who led the movement into guerilla warfare and had been imprisoned since 1966. (Ya Toivo took up the post of SWAPO Secretary-General after his release.)[95] There was no diminution of repression and detention without trial, however. During the course of the year more evidence came to light of continuing detentions, torture and atrocities, especially at the hands of the notorious Koevoet police COIN unit.[96]

Throughout the first half of 1984 guerilla activities continued to increase. In an interview in the PLAN journal *The Combatant*, the Chief of Staff of the liberation army commented:

> In the past we were most active during the rainy seasons, but now our military activities are being conducted throughout the year . . . By signing the Lusaka Accord, the Pretoria regime thought the ground would be cut from under out feet and that it would bring SWAPO off the battlefield. But they are failing to stop our advance. Our forces are battling the enemy troops deep in the south of our country. We have never and do not intend to upset the agreement reached between Angola and the apartheid regime of South Africa. But this cannot prevent us from fighting inside Namibia where our forces are based . . . We have permanent forces in the north, north-western and north-eastern areas of Namibia.'

He added that PLAN's immediate strategic objective was to 'advance the war towards industrial and commercial areas', a strategy reflected in a sharp increase in sabotage on industrial targets.[97]

Deepening 'Security' Crisis

The SADF's weakening position in Namibia was reflected in the minutes of a secret meeting held by military intelligence officers in Windhoek in May 1984. The minutes listed a wide range of factors as a threat to security, complained of low morale in the SADF, and confirmed that SWAPO was 'constantly' carrying out sabotage operations. The secret minutes admitted:

> SWAPO internally is organised on a wide terrain on different levels and possesses the infrastructure to collect information over a wide spectrum . . . it has an extensive intelligence gathering network whereby the public, especially the hundreds of cuca shops in Ovambo and Kavango are involved and keep it informed as to the movement of the security forces.[98]

The document also noted that the 'unstable political situation' and the 'squabbling between political parties in SWA' were factors assisting SWAPO.[99]

The leaked minutes provided a rare insight into the real thinking of the SADF and the actual state of the conflict. They contradicted official press releases and public statements by SADF officials, who were insisting that SWAPO's military capability had been destroyed. In November 1984, for example, Major General Meiring announced that the Kaokoveld had been 'completely cleared' of PLAN while there were only 23 guerillas in the Kavango and Ovambo bantustans.[100]

General Meiring also announced that more than five hundred guerillas had been killed in Namibia during 1984 for the loss of only 26 members of the 'security forces' – a ratio of 21 to 1.[101] Such 'kill ratios' have been rising steadily over the past few years, and are given by the SADF as an indication of the increased efficiency of the occupation forces. They are probably a better indicator of the increasingly exaggerated and unreliable nature of official communiques and statistics.

Almost all commentators on the Namibian situation agree that SWAPO guerillas are well trained, well armed and well motivated. On the other hand, a large percentage of the 'security forces' consists of poorly trained auxilliaries such as Special Constables. It is thus most unlikely that SWAPO deaths should outnumber SADF casualties by more than twenty to one, unless, that is, the SADF includes civilians in its totals. Furthermore, by 1984 the SADF claimed to have killed a total of over 8,000 guerillas – more than the estimated field strength of SWAPO. It is unlikely that SWAPO would have been able to sustain the liberation war if these figures were correct.[102]

It was clear a year after the Lusaka undertaking that PLAN activities in Namibia had not been substantially reduced by the attempt of the SADF to establish a 'cordon sanitaire' in southern Angola. *(See Table XVI for official figures on PLAN operations 1977-1984.)* In March 1985, the continuing escalation of the struggle led the occupation authorities to seal off the northern bantustans of Kaokoland, Ovambo, Kavango and Eastern Caprivi as well as the easterly bantustans of Bushmanland and Hereroland East, isolating over half of Namibia's population from the rest of the country. All civilians not normally resident in these areas were forced to apply for police permits before entering, with a penalty of a fine or a 12-month prison sentence for failing to produce a permit. The new restrictions were introduced alongside increased penalties for failure to carry indentity cards – proof of residence in one of the 'security districts' would be dependent on details provided in the identity card.[103]

Despite these restrictions, it became clear that PLAN activities increased once again in 1985. The President of SWAPO stated that by the end of June the liberation movement's military actions represented a three-fold increase compared to the whole of 1984, while the SADF itself admitted to a huge increase in sabotage attacks – a total of 58 incidents were recorded in the first five months of 1985. PLAN actions included attacks on the Rundu, Ruacana and Eenhana military bases, the bombardment of Oshakati, and a number of major sabotage actions on the territory's road, rail, communications and power networks.[104]

At the end of 1985 a Namibian newspaper commented:

> Although the SWA Territory Force claims that SWAPO's military effort is 'winding down', a look at newspaper and SWATF reports over the past year reveals that the security forces have been engaged in a constant battle . . .
>
> Incidents of sabotage by SWAPO guerillas, as well as 'contacts' with the security forces, have occurred at the rate of two or three a week.[105]

A wave of repression against SWAPO members and other Namibians supporting the implementation of UN Resolution 435 was unleashed in June 1985 when the South African regime established a new administration which it called a 'Transitional Government', composed of the six small parties in the Multi-Party Conference. The new administration consisted of a legislative authority, an executive authority and a constitutional council charged with drawing up a constitution for a nominally independent Namibia. No elections were held and the parties involved soon fell into disagreement over how to deal with the bantustan system. The MPC administration was condemned as 'null and void' by the United Nations and the Western Contact Group, and marked a clear break with Resolution 435.[106]

The Security Police special force, Koevoet, was responsible for the brutal suppression of a demonstration against the new administration in Windhoek on the day it was inaugurated, and many observers predicted that military and police repression would intensify under the MPC administration. SWAPO and Namibian church leaders pointed out that there was 'no prospect for peace' given the South African regime's refusal to implement UN Resolution 435 and allow internationally supervised elections in the territory.[107]

Military Occupation Structures

South African military structures and operations in Namibia have undergone a number of changes as the war of liberation has progressed. SADF commanders distinguish four phases, reflecting changing military and political situations.

During the **first phase**, from 1966 to 1973, the war was one of very low intensity, and its conduct was left almost entirely to police COIN units brought from South Africa. Military units remained under the control of SWA Command in Windhoek but were not involved in any major operations until the general strike at the end of 1971. In the **second phase**, the SADF took over full control in the war zones of the north, and operations were placed under the command of 101 Task Force in Grootfontein, which was in turn directly responsible to military headquarters in Pretoria. During this period, in an effort to counter growing support for SWAPO, the occupation forces instituted the strategy of 'winning hearts and minds', engaging in a number of civic action programmes and taking over administrative and service roles.[108]

In the **third phase**, from 15 August 1977, military authority for the whole of Namibia was again centralised in Windhoek, in preparation for the establishment of the SWA Territory Force two years later. These administrative and organisational changes were aimed at reinforcing the 'internal parties' and giving the impression that the territory was acquiring its own independent military force. Intensified recruiting for black units took place, leading to the introduction of black conscription in October 1980. The local Commandos or Area Force Units (AFUs) were also upgraded.

Since the third phase the Namibian war has to some degree been characterised by the abandonment of the 'hearts and minds' strategy and the adoption of more direct and brutal counter-insurgency methods. It has also been marked by an escalation of aggression against Angola and strikes against Namibian refugee settlements there.

SADF commanders identify a **fourth phase** of the war after the Lusaka Understanding with the Angolan government at the beginning of 1984. Although this did not result in a ceasefire between Angolan and South African forces, and had no marked effect on SWAPO operations inside Namibia, it led to a reduction of SADF operations in Angola during 1984. The conduct of the war in Namibia itself continued in much the same way as it had since 1978. In 1984 and 1985 renewed efforts were also made to 'Namibianise' the conflict by extending black conscription and passing formal administrative responsibility for SWATF to the new Multi-Party Conference administration.

The 'Operational Area'

The northern war zone or 'Operational Area', falls under direct SADF control and is intensively patrolled by units consisting of both South African and Namibian personnel.[109] It is divided into three zones: Sector 10 which covers the Ovambo and Kaokoland bantustans and is headquartered at Oshakati; Sector 20 covering the Kavango bantustan and the Western Caprivi Strip (HQ Rundu); and Sector 70 covering the Eastern Caprivi Strip (HQ Katima Mulilo).[110]

Since the mid-1970s most military activity has taken place in Sector 10, in which at least eighty permanent army and police bases have been established.[111] Three infantry battalions are based in this sector, each with a permanent headquarters structure. Most of the patrolling and deployment is organised from the company-strength bases attached to each battalion. Each of these bases maintains a standard force of about three hundred men, approximately one-third of whom are engaged in back-up and logistical activity (mechanics, sappers, drivers, storemen, etc) and the rest deployed in infantry combat roles. From time to time, depending on operations, specialist reaction forces such as Koevoet share the facilities.[112]

Armoured cars and a mortar section are usually attached to each company base, but most of the activity consists of intensive daily foot patrolling. Small groups of men – between 10 and 25 strong – set off on patrols of up to a week in duration, scouring the bush for signs of PLAN guerillas and checking on local kraals (settlements) and cuca shops. Once contact is made, the patrols attempt pursuit or lay an ambush and radio their base for reinforcements if necessary. In the case of a large PLAN presence, mobile reaction forces in armoured personnel carriers (code named 'Romeo Mike' groups) will be despatched from the battalion

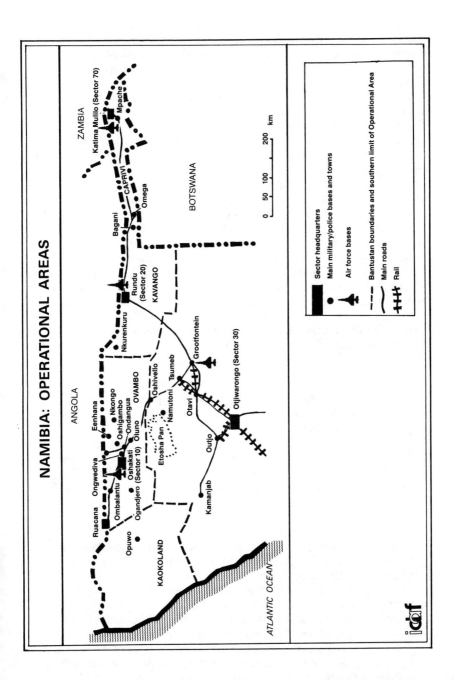

NAMIBIA: OPERATIONAL AREAS

195

headquarters where they wait in readiness.[113] Helicopters may also be despatched to co-ordinate battle activities and carry out strafing operations or reconnaissance. The acute shortage of helicopters in the SADF – a result of the arms embargo – leads to many of them being earmarked for priority casualty evacuation.[114]

Army patrols are supported by police operations mounted from small but numerous police bases scattered across the war zones. With the exception of specialist units, the police do not usually share bases with the army. Separate patrols are mounted from police bases, which usually house forty to sixty men, most of them black 'Special Police' operating under white command. The police, who are trained in counter-insurgency warfare and equipped with army weapons, specialise in intelligence gathering. Security police, an active component at many bases, are responsible for the torture and interrogation of prisoners and suspects.[115]

Oshakati, the nerve centre of Sector 10, is also the headquarters of a number of army and police units, including Koevoet, and the site of a large logistical and support establishment. Ondangua, some 30 km to the south, provides the main air base for operations in Namibia. It has extensive facilities for Puma and Alouette helicopters, Impala jet aircraft and light reconnaissance aircraft.[116] The atmosphere of siege in these garrison towns has been remarked upon by many commentators. The following report, from a South African daily newspaper, gives some indication of the beleaguered position of the occupation forces in the Ovambo and Kavango bantustans:

Oshakati, a dull fortified village lying about 60 km south of the Angolan border, provides a grimly accurate reflection of [the South African army's] position.

High fences circle the entire town where rows of dreary prefabricated houses line dusty streets. Bomb shelters are a bizarre, yet realistic, feature of each garden.

Anti-aircraft guns on towering stands point menacingly into the African sky and at the nearby Ondangua air base jet fighters and radar provide additional protection. It is a 'white' village with gates manned by military policemen and a dusk-to-dawn curfew.

At its only hotel, members of the police Counter-Insurgency unit Koevoet . . . exchange stories of 'kills' while quaffing generous quantities of Windhoek beer . . .

Beyond Oshakati's tenuous security South African soldiers are treated with cold civility. Outside the fences the town's other face is pimpled with the delapidated tin shanties of the slums built by hundreds of rural people trying to escape the war.

Hygiene is basic, while sanitation is almost non-existent. Teenage members of Koevoet slouch around the market places where bloody portions of cattle are offered on pieces of rusty corrugated iron.[117]

Military Structures Outside the War Zones

South of the war zones, which coincide with the bantustan boundaries, the nature of military deployment is different, although often no less intensive *(See Table XVI)*. Towns such as Grootfontein and Okahandja contain large military bases and logistic facilities. Almost all centres of any size have **Area Force Units** (AFUs) attached to them, into which farmers and white civilians are mobilised on a part-time basis. Some blacks participate in some of the AFUs, and in certain areas all-black AFUs have been established, but they remain largely the preserve of whites.

Area Force Units provide close support and advice to the estimated five thousand white farmers in Namibia who are regarded as a first line of defence against guerillas. Many farmers have been issued with two-way radios linked to the MARNET (Military Area Radio Network) system, so that they can provide the SADF with intelligence information and summon assistance.[118] Farmers who belong to the AFUs are issued with automatic weapons and camouflage uniforms, and some of them wear uniforms and carry arms as a matter of course. In the event of guerilla operations south of the Red Line, farmers in the affected area are placed on alert. They are expected to patrol their farms and 'take certain predetermined cautionary measures'. Troops may also be deployed on key farms, and the local Area Force Units are mobilised for patrols, either on foot or in armoured vehicles.[119]

Owing to the great distances in Namibia, and the dangers of mines on the roads, many white farmers use private light aircraft for personal transport. They are encouraged to join the 'SWA Air Force' – **1 SWA Squadron** – which carries out reconnaissance and other tasks for the SADF, making use of private aircraft.[120]

An article in the SADF journal *Paratus* described the integration of white farmers with the military effort in the following way:

> Each home becomes a stronghold in itself. The local population provides intelligence by reporting any suspicious movements . . . to implement a farm protection system, representatives of the SADF are sent to the farmer. The farm's layout is assessed and a suggested strategic plan is recommended to the farmer . . . There are five basic recommendations regarding farm protection;
> – installation of a radio communications system;
> – erection of security fences;
> – use of guard dogs;
> – removal of undergrowth;
> – a house plan . . .[121]

Businessmen and private companies also contribute directly to the military occupation, both through tenders and other work carried out for the SADF – road construction, defoliation, military housing – and through the establishment of **private security bodies**. These bodies are usually set up in terms of South African Key Points legislation which is in force in Namibia. For example, a security document from Rossing Uranium Ltd which was obtained by SWAPO in 1980, described the procedures to be followed by a security force established at the mine. The unit was set up 'to maintain a state of preparedness against civil or labour unrest or terrorist attack'. The document revealed that the private force could draw on the resources of a local industrial commando called the Swakopmund Industrial Protection Unit. [122]

Private security firms supplement police activity south of the war zones. The **SA Police** and **SWA Police** are active in 'normal' policing as well as the suppression of political protests and in paramilitary operations. As in South Africa, two reserve forces, the Reserve Police, consisting of part-time volunteers, and the Police Reserve, drawn from ex-policemen, carry out back-up tasks. **Security Police** are active in carrying out detentions and interrogations in the south as well as in the north. The **Railways Police**, backed by their own reserve, are included in the definition of 'security forces' and equipped with automatic weapons. 'White' towns have their own **Municipal Police** forces, including traffic police, who are also armed. A special police force has also been established in the **Katutura hostel** compound outside Windhoek, and has been responsible for a number of violent attacks on residents. Considerable effort has been put into the recruitment of black policemen, referred to as **Special Police**, who have established a reputation for intimidation and brutality. [123]

For military purposes, the south, like the Operational Area, is divided into military zones, the most important of which is Sector 30, covering the areas to the north of Windhoek affected by emergency legislation. Its headquarters are at Otjiwarongo. Sector 40 covers the central area around Windhoek, Sector 50 the east (HQ Gobabis) and Sector 60 the south (HQ Keetmanshoop). The enclave of **Walvis Bay** is excluded, as the South African regime adminsters it as part of the Cape Province. An estimated 3,500 troops are permanently based in Walvis Bay, which is one of the most militarised areas in Southern Africa. The rail head for Windhoek and the north, Walvis Bay is of vital strategic significance. Its importance has been further increased by the discovery of large oil and natural gas reserves off the coast. [124]

Walvis Bay is home to the 2 SA Infantry Battalion Group, the only SADF unit combining infantry and armour, which has played an important role in attacks on Angola. It is also the site of the Rooikop military airfield from which Mirage and Buccaneer jets operate. Its port is protected by a Marine unit and regularly visited by South African warships. [125] As the main centre for the training of Namibian conscripts, the facilities at Walvis Bay are being continually expanded. [126]

Conscription and Recruitment

For more than a decade the SADF has attempted to sow division amongst the Namibian people by incorporating sections of the population into the occupation army. This 'Namibianisation' process is aimed at transforming the independence struggle into a civil war, alleviating the SADF's manpower shortages and reducing the casualty rate amongst white South African soldiers.

'Namibianising' the War

The incorporation of blacks into the occupation army was long preceded by their recruitment into the police force – a policy employed by the Germans and continued by the South Africans after their occupation of the territory in 1914. With the onset of the armed struggle in the mid-sixties black police began to be armed in significant numbers, and counter-insurgency training began in 1972. In that year the first detachments of trained black policemen were despatched for operational duties in Rhodesia and Namibia.[127]

The first black army unit was formed in 1974, with the establishment of **201 Battalion** consisting of men classified as 'Bushmen'.[128] *(See section on Civic Action)* The establishment of 201 Battalion was followed by the inauguration of units in the Ovambo and Kavango bantustans the following year. The lack of jobs in the war zones, and the relatively high salaries and privileges associated with the military service reportedly facilitated recruiting. Further **bantustan-linked units** were established in 1976 and 1977.[129] During this period the SADF projected an 'ethnic' character on the various units and built them up as a way of strengthening compliant leaders installed in the bantustans.

With the introduction of the Turnhalle system, and its eleven different administrations federated under a central council in Windhoek, the bantustan-based units were incorporated into the **SWA Territory Force**. A central training and operational unit, **911 Battalion**, was established with headquarters in Windhoek. This battalion was presented as a 'multiracial' unit – but the constituent companies of the unit tended to be segregated and exclusive.[130]

Efforts were made to establish **Special Police**, bantustan police forces, which now fall under the command of the SWA Police.[131] Such units have been set up in almost all the bantustans, where they have been deployed mainly to protect bantustan leaders. The Special Police are especially numerous in the Ovambo bantustan, where bantustan leaders are under constant guard.[132]

The Special Police are also used for patrolling duties, and are trained in counter-insurgency warfare mainly at a base near Ondangua. Their training is rudimentary and lasts for only two months. This, coupled with the youth of many recruits – often as young as 16 – has led to widespread indiscipline amongst the units. Recruits who show 'leadership qualities' are taken to South Africa for further instruction at the police counter-insurgency centre at Maleoskop, after which they may be signed up for the Koevoet unit.[133] Special constables are usually equipped with G3 automatic rifles. They number 9,000, about a third of whom are based in the Ovambo bantustan.[134]

The behaviour of the Special Police – sometimes called Home Guards – was reflected in an editorial in the *Windhoek Observer* on 6 February 1982:

A look at the records of 1981 discloses that this country has institutionalised terror, government sanctioned, trained and supported gangsters, who are issued with G3 sub-machineguns or assault rifles as the deadly weapons are called, and then given a free hand to embark upon a campaign of terror.

These people are called Home Guards, and are dressed in camouflage uniforms, the overwhelming bulk of them consist of undisciplined vagrant youths, some 15 or 16 years of age. Their training is poor and their backgrounds would preclude them from the military or police organisation of any civilised state . . .

Has the Home Guard system been created in order to build a counter insurgency arm? Has it been created to serve as the front end of a strike force so as to curb losses on the part of white soldiers and police? Or has it been created with the explicit objective to sow terror and to murder people, and thereby to institute civil strife and war? With rare exceptions one can only call the Home Guards gangsters. The record is an ugly one and their appearance at Court trials even more ugly. They convey the impression, if one must judge on the strength of court reports, of vagrant drunkards, armed and wandering aimlessly around to shoot at random and to kill. They can be termed official exterminators . . .

The SWA Territory Force

In April 1980 the then Administrator-General of Namibia, Dr Gerrit Viljoen, declared that devolving 'some control' over army and police forces would be a 'top priority' once executive powers had been accorded to the DTA-controlled National Assembly in Windhoek.[135] Four months later a 'Department of Defence' was established and administrative control over 66 SADF units – some 20,000 troops – was transferred to the newly established executive, the Council of Ministers.[136] The South African military commander in Namibia, Major General Lloyd, adopted the title of 'Secretary of Defence' and doubled as head of the 'SWA Department of Defence'.[137]

In August 1980 the SWA Territory Force was formally inaugurated and new uniforms, rank structures and pay scales – differing only slightly from those of the SADF – were unveiled.[138] Despite these trappings, it was evident that command structures remained little changed. In operational matters, Major General Lloyd was still required to refer to the Chief of the

SADF, and the SADF itself maintained direct control over the conduct of the war in the Operational Areas and in Walvis Bay. The functions of the SWATF were limited to executing administrative control outside the war zones over units with Namibian personnel. [139]

The collapse of the Council of Ministers in 1983 and the reversion to direct rule through the Administrator-General, meant that in effect SWATF reverted to direct SADF control. The force was nevertheless kept nominally separate, and when the MPC administration was inaugurated in mid-1985, it was given formal, though not real, control of the SWATF.

SADF commanders have indicated that they regard the SWATF as the nucleus for the armed forces of an independent Namibia. Major-General Lloyd has declared that as 'part of the SWA independence process', the SWATF should 'form the basis of the defence force of the new state'. According to Lloyd, the demilitarisation process laid out in the UN Plan and Resolution 435 would only be 'a temporary phase that should last only for the duration of the election campaign . . . After the election the new constitution will provide for a defence force which will incorporate the SWATF as we know it today.' [140]

In addition to the SWATF an **SWA Police** force (SWAP) was formally inaugurated in 1981 with uniform and other cosmetic changes. South African police serving in Namibia were given the option of joining the SWAP or remaining 'on secondment'. [141] SWAP fell under the nominal control of the DTA and later the MPC administration. The Security Police and Koevoet remained directly under the SADF and SA Police during the period of the DTA administration, but became part of the SWAP in May 1985. [142]

The establishment of the SWAP had potentially serious consequences for the independence procedure as the UN Plan did not provide for the demobilisation of local police forces, which would be expected to carry out 'normal policing duties'. This would mean the Koevoet, as a police unit, could be excluded from demobilisation under the plan. [143]

Changes in police and military command structures have had little effect on the conduct of the war in Namibia. The large numbers of South African police and military personnel 'on secondment' to the SWAP and SWATF, coupled with direct SADF control over operations, and Pretoria's overall political and economic control in the territory, have ensured that the SWATF and SWAP have remained in effect administrative sub-sections of the SADF and SAP. This much was admitted by the chairman of the 'cabinet' of the MPC administration, David Bezuidenhout, in August 1985, when he stated that it was impossible to establish a separate military command structure – let alone a fully independent force – as the SWATF had only administrative and not operational responsibility. He also pointed out that Pretoria had refused to pass responsibility for military affairs to the MPC administration. [144]

Conscription

In October 1979 General Geldenhuys, then commander of the Namibian occupation forces, announced that the number of South African troops in Namibia would be cut back by as much as fifty per cent over the following two years. They would be replaced by 'local black and white personnel' in the SWATF.[145] Such a cutback did not occur, but the ranks of SWATF were enlarged by the introduction of conscription for black Namibians from January 1981.

After carefully orchestrated demands for conscription from the DTA, in October 1980 the South African State President issued a proclamation extending liability for military service to all Namibian males between the ages of 16 and 25.[146] The Administrator-General declared that conscription would 'give expression to the feeling that . . . the entire population of South West is handling its own interests, [it is not] as some hostile elements put it, . . . the Boers who are defending SWA.'[147]

Circulars were sent to school principals, instructing them to register all boys of 16 or over for military service, and in November 1980 call-up orders were posted to selected young men.[148] While all young Namibian males were eligible for call-up, a careful selection took place and residents of the four bantustans in the north were excluded from the process. Military spokesmen argued that this was because the bantustan battalions in these areas were already up to strength, and there were no plans to establish Area Force Units. A more likely reason for the exclusion of the war zones was that in these areas support for SWAPO was strong and resistance to conscription would have been overwhelming.[149]

Fearing military call up, large numbers of contract workers were reported to have left the Katutura hostel near Windhoek, returning to their homes or crossing into Angola or Botswana as refugees.[150] Protests against conscription spread, uniting many diverse sectors of the country. At a mass rally in Katutura in December, about three thousand SWAPO supporters met to condemn the call-up and mobilise opposition to it.[151] The Namibian Council of Churches, representing most of the major Namibian churches, petitioned the South African State President to review the legislation and warned that conscription would lead to an exodus of refugees, industrial strikes, an increase in sabotage attacks and school boycotts.[152]

By the second week of January 1981 the Lutheran World Federation reported that 5,000 refugees had arrived in Angola in order to avoid conscription. New refugees – including women and children, who were not conscripted, but feared the effects of men being called up – were reported to be arriving in Angola at the rate of 500 a week.[153]

About two thousand men were called up in the January 1981 intake[154] but it was later revealed that only three companies were under training (an estimated nine hundred men), suggesting that over half those called up did not obey their instructions. Although supposedly integrated – about twenty per cent of the first intake was white – all but one tent at the training base were reported to be segregated.[155] All conscripts were initially allocated to

2 SA Infantry Battalion Group based at Rooikop in the Walvis Bay enclave. After basic training with the SADF, some of them were sent to a newly established SWATF junior leadership school at Okahandja, after which they were posted to various SWATF units to complete their second year of service.[156]

Faced with massive resistance to conscription, the military authorities apparently turned to press-gang tactics. There were reports of young men being taken off the streets of Windhoek by the police or army and forcibly sent off for military training. Students at secondary schools in the north were forcibly enlisted. South African soldiers accompanied by municipal police toured black areas in Windhoek and other major towns, serving registration papers on eligible males.[157] There were also reports that contract workers were being forced to sign undertakings that they would serve in the occupation army before being allowed to take up employment contracts.[158]

At the Okahandja Junior Leadership School another problem arose. After being asked to declare their political affiliations, 32 of the trainees announced that they supported SWAPO. They were removed from the rest of the group and put into virtual isolation, after which they were allegedly sent without weapons to the Operational Area for 'reorientation'.[159] When the parents of the young men heard of their plight, they organised themselves into a People's Action Committee and arranged a public meeting in Katutura.[160] The attention of those campaigning against conscription was also directed at an official announcement that a cadet training system would be introduced into Coloured schools to prepare secondary school pupils for 'national service'.[161]

In the face of such strong resistance, no significant expansion in the annual intake was recorded. The issue of conscription remained an important one in Namibia, however, and each intake led to renewed calls for the abolition of conscription.[162]

In June 1983, a young Namibian, Eric Binga, who had failed to gain exemption from conscription on the grounds of his long-standing membership of SWAPO, filed a declaratory order before a Judge President in Windhoek to have his call-up orders invalidated.[163] Binga, who was supported in court by his father, attested that he had a brother fighting for PLAN. He argued that as the South African occupation of his country was illegal, and the terms of the original mandate granted to Pretoria specifically prohibited the conscription of the indigenous population, it followed that his call up orders had no legal basis.[164] The Windhoek Supreme Court rejected Binga's argument, but he was given leave to take his case to the Appeal Court in Bloemfontein.[165]

In 1982, when an estimated 800,000 white South African men aged up to 55 became eligible for conscription into the Commandos, the SADF indicated that the new system would not be applied to Namibia.[166] Nevertheless, at the end of October 1984 the commander of the Namibian occupation forces, General Meiring, announced that all Namibian men between the ages of 17 and 54 years of age would have to register for military service. The aim was to gain 'personal information about all males living in Namibia . . . and the determination of each person's service commitments' in order to set in motion 'the allocation of these persons to a unit for service, or if not allotted, the checking out of persons on a waiting list for subsequent allocation for service, or to one of the Reserves'.[167].

The move was immediately condemned in the strongest terms by a wide range of Namibian organisations. The Namibian Council of Churches joined with SWAPO in warning that the drive would sow the seeds of civil war and undermine prospects for peace and independence. The Council extended its support to those refusing to register and noted that in some 'deplorable cases' people had lost their jobs for refusing to comply with the order.[168] SWAPO described the move as amounting to 'the practical establishment of civil war . . . and an attempt at subjugating the Namibian people militarily'.[169]

When the registration drive was announced it was made clear that 'for practical reasons it is not possible for the SWATF to obtain the personal details of all male citizens in SWA between the ages of 17 and 54 simultaneously' and that registration would take place in phases over the following year.[170] In the first phase, all members of the reserve – that is, any Namibian who had ever served in the army – were obliged to register. Then a general registration was embarked upon in Sector 30, covering Tsumeb, Otavi, Otjiwarongo and Grootfontein. Registration centres were established at farms, commando headquarters, nature conservation stations and military bases, and warnings were issued that those refusing to register, or encouraging others not to, would be prosecuted.[171] Farmers and businessmen were accused of threatening to sack employees who did not register.[172]

By the middle of November 1984 the SADF claimed that 17,000 men had registered in Sector 30[173] and it was made clear that the process would be extended until the entire country had been covered.[174] However the registration scheme was halted during 1985. General Meiring, indicated that this was partly a result of a lack of financial resources.[175]

The UN Council for Namibia warned that conscription was not only 'illegal and reprehensible', but that it was 'aimed at further delaying the independence of Namibia'.[176] SWAPO President, Sam Nujoma, alluding to the role that SWATF could play after independence, denounced military conscription as 'sowing the seeds for a harvest of future destabilisation . . . thus perpetuating the dependence and exploitation conditions'.[177]

The Battle for 'Hearts and Minds'

The refrain that counter-guerilla warfare is eighty per cent social and political and only twenty per cent military has been echoed by South African military and political leaders time and time again over the past decade. But the occupation of Namibia has been markedly devoid of viable social, economic and political strategies to counter the liberation movement. Increasingly, the SADF has reverted to brute force to maintain its grip over Namibia. The South African regime's initiatives in attempting to create a strata of allies in the territory have floundered and collapsed.

Civic Action
Specific Civic Action programmes – sometimes referred to as social or psychological action – were first introduced into Namibia in 1974 after the failure of police and then military efforts to 'clear' the northern areas of guerillas. From the outset, localised development projects were closely related to the overall aim of building up an administrative infrastructure in the bantustans as part of the drive to balkanise the territory. Areas regarded as militarily sensitive were prioritised for development – at the same time, there was no decrease in general repression or military activities against the guerillas. In many cases, the implementation of 'social action' programmes coincided with major military operations. As a result the social programmes were undermined by the alienating effects of military brutality.

A major factor behind the failure of the programmes is that they have been closely indentified with the unpopular and repressive bantustan system. Furthermore, in many cases SADF personnel – doctors, nurses, teachers, argriculturalists – have simply filled vacancies left by white civilians who were increasingly reluctant to take up posts in war zones. They have thus been perceived both to be blocking local job advancement and to be perpetuating the structures of white domination and colonial oppression.[178]

The showpiece Civic Action project has been **201 Battalion** at Omega in the western Caprivi. In 1974 the SADF began recruiting as trackers nomadic men classified in apartheid terms as 'Bushmen', and during its operations in Angola the following year gained additional recruits from men in the service of the disintegrating Portuguese army. These men and their families were settled around a training base in the Western Caprivi, initially called Alpha but soon renamed Omega.[179] They were joined by other family groups from Angola whose nomadic lifestyle was being made impossible by the pressures of the war.[180] A condition for making use of the facilities at the base was service in the SADF for all fit men of military age, while employment in auxilliary tasks was offered to some of the families of men who signed up.[181]

The Omega project was kept secret until 1977, but since then the SADF has lavished publicity on the scheme as a successful example of 'winning hearts and minds'. With about 850 troops, 201 Battalion has a complement of 200-300 white officers, NCOs and National Servicemen – a high white-black ratio reflecting the SADF's belief that the black troops 'will always need white leadership'. The unit's emblem, a crow with a white breast set against a white background, is said to symbolise black/white relationships in the camp. The white breast is meant to signify white leadership, and the white background 'western civilisation'.[182]

Settled at the base with the soldiers are nearly four thousand others – eight hundred and fifty wives, over two thousand children, hundreds of dependants and a number of 'illegal squatters'. Omega is reported to make up eighty per cent of the population of the remote Western Caprivi area. Life at the base is utterly dependent on the SADF. The inhabitants are taught Afrikaans and subjected to the exclusive ministrations of the Dutch Reformed Church. Children are taught by soldiers according to the South African Cape Province syllabus. The army runs the only shop and administers civil justice in cases such as divorce.[183] Alcoholism is reported to be endemic.[184]

Salaries are high and Omega offers virtually the only employment in the region, leading many observers to question what will happen after the SADF withdraws. An entire community, made totally dependent on the SADF, has grown accustomed to relatively high pay as a result of their service in the occupation army. A new generation of children is growing up at Omega knowing nothing but the peculiar conditions at the camp and thoroughly indoctrinated with the ideology of racist South Africa and its armed forces. The SADF is continuing to expand the programme – in 1980 it was announced that the accommodation at Omega would be almost doubled by the construction of a further 800 buildings.[185] At the end of 1985, the area around Omega was declared a 'Bushman development zone' and it was announced that essential services would be withheld from people living outside the designated area, in order to further concentrate the San-speaking population around Omega.[186]

A second San battalion has been established in the Bushmanland bantustan. Small bases have been established at various centres in this arid and underpopulated region. At each of these bases 'mini-Omegas' are under construction with the establishment of army-controlled shops, housing and schools.[187]

Although Omega has been presented as an example of 'winning the hearts and minds' of the Namibian population, in fact almost all the people involved were recruited from Angola. This was admitted by General Meiring in 1985: 'There is no real Civic Action programme [in the western Caprivi] . . . there is only a number of bushmen . . . who fled Angola in 1975 and established a base at Omega'.[188]

The **Kavango bantustan** adjoining the western Caprivi was prioritised for Civic Action during the mid-1970s, when a number of projects aimed at building up the bantustan infrastructure were started. Almost all the projects had both military and political objectives – the SADF regarded the construction of roads and communication facilities as essential for the conduct of the war. Extensive use was also made of the system of deploying National Servicement with appropriate qualifications in local schools, both as a way of familiarising the population with the army, and for intelligence functions. At least one school had a staff entirely composed of National

Servicemen.[189] The occupation authorities also attempted to entrench the authority of the appointed bantustan through the establishment of a youth movement, Ekongoro. Membership of this movement was made compulsory for all 30,000 schoolchildren in the area. Ekongoro aimed to instill 'Christian Nationalism' amongst the children and encouraged 'the development of a Kavango nationalism'.[190]

Another 'cultural organisation' consisting mainly of members of the 'security forces' and the bantustan administration, was also established. Called Ezuva, this organisation became the principal front for SADF 'hearts and minds' activities during 1985. A wide range of propaganda was produced under its name and government employees were sent to Ezuva training courses.[191]

In 1978, the SADF invited selected press reporters to the Kavango bantustan to inspect the result of the Civic Action programme. A number of reports appeared in the South African press praising the occupation forces for their good works. Typical of these reports is that which appeared in the *Rand Daily Mail* on 18 June 1978:

> Kavango . . . is a vast, sparsely populated area bordering Angola. The SA Defence Force has initiated an extensive civil action programme serving the 80,000 tribesmen in Kavango and securing the border from any possible SWAPO threat.
>
> In counter-attack to SWAPO's methods of intimidation and indoctrination, the Defence Force has built hospitals, schools, irrigation projects – and a sense of pride – for the five tribes of Kavango.
>
> After training, a seasoned Kavango battalion serves side by side with white soldiers guarding the area. And it's all working . . .

Only a few years later Kavango had become one of the principal sites of SWAPO activity and the army had reverted to more overt methods of oppression – mass arrests, forced removals and the poisoning of water supplies.[192] In 1983 a senior Koevoet commander admitted in a court case: 'The entire western Kavango is rotten [with guerillas] and we get no co-operation from the local population'.[193]

'Development' projects aimed at establishing an infrastructure for the military and the bantustan administrations have also been instituted in the **Ovambo bantustan**. Widespread use has been made of the soldier-teacher system, whereby qualified National Servicemen have been seconded to bantustan administrations. From the outset the programme met considerable resistance, and there were repeated protests at the presence of soldiers in classrooms.

In August 1978 seven hundred pupils at the Petrus Kaneb Secondary School went on strike to back a demand for the withdrawal of SADF teachers. Their parents, who supported their stand, formed a Black Parent Society to step up the pressure.[194]

Other Civic Action projects in the Ovambo bantustan included the establishment of an army-run agricultural college at Ogongo[195], a few irrigation projects[196] and a number of very small-scale projects such as building bridges over streams.[197]

Etango, an organisation similar to Ezuva in the Kavango bantustan, has been established to build support for the SADF and the bantustan authorities. A delegation from the Southern African Catholic Bishops' Conference which visited Namibia in 1984 reported that the organisation, 'seemed to be a project promoted by the security forces to win "the minds and hearts" of the Ovambo people'. The Bishops noted that a document attributed to Etango and distributed by the army promised rewards of up to R20,000 for reporting the presence of SWAPO guerillas to 'Etango the protector'.[198] The organisation, which was established by the army and police, drew most of its initial membership almost entirely from the 'security forces'.[199] By 1985, it was reported to have 5,000 members.[200]

Given the needs of the communities in the war zones, SADF civic action initiatives have been hopelessly inadequate to win local support for the occupation army. Of the tens of thousands of troops deployed in Namibia, probably fewer than five hundred are involved in civic action projects, mostly as teachers.[201] There is no indication that the projects have managed to halt the social and economic decline in the war zones, far less provide a basis for undermining the liberation movement by removing social, political and economic iniquities.

In Sector 10, the principal war zone, the SADF has been particularly unsuccessful in winning hearts and minds. In February 1981 an army officer admitted to the press; 'In Ovamboland I'm not sure if [Civic Action] does much good because of the large number of SWAPO there'.[202] By 1985 the number of SADF teachers deployed in the Ovambo bantustan had dropped to 23 from a reported 90 in 1978. All these were withdrawn in August 1985 after protest that soldiers had organised extra-mural activities in schools without obtaining permission, and allegations that the SADF had bombed the Ongwediva Training College and blamed the attack on SWAPO.[203]

Deteriorating Conditions

Apart from a few localised projects, Civic Action in Namibia has consisted mainly of propping up collapsing bantustan structures by the deployment of National Servicemen, a situation that has led to a military takeover of some government functions. As a result of years of neglect, military occupation and colonial policies, the vast majority of Namibians live in deteriorating social conditions characterised by overcrowding, poor housing, bad lighting and drainage, untarred roads and totally inadequate health, educational and community facilities.[204]

In 1978 a United Nations study estimated that the per capita income for Namibian whites was around R3,000, while the corresponding estimate for blacks was R125 – a ratio of 24 to 1.[205] With high inflation, real black wages have been falling considerably in recent years, while unemployment has been rising. Nearly one-third of the labour force is unemployed or underemployed.[206] A survey in 1983 showed that 86 per cent of wage earners in Windhoek were living below the household subsistence level while in the war zones of the north this figure increased to 99 per cent.[207]

These appalling social and economic conditions – a direct result of the military occupation – have been exacerbated by the war. In the Ovambo bantustan, despite the deployment of soldier-teachers, 19 schools were reported to have been closed by 1981, and the classroom shortage was put at 2,600.[208] Only one per cent of black Namibians have secondary school qualifications – two thirds have had only nominal formal education or none at all.[209]

In many cases, the decline in services, particularly in the health field, has been the result of the deliberate destruction of facilities by the SADF, on the grounds that they were being made use of by SWAPO. Mission hospitals have been a particular target of the police and army. The Lutheran Hospital at Ondangwa, St Mary's Anglican Mission at Odibo and the Lutheran Hospital at Onandjokwe have all been subjected to SADF harrassment. Doctors, nurses, patients and even the directors of the institution have been detained under security legislation, landmines have been planted in hospital grounds, police raids have been conducted and on some occasions buildings have been blown up.[210]

Health problems have been exacerbated by the curfew and prohibitions on movement in the war zones, and by the migration of people from the war-ravaged countryside to the urban areas, where vast squatter settlements have sprung up. An estimated two hundred and fifty thousand people live in a 30 km wide strip between the garrison towns of Ondangua and Oskhakati. This strip of squalid shanties, which has no water-borne sewage or toilet facilities, has been identified as a breeding ground of disease, including an epidemic of bubonic plague which broke out in 1983.[211] The official response to the outbreak of the plague is instructive. The SWA Territory Force airlifted five tons of rat poison to the area which it distributed around the perimeters of military bases – but it did nothing to help prevent the disease spreading in the black squatter settlements.[212]

A further deterioration in health and other facilities resulted from the attempt to establish eleven different administrative departments in Namibia – one for each 'population group'. Ten separate health services were set up under the Turnhalle plan, resulting in 'chaos, corruption and inefficiency'. By 1984, all but three of these 'ethnic' services had been taken over by the wealthy Administration for Whites. In the Ovambo bantustan, on the pretext of preventing the total collapse of the health system, the army took over direct control at the end of 1983. There was considerable resistance to this move, especially from nurses and other health workers.[213]

Almost all the doctors working in the Ovambo and Kaokoland bantustans are SADF personnel, as are all the vets, dentists and psychologists.[214] The SADF claims that the military takeover of the health service has been appreciated by the local population: most of the evidence shows that in fact the uniformed health personnel are feared and distrusted.[215]

The army's claim to be 'winning hearts and minds' through social and political development is belied by the apparently irreversible deterioration in virtually all social facilities in Namibia. On the other hand, there has not been the slightest sign that the process of militarisation is being halted. In the words of one commentator, although the SADF regards the solution to the Namibian conflict as 80 per cent social and political and only 20 per cent military, it appears to spend 80 per cent of its efforts chasing the 20 per cent of the solution.[216]

Atrocities

The progressive failure of the 'hearts and minds' campaign in Namibia has been accompanied by an increase in police and army atrocities. In the early 1970s regular SADF units carried out mass round-ups of hundreds of Namibians in the northern areas, many of whom were tortured. Torture is still rountinely carried out at police and army bases, but the rise in atrocities in recent years is mainly – but not entirely – due to the increased activities of the Special Police and Koevoet, now known as the Counter-Insurgency Unit of the SWA Police.[217] *(See Chapter 6)* It has been stated in the Windhoek Supreme Court that up to 90 per cent of murder cases dealt with by the court have involved Special constables and Koevoet members.[218] Furthermore, units such as Koevoet keep no records of who they kill.[219]

Atrocities have been encouraged by the official policy of offering 'bounties' or *kopgeld* (literally 'head money') to members of units such as Koevoet for each killing they carry out. The sums involved are considerable – up to five times the usual monthly salary. Similar 'bounties' are offered to civilians.[220]

Police and army atrocities in Namibia may broadly be broken into two types: officially-sanctioned terror and torture operations, and ad hoc terrorism and rape by 'rampant' police and army members, often carried out under the influence of alchohol. There can be little doubt that the torture carried out in army and police camps is approved at officer level, and that the methods of groups like Koevoet are authorised at the very highest level. A Koevoet commander has asserted that his men are trained exclusively as 'killing machines' and that the unit has a policy of taking no prisoners.[221]

Koevoet, the 'Takkie Squad' and other irregular units have engaged in 'pseudo-operations' using tactics learnt from the Rhodesian Selous Scouts. Disguised as SWAPO guerillas, the troops have entered kraals and requested food and shelter, and then carried out brutal reprisals against those who have assisted them.[222] It has also been alleged that they have carried out attacks on civilians when disguised as SWAPO guerillas in order in to discredit the liberation fighters. Such deception is facilitated by the fact that Koevoet and similar units have often made use of AK 47 rifles, which are standard issue to SWAPO guerillas.[223]

A Koevoet pseudo-operation took place at the settlement of Oshikuku, some fifty kilometres from Oshakati, in March 1982. Armed men dressed as SWAPO guerillas entered the settlement, lined villagers up against a wall and raked them with automatic fire, killing eight. The military authorities blamed the attack on SWAPO, but survivors claimed the Koevoet was responsible, and said that they had recognised a police commander amongst the men.[224]

Koevoet members have been accused in the Namibian courts of a number of atrocities over the past few years. Cases that have been brought before the courts represent only a small proportion of atrocities. However, as the vast majority go unreported or are not acted upon. According to the Namibian lawyer Anton Lubowski, as there are no lawyers based in the war zones and victims of assault are often too frightened to report incidents to the authorities for fear of reprisals, only an estimated ten to twenty per cent of all violent incidents against civilians have ever been brought to public attention.[225] Every year about five hundred inquests are heard in the Namibian courts for which no proper investigations are carried out. In many of these inquests, the deaths are ascribed to 'persons unknown'.[226]

In April 1985, in an attempt to defuse rising protest about atrocities, the SWATF issued what was referred to as a 'comprehensive list of transgressions' by the military and police in Namibia. The list contained only incidents between 1982 and 1984 which had resulted in prosecutions of police and army personnel – nevertheless it listed 68 cases ranging from murder and rape to assault, theft and robbery. Sentences for police and army members convicted of such offences were generally very lenient, often only a reprimand or fine.[227] Two Koevoet members who were accused of killing a detainee, Kadimu Katanga, in November 1983 by beating him with an ox yoke and forcing him to run several kilometres in intense heat were fined R30 and R60 respectively.[228] In 1984 two SWATF soldiers were fined R50 each after being found guilty of assaulting Ndara Kapitango, a 63 year old man they had tortured by roasting over a fire.[229] In many cases where police and army members have been charged with atrocities, they have reserved the right to invoke Section 103 of the Defence Act, which grants immunity from prosecution to members of the 'security forces' for acts carried out 'in good faith' under operational conditions.

Most of the cases listed by the SWATF in April 1985 involved incidents in which police and army personnel acted outside orders and took their own initiatives in torturing and intimidating civilians, or engaged in random acts of murder or serious crime. Two Koevoet members, Jonas Paulus and Paulus Matheus, for example, were accused of eleven counts of murder, rape, attempted murder and robbery after a night 'on the rampage' when, dressed in SWAPO uniforms, they terrorised a number of civilians. Paulus was sentenced to death and executed; Matheus was imprisoned for 12 years.[230]

The vast majority of incidents of torture and intimidation have gone unprosecuted as they have been carried out under orders. In recent years, a number of church delegations which have visited Namibia have reported on the brutal methods of the police and army, and their terrorisation of the Namibian population.

Church Reports

A report issued by the British Council of Churches (BCC) of a visit by a delegation to Namibia in November 1981 referred to the South African military presence in Namibia as a 'reign of terror' to which local people had no redress. It documented details of 20 individual cases of brutalities, and described how troops dragged corpses of people they had killed behind their vehicles as they drove through villages.

A similar report was made by two leaders of the South African Council of Churches, Bishop Desmond Tutu and Rev Peter Storey, who visited Namibia in February. They reported that the majority of Namibians regarded the South African occupation troops as 'terrorists', and that any contribution made by the Civic Action programme towards 'winning hearts and minds' had been far exceeded by the atrocities committed against the Namibian people. The churchmen noted a long catalogue of killings, the burning of huts, rapes and detention without trial.[231]

In 1982 a group from the Southern African Catholic Bishops Conference, led by Archbishop Hurley, interviewed 180 Namibians and detailed cases of South African atrocities and torture, including electric shock torture, hangings and beatings. The bishops noted:

> The Security Forces stop at nothing to force information out of people. They break into homes, beat up residents, shoot people, steal and kill cattle and often pillage stores and tea rooms. When the tracks of SWAPO guerillas are discovered by the Security Forces the local people are in danger. Harsh measures are intensified. People are blindfolded, taken from their homes and left beaten up and even dead by the roadside. Women are often raped. It is not unknown for a detachment to break into a home and while black soldiers keep watch over the family, white soldiers select the best-looking girls and take them into the veld to rape them. There is no redress because reporting irregularities or atrocities to commanders is considered a dangerous or fruitless exercise . . . A dusk to dawn curfew is imposed in the operational area. Anybody moving after dark is shot. A person cannot even go to the help of a sick neighbour or woman in childbirth. A priest risks his life in going on a sick call . . . The whole complex of Security Forces in the operational area is designated by the (Ovambo) word *omakakunya*. We found it hard to determine the literal meaning of the word but its implications are by no means flattering – 'bloodsuckers', 'bone-pickers' and so on.[232]

After the Catholic bishops' visit, Archbishop Hurley held a press conference in South Africa in which he publicly accused Koevoet and other military units of carrying out atrocities. He was subsequently charged under Section 27B of the Police Act, which makes it a crime to publish 'any untrue matter in relation to any action by the South African Police Force' and puts the onus on the defendant to show that the allegations could be proved. Newspapers were warned that publication of the Archbishops' statements would lead to prosecution – the maximum penalty is five years' imprisonment. The charges were dropped after the case attracted international attention and Archbishop Hurley made it clear that he intended revealing further details of atrocities during his trial.[233]

In January 1985 a report produced by the Catholic Bishops' Conference following another fact-finding visit to Namibia confirmed the findings of the earlier report and documented further cases of torture and intimidation.[234]

A six-member international delegation from the Anglican church which visited Namibia in 1983 reported that:

> The curfew in operation in the north, the undoubted intimidation, the restriction of movement, the spreading of distrust through informers, the divisions in family life, the cases of abduction, torture and beatings, the total massive armed presence of the SADF, cause the community to live in a state of perpetual fear and repression.[235]

The findings of church delegations to Namibia have been corroborated from many other sources. To allay mounting international pressure, in 1982 the SADF established a Board of Inquiry to investigate allegations of atrocities on the part of the police and army.[236] Later a permanent military law office was established and a liaison committee between the SADF and the bantustan authorities set up.[237] As all these structures involved the SADF and could not be regarded as independent, Namibian church and community leaders declined to co-operate with the investigations.[238]

At the end of 1982, the Namibian Bar Council, which represents advocates in the territory, issued a statement expressing concern at the increasing number of deaths in detention, the destruction of property and abuse of power by administration officials and military and police personnel, and the increasing number of unsolved cases of people 'disappearing'. It expressed shock at 'instances of abuse of detainees and some recent cases of even rape and death in detention', and highlighted the wide power invested in the police and army through Proclamation AG9, which allows any authorised police or army member to detain and interrogate Namibians for renewable 30-day periods. It also noted the immunity given to police and army personnel under Section 103 of the Defence Act and stated that 'the rule of law is in jeopardy, particularly in the operational area'.[239] It called for an independent inquiry, a call that was taken up by church and community leaders.

A Commission of Inquiry into Security Legislation was duly established by the occupation authorities. It was immediately criticised for its narrow scope and the evident bias of its terms of reference, which referred to a 'terrorist war' and a 'revolutionary onslaught on the territory of South West Africa'. The Council of Churches in Namibia labelled the commission 'an insincere and manipulatory effort to further entrench existing security legislation'.[240]

The Bar Council submitted evidence to the inquiry focussing on the unchecked powers of police and army personnel, the immunity and secrecy under which they operated and the growing numbers of atrocities. It noted that hundreds of people had disappeared without trace, been murdered by 'persons unknown', or killed and buried without inquests being carried out.[241]

The Bar Council noted that only a very few cases of torture and brutality ever reached the courts. However, many individual Namibians have attested inside and outside the courts that they have been brutally tortured at army and police bases. They have reported being the victims of many of the tortures used in South African police stations – sleep deprivation, repeated beatings, electric shocks, strangulation, being suspended from beams and walls. More horrific forms of torture have also been reported such as being tied to the exhaust outlets of vehicles or helicopters, being shown the heads of previous victims and being threatened with poisonous snakes. Detainees are commonly kept in makeshift corrugated zinc and barbed wire detention cells, often in appalling conditions.[242]

Rape and 'Disappearances'

Rape has been an increasingly common feature of the military occupation. According to the Attorney General, 42 per cent of criminal cases brought before the Windhoek Supreme Court in 1982 involved rape, the majority from the war zones.[243] Cases brought to the courts represent only a tiny minority of rapes. For most Namibian women living in remote areas, there are minimal opportunities for bringing a court action against a member of the 'security forces' who has the power of arrest and carries the full weight of the administration and armed forces behind him. Even when rape cases appear before the courts there is no guarantee of a conviction. In one case, a white South African soldier who raped an 80 year old woman who subsequently spent two weeks in hospital because of profuse bleeding walked free from the court after the judge accepted his plea that his victim had 'consented'. He later admitted to a reporter that he had lied in court.[244] When convictions are delivered the sentences are often extremely lenient – fines of a hundred rand are not uncommon for violent rape by police and army members.[245]

Under martial law conditions, which allow for *incommunicado* detention, 'disappearances' are not uncommon. Many of these cases are simply the result of people slipping off to join SWAPO, keeping their decision secret so as to prevent recriminations. However, there are many incidents on record of people being arrested by the army or police and then never being seen again. In some cases relatives were told that detainees were 'abducted by SWAPO', even though witnesses had seen them being arrested.[246] The SADF hardly ever mentions capturing guerillas but it is widely believed that such individuals are held secretly in detention and tortured for information. The only prospect for release appears to be to join up with Koevoet or similar units. In 1981, a representative of the International Red Cross expressed his concern about the complete lack of information on captured guerillas. He noted that 'it simply does not happen in any conflict or battle that you have a clash with 200 people and 45 killed and no prisoners or wounded are taken'.[247]

Strategic Implications

As SWAPO, the Namibian Council of Churches and many other organisations have repeatedly stressed, the overwhelming majority of the Namibian population wants independence on the basis of UN Resolution 435, which provides for a ceasefire and free internationally supervised elections.

There are compelling reasons for Pretoria to remove what has been referred to in the South African press as 'the Namibian albatross'. It is thought in Pretoria that the issue of Namibia has been an important factor behind the failure of the Western powers to move into a closer relationship with South Africa. Another concern in Pretoria is the economic drain of the war. In 1983 the apartheid economy entered a period of deep recession, the most serious since the 1930s. The war in Namibia, and the allied cost of propping up the elaborate bantustan administration system, has absorbed an increasingly large percentage of the South African budget, while returns from uranium and diamond mining and the exploitation of other Namibian resources have declined.

Against these factors Pretoria must balance its military interests in Angola, the political effect of a SWAPO victory inside South Africa, and the long-term strategic implications of losing the last of the 'buffers' against independent Africa. There is little doubt that the apartheid regime would withdraw from Namibia if it could sufficiently weaken the MPLA government of Angola and ensure that SWAPO would be economically and politically crippled. Should the South African regime manage to achieve these conditions it will have done so at a terrible cost. Namibia today lies almost in ruins, on the brink of economic and social collapse. The South African forces are almost universally despised in the country. The population is either demoralised, or supports SWAPO.[248]

The South African regime has carried out a huge and sustained military operation in Namibia, absorbing billions of rand, involving up to half the SADF's active strength, and entailing the invasion and partial occupation of Angola. Despite this, PLAN guerillas continue to operate over wide areas of the country and SWAPO's political support has grown. In a war that the apartheid generals have characterised as 80 per cent political, the SADF has stood sentinel over the complete collapse of the regime's political initiatives and has palpably failed to win the hearts and minds of the Namibian people.

9. THE BATTLE FOR SOUTH AFRICA

South Africa was conquered by force and is today ruled by force. At moments when white autocracy feels itself threatened, it does not hesitate to use the gun. When the gun is not in use, legal and administrative terror, fear, social and economic pressures, complacency and confusion generated by propaganda and 'education' are the devices brought into play in an attempt to harness the people's opposition. Behind these devices hovers force . . .

– From *Strategy and Tactics of the South African Revolution*, Consultative Conference of the ANC, Morogoro, Tanzania, May 1969.

It was an analysis of the kind expressed above that lay behind the decision of the leadership of the South African liberation movement in 1961 to make up an armed struggle. This analysis has been borne out by events since then. The strength and powers of the police and army have been drastically expanded and deployed with increasing frequency in attempts to suppress resistance.

Liberation Struggle

The decision to take up armed struggle was taken only after the methods of peaceful struggle had been exhausted by state repression and after careful assessment. Since 1961 the ANC has restructured itself underground in South Africa as well as in exile. It has built up a guerilla army that has carried out operations in all parts of the country, attacking strategic, military and economic targets. It has achieved this military capacity at the same time as broadening its support base and extending political mobilisation. There is every indication that the ANC has gained support by its willingness and ability to mount an armed struggle against the apartheid regime.

Surveys of black opinion have shown that even after a quarter of a century of being banned and operating underground, the ANC is still the most popular political organisation in South Africa. The ANC leader, and first commander of Umkhonto we Sizwe, Nelson Mandela, is by far the most popular South African leader.[1]

As was shown in Zimbabwe during the independence elections, it is more than likely that the real level of support for the liberation movement is much higher than revealed by polls or assessed by researchers. Support for the ANC is further demonstrated by the widespread use at political rallies and funerals of the movement's slogans, its black-green-and-gold colours and freedom songs, and by countrywide support for the Freedom Charter of the Congress Movement, to which hundreds of South African organisations have declared their allegiance. Commitment by the black majority to the armed struggle is underscored by the huge attendances at funerals for guerillas killed in action or at memorial services for those hanged after capture.

Armed Struggle

Even official government statistics demonstrate the increasing ability of the ANC to carry out military actions against the apartheid regime. According to the head of the Security Branch, Major General Steenkamp, there were four guerilla attacks in 1976, 20 the following year, 13 in 1978, 12 in 1979, 19 in 1980, 55 in 1981, 39 in 1982 and 55 again in 1983.[2] During the second half of 1984 there was a reduction in the number of attacks, resulting in a total for 1984 of 44 operations.[3] In 1985 ANC armed actions increased dramatically, and the 1983 peak of 55 attacks had been surpassed by September.[4] By the end of the year, 136 actions had been recorded.[5] The situation goes even beyond what these statistics suggest, as information on many incidents is either suppressed or deliberately played down.[6]

ANC guerillas have dealt major blows against strategic targets – the Koeberg nuclear power station, the SASOL oil-from-coal plants, military headquarters in Pretoria, power stations and key industrial plants. In 1984 Major General Steenkamp claimed that such attacks had caused R600 million damage – the real figure is likely to have been several times that amount.[7]

The armed struggle in South Africa may be seen as having progressed through four phases.

In the **initial phase**, from 1961, members of the ANC and PAC carried out a large number of operations which, in the case of the ANC, were limited almost entirely to sabotage attacks avoiding loss of life. By 1965, following ruthless police repression, the fledgling underground structures had been seriously damaged and many of the leaders of the struggle captured and imprisoned or executed. In a **second phase** from 1965 the ANC, and to a lesser extent the PAC, concentrated on rebuilding underground structures and organising military training abroad. This was slow and painful work until 1975 when the independence of the former Portuguese colonies in Southern Africa and a new militancy inside South Africa laid the basis for an expansion of operations.

A **third phase** followed the 1976-77 uprisings. There was a dramatic increase in the number of people leaving the country for guerilla training, as young blacks were radicalised in confrontations with the police. During the following years the armed wing of the ANC, Umkhonto we Sizwe, carried out many attacks on strategic installations, and assassinations of individuals collaborating with the Security Branch. Assaults on police stations became increasingly common and there were also attacks on SADF targets.[8]

An analysis of armed actions between January 1977 and October 1982 revealed 33 attacks on railway installations, 25 on industrial and power installations, 14 on administrative buildings, 13 on police stations, three on military bases and 19 clashes between guerilas and army units as well as other actions. Many guerilla operations were directly tied to particular struggles – for example, the destruction of railway lines at the time of 'stayaway' actions, the bombing of company installations during strikes and attacks on administrative offices during rent strikes.[9] The ANC has characterised many of its actions during this period as 'armed propaganda' designed to restore the confidence of the people.

During 1984 and 1985, the armed struggle entered a **fourth phase** with the move from 'armed propaganda' to a more generalised offensive aimed at making South Africa ungovernable and stressing the prospects for a popular insurrection. The distinction between armed actions carried out by trained guerilas and attacks of a more spontaneous character arising out of mass resistance – using mainly stones, petrol-bombs and small arms – became less sharp. The ANC's National Consultative Conference held in Zambia in June 1985 issued a call for a 'people's war' to forge closer links between guerilas and political activists and to actively engage the enemy.[10]

The ANC President, Oliver Tambo, declared: 'We will confront the armed police and the soldiers and anyone else identified with the police or soldiers.' Such confrontations took place on a daily basis in South African townships throughout 1985, and both before and after the State of Emergency, apartheid administration in many black areas was destroyed and the police and army could enter only in considerable strength.[11]

Mass Resistance

The armed struggle has been accompanied by both underground and legal organisation. After the banning in 1977 of almost all the legal resistance organisations, there took place a broad and deeply rooted growth of new legal and semi-legal structures of open resistance. The initial stage consisted of the formation of a large number of local, community-based organisations. The organisations mobilised support around specific aspects of the apartheid system affecting the lives of the majority of the population – high rents, transport costs, low wages, and inferior education. National organisations of pupils and students were also formed and there was a tremendous growth of independent black and non-racial trade unions.

Over the next few years, particularly in the course of mass political

218

campaigns such as the boycott of elections to apartheid institutions, links between the new organisations were strengthened. Specific struggles were integrated into the overall struggle against the apartheid system. This took place at first on a regional and ad hoc basis, and then in 1983 took a national and more permanent form in the emergence of the United Democratic Front (UDF). The UDF was formed specifically around opposition to the new apartheid constitution. It campaigned for boycotts of elections to the Black Local Authorities in November 1983 and to the first elections to the Indian and Coloured chambers of the segregated tricameral parliament in August 1984.

This process was an indication that the repression of the 1960s and '70s had failed to destroy the movement for liberation. The UDF grew to incorporate over six hundred organisations, collectively representing two million South Africans. It united youth and women's organisations, trade unions, student, community and religious organisations at both local and national level.

By the end of 1984 the state's carefully laid plans to create a 'military defensible' system faced a major challenge. The months of unrest which began in early 1984 and intensified after the August elections in many ways resembled the 1976 uprising. However, the mobilisation and organisation of resistance was far more extensive and the strategic understanding and the depth of commitment of those leading the community, youth and worker struggles was manifestly more advanced than eight years previously.

Faced with the destruction of administration in black urban areas, and an unprecedented nationwide anti-apartheid mobilisation, the South African regime imposed a State of Emergency on 21 July 1985. Despite violent repression on a scale not seen before in South Africa, the regime had difficulty in restoring its grip and it was evident that the struggle against apartheid had entered a new phase. To Prime Minister Botha's supporters, the crisis of 1985 was a vindication of his warning that the apartheid system was facing a 'total onslaught'. But it was an 'onslaught' not from an external 'communist aggressor', as portrayed in state propaganda, but from the oppressed majority of the South African population itself, whose determination to end decades of oppression was growing.

The internal crisis was exacerbated by a rapid deterioration in the regime's international position. By September 1985, with even the United States government imposing limited sanctions, gains made in the first half of 1984 as a result of new regional arrangements had disappeared almost entirely.

The 1984 breakthrough in the regional and international arena had been achieved with the backing of the United States administration and was facilitated by a more flexible and differentiated approach to regional problems. This was symbolised by the virtual disappearance of the phrase 'total onslaught' from Pretoria's vocabulary during 1984 and by the description of its regional policy as a 'peace offensive'.

Chester Crocker, President Reagan's Africa adviser, was opposed to 'total onslaught' propaganda which he felt blinded the South African regime to the tactical opportunities which existed in the region.[12]

Dr John Seiler, visiting professor at the J F Kennedy Special Warfare Centre in Carolina, USA, who conducted a number of interviews with SADF officers and State Security Council personnel, has argued that:

> By 1983 the concept [of a 'total onslaught'] was entrenched in the structure of the advanced interdepartment joint courses at the SADF's defence college, in which high ranking officials from the SADF, the SAP and a wide range of government departments considered its implications for joint planning and programme management both in theory and through case studies.

However 'a small cadre of strategic studies scholars who had access to the SADF and the State Security Council' had persuaded General Malan and P W Botha to drop the concept as it 'generated an exaggerated and fearful assessment' of the challenges to the apartheid regime. According to Seiler, a secret memorandum to minimise references to the 'total onslaught' was issued by General Malan towards the end of 1983.[13]

Discarding the term 'total strategy' in the search for respectability and a more sophisticated approach to internal, regional or international relations did not, however, alter the overall strategic approach of the regime. This approach rests on a trilogy of foreign policy, military policy and domestic policy. Although eighty per cent of the struggle is supposedly political – or socio-economic – the military aspect is absolutely indispensable. 'Reform', it is believed in Pretoria, can only be carried out under carefully controlled conditions which may necessitate increased repression. The basic task of the armed forces – and this assessment is shared by virtually all sections of the white power structure, including the parliamentary opponents of the National Party – is to 'buy time' or 'hold off the onslaught' while the necessary adjustments are made to the system to make it more 'defensible'.

Crocker has summed up this approach:

> While the SADF and the police can hold the line for now, the top officers see their role as one of buying time for domestic political evolution that will make the Republic more 'defensible', less internally vulnerable to violent disorders, and better able to generate the identification and support of the majority. This is precisely what General Magnus Malan . . . means when he reiterates that the strategy for South Africa must be 90 per cent political.[14]

The emphasis placed by P W Botha and his generals on the political aspects of counter-insurgency warfare could not therefore be taken as an indication that the regime was in any way abandoning force or scaling down its military and security effort. Quite the contrary. In the words of General P J Coetsee, the Commissioner of Police: 'In circumstances of political adjustment and development, the exercise of a strong centrally-based authority is the *sine qua non* to maintain stability'. General Coetsee makes it clear that this 'centrally based authority' rests on firm action by the army and police.[15]

Major-General Steenkamp, the head of the security police, has also underlined the state's commitment to violent repression:

> The key to effective counter-revolutionary action is fast and effective measures by the forces of law and order. Law and order must be maintained and the revolutionary leadership and their political support apparatus must be isolated. Some students of political violence have told us that strong action by the authorities at an early stage merely leads to further counter-violence by the terrorists. They also tell us that firm police action alienates the community. This is not so . . .[16]

Both General Steenkamp and General Coetsee have steadfastly refused to acknowledge that the South African liberation struggle is rooted in the injustices of apartheid – they persist in claiming that it is the effect of manipulation by external forces.

The generals have also insisted that guerilla warfare is a criminal matter and not a military one. In doing so they have been reflecting a long-standing policy of the apartheid regime, most clearly articulated in 1982 in the report of the Rabie Commission.

Legal Apparatus of Repression
The Rabie Commission was established in 1979 in the context of a rising level of resistance, to review the country's 'security legislation'. Its recommendations resulted in the streamlining and consolidation of existing repressive legislation, in the form of the Internal Security Act of 1982. A number of other new laws were also adopted in the same year. In advising the government on what legal powers it needed to suppress opposition, the commission paid specific attention to the use of the military in dealing with resistance in general and the armed struggle in particular. The commission recommended that:

> activities which threaten the internal security of the Republic should, as far as circumstances permit, be combatted as crimes. Such a line of action is, so long as it can be maintained, preferable to a situation where subversive activities are combatted by military measures.[17]

The Rabie report noted that the state's policy in relation to the armed struggle had been to treat the actions involved:

as crimes rather than acts warranting action by the Defence Force. In practice this means that acts . . . committed by the ANC in the course of what it describes as guerilla war are combatted as crimes that are tried by courts of law.[18]

The commission concluded that as long as this approach remained policy, exceptional legal procedures were necessary. Detention without trial of suspects for purposes of interrogation and of potential state witnesses, and refusal of bail, it urged, were necessary instruments in the hands of those who were given the task of maintaining 'security'.[19]

Political trials have been a key element in the repressive strategy of apartheid. Since the 1960s tens of thousands of people have been arrested and charged with a variety of offences. They range from common-law offences such as treason, sedition, public violence, damage to property, murder and arson, to offences specifically defined under the Internal Security Act (such as terrorism, sabotage and subversion).

The Rabie Commission presented the state's approach as one which preserved civil liberties. In reality, the courts, always regarded by the black majority as an integral part of the oppressive system of apartheid, have more openly been used as instruments of repression. The exceptional legal procedures identified by the Commission have given scope to the Security Branch to play a decisive part in trials. The provision for detention of suspects and potential witnesses allow the police to extract statements by pressure, violence and torture which, regardless of their truth, produce convictions in court.

In particular, trials of people suspected of being involved in the armed struggle have been characterised by tight security, censorship, and evidence of systematic violence and torture.

Despite international legal opinion and repeated calls by the United Nations and other international bodies that ANC and SWAPO combatants be accorded Prisoner-of-War status in terms of the Geneva Conventions, the apartheid regime has continued with its policy of executing captured liberation fighters. In November 1980, the President of the ANC, Oliver Tambo, deposited at the Geneva headquarters of the International Red Cross a declaration that the liberation movement would as far as possible abide by the Geneva Conventions on the Humanitarian Conduct of War.

The ANC undertook this pledge on the basis of a Protocol which was added to the Conventions in 1977 to extend their provisions to 'armed conflicts in which people are fighting colonial domination and alien occupation and against racist regimes in exercise of their rights to self-determination'. The Pretoria regime, which acceded to the Conventions in 1952, has refused to recognise this Protocol, which in effect provides international legal recognition of the right of the Southern African liberation movements to take up armed struggle. The regime has thus acted in violation of international law in executing ANC combatants.[20]

Armed Force: Police and Army
While the police and the courts have continued to be used as instruments of repression, they have proved inadequate to deal with the rising tide of resistance. As the South African state has come under increased pressure, the SADF has increasingly been deployed to suppress resistance. The 1977 White Paper on Defence formulated the relationship between the police and the military in this way:

> The responsibility for combatting internal and especially urban unrest rests primarily on the SAP. Nevertheless, the SA Army must at all times be ready, on a countrywide basis, to quickly mobilise trained forces to render assistance to the SA Police.

Since then the roles of the police and army have converged to such an extent that in many ways they are indistinguishable. The paramilitary nature of the police and the policing roles adopted by the army, combined with their joint functioning under co-ordinated command, has considerably blurred the distinction. During the 1985-86 State of Emergency, joint SADF/SAP patrols were routine, and military and police personnel commonly shared the same transport. The deployment of the army in policing roles began in earnest some years earlier. The 1982 White Paper disclosed that:

> In respect of the internal situation there has been particularly close co-operation between the SADF, the SAP and SA Railways Police. Joint action, the determination of areas of responsibility and supporting doctrines are some of the facets that have already been formulated jointly to unite the Security Forces into a well-knit community . . .[21]

An editorial in *Paratus* in June of that year described the SADF and the SAP as 'an unbeatable team' and explained how the army was involved in 'routine police operations'.[22]

Military involvement in police tasks is integral to the regime's National Security Doctrine which, as explained in Chapter 2, makes little distinction between external defences and internal 'security'. The implications of this doctrine were set out by Lt General Dutton in 1977:

> The traditional dividing line between national security and national defence would appear to have become obliterated. According to the classical concept, the military aspect of national security comprised two distinct and separate functions, namely, national defence to ensure that the integrity of the state will be defended against foreign aggression, and support to the civil authority in the maintenance of law and order internally. In the new perspective, however, civil riots, strikes accompanied by violence and urban terrorism are seen as

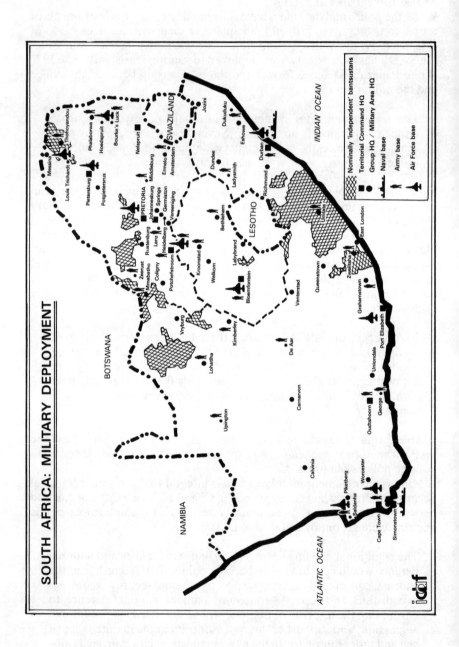

SOUTH AFRICA: MILITARY DEPLOYMENT

Nominally 'independent' bantustans

Territorial Command HQ

Group HQ / Military Area HQ

Naval base

Army base

Air Force base

NAMIBIA

BOTSWANA

SWAZILAND

LESOTHO

ATLANTIC OCEAN

INDIAN OCEAN

Messina

Thohoyandou

Louis Trichardt

Phalaborwa

Hoedspruit

Bourke's Luck

Pietersburg

Potgietersrus

Nelspruit

Middleburg

Ermelo

Amsterdam

Jozini

Dukuduku

PRETORIA

Johannesburg

Springs

Germiston

Vereeniging

Rustenburg

Lanz

Heidelberg

Zeerust

Mmabatho

Coligny

Potchefstroom

Vryburg

Lohatha

Kimberley

Welkom

Kroonstad

Bloemfontein

Ladysmith

Dundee

Bethlehem

Ladybrand

Eshowe

Durban

Richmond

Ulundi

East London

Zwelitsha

Queenstown

Grahamstown

Port Elizabeth

Uniondale

George

Oudtshoorn

Carnarvon

De Aar

Ventersdorp

Upington

Calvinia

Worcester

Piketberg

Saldanha

Cape Town

Simonstown

guerilla actions aimed at military, political, economic or psychological objectives as part of the overall assault. Moreover, such ostensibly civil manifestations carry within them the ingredients for escalations to levels of force beyond the capabilities of the civil forces of law and order. The suppression of civil disturbances within this category no longer provides a solution . . . .

The role of the armed forces in the maintenance of national security would therefore appear to be a simple extension of their classical role in national defence. There would be a difference in the means employed, in the force levels, the choice of weapons and tactics – but one overall strategy.[23]

In other words, the suppression of strikes, protests, demonstrations and other anti-apartheid activities is a legitimate concern of the military, entirely consistent with and integrated into its external tasks. A similar logic can be applied to the police, whose role is thus extended from that of the maintenance of law and order to internal warfare.

In an effort to play down the level of the threat and the political aspects of the armed struggle, the police have been used in counter-insurgency roles in South Africa and Namibia since the early 1960s, and were extensively deployed in Zimbabwe during the independence war. Even after the SADF took over command from the police in Namibia in 1974, thousands of police remained engaged in operational duties there.

The South African Police has the character of a paramilitary counter-insurgency force rather than an anti-crime force. As has been discussed in Chapter 6, riot squads have been established in each of the 19 regional police divisions. Armed with both military and police equipment and transported in armoured cars, these units have borne the brunt of front-line activity during the 1976, 1980-81 and 1984-86 uprisings, and have been rapidly expanded and re-equipped over the past few years. The squads are backed by the highly trained Special Task Force. All police now receive counter-insurgency training which differs little from that given to SADF infantry units, and almost all of them are eligible for call up for active service either in Namibia or along South Africa's borders.

The close 'partnership' between the military and the police in operational conditions to some extent covers up tactical differences in approach between SADF and SAP commanders. During the 1976 uprising P W Botha and the military generals regarded the conduct of the police as unsophisticated, and criticised their lack of effective anti-riot equipment and methods.[24] Minister of Police, Jimmy Kruger, responded that it would be 'ridiculous' to equip the force with 'anti-riot' equipment as 'a police officer will hardly be able to handle his rifle if he is also wearing a heavy flak jacket and a face guard'.[25] By 1984, with Botha and his generals firmly in power, the police had been fully equipped with modern 'anti-riot' equipment.

As a result of the introduction of the unified National Security Doctrine and the vastly increased political influence of the military under P W Botha's premiership, police-army competition has waned and the tactical differences of the 1976 period have declined. However, the residue of crude 'maximum-force' advocacy remains strong in the police, especially at a local level. This was demonstrated on numerous occasions during the unrest of 1985.

Deployment of Forces

Sealing the Borders: 'A Ring of Steel'

While the prospect of an internal insurrection has always been a dominant factor in apartheid security planning, the regime has at the same time devoted considerable attention to preventing guerilla infiltration from neighbouring countries. During the 1960s and early 1970s, Pretoria felt safe in the knowledge that it was protected by sympathetic regimes to the north. The independence of Angola, Mozambique and Zimbabwe clearly called for new measures. In the late 1970s the SADF took steps to establish what it called 'a ring of steel' around the northern borders.

According to the Deputy Defence Minister, H J Coetsee, the defensive 'ring' would include 'a chain of protected villages doubling as military bases' and fortified strongpoints in which white farmers could spend the nights.[26] A 'living fence' of sisal – a cactus-like plant – was planted along most of the Zimbabwean border and the construction of patrol roads commenced. Legislation passed in 1978 gave the SADF the power to clear any land within 10 km of South Africa's borders of inhabitants, buildings or foliage.[27]

In 1979 a commission with SADF representation was established to investigate the density of the white population in border areas. The study showed that nearly half the farms bordering Botswana, Rhodesia and Mozambique had no white occupiers. Many of them were run by absentee white landlords, who used the properties mainly for weekend game-hunting.[28] Resident white farmers were increasingly selling up to absentee owners, partly through fear of guerilla war but primarily for economic reasons. The SADF viewed the situation with considerable alarm. Various schemes were advanced to repopulate the area, including the recruitment into government-assisted farming ventures of young white men who had recently finished their National Service.[29]

The main government initiative was to offer financial and other assistance to white farmers wishing to settle in border areas and to oblige the farmers to participate in military structures. The 1979 Density of Population in Designated Areas Act offered interest-free loans and other incentives to whites wanting to establish farms in areas up to 50 km from the north and north-west Transvaal border and 30 km from the eastern Transvaal border.[30] The act provided for obligatory white occupation of the properties and other 'security' measures, but these were not initially enforced.[31] In the following three years more than R35 million was granted to farmers, but the situation did not improve and in some areas it deteriorated.[32]

A special cabinet committee was appointed to look again into ways of repopulating the border areas in 1982.[33] The committee recommended that steps should be taken to implement sections of the 1979 Act which empowered the government to force farmers to occupy their properties. In May 1983 regulations were introduced requiring farmers to occupy their farms for 300 days a year if they took advantage of government loans for properties situated less than 10 km from the Botswana and Zimbabwe borders, or else to ensure that another white person occupied them during the period. Farmers were also obliged to maintain fences and roads and to keep written records of all the people, both black and white, living on their farms. Contravention of the regulations could lead to imprisonment for up to five years.[34]

Many of the farmers resettled in the designated zone were veterans from the Rhodesian army deserting independent Zimbabwe. Almost all the farmers were issued with semi-automatic weapons and integrated into Commandos. According to one farmer: 'The idea was that it was cheaper to put us here than a large military force'.[35]

At the end of the 1984, the 10 km designated zone along the Botswana and Zimbabwe borders was widened to 50 km, and the regime announced another multi-million rand 'stabilisation' programme. This reflected increasing concern at the continuing rise of guerilla activity and the politicisation of the rural population.[36]

The SADF has also undertaken an extensive deployment of military and police counter-insurgency units along the borders. In addition to building up the Commando system and establishing major army bases at which National Servicemen can be both trained and deployed, company size or smaller operational bases similar to those dotted around northern Namibia have been set up. An indication of the establishment of such bases was given by P W Botha in 1980, when he announced the formation of African regional units in the northern areas. New measures had been authorised, he said, including 'the formation of a number of area headquarters and battalion headquarters for counter-insurgency and the creation of strong points on a decentralised basis at strategic places . . .'[37]

According to the Minister of Law and Order, in 1984 there were 'approximately 27' police 'border bases' along South Africa's northern borders and around Lesotho. These were usually platoon-sized bases from which vehicle and foot patrols were sent out.[38] The bases along the Kruger National Park/Mozambique border and the Zimbabwe border east of Beit Bridge were manned primarily by the military, but the police remained responsible for the other borders. At the end of 1985 all the six thousand remaining police along this border were replaced by troops and redeployed 'to help with the unrest situation in the interior'.[39]

Following the planting of landmines in border areas by ANC guerillas after November 1985, further steps were announced to militarise the areas. Weapons were issued to farmers' wives, soldiers were posted to every white farm, and subsidies were provided for farmers to buy mine-proofed vehicles and install security fences, alarms and floodlights. It was also announced that a high-voltage electrified fence would be established along the entire Zimbabwean border, and that there were plans to 'repatriate illegal migrants and workers' from Zimbabwe who were 'suspected of aiding the ANC'.[40]

Area War

With the intensification of the liberation struggle in South Africa, the SADF's emphasis on sealing the borders against guerillas has been extended to a more comprehensive strategy of rural counter-insurgency. Notwithstanding the increased levels of border patrolling, army strategy now accepts that guerillas will be able to cross into the country regardless of measures taken at the borders and that there are guerilla forces based inside the country. 'Area Defence', rather than 'border defence' is thus the term the regime uses to describe its rural counter-insurgency strategy. Officially launched in 1982, the doctrine of Area Defence has in fact been the basis of SADF planning since the 1970s.

As early as 1968 P W Botha, then Minister of Defence, warned that the state needed to prepare for 'unconventional warfare' and that the local Commandos would be upgraded to deal with guerilla warfare in the countryside.[41] In the 1973 Defence White Paper Botha stressed the important roles of local Commando units in acting 'immediately in support of the SA police [and defending] the territorial area allocated to them against insurgency'.[42] The Commandos, he argued, needed to be considerably expanded and improved, and a reaction force of National Servicemen established to be deployed 'at any place they might be needed' to back them up.[43] The basic outline of the Area Defence system was beginning to take shape.

In 1974 it was announced that 'great strides' had been taken 'in installing what amounts to an integrated "burglar alarm" system in the Transvaal, with outposts in the smallest and most isolated villages'. Pamphlets on security protection had been issued to farmers and householders and Commando activity had been stepped up.[44] Further decentralisation took place in the following few years. The 1975 Defence White Paper noted:

> The planning and conduct of Counter-Insurgency operations have been decentralised to the existing nine territorial Commands . . . Every officer commanding a territorial command is responsible for measures to prevent insurgency as well as the conduct of active Country-Insurgency within his territorial boundaries. For this purpose the Commandos in the area, as well as a number of specially allocated Citizen Force units, are under his direct command, thus forming an independent Country-Insurgency force. Commandos

have the capability of rendering limited aid to the SA Police and, during disasters, to local authorities without the formal mobilisation of troops. Thus the total area of the RSA is covered by a military presence . . .[45]

In a widely reported speech in October 1981 General Malan announced that 'a second front' was being 'opened up'. He did not specify which area he was referring to, but it was understood that he was referring to the start of generalised guerilla warfare in South Africa itself.[46] Malan later revealed in parliament that 'the number of troops deployed in the various operational areas in South West Africa and South Africa increased by more than 5,000 per cent between 1975 and 1981'.[47]

A new stage in the implementation of the Area Defence system was reached in 1982, with the introduction of conscription into the Commandos for older white men. The move was preceded by a statement by General Viljoen, then the SADF Chief, in which the term 'Area Defence' was first used publicly. According to Viljoen, Area Defence was a response to the growing countrywide activities of Umkhonto we Sizwe and the political mobilisation of the black population. Referring to the ANC, Viljoen declared:

> They apparently do not have a border war in mind. They are going to fight an area war . . if we had to deal with this using the full-time force, the demands on the system would be too great. But we are going to deal with it by using Area Defence . . . people living in an area must be organised to defend themselves. They must be our first line of defence. Our full-time force must be a reaction force. The first line of defence will contain any terrorist threat and the better equipped and trained reaction forces will deal with insurgents.[48]

General Malan expanded on Viljoen's statement when he warned that 'the revolutionary effort' had 'reached an extremely dangerous phase' and that 'the permanent force and the present number of national servicemen' could no longer guarantee the protection of the white population. 'It has therefore become imperative that each citizen be involved, in one way or another, in the process of countering the onslaught', he said.[49]

The basic principle of the Area Defence system involves the mobilisation of the white population into military formations responsible for a blanket early-warning and first-response system capable of dealing with both political, civil and guerilla threats to the apartheid system. If not in the Commandos, other SADF structures or the Reserve Police, whites are involved in the regime's defence system through schools, civil defence organisations, local authorities and SADF support groups.

As discussed in Chapter 4, in March 1982 the government introduced legislation enabling the SADF to call up virtually every white man under the age of 55 for some form of military service. The period of Citizen Force service was almost doubled to 720 days over a ten-year period, and provision was made for older men who had not been called up to serve up to 20 days a year in the Commandos. The military net was thus spread over almost a million white males, potentially involving almost all of those who had previously been exempted from military service.[50] The initial plans called for a countrywide military census to be conducted to ascertain exactly what manpower was available – this was later adapted to allow regional censuses as each area was mobilised.[51]

The new measures were widely regarded as an overreaction. One newspaper report commented:

> Suddenly, one day we [white males] were all in the army. Henceforth we would be living like the Israelis, all trained in some aspect of combat, all available for instant call-up. This represents a definitive change in the state of our society.[52]

To counter criticism, the SADF assured the white public that the scheme would only be implemented in stages and would be unlikely in the first few years to affect the white population in urban areas. Nevertheless, many northern areas were mobilised in the following year and by the end of 1985 a large part of the country had been called up. *(See map)* It is likely that the mobilisation will continue in stages until all of South Africa has been covered, except for the nominally 'independent' bantustans which for political reasons have been excluded. In April 1983 an SADF spokesman indicated that all districts in the country would be called up by 1988.[53]

The Commando mobilisation was made necessary both by the rapid escalation of the liberation struggle and by the failure of the government's campaign to induce whites to volunteer for Commando service. By the time the 1982 legislation was introduced the Commandos were almost forty per cent under their authorised strength. Army commanders were complaining that white South Africans preferred sport and social life to military duties. 'The attitude of the man in the street is that the Defence Force and the police are responsible for the defence of the country for which they have to pay taxes. So why should they serve in the army?', one commander complained.[54]

In one case a Commando near Pretoria was so undermanned that when it was mobilised for an operation the officer in charge had to make use of National Servicemen who had just returned from a three-month stint in Namibia. Another Pretoria Commando chief reported that in an emergency mobilisation only 26 of his 218 members had turned out. In 1982 a Nationalist MP complained that a Commando unit in his constituency had been compelled to call out its volunteers for 139 days in one year to make up for manpower shortages.[55]

The call-up of white men has significantly bolstered the Commandos, albeit at the expense of the 'spirit of voluntarism' through which the SADF was hoping to build what General Malan likes to call a 'people's army'. The

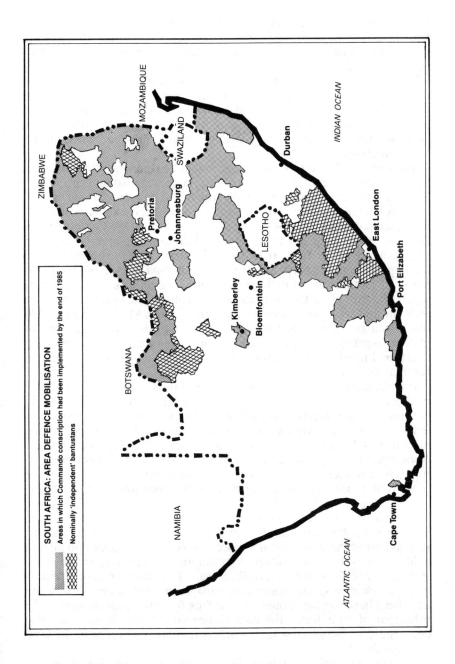

SOUTH AFRICA: AREA DEFENCE MOBILISATION

Areas in which Commando conscription had been implemented by the end of 1985

Nominally 'independent' bantustans

ZIMBABWE

MOZAMBIQUE

SWAZILAND

Pretoria

Johannesburg

LESOTHO

Durban

BOTSWANA

Kimberley

Bloemfontein

East London

Port Elizabeth

NAMIBIA

Cape Town

INDIAN OCEAN

ATLANTIC OCEAN

231

Commandos have been further strengthened by the unit allocation system known as the 'area bound' system. Under a provision of the 1982 legislation, young conscripts who have completed their initial period of two years' National Service may apply to become 'area bound'. If they have adequate reasons for not wishing to be called up for long periods of operational duty (for example, if they have business or farming commitments), they will be allotted to their local Commando rather than a standard Citizen Force unit. Instead of being called up for 'camps' every year they will be eligible to serve 50 days a year in the Commando for the following 20 years.[56]

The Commandos still contain a large volunteer component including the 10,000 white women who have joined up in non-combatant capacities.[57] Since 1978 black men have also been entitled to volunteer for Commandos, but only limited numbers have done so. The issue of the admission of blacks has posed political problems for the SADF, as many of the Commandos in the most strategically sensitive parts of the country lie in areas in which white political parties to the right of the National Party have become active. These parties oppose black participation in the SADF, even in segregated units. In some areas, prior to conscription, the ultra-right wing parties urged a boycott of the Commandos, while in others attempts were made to infiltrate and seize political control of units.[58] The SADF has insisted that black men be allowed to join – usually in separate command units or platoons – partly because it evisages them playing a useful role in 'winning hearts and minds' and gathering intelligence through their links with the community.[59]

Intelligence is one of the principal tasks of the Commandos, and every member is instructed to keep an eye on local events. Farmers and businessmen are expected to monitor their black employees and report any out of the way occurrences. Commandos also support the police and regular SADF units at roadblocks, patrol areas in which guerillas are suspected to be operating, and carry out 'pacification' operations to suppress resistance in black townships and settlements.[60]

Many of the men mobilised for Commando service are farmers, a section of the population which has been targeted for special attention by the SADF. General Viljoen has stated that residents of rural areas should be involved in military activities '365 days a year' and that agriculture has to be seen as part of the state's 'Total Strategy'. Farmers are expected to make a political as well as a military contribution.[61] According to an army commander in the north eastern Transvaal: 'The farmer in his capacity as manager, planner, specialist and economist, must now become a leader and a soldier'. In particular, farmers should look for 'suspicious changes in the behaviour of their staff', the commander said. White farmers are also encouraged to recruit their farm workers into black platoons in the local Commandos.[62]

Farmers and other civilians in isolated areas are linked to the Commandos and military bases through the MARNET (Military Area

Radio Network) system, which covers three quarters of the country. Apart from providing protection to farmers as an SOS system, MARNET also functions as an intelligence warning system. As the Namibian experience has shown, it is an important aspect of the SADF's campaign to integrate white farmers into its rural counter-insurgency programme.[63]

MARNET is backed by a comprehensive SADF telecommunication system using Marconi tropospheric scatter equipment, codenamed Ebbehout. The scatter system runs from Durban to the Swaziland border and then along the northern borders until it cuts south to terminate at Upington. This system is in turn interfaced with a mobile army telecommunications system (Netor) based at brigade and some command headquarters and with the civilian microwave network which links all the country's major centres. Long-distance communications are provided by the Silvermine centre at Simonstown. In this way the sensitive border areas are comprehensively linked to the SADF communications network, allowing the rapid deployment of forces and transfer of information.[64]

In the parts of the country in which the Area Defence system has been implemented, the upgraded Commandos carry out regular exercises in conjuction with various police forces, other SADF units and Civil Defence organisations. In this way the integration of virtually all state structures in a particular area is achieved and the maximum level of white participation in the military effort ensured.[65] The militarised character of these areas and the ability of the authorities to mobilise at short notice a wide range of military and paramilitary organisations is disguised by press censorship and by the refusal of the SADF to give anything but the barest details of operations.[66]

Area Force mobilisation has been accompanied by the construction of strategic bases and airfields and the upgrading of security around key rural installations such as dams and power stations. All dam walls are being fenced off and lines of buoys are being placed along the walls to prevent approach by boats.[67] Detailed guidelines have been issued for the protection of fuel storage facilities, and security at power stations, sub-stations and other power facilities has also been prioritised.[68] Escom, the state electricity corporation, has established its own private intelligence agency 'to determine specific threats against the people of Escom and its installations, so that the necessary preventive measures may be taken in good time'. The corporation admitted in a recent annual report that protecting installations from attack was a major headache. According to the report, 'security measures at all Escom's installations account for a significant percentage of total expenditure' – which totalled R1,600 million in 1984.[69]

An innovation in the rural military programme has been the conversion of roads to double as aircraft runways. By 1983, two such dual-purpose 'roadways' had been constructed near the Botswana and Mozambique borders and more were planned to facilitate the swift deployment of reaction force troops.[70]

Bantustans

Military deployment and organisation in the bantustans, while clear in its basic principles, has not been as consistently and rigorously formulated and implemented as the Area Defence system in other rural areas. Different approaches appear to have been adopted in the various bantustans in somewhat hasty attempts to prevent the re-occurrence of what, from the SADF's point of view, can only be regarded as a disastrous process in the Transkei. *(See Chapter 6)*

In outline, it is clear that the military forces of the bantustan have two main functions. Firstly, they function in the same way as the Area Defence structures in other rural areas as a first line of defence against guerilla activities or rural unrest and as a 'trip-hammer' for the mobilisation of more powerful reaction forces. Secondly, they perform repressive functions for the bantustan authorities and thus, indirectly, for the central government in Pretoria. A possible third role is that of maintaining Pretoria's grip over the bantustan regimes themselves.

As has been explained in Chapter 6, the bantustan military units consist principally of infantry companies trained in counter-insurgency warfare along SADF lines. Small elite 'reaction forces' modelled on the Reconnaissance Commandos are being built up in the Transkei and Ciskei bantustans, and in all four of the 'independent' bantustans legal provision has been made for a form of 'national service'. It is unlikely, however, in view of the increasingly militant opposition to the bantustan authorities and the very limited resources at their disposal, that any attempt will be made in the near future to create mini 'people's armies' along the lines of the SADF's Area Defence system.

In each of these bantustans it is evident that SADF doctrine on the need for unified operational command of the 'security forces' has been followed. There is close co-operation between police and military units in manning roadblocks, carrying out patrolling duties, protecting the authorities and suppressing protests and demonstrations. As in the rest of South Africa, the bantustan authorities rely in the first place on repressive legislation and the police to enforce their rule. Virtually all the provisions embodied in the repressive legislation of the central government apply in the bantustans. Until central government 'security' legislation is repealed by a particular bantustan authority, it remains applicable in the area. Where such legislation has been repealed, it has been simultaneously replaced by laws embodying the same or strengthened provisions.[71]

When local bantustan forces have shown themselves inadequate to deal with challenges to apartheid rule, the SADF and SAP have been deployed in strength. In the Bophuthatswana and Venda bantustans 'joint forces' of SADF, SAP and bantustan police and military units have been mobilised to deal with guerilla attacks, while SADF and SAP actions in the Transkei and Ciskei bantustans are formalised by agreements providing for police and army units to ignore the official boundaries.[72] The nature of SADF control over the bantustan forces is perhaps best indicated in the 1982 Defence

White Paper:

> In order to further mutual interests and to help ensure the national security of the Independent States, military agreements are entered into with these States when they attain their independence. This leads to the creation of a joint management body to co-ordinate co-operation and aid in the field of training and standardisation with a view to joint action. The SADF recognises the supportive capabilities of the Independent States and encourages their participation in an overall Southern African military treaty organisation against a common enemy.[73]

Characterised by extreme repression and poverty, the bantustans have been sites of almost continuous conflict over the past decade or more. In Bophuthatswana the army and police have been engaged in extensive cordon, roadblock and other counter-insurgency operations, undertaking both rural and urban operations and raiding poverty-ridden 'resettlement' camps. The Transkei military unit has been involved in quelling student protests and other repressive operations.[74]

The military and police forces of the Ciskei have been responsible for some of the most severe and brutal repression, particularly during a bus boycott in the principal township, Mdantsane, in 1983. The Ciskei authorities attempted to break the boycott – a protest against increased fares – by deploying a combination of police, military and 'vigilante' forces. Roadblocks were set up to block car and taxi traffic and the railway stations were cordoned off in an effort to prevent commuters from reaching the trains. When this failed to break the boycott, the 'security forces' opened fire on commuters who tried to catch trains, on one occasion killing ninety people, according to eyewitness reports.[75]

Hundreds of Mdantsane residents were incarcerated in a football stadium and those suspected of taking part in the boycott were brutally tortured. A State of Emergency was declared and army and police units were deployed at hospitals, schools, crossroads and other 'strategic' points. Co-operation between the Ciskei bantustan and South African security forces was evident.[76]

In general, the establishment of bantustan police and military forces has allowed the South African regime to devolve politically sensitive tasks of repression and to establish a secondary military structure responsible for front-line operations. At the same time the SADF and SA Police have retained the power to intervene and ensure that operations are conducted to their satisfaction. The strategic buffer role of the bantustans is evident by the semi-circle they form around the industrial heartland of South Africa.[77]

The system has presented the SADF with a number of problems, however. White farmers living near bantustan boundaries have complained of 'a climate of instability and mistrust on the homeland borders' with stocktheft a major problem. After a farmers' conference at which these issues were discussed, the white president of the Commercial Farmers Union of Zimbabwe, who was an invited guest, remarked:

> Just listening to the debate on stocktheft on the border I got the feeling that I had heard it all before. I am loath to prescribe to this government how it should run the country, but it is history in Zimbabwe that internal rural strife paved the way for terrorism . . .

He pointed out that stocktheft was a standard tactic of the liberation forces in Zimbabwe. To counter this, white farmers have called for the erection of more boundary fences, SADF patrols and other measures.[78] At least a dozen permanent paramilitary police stocktheft units have been established around South Africa.[79]

The SADF has shown a keen interest in government plans for re-drawing bantustan boundaries. Military representations were made to the Van der Walt commission which investigated bantustan 'consolidation' and in 1974 the then Army Director of Operations went as far as publicly urging the regime to allocate more land to the bantustans in the interests of reducing the number of 'borders' to be patrolled.[80]

Civic Action

Apparently undeterred by the failure of its Civic Action programme in Namibia, the SADF has expended considerable efforts in its campaign to 'win hearts and minds' in South Africa. The failure of the Namibian campaign has been put down by the military to the fact that it started too late and was not implemented rigorously enough.

SADF doctrine accepts that Civic Action can only work in a preventive fashion. According to General Lloyd, the SADF commander in Namibia from 1980 to 1983, once guerilla activities have begun in a specific area, 'the time has run out for most other strategies' and military forces have to rely on their firepower and military strength.[81] Captain W Steenkamp, the defence reporter on the *Cape Times*, has echoed this theme:

> Ultimately a hearts and minds strategy can't win a campaign, it can only contribute. It's better to get in on the early stages before insurgency starts and before the politicisation process begins, otherwise you start with a credibility gap. In Ovambo it didn't work that way. You should start with the hearts and minds campaign before the political action begins.[82]

Apartheid military strategists have argued for the early implementation of a comprehensive Civic Action programme in South Africa as a 'deterrent' to guerilla warfare. As early as 1968 the SADF was asserting: 'The objective for both sides in a revolutionary war is the population itself. . . military tactics are well and good, but they are really quite useless

236

if the government has lost the confidence of the people among whom it is fighting.'[83]

A 1975 manual issued to members of the Permanent Force was more explicit. 'Liberalistic negrophiles and others have too often in the past presented themselves as the only well-doers and friends of the non-white community', it stated. 'In this way they have done more harm than good. It is now our duty to ensure that that time is once and for all past'. The document continued: 'If we want the policy of separate development to be generally accepted and implemented, we will simply have to win the goodwill of the non-white nations – and this, in the first place will have to take place on a personal level'.[84]

What exactly the SADF meant by establishing goodwill on a personal level was spelt out in an 11-page guide for army personnel. The document declared:

> The co-operation, especially of Bantu is of the utmost importance, and where they are not involved at present with the armed forces, we should acquire sufficient knowledge of them to get them involved. . . Any person who does not take the Bantu into consideration as an important factor in the defence of South Africa lives in an ivory tower, particularly as it is the Black man, and sometimes our own Bantu, who is the terrorist in Africa.[85]

SADF 'hearts and minds' projects have taken four main forms. Firstly, units of the SADF have been allocated Civic Action tasks – for example, assisting in drought relief in the bantustans. Secondly, specially trained individual national servicemen have been deployed in bantustan and government departments, mainly as teachers and medical personnel. Thirdly, special SADF 'task forces' have been established for specific projects – for example, army-run rugby clinics in the Western Cape. The final aspect of Civic Action has been the development of black military, paramilitary and Civil Defence organisations and the use of these structures in attempts to 'win hearts and minds'.

The Civic Action programme is closely bound up with the development of the bantustan system. A number of visits to 'the border' (the war zones of Namibia) have been arranged for bantustan leaders and officially sanctioned leaders of black urban authorities. For example, the Chief Ministers of the Venda, Gazankulu and Qwa-Qwa bantustans were taken on a visit to Namibia in 1978, which concentrated on the Civic Action programme there.[86] At the same time the chairmen and deputy chairmen of urban Community Councils were taken on tours of various SADF bases in South Africa and occupied Namibia.[87] The establishment of black units like 21 Battalion, the Cape Corps and the Indian naval unit has given the SADF further opportunities in this field. These units have been regularly inspected by officially approved black leaders. Black employees of the state's propaganda organs, notably the SA Broadcasting Corporation, have also been taken on visits to the units.[88]

According to *Paratus*, the appreciation of 'the common people' for SADF health services is 'simple and sincere' and the men are known in the KwaZulu bantustan as 'our soldiers'.[89] Most of the health work has been carried out by the SADF's Medical Services – since 1978 doctors undergoing National Service have been seconded to various state and bantustan medical institutions. The Medical Services are now supposed to 'emphasise the national aspects rather than only the military aspects of its personnel'.[90] Civic action programmes have also been used to undermine opposition to the establishment of the SADF's regional units, to which some of the bantustan leaders were initially opposed.[91]

By 1983 an estimated two hundred National Servicemen were seconded to the bantustans.[92] The vast majority of them served as teachers, but they were also employed as engineers, sports organisers, medical and veterinary personnel, agricultural, legal and financial advisors, radio technicians and in one case a director of tourism.[93] There have also been indications that the army has been involved in literacy programmes.[94] The idea behind these deployments is:

> To project the image of the soldier as man of action but who is nonetheless a friend of the black man and who is prepared to defend him. We want the National Serviceman to teach the black man whilst his rifle is standing in a corner of the classroom.[95]

After undergoing their basic training, National Servicemen with the required skills for Civic Action tasks (usually university graduates) are sent on a six-month course at 11 Commando in Kimberley. They are then despatched to the area in which they are to complete their two years' National Service. They continue to draw army pay, wear army uniforms and to be subjected to military discipline. In KwaZulu following complaints from the authorities there, Civic Action personnel use 9mm pistols instead of rifles and wear parade uniforms instead of combat gear.[96]

With the possible exception of KwaZulu, Civic Action activity is most concentrated in the Bophuthatswana bantustan in the strategically important north western Transvaal. Apart from serving as teachers, National Servicemen are engaged in a number of agricultural projects under the auspices of the Bophuthatswana Agricultural Corporation. SADF school teachers are also active in the Ciskei, where army personnel are involved in training the 'Pillar of the Nation' youth movement.[97]

In other parts of the Transvaal, particularly areas near the borders, the SADF has taken a variety of 'hearts and minds' initiatives. Thousands of leaflets have been distributed in rural areas bearing slogans like 'Live your life as your forefathers did'; 'Don't listen to the evil talk of the troublemakers. It is poisonous'; 'The South African Army is the guardian of the people' and 'The South African soldiers help you grow [maize]'. The slogans have been accompanied by crudely drawn pictures showing guerillas stealing food or with snakes coming out of their mouths, and soldiers holding babies or standing proudly next to maize fields. The army has been making extensive use of its black troops in its 'hearts and minds' campaign in the Transvaal. According to one report, black soldiers have been left near villages in plain clothes and instructed to 'mix with the locals'.[98]

In the Lebowa bantustan SADF troops have regularly handed out copies of the army publication *The Warrior* at schools. A pupil reported that they were 'told to read nothing else in case they were influenced by communism'. The SADF has also distributed *Warrior* T-shirts and circulated photographs of local people who had left the area, warning that they could be 'communists' and should be reported to the authorities.[99]

The pattern of Civic Action that has emerged in the rural areas of South Africa is a multifaceted and partly experimental one. The primary task is to prop up the bantustan regimes through assistance with education, health, rural development and administrative functions. A second equally important function is that of intelligence gathering. All civic action personnel are expected to fill out regular questionnaires and 'keep their eyes and ears open'. Their third task is that of direct propaganda for the SADF – distribution of leaflets and SADF publications.[100]

Soldier-teachers have been increasingly deployed in schools in urban areas, both as a means of alleviating the teacher shortage and of 'winning hearts and minds'. The presence of SADF personnel in urban African schools was first revealed in 1979, when a row broke out over the distribution to students of copies of *The Warrior*. It was subsequently admitted by the Transvaal Regional Director of Education that National Servicemen were being 'loaned' to his department. Public meetings were called by the Congress of South African Students (COSAS) and community organisations, and boycotts were threatened.[101] Subsequently, there have been a number of walk-outs and protests at schools where soldier-teachers have been deployed. Despite these actions, National Servicemen have been installed at schools in all the major African townships. However, deployments have been very limited due to strong opposition, and troops have often been withdrawn after relatively short periods.

The SADF has also organised visits to army bases for schoolchildren and run 'adventure camps', as discussed in Chapter 3. Black schoolchildren from the Transvaal have been taken on excursions to the SADF headquarters at Voortrekkerhoogte and to 21 Battalion where they have been given lectures and issued with T-shirts. Many schools have been visited by SADF recruiting teams.[102]

National servicemen have been deployed in small numbers in Indian and Coloured schools in the Transvaal and Natal. There do not appear to be any National Service teachers in the Western Cape, where the emphasis has instead been on running 'adventure camps' and sporting or 'social' events. Between 1,500 and 2,000 students aged from eight to 18 and chosen on the basis of 'leadership abilities' have passed through SADF camps in the

Western Cape area every year since 1976. This represents a significant proportion of the school-age population which has been exposed to the apartheid regime's 'hearts and minds' programme.[103]

The camps programme has been met with considerable and growing opposition. On one occasion, after a mass meeting in Mbekweni called by the local branch of the United Women's Organisation and the Western Cape Civic Association, parents drove to the 'adventure camp' at Hermanus and removed their children, who had been sent to the camp without their permission. On another occasion, after pupils had been lured to an SADF camp under false pretences, a pamphlet was distributed in the townships urging the community to 'unite in our efforts to stop the army from interfering with the minds of our children'.

Although concentrated in the Western Cape, the school camps have been extended to other areas of the country, particularly southern Natal. Youth camps for Indian and Coloured children in the Johannesburg area have also been planned, and similar moves have taken place in Bloemfontein.[104]

In some townships the army has provided facilities which are denied by civilian departments of the government. For example, the chronic shortage of entertainment facilities for children during school holidays has been alleviated by the Civic Action department which has set up tents in Western Cape communities and shown free propaganda movies. Sports facilities have also been provided by the SADF teams who have established coaching teams for rugby, netball and other school-based sports.

Given the SADF's ideological emphasis on winning hearts and minds, the Civic Action programme has been very limited. While it may be extended, it is evident that the programme did not get under way before the 'politicisation process' had begun. As the liberation struggle inside the country advances, the SADF is likely to make more intensive use of direct repression. The response to township uprisings is a clear indication that when the 'preventative' strategies of 'winning hearts and minds' fail, the police and army do not hesitate to fall back on the use of force. But even during the State of Emergency the SADF maintained some pretence at 'winning hearts and minds'. While patrolling and occupying the townships, breaking up protests or boycotts and shooting and teargassing residents, the army distributed leaflets and stickers claiming to be a 'friend' of the people.

According to Major Britz, the Cape director of the Civic Action programme, civic initiatives by the SADF increased by three hundred per cent between 1980 and 1983. Most of these initiatives were in the Western Cape, especially aimed at the Coloured community which the apartheid regime had targeted for incorporation into the structures of apartheid rule. Yet it was in precisely these areas that resistance to the tricameral elections was highest, where some of the sharpest opposition to black conscription was manifested and where some of the strongest resistance to the State of Emergency took place.[105]

The limited steps taken by the SADF to show itself as a 'friend of the people' have done little to overcome the resistance of the overwhelming majority of the South African population which has been alienated from the apartheid state by years of repression and suffering. As Captain Steenkamp has admitted:

> When the Administration Board knocks down your shanty you're not going to be very sympathetic to the state. . . the Admin Boards are in charge and the army is subordinate and the Admin Boards aren't always aware of the problem. While apartheid is still around the credibility gap remains large. . .[106]

Steenkamp has ascribed the failure of Civic Action to the problem of 'civilians running the show', and has claimed that 'in the operational areas' where the SADF has taken command of most civilian functions the Civic Action programme would be more likely to succeed. But the experience of Namibia, where the army has been caught in a cycle of increasing repression, has indicated otherwise

Urban Areas

Since the 1940s, when the urbanisation of the black population began to gather pace, South Africa's townships and cities have been a site of ceaseless struggle between the oppressed population and the apartheid authorities.

In the period since the 1976 uprisings hardly a single African township has been untouched by demonstrations, protests, attacks on government installations, guerilla actions and confrontations with the police and army.

Suppressing Urban Resistance

As discussed in Chapter 1, the army was actively involved in the suppression of urban protests during the 1960 State of Emergency, notably in the Cape Town township of Langa. The following year a massive deployment of troops accompanied the declaration of the Republic.[107]

But it was not until the 1976 uprisings that the army was again reported to have been involved in the suppression of urban resistance. On 18 June, as the revolt began to spread from Soweto to other Rand townships, and it became clear that police were stretched to their limit, National Service army units were called in to secure strategic points in Alexandra township. According to one eyewitness report:

> The army had to move in quickly. . . they used small armoured cars, other armed cars with machine guns mounted on top, to guard the Toyota and other factories, and areas like Lombardy and white residential areas [adjoining the township].

The SADF denied that its troops were involved. Nevertheless, evidence of SADF involvement in Alexandra and other areas, notably in the Western Cape, emerged later.[108]

The regime's strategy during the 1976-77 uprisings was to attempt to play down the seriousness of the revolt by ascribing it to a small number of 'agitators and intimidators'. For this reason it was determined to mobilise the army only as a last resort, although many SADF units were put on immediate standby during the second half of 1976. It has been argued that there was another reason for the decision not to mobilise the SADF – the army itself was severely stretched at the time. The war in Namibia was intensifying and the situation in both Angola and Mozambique remained tense, resulting in the SADF's resources being tied up with regional priorities.[109]

While the police, spearheaded by riot squads, largely succeeded in suppressing the 1976-77 revolt through brute force, it was becoming evident that the military would be deployed to suppress popular resistance. The tactical change was probably the result both of the accession to power of P W Botha and the introduction of a more integrated 'security' approach, and of the simple fact that the understrength police force could no longer hold the front line. By April 1978 the government was openly admitting that the SADF was involved in police tasks, and that its role in these tasks would increase.

The change in policy was shown in a wave of massive army and police 'sweeps' that began in April 1978. Troops and police threw a cordon around Soweto, Alexandra and other Reef townships and Hillbrow in central Johannesburg. Hundreds of troops and police set up roadblocks and searched all vehicles and individuals entering or leaving the cordoned areas. Thousands of arrests were carried out. The head of the exercise, a Johannesburg police commander, announced that the army would be called in 'on all future operations to assist the police in combatting many offences'. Another police officer described the operations as 'the first ever operation to combat crime by police and army and designed to pioneer combined operations between police, army and traffic officers.'[110]

Similar cordon and roadblock operations were soon reported to be taking place in other parts of the country, notably in the Cape Peninsula and other parts of the Transvaal.[111] Although described as 'crime sweeps', these operations were perceived by township residents as an exercise in political intimidation.

The twentieth anniversary of the declaration of the republic, in May 1981, which was met by massive protests and a wave of ANC sabotage operations, led to a state of alert and the establishment of roadblocks throughout the country. The streets of Durban, the centre of the regime's celebrations, were patrolled by hundreds of police and troops.[112] Police and army units sealed off Soweto in what was described as a show of 'formidable strength'. Inside, the township suffered 'its biggest crime weekend for a long time' – effectively refuting police claims that the operation was designed to prevent crime. An editorial in the black readership newspaper, *Sowetan*, commented that the operations clearly had a 'political bearing' and were leading to 'an aggressively negative' attitude amongst residents towards the army and police.[113]

The most widely publicised joint police-military operation – that is, until the township sweeps which began in October 1984 – occurred in June 1981 when a combined force of police, traffic police and troops launched an operation to 'capture' the leaders of a schools boycott which was sweeping the Rand. Westbury township was sealed off by heavily armed soldiers while police conducted systematic house-to-house searches and stormed the local high and junior schools.[114] The troops were drawn both from local Commandos and the SA Army Gymnasium.[115]

The Army in the Townships

The army was increasingly involved in a series of confrontations escalating through 1983 and 1984. The confrontations centred around township protests over bus fares and rents, struggles against the black urban authorities and the segregated tricameral parliament, and the on-going education struggle which had been simmering since 1976.

During 1983 bus boycotts led to violent confrontations with the police, army and bantustan paramilitary forces in townships near Durban and East London and similar confrontations developed in other areas of the country in 1984. Protests were also mounted against the Community Councils in African townships. After a successful boycott campaign, the councils were elected on a national average poll of only seven per cent.

Struggles in schools predominantly took the form of classroom boycotts, which led to increasingly violent clashes with the police. Tension in the country grew as the elections to the new Coloured and Indian parliamentary chambers approached and the UDF intensified its boycott campaign. On the eve of the Coloured elections at the end of August the leadership of the UDF was arrested.[116]

On 3 September 1984, the day the new constitution was implemented and P W Botha took his seat as Executive President, the Vaal townships rose in protest. Thousands of residents attacked apartheid targets. Sharpeville, the scene of the most violent confrontation, was sealed off by the police the following day, and police shootings and the use of tear-gas spread to other areas. General Constand Viljoen, the SADF chief, flew in from the parliamentary ceremonies in Cape Town and toured the townships by helicopter.[117]

On 7 September the Transvaal congress of the National Party was informed by the Minister of Law and Order, Louis Le Grange, that 'elements of the South African army will be utilised to a greater extent in a support role for the South African police' and that the police and army had been 'working on formalising army support'. He also revealed that the SADF had already been assisting the police in 'controlling the unrest', but that this had been limited to roadblocks and helicopter support.[118]

As Le Grange spoke, columns of armoured personnel carriers entered Soweto and townships outside Grahamstown and Port Elizabeth in the Cape Province. In Grahamstown a military spotlight was erected on a hill and at night it was trained onto black residential areas to assist police and army operations. Troops were issued with police 'quirts' (metre-long flexible batons) in order to break up demonstrations.[119]

The deployment of troops was met with considerable protest. The End Conscription Campaign, which had just launched a national campaign against compulsory military service, declared that it was 'immoral and unjust' that 'thousands of young South Africans are being forcibly conscripted to fight against fellow South Africans who daily suffer the hardships of apartheid'.[120] The SADF responded by assuring the public that it was 'normal'. In a joint statement, the Ministers of Law and Order and Defence declared:

> Just as the police force support the Defence Force on the border, so the Defence Force is supporting the police in internal unrest situations, and . . . this has been done on a number of occasions.[121]

Demonstrations, protests and attacks on local authorities continued to spread through black townships, especially in the Vaal Triangle.

On the night of 22 October a force of five thousand army personnel (mostly conscripts undergoing National Service) and two thousand police was assembled outside the Vaal Triangle townships. Just before midnight columns of armoured cars surrounded and entered the township of Sebokeng. The operation – called 'Operation Palmiet' – was planned and initially conducted in total secrecy. Reporters were not allowed into the area until daybreak, by which time virtually every house in Sebokeng – which has a population of well over 100,000 – had been systematically searched by teams of armed police.[122]

One resident described how he had experienced the operation:

> At about midnight I saw there were soldiers all over the streets. I never thought they were going to make house-to-house searches. But about four o'clock they knocked on the door as if they wanted to kick it in. When I opened they didn't greet me or ask if they could search. They just asked for the house permit, then walked past me into the room where my mother and father and younger brother were sleeping. They switched on the light and demanded to know who they were. They said we have come in peace. Before they left, the took a sticker and stuck it on a cupboard. It said 'Trust me, I am your friend'. . .[123]

Pamphlets prepared by the SAP and SADF, which were described as 'The Friendly Forces', were issued to residents, calling on them to 'Unite for a safer community' and to 'Go back to school'. Another pamphlet stated: 'We are here to promote normal social life, continued education, safe travel, stability, a healthy community and the delivery of food.'[124] Police moved around with loudhailers repeating these messages and threatening that unless residents paid their rents and bills their electricity and water would be cut off. After searching Sebokeng, the troops and police were redeployed to the nearby townships of Boipatong and Sharpeville.

The aim of the operation, according to the Minister of Law and Order, Le Grange, was to root out 'revolutionary, . . . criminal and intimidatory forces'. By sunrise, nearly four hundred people had been arrested. Not one of them was charged with any offence of an overtly political nature – the vast majority were prosecuted for pass law violations or minor criminal offences such as possession of cannabis or illegal crates of beer.

Some observers described the operation as 'a glorified pass raid'. The UDF and other representative organisations described it as 'a declaration of war' and an 'occupation'. The Southern African Catholic Bishops' Conference expressed 'utter disbelief' at the action and declared it an 'unwarranted military siege'. A statement from the Congress of South African Students (COSAS), which was leading the education boycotts in the region, declared: 'Students and many of our countrymen have been killed by the army and the police, and now the same army and police say, trust me I am your friend'. The operation also met with a hostile international reception.[125]

The SADF presented Operation Palmiet as a resounding success and a good example of an urban counter-insurgency exercise, designed to raise the profile of the SADF and test the effectiveness of large-scale joint police and army operations. By the tone of the propaganda material distributed during the operation, the military planners clearly expected some level of township support for restoring 'law and order'. A few days later, troops and police manning roadblocks were distributing leaflets saying:

> The members of the combined SAP and SADF security forces want to thank the peoples of Sebokeng, Sharpeville and Boipatong for their co-operation and support in the actions to make the area safer for all to live in. Although the peoples of these areas had some discomfort in the house-to-house searches and roadblocks, they accepted the steps as a necessity from which they all would benefit. We appreciate your dignity, kindness and support. Our heartfelt thanks. You earned the respect of all our members.[126]

After Operation Palmiet, hundreds of troops remained deployed in the Vaal townships. In response to increasing repression, the detention of leading trade unionists and the continued refusal of the regime to make any economic or political concessions, trade unions and many other anti-apartheid groups called a two-day stayaway from work in the Transvaal for 5 and 6 November. One of the demands made was for the withdrawal of police and troops from the townships.

The SADF handed out thousands of pamphlets at roadblocks and dropped them from helicopters in the days leading up to the strike. These leaflets apparently accepted that the police and army were not regarded as 'friends'. Instead they tried to blame atrocities on the UDF, the Release Mandela Committee and other groups.

Despite these efforts, the 5 and 6 November saw the largest ever political stayaway in South Africa, with over a million workers and students obeying the call. Significantly, it was most successful in townships that had just been 'pacified' by 'Operation Palmiet'. In Sebokeng it was one hundred per cent successful, and in the Vaal Triangle and East Rand as a whole, ninety per cent of workers and students stayed away, paralysing the industrial heartland of South Africa.[127]

On the first day of the stayaway, nearly three thousand troops moved into the East Rand township of Tembisa, where they set up headquarters at the police station. From there they patrolled the township and established roadblocks, distributing leaflets and urging people through loudspeakers to go to work and school. At the end of the strike most of the troops withdrew, but residents reported that the SADF continued to keep a noticeable presence in the area.[128]

Troops were also called in to crush the strike at the strategic Sasol plant, which like the state's Iron and Steel Corporation, Iscor, was paralysed by worker action. Six thousand Sasol workers obeyed the strike call, although they were given a special exemption by their union on the grounds that strike action at Sasol is illegal. The hostel where shop stewards met on the first day of the strike was surrounded by police and army personnel who stormed the building, forcing the shop stewards to flee. All six thousand workers were them dismissed and paid off at gunpoint.[129]

During the stayaway, the police refused to provide any information on SADF involvement in joint operations. The head of the police public relations division announced: 'We will no longer confirm or deny any reports that the military has assisted us in operations in any townships or other areas'. Henceforth, all information on combined operations would be restricted.[130]

This blackout on information on army operations was widely condemned as yet another indication that, under a veil of secrecy, the regime was engaged in a strategy of suppression akin to civil war. It was also taken as evidence that the SADF was embarrassed by the negative reaction to 'Operation Palmiet' and would not in future allow publicity for such exercises.[131]

The authorities began to deny reports of army operations in townships, even when eyewitnesses attested to the presence of troops. For example, at the end of November 1984, residents of Thokoza township on the East Rand were quoted in the press about army raids on their houses. The police flatly denied any SADF involvement. When the eyewitness accounts were put to them by journalists, the police simply responded that it was no longer policy to comment on 'day-to-day activities' of the SADF.[132] On another occasion, after more than 2,000 Sebokeng hostel residents had been rounded up and arrested for refusing to pay rents, police spokesmen simply 'refused to confirm or deny' SADF involvement.[133] This refusal to comment became the norm, especially after the State of Emergency was declared in July 1985.

After the township uprisings of August-November 1984, the Southern African Catholic Bishops' Conference released a report on the conduct of the police, based on interviews with victims of police brutality and a number of affidavits and statements. Documenting cases of brutality, victimisation, torture, rape and unprovoked aggression, the bishops accused the police of: 'indiscriminate use of firearms; assaults and beatings; damage to property; provocation, callous or insensitive conduct [and] indiscriminate or reckless use of teargas. . .'.

Cases were recorded of police firing into houses for no apparent reason, shooting pedestrians from armoured vehicles, invading a mineworkers' hostel and beating the workers in their beds, looting shops, discharging teargas into classrooms and houses, attacking mourners at funerals, and countless beatings and shooting of students and others protesting in the streets.[134] While the Catholic Bishops confined their report to the police, the army was increasingly becoming involved in similar repressive activity.

State of Emergency

Resistance to local authority structures in black residential areas, education boycotts, worker strikes and stayaways, attacks on police and other manifestations of resistance to apartheid continued with renewed intensity in the first three months of 1985. By the end of March, over 10,000 people had been arrested on charges arising out of the conflicts which had spread across the country since September the previous year.[135] Between January and April 104 people were killed, mostly by the police, in confrontations between township residents and police or military forces. On 21 March, the anniversary of the Sharpeville massacre, police opened fire on an unarmed crowd in the township of Langa outside Uitenhage in the Eastern Cape. Twenty people were killed, eleven of them juveniles, 17 of them shot from behind.[136]

In the fortnight following the Uitenhage massacre, large concentrations of troops were moved into the Eastern Cape and East Rand townships to back up the police.[137] Apart from joint patrolling with the police in armoured vehicles, troops were widely used in house-to-house search operations in various townships, following the model established by Operation Palmiet. At the end of June the military authorities announced that 30-day call-ups for members of the Citizen Force would be doubled to 60 days to cope with the increased deployments in townships.[138]

The massive use of troops, the occupation of townships, the arrests,

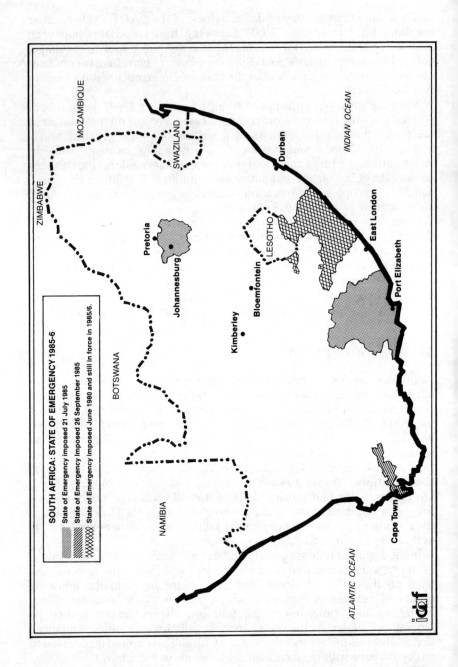

SOUTH AFRICA: STATE OF EMERGENCY 1985-6

State of Emergency imposed 21 July 1985

State of Emergency imposed 26 September 1985

State of Emergency imposed June 1980 and still in force in 1985/6.

ZIMBABWE

MOZAMBIQUE

SWAZILAND

BOTSWANA

NAMIBIA

LESOTHO

INDIAN OCEAN

ATLANTIC OCEAN

Pretoria

Johannesburg

Kimberley

Bloemfontein

Durban

East London

Port Elizabeth

Cape Town

idaf

detentions and the deaths inflicted by the police and army fuelled protests. Workers and students organised stayaways and demonstrations to demand the withdrawal of police and army units. Protests spread from the major metropolitan areas to smaller centres and rural areas, while resistance in the Witwatersrand and the Eastern Cape remained almost continuous. Attacks on police, administration and other government targets increased. In some areas consumer boycotts were launched in addition to the widespread education boycotts. Guerilla activities escalated, with more acts of sabotage recorded in the first half of 1985 than in the whole of the previous year. Government ministers claimed that the ANC and the UDF were trying to make the country ungovernable and were establishing alternative forms of power in black areas.[139]

On 21 July President Botha declared a State of Emergency in the Witwatersrand and the Eastern Cape, covering a third of the South African population.

The emergency proclamation, issued in terms of the Public Safety Act of 1953, conferred far-reaching powers on police and military personnel. All members of the SAP, Railways Police, SADF and Prison Service were empowered to carry out arrests without warrant and detain individuals for up to 14 days for the purposes of interrogation. Detention orders could be renewed with the permission of the Minister of Law and Order for an indefinite period until the end of the State of Emergency. Police, SADF and Prison Officers and NCOs were further empowered to 'apply or order the application of such force as [they] under the circumstances may deem necessary in order to ward off or prevent. . . suspected danger'. Troops and police were indemnified against any civil or criminal proceedings in the courts over actions carried out under the terms of the emergency, unless it could be proved they did not act 'in good faith'.[140]

Police commissioners or any person acting with their authority, were empowered to invoke further regulations in any of the areas falling under the State of Emergency. These could include curfews; cordoning off of areas; closure of any public, private or business place; forcible removal of people from any areas; control of key services or installations; and 'control, regulation or prohibition' of news and information. Within a month of the declaration of the emergency, regulations of this nature had been imposed in 48 townships. These included curfews, provisions used to suppress school and consumer boycotts and restrictions on the media.[141]

The State of Emergency was extended to cover parts of the Western Cape on 26 October 1985. The Transkei bantustan was already under a State of Emergency imposed in 1980, and throughout the country legislation was in force embodying many powers first used in previous emergencies. In areas not covered by the State of Emergency, more intensive use was made of the Internal Security Act and other legislation providing for detention and interrogation. Furthermore, on 1 November 1985 the indemnity given to police and troops in the emergency areas was extended to cover the whole of South Africa.[142]

In December 1985 further permanent powers were extended to SADF personnel over the entire country. SADF officers above the rank of Warrant Officer were empowered to prevent and break up meetings and order the detention of any person for 48 hours – a period which could be extended. All SADF personnel were given wide powers of arrest, and empowered to search buildings and cars and control roadblocks without assistance from the police.[143] In effect, this meant that the most draconian aspects of the emergency powers were made permanent and extended over the whole country.

Forces Deployed under the Emergency
As a result of rigorous restrictions on the media, little information was made available regarding the command and control of military and police forces under the State of Emergency. It is likely that major policy decisions – including the decision to impose the emergency – were taken in the State Security Council, but there was little indication to what extent the National Security Management System was brought into operation. With its pyramidal structure of Interdepartmental Committees and Joint Management Centres the system was apparently tailor-made for dealing with a situation such as the State of Emergency.[144] However, only in rare cases was any mention made in the media of the involvement of National Security Management System structures – for example, it was reported in November 1985 that a 'Mini Joint Management Committee' in Queenstown had decided to withhold government food aid from a local township as part of efforts to break a consumer boycott of white shops.[145]

During 1985 police-military liaison was regulated through Joint Operational Centres established at army territorial command levels and below. While police and army units remained under the command of their respective officers, overall authority was vested in the police, exercised through the police divisional command system.[146]

In most, if not all areas where the army was deployed for long periods of time, the local Commando assumed direct command of all troops active in the area. For example, during May 1985 the township of Kwanobuhle in the Eastern Cape was occupied by a military force consisting of elements drawn from 4 and 7 Infantry Battalions from the Transvaal, the School of Armour in Bloemfontein, the State President's Guard from Pretoria and an armoured car unit from Port Elizabeth, as well as members of the local Commando. The whole force fell under the control of the leadership and headquarters element of the Commando.[147]

While troops were used to an increasing extent, the police remained in the front-line of operations throughout 1985. In an effort to reduce the number of troop reinforcements needed, to increase the number of police with combat experience for deployment in metropolitan areas, and simultaneously to militarise border areas, police undertaking military duties along South Africa's northern borders were replaced by troops at the end of 1985.[148]

During the State of Emergency police riot squads were greatly strengthened by the transfer of regular police, while the police force itself drew heavily on its reserve formations. *(See Chapter 6)*[149] As resistance spread from one part of the country to another, so police reinforcements were despatched to bolster the local police forces. There were also reports that the Koevoet unit, usually deployed in the Namibian war zones, had been brought into the Western Cape, but these were denied by the authorities.[150]

SAP forces and their reserves were supplemented by Railway Police, armed Traffic Police, Mine Police controlled by the mining companies, and paramilitary and vigilante groups. In bantustan areas bantustan police were deployed in similar roles to the SAP. In townships around Durban paramilitary groups of the Inkatha bantustan movement actively suppressed demonstrations and attacked UDF supporters with the backing of the police.[151]

The formation of vigilante groups was encouraged by the police in some areas. In Queenstown police approved the formation of an armed group loyal to the local Coloured Management Committee and approached the SADF to have the group properly armed and trained up to the status of a Commando.[152] Ninety-three men were subsequently deployed in the Commando after only six days' training.[153]

Police controlled by Development Boards were also used to suppress resistance, but were being replaced by police financed and nominally controlled by black town councils. Town council police, unlike those they were replacing, were equipped with the same anti-riot equipment as the SAP, including automatic rifles. During 1985 over R2,000 million was allocated to black local authorities to establish police forces, and 5,000 policemen were due to be trained in the first six months of 1985.[154] Town councillors themselves – those who did not resign in response to residents' demands – were placed under police guard or removed to specially fortified encampments.[155]

Apart from the Commandos, the majority of the troops deployed in the townships during the State of Emergency were Citizen Force members called up for special two-month periods of duty in the townships. As these call-ups were instituted at a Territorial Command level, local military commanders were able to mobilise troop reinforcements at short notice. National Servicemen were also deployed in the townships.[156]

Military and Police Operations
Day-to-day army operations in black metropolitan areas consisted mainly of patrolling the streets in armoured vehicles – usually police Casspirs (originally designed for Koevoet use in Namibia) or army Buffels. The patrols would break up gatherings, destroy barricades and attack residents.

Weeks of violent confrontations were followed by 'pacification' operations in which large numbers of troops sealed off areas which were then systematically searched by contingents of police. Suspects and people whose papers were not in order were arrested. Dozens of townships were subjected to these operations.[157]

Troops became increasingly involved in breaking consumer or education boycotts. Black-owned shops near townships were closed down in efforts to force residents to shop in white areas, and delivery vans turned back at roadblocks. Steps were taken to force pupils to attend schools by troops patrolling the streets warning students with loudhailers to attend classes, and in some areas by obtaining lists of boycotting pupils from headmasters and then driving to their homes to pick them up and ferry them to school at gun point.[158]

Police and troops also attempted to break student organisation and resistance by raiding schools at which pupils were holding meetings. Students were whipped, beaten and shot and hundreds were rounded up and detained. In some areas schools were closed to prevent them being used as centres of resistance, and in the Western Cape police and troops occupied schools and attacked teachers and students attempting to enter them. The principal students' organisation, the Congress of South African Students (COSAS) was banned in August 1985.[159]

Troops enforced night curfews which were imposed on many townships in and outside the emergency areas, and broke up meetings and funerals of victims of police and army violence. Troops manning roadblocks were also responsible for enforcing regulations preventing non-residents from entering certain townships, particularly at times of mass funerals.[160]

All these operations were accompanied by the widespread distribution of propaganda material describing the SADF and SAP as 'friends' and urging residents not to support those described as 'troublemakers', to return to work or school and to assist in the 'maintenance of law and order'. These messages were projected through leaflets dropped from armoured vehicles, helicopters or light aircraft, and by announcements made through loudhailers or speakers mounted on armoured vehicles, helicopters and aircraft. In some areas toy models of Casspirs and army vehicles were distributed to children.[161]

The widespread dissemination of political propaganda by the SADF and police was only occasionally backed by Civic Action initiatives. In some areas the SADF made efforts to restore essential services by attempting to organise residents into work squads to clear the streets of barricades, but these initiatives were not widespread. On other occasions soldiers attempted to 'win hearts and minds' by arranging 'spontaneous' games of soccer with local children. (On at least one occasion youths used the opportunity to steal the troops' rifles.)[162]

All over the country township residents reported widespread and often indiscriminate brutality by the regime's forces, including beatings, tortures, assaults, rapes, abductions, attacks on children and interference with injured people. Press reports and affidavits drawn up by victims reveal a pattern of police and army brutality which was repeated over and over in townships across the country.[163]

Attacks on meetings and gatherings usually took the form of police or army vehicles driving at the crowd firing teargas, rubber bullets, shotguns or rifles. In some cases, especially when demonstrations took place in 'white' areas such as the centres of major cities, police used whips (sjamboks) and batons to disperse demonstrators. Water cannons and automatic rubber bullet devices were employed for the first time in October 1985.[164]

Many incidents were reported of police and troops driving through townships and firing indiscriminately at houses or people on the street, even when there was no question of them being engaged in any demonstration or political activity. Many cases of children being fired at and killed in this way were reported. Police and troops also deliberately provoked attacks so that violent responses could be made. For example, in Bongweni near Colesburg, police placed a youth on top of their armoured vehicle and repeatedly assaulted him in view of a group of young people. When the young people responded by throwing stones at the vehicle, the police opened fire. In the same township, police set up an ambush by hiding in a house and firing on people as they walked past. In Cape Town, Railways Police hid themselves in crates on the back of a municipal truck and drove slowly past groups of young people, inviting attack. When stones were thrown, they opened fire, killing three.[165]

Torture, beating and intimidation of detained or abducted people was widely reported. Many detainees reported being beaten in police and army vehicles and then being further beaten and tortured in police stations and detention centres. Children were caught by police or soldiers, taken into armoured vehicles, beaten and intimidated and then released.

A National Serviceman who was engaged in joint township patrols with the police reported: 'The majority of [police and troops] are not afraid or confused. They are in turn bored and excited, they want action, they are callous, they are enormously arrogant.' The National Serviceman described the type of activity he had been engaged in:

We come on a pick-up truck loaded with children and youths who show us the clenched fist salute.

The cops go into action. The pick-up is overtaken and forced to stop. Black bodies spill off in all directions as the cops tumble out in pursuit. Soon, they return with their catch: a boy of about 10 whom they hit and slap as they drag him into the vehicle where they continue to slap and punch. . . We trundle on. . . There is a loud 'dong' as a stone hits the armour and bounces in through the roof opening. The sergeant acts immediately, sending off a 37mm gas canister. It lands on a house and the residents pour out coughing, eyes streaming. We go and watch briefly, the cops laugh loudly. . .

The funeral is over. The returning crowd starts to break up. Knots of people on street corners sing and shout defiance. . . We launch into a hurtling, lurching circuit, past streams of panicking, running people, pumping out gas and rubber bullets.

It's over in a couple of minutes. The cops prepare for the second round but the crowd has dispersed. There is an atmosphere of sport.

Eventually we return to the police station. The police have brought in a man (ostensibly a stone-thrower) and derive much sport from beating and poking him with the sjamboks and truncheons in front of the station and in the back of a van. . .[166]

Such attitudes and behaviour on the part of police and army help explain how so many were killed by apartheid forces during township confrontations. Nine years earlier, after the uprisings which began in Soweto in June 1976 had left hundreds dead, the large number of people killed was partly ascribed to the fact that the police lacked modern anti-riot equipment and were obliged to use their rifles. However, by 1985 the police – and in some cases, troops deployed alongside the police – were equipped with a wide range of anti-riot equipment including rubber bullets and teargas. Protective clothing in the form of helmets, visors and shields, was also issued to police and troops. The police regarded the new equipment as inefficient and did not always use it. Before the Uitenhage massacre, for example, anti-riot equipment was withdrawn on the instructions of the local police commander and police were issued with heavy-gauge ammunition.[167]

During the course of 1985 various tactics and weapons were tried out. Dogs were on occasion used to break up crowds and SADF mounted units were deployed for the first time. Experimental use was made of military searchlights mounted on hills near townships for night operations. Helicopters and light aircraft were widely used, mainly for surveillance and to distribute propaganda leaflets. In November 1985 helicopters were for the first time used to fire teargas on crowds, during demonstrations in Mamelodi, near Pretoria in which 13 people were massacred.[168]

Use has also been made of the 'sneeze machine', a teargas dispersant mounted on a vehicle, a smoke generator and water cannons, but standard police and army 'anti-riot' equipment has consisted of rifles (often fitted with teargas cap dischargers), shotguns and the Stopper, a 37mm gun capable of firing rubber bullets or teargas canisters. In October 1985 an automatic weapon capable of firing a continuous stream of rubber bullets was demonstrated.[169]

An insight into the thinking behind police tactics and the use of specialised equipment was provided in an article in the September 1985 issue of the official SAP journal, *Servamus*. The writer, H R Heitman, who has close links with the SADF establishment, argued that the application of 'European' anti-riot equipment and tactics had proved inadequate in South Africa as a result of climate, terrain and the nature of the conflict. He concluded:

. . .Various circumstances. . . conspire to make 'ideal' riot control well-nigh impracticable in South Africa today. Had we three times the police force we might see fewer fatal casualties. In present circumstances there are probably only two ways in which the number of fatal casualties can be reduced: either the rioters must exercise firmer control over their own activities. . . or the police will have to act far more strongly earlier in the proceedings. . .[170]

Similar views were expressed by Major-General A J Wandrag, a Deputy Commissioner of the SAP and head of Riot Control. He argued that 'firm police action' was necessary as 'riots' were well-organised aspects of the 'total communist onslaught'. He ascribed casualties among children to the fact that 'agitators' placed 'women (many of whom are pregnant) and children to form the front line of rioters'.[171]

Police and military tactics had not ended resistance in the townships by the time the State of Emergency was lifted in March 1986. After eighteen months of almost continuous conflict, many townships had the atmosphere of war zones. Sophisticated community defence structures had been organised in response to police and military deployments, and patrols were being attacked with greater effectiveness.[172] Structures of 'people's power', including area and street committees, had been established in many townships, and some civic affairs were being administered by these structures.

In the face of occupation of townships by the police and army and the reign of terror instituted by the apartheid regime under the State of Emergency, growing support for the armed struggle among the black population became evident. Despite the dangers of doing so, 36 per cent of black respondents surveyed in September 1985 said that they supported armed resistance against the South African regime.[173]

By the time the State of Emergency was lifted, it was evident that a 'people's war' against the apartheid regime of the kind called for by the ANC was being concretely manifested across the breadth of South Africa. Guns, handgrenades and bombs were increasingly being used to supplement the standard township weapons of petrol bombs and stones.[174]

The restrictions on meetings; the banning of the Congress of South African Students (COSAS); the detention of an estimated eight thousand people and the death of over eight hundred;[175] the arrest and torture of anti-apartheid leaders and organisers; the deployment of tens of thousands of police and soldiers and the occupation of townships – all this failed to destroy anti-apartheid organisation in black areas or break resistance.

P W Botha, addressing the apartheid parliament shortly before the lifting of the State of Emergency, made it clear that from the regime's perspective, the battle for South Africa had entered a decisive phase. Despite verbal commitments to reform, he refused to contemplate any move away from the basic structures of apartheid and called for the further strengthening of bantustan and other segregated structures.[176] This perspective underscored the build-up of military and police forces which had taken place over the previous decade or more, and, in the context of the quickening tempo of the struggle for freedom from apartheid, laid the basis for a further escalation of war in Southern Africa.

In the report of the National Executive Committee of the ANC on 8 January 1986, the 74th anniversary of the founding of the movement, President Oliver Tambo declared:

> Realising that power is slipping out of its hands, the Botha regime could not rule in the old way any longer. Hence it has adopted new and more brutal ways of governing our country to save itself from destruction. These include the proclamation of martial law, handing over administration of large areas of our country to the murderous army and police, the use of secret death squads, the assassination of our leaders, massacres, mass arrests, stringent control of the press, continuing external aggression and the murder of our people outside our country.
>
> Despite the extraordinary measures designed to safeguard racist rule and reassure the white minority, the reality is that the white power bloc has never been as divided as it is today. . . The Botha regime has lost the strategic initiative. That initiative is now in our hands. . .
>
> . . . Through our sacrifices, we have prepared the conditions for us further to transform the situation to that position when it will be possible for us to seize power from the enemy. Thus the central task facing the entire democratic movement is that we retain the initiative until we have emancipated our country.[177]

Tables

TABLE I: Members of the State Security Council 1985

Statutory Members

President	P W Botha
Minister of Defence	Gen M A de M Malan
Minister of Foreign Affairs	R F 'Pik' Botha
Minister of Law and Order	Louis le Grange
Minister of Justice	H J Coetsee
Senior Cabinet Minister: Minister of Transport Affairs	H Schoeman
Chief of the SADF	Gen Johan J J Geldenhuys
Commissioner of Police	Gen P J Coetzee
Head of the National Intelligence Service	N L Barnard
Director General Foreign Affairs	J van Dalsen
Director General Justice	J P J Coetzer
Secretary of the State Security Council	Lt Gen P W van der Westhuizen

Probable Members

Deputy Minister of Law and Order and Defence	A J Vlok
Minister of Constitutional Development and Planning	J C Heunis
Minister of Industries, Commerce and Tourism	D J de Villiers
Head of Atomic Energy Corporation	Dr Roux
Chairman of Armscor	Cmdt P Marais

TABLE II: SADF Command Personnel December 1985

Statutory Members

Chief of SADF	Lt-Gen Johan J Geldenhuys
Chief of Staff	Lt-Gen I R Gleeson
Chief of Staff Operations	?
Chief of Staff Personnel	Lt-Gen R F Holtzhausen
Chief of Staff Intelligence	Lt-Gen P W van der Westhuizen
Chief of Staff Logistics	Lt-Gen I Lemmer
Chief of Staff Finance	Vice-Adm M A Bekker
Chief of Army	Maj-Gen A J Liebenberg
Chief of Air Force	Lt-Gen Earp
Chief of Navy	Vice-Adm. G Syndercombe
Surgeon General	Lt-Gen N J Nieuwoudt
General Officer Commanding SWA	Maj-Gen G L Meiring

TABLE III: South African Military Expenditure 1960–85
(Millions of rand)

Fiscal year	Defence cash vote (budget)	Special defence account	Total defence spending (all departments)
1960/61	44		
1961/62	72		
1962/63	129		
1963/64	157		
1964/65	210		
1965/66	229		
1966/67	255		
1967/68	256		
1968/69	252		
1969/70	271		
1970/71	257		
1971/72	321		325
1972/73	335		351
1973/74	472		502
1974/75	692	311	707
1975/76	970	596	1043
1976/77	1350	897	1407
1977/78	1654	1000	1940
1978/79	1899	799	1976
1979/80	1972	1189	2189
1980/81	1970	1160	2300 est
1981/82	2465	1330	2800 est
1982/83	2668	1754	3400 est
1983/84	3093	2024	3800 est
1984/85	3755	2224	4300 est
1985/86	4274	?	4800 est

Source: White Papers on Defence; Annual Estimates, press reports. Total defence spending figures for 1980/81 onwards are conservative estimates and include additional appropriations and transfers.

TABLE IV: Comparative Police and SADF Budget Increases 1974–85
(Millions of rand)

Fiscal year	Military		Police	
	Budget*	% Increase	Budget*	% Increase
1974/75	692	46.6	119	6.3
1975/76	970	40.2	153	28.6
1976/77	1350	39.2	168	9.8
1977/78	1654	22.5	177	5.4
1978/79	1899	14.8	204	15.3
1979/80	1972	3.8	221	8.3
1980/81	1970	–	245	10.9
1981/82	2465	25.1	310	26.5
1982/83	2668	8.2	482	55.5
1983/84	3093	15.9	564	17.0
1984/85	3755	21.4	796	41.1
1985/86	4274	13.8	954	19.8

* *Note:* Cash votes to departments, actual expenditure is considerably higher.
Sources: Annual Estimates 1974/75–1985/85; press reports.

TABLE V: Breakdown of SADF Personnel Strength at 31 July 1983

While the SADF does not give any detailed breakdown of personnel strength, these figures have been calculated on the basis of percentages provided in the *1984 Defence White Paper* (Col A) and from other official sources (Col B), using as a base the figure of 62,500 National Servicemen. (See Notes 7, 8 and 10.)

Force Components	A[6] % of full-time force	B % of total force	C[9] Estimated strength	D[11] Minimum strength	E[12] Maximum strength
(1) Permanent Force	25.5		37,900	36,000	40,000
(2) Auxiliaries[1]	3.1		4,600	4,000	5,000
(3) National Service[2]	42.1		62,500[10]	60,000	65,000
(4) Voluntary National Service[3]	2.2		3,300	3,000	4,000
(5) Full-time Armed Forces $[(1)+(2)+(3)+(4)]$[4]		20[7]	**108,300**	**103,000**	**114,000**
(6) Civilians[5]	27.1		40,000	38,000	42.000
(7) Full-time Force $[(5)+(6)]$	100.0		**148,300**	**141,000**	**156,000**
(8) Citizen Force		47[8]	254,000	242,000	268,000
(9) Commandos		33	179,000	169,000	189,000
(10) Part-time Force $[(8)+(9)]$		80[7]	**433,000**	**411,000**	**457,000**
TOTAL $[(7)+(10)]$		100	**581,300**	**552,000**	**613,000**
Standing Force [13] $[(5)+16.7\%$ of $(8)+3.3\%$ of $(9)]$			157,000	148,000	166,000
Combat Force [14] $[(11\%$ of $(7)+10\%$ pf $(8)]$			42,000	39,000	44,000

These figures do not include the strengths of the SWA Territory Force or Surrogate Forces nor the nominally 'independent' Bantustan forces.

TABLE V continued

Notes

1. This category includes the regional African battalions *(1982 Defence White Paper*, p.12).
2. White males undergoing two-year National Service.
3. White women and Coloured and Indian males undergoing two-year Voluntary National Service *(1982 Defence White Paper*, p.12).
4. This sub-total excludes civilian employees of the SADF.
5. Includes labourers as well as administrative staff.
6. Percentages given in *1984 Defence White Paper*, p.13, rounded to the nearest tenth.
7. The approximate ratio of 1:4 between full-time (assumed to exclude civilians) and part-time forces is given by H R Heitman, a serving officer in the CF, in Heitman [1985], p.24. In 1977 the ratio (including civilian administrative staff, but not labourers) was 17:83 *(1977 Defence White Paper*, p.18).
8. Cited by MP P C Cronje in *Debates* 2.4.82 col 4263.
9. Full-time force figures have been calculated on the basis of the *1984 Defence White Paper* percentages in Col A using the estimate of 62,500 National Service (ie. 31,125 per year intake) as a base. Part-time force figures have been calculated on the basis of the percentages in Col B using the full-time armed force strength of 108,300 as a base. Figures, including the SADF total, have been rounded to the nearest thousand.
10. In 1980 there were approximately 60,000 National Servicemen (*Hansard*, 2.3.79; *Proceedings of the US Naval Institute*, December 1981; IISS *Military Balance* 1981–2; Jaster [1980], p.13.). Numbers have increased since then owing to demographic trends, the conscription of white immigrants (up to 2,000 a year — *SA News* July 1984) and the call-up of men previously disqualified on medical grounds (*Uniform* 1.12.85).
11. Cols D and E provide a window of error in which the estimates in Col C can be viewed. Col D is calculated using the same procedure as for Col C, using 60,000 National Servicemen as a base. Figures rounded down to nearest thousand.
12. Same as D, using 65,000 National Servicemen as a base. Figures rounded up to nearest thousand.
13. Standing Force is an estimate of the number of troops under arms at any given time under 'normal' circumstances (ie. not involving emergency mobilisation beyond the limits set in the 1982 Defence Amendment Act). This is made up of the full-time armed force, one-sixth of the Citizen Force (each member is required to serve four months in every 24) and one-thirtieth of the Commandos (each member must serve a minimum of 12 days per year).
14. Combat Force. This is an estimate of the number of troops available for combat deployment *excluding* supporting infrastructures. It is based on 11% of the full-time force (*1982 Defence White Paper*, p.12) and 10% of the Citizen Force (*1982 Defence White Paper*, p.13).

TABLE VI: Estimated Personnel Strength of Apartheid Armed Forces December 1985

The figures in this table are based on those calculated in Table V. This Table does not include the surrogate forces UNITA, MNR, LLA and Zimbabwean units trained, equipped and deployed by the SADF.

Component	Total	Standing[19]
SADF Permanent Force [1]	43,000[6]	43,000
SADF National Service[2]	67,000[7]	67,000
SADF Citizen Force	265,000[8]	44,000[20]
SADF Commandos	200,000[9]	6,000[21]
SADF Civilians	40,000[10]	–
'Independent' Bantustan Military Units[3]	3,000 [11]	3,000
SWA Territory Force	21,000[12]	15,000[22]
Total Military	**639,000**	**178,000**
SA Police (Regular)	46,000[13]	46,000
SA Police (Reservists)[4]	40,000[14]	1,000[23]
Bantustan Police[3]	3,000[15]	3,000
Railway Police	7,000[16]	7,000
SWA Police	10,000[17]	10,000
Auxiliary Police Forces[5]	10,000[18]	10,000
Total Police	**116,000**	**77,000**
TOTAL ARMED FORCES	**755,000**	**255,000**

Notes:
1. Including the Auxiliaries listed separately in the 1983 Table (Table V).
2. Including the Voluntary component listed separately in 1983 Table (Table V).
3. Transkei, Bophuthatswana, Venda and Ciskei.
4. Reserve Police and Police Reserve.
5. Traffic Police, Mine Police, Town Council Police, etc.
6. An increase of 500 from 1983. According to the 1984 Defence White Paper PF recruitment was continuing (*1984 Defence White Paper*, p.13).
7. An increase of 1,200 from 1983 due to conscription of immigrants and a larger intake of Coloured volunteers.
8. An increase of 11,000 from 1983. The CF will gradually increase in strength until it reaches its maximum of 360,000 (based on 12 yearly groups of 30,000) under the 1982 Defence Amendment Act measures. The increase occurs by more members joining each year than the number completing their commitment.

TABLE VI continued

9. An increase of 21,000 from 1983 due to implementation of conscription of older men into the Area Defence system. The Commando strength is likely to increase annually by approximately 15,000 as this system is established. Swifter expansion is unlikely due to the lack of training facilities and personnel.
10. No increase from 1983.
11. No figures are available, but each of the four 'armies' is not much stronger than battalion strength.
12. In 1980 SWATF strength was estimated at 20,000 (*WO* 9.8.80). It was officially put at 21,000 in 1985 (*GN* 19.6.80).
13. SAP strength in 1984 was 45,500 (*Cit* 17.10.84). Strength is planned to increase to 68,000 in the next decade (*Servamus* June 1983, p.4).
14. Total Reservists in 1983 was 40,029 (Commissioner of the SAP, 1983).
15. No figures available. This is a conservative estimate, which also includes a small number of police attached to non-'independent' bantustan police forces.
16. Authorised strength in 1981 was 6,891.
17. Estimate based on IDAF [1982a], p.42, allowing for an expansion of 2,000 since 1980.
18. No figures are available. This is a rough estimate.
19. The number of troops usually under arms at any given time, excluding emergency deployment.
20. One-sixth of strength (members serve four months in every 24).
21. One-thirtieth of total strength (members serve at least 12 days a year).
22. An estimate based on 14,000 regulars and conscripts and 1,000 Citizen Force and Area Force (Commando) unit members.
23. One-twelfth of the Active Police Reserve Strength of 4,000 and one-thirtieth of the Active Reserve Police Strength of 16,000.

TABLE VII: South African Police Personnel Strength 1973–83

	1973	1975	1977	1979	1981	1983
Regular Police (Actual)	31,588	33,082	35,019	34,076	34,271	42,526
Active Police Reserve	886	2,171	3,318	4,283	4,666	4,053
Active Reserve Police	10,926	11,656	15,320	15,325	13,444	16,199
Sub-total: Active Police	**43,400**	**46,909**	**53,657**	**53,684**	**52,381**	**62,778**
Non-Active Reservists	14,283	18,032	18,424	18,572	20,511	19,777
Total Police Strength	**57,683**	**64,941**	**72,081**	**72,256**	**72,892**	**82,555**

Source: All figures are for establishments on 30th June of each year from Commissioner of the SAP.

TABLE VIII: Estimated Numbers of Black Troops in SADF and Bantustan Units December 1985

African:	Bantustan units	3,000
	Regional battalions	3,000
	21 Battalion	1,000
	Commandos (part-time)	500
Coloured:	Cape Corps ('Voluntary National Service')	3,000
	Army Permanent Force	1,500
	Navy/Air Force	1,000
	Commandos (part-time)	2,000
Indian	Navy ('Voluntary National Service')	200
	Navy (Permanent Force)	400
	Commandos (part-time)	1,000
	ESTIMATED MAXIMUM TOTAL	**16,600**

There are also at least 10,000 black Namibians serving in the SWA Territory Force.

Source: Grundy [1984], p.275; SAIIR *Survey 1984*, p.746; *Debates*, 12.3.85.

TABLE IX: SA Army Weapons and Equipment

Weapon/System	Manufacture	Note	Refs.
PISTOLS			
9mm Super Star	Spain		3/36
9mm Walther P38	FRG		36
9mm Beretta M 1951	Italy		36
9mm Browning/FN GP35	Belgium		2/3
9mm Beretta M92 Luger	Italy	1	36
9mm Mamba	South Africa		39
SUBMACHINE GUNS			
9mm Uzi	SA(Belg/Isr)	2	2
9mm Sterling L2A3	UK		3
9mm BXP	SA	3	20
9mm Beretta M12S	Italy	4	
mm Sanna 77	SA	5	8

TABLE IX continued

Weapon/System	Manufacture	Note	Refs.
RIFLES			
7.62mm R1	SA(Belg)	6	3/33
7.62mm R2/G3	FRG	7	2/33
7.62mm R3	SA(Belg)	8	
5.56mm R4	SA(Isr)	9	
5.56mm R5	SA(Isr)	10	38
5.56mm LM5	SA(Isr)	11	57
5.56mm M16	US	12	
MACHINE GUNS			
7.62mm FN MAG 58	Belgium	13	2/3/33
7.62mm BREN L4A1	UK		33
7.62mm MG4	SA(Belg)	14	3/8
7.62mm/30 Browning M19 19 A4	Belgium		2/33
7.62mm Vickers	UK		
12.7mm/50 Browning M2 HB	Belgium		2/7/33
GRENADES			
75mm HEAT rifle grenade	SA		3
65mm Energa HEAT rifle grenade	SA(Belg)	15	3
65mm STRIM FN HEAT rifle grenade	Belgium		
40mm STRIM FN rifle grenade	Belgium		
Zulu/PRB 103 rifle grenade	SA(Belg)		2/33
M26 hand and rifle grenade	SA(US/UK)	16	3
GRENADE LAUNCHERS			
40mm M79	US		2
40mm grenade launcher	SA(US)	17	20
RIOT CONTROL MUNITIONS			
37mm 'Stopper' grenade launcher	SA	18	20
12-gauge combat shotguns (various)	SA/US/Italy	19	3/8/12
MORTARS			
60mm M1	SA(Fr)	20	2/3/49
60mm Commando M4	SA		3
81mm M3	SA(Fr)	21	3
120mm M5	US(Isr)	22	59
RECOILLESS GUN			
106mm M40	US(Isr)	23	59
ROCKET LAUNCHERS			
68mm SARPAC RL	Fr	24	12
88mm/3.5in 'Bazooka'	US/Belg		53
89mm LRAC 89 F.1	Fr		2

TABLE IX continued

Weapon/System	Manufacture	Note	Refs.
ANTI-TANK GUIDED WEAPONS			
ENTAC	Fr		58
SS-11	Fr		58
Milan	Fr/FRG	25	60
TANKS			
Olifant	UK/SA(Isr)	26	2/61
Centurion	UK		2
Merkava (allegedly on order)	Israel	27	70
RECONNAISSANCE VEHICLES			
Eland 90/Panhard AML-90	SA(Fr)	28	2/7/50
Eland 60/Panhand AML-60	SA(Fr)	28	2/7/50
Eland 20	SA(Fr)	29	6/7
ARMOURED PERSONNEL CARRIERS			
Ratel 12.7mm Command Vehicle	SA(Belg)	30	3/7
Ratel 20 & 60 IFVs	SA(Belg)	30	3/7
Ratel 90 FSV	SA(Belg)	30	3/7
Saracen	UK	31	7
Buffel	SA(FRG)	32	2/11
Bulldog/Rhino	SA(FRG/Jap)	33	11
Casspir/Hippo/Ribbok	SA(?)	34	62
ARMOURED SUPPORT VEHICLES			
Ratel 8x8 Logistics Support Vehicle	SA(Belg)		
Rinkhals Armoured Ambulance	?		40
Kwevoel Logistics Vehicle (Samil 100)	SA(FRG/Jap)		43
Gemsbok Recovery Vehicle	SA(?)	35	62
Albatros Tank Transporter	SA(?)	35	62
AFV (ARMOURED FIGHTING VEHICLE) ARMAMENT			
105mm tank gun	SA(UK)	36	7
90mm F-1 DEFA D921 gun	SA(Fr)	37	3
20mm M693 (F-2) cannon	SA(Fr)	38	3
20mm G12 cannon	?		14
SELF-PROPELLED GUN/HOWITZERS			
155mm G6 Rhino (under development)	SA(Can/etc)	39	1/7/18/19/34
155mm M109A1	US	40	60/63
105mm M7 (in reserve)	US		60
88mm Sexton (in reserve)	Canada		58
SELF-PROPELLED ANTI-AIRCRAFT MISSILES			
Cactus/Crotale S-A-M	Fr	41	4/7

TABLE IX continued

Weapon/System	*Manufacture*	*Note*	*Refs.*
TOWED GUNS/HOWITZERS			
155mm G5	SA(Can/etc)	39	1/5/16/19/29
140mm G4	SA(UK)	42	2/5
5.5in G2 (in reserve)	UK		2/5
90mm anti-tank gun	SA(Fr)	43	7
88mm 25 pdr field gun G1 (in reserve)	UK		2
76mm 17 pdr anti-tank gun (in reserve)	UK		58
57mm 6 pdr anti-tank gun (in reserve)	UK		58
SURFACE-TO-AIR MISSILES			
Tigercat	UK		4
TOWED ANTI-AIRCRAFT GUNS			
3.7in AA Gun	UK		58
40mm Bofors L/70 LAAG	Switz		58
35mm K-63 twin GDF-002 LAAG	Switz		58
20mm GA1-BO1 LAAG	Switz		64
20mm GA1-CO1 LAAG	Switz		64
MULTIPLE ROCKET LAUNCHERS			
Valkiri 127mm MRL	SA/Taiwan		1/2/9/42
ARTILLERY EQUIPMENT			
AS80 Fire Control System	SA(Isr/US)	44	1/13/16
EMVA Mk10B Muzzle Velocity Analyser	SA		1/13
S700 Meteorlogical Ground Station	SA		1/13/30
MLS80/MLS2 Mortar Locating System	SA		48/50
MINES AND DEMOLITIONS			
Anti-tank Mine No.8	SA		3/10
Anti-personnel Mine HE R2M2	SA		3/10
Shrapnel Mine No.2 (Claymore)	SA(US)	45	3/10
Charge Demolition SC 450g	SA		3/10
Charge Demolition Clam HE 450g	SA		3/10
AMMUNITION			
155mm M57 (5 types) for G5	SA(Belg/US)	46	5/16/7
90mm F1 (4 types) for Eland/Ratel & ATG	SA(Fr)		3
81mm & 60 mm mortar bombs	SA(Fr)		3
Various other ammunition from 140mm down to 5.56mm	SA		3/7/20
LIGHT VEHICLES			
Light & Longwheelbase Land Rover	U/K		
Willy's Jeep	US		
Toyota Land Cruiser	Japan		
Jackal Crosscountry combat vehicle	SA(UK/Jap)	47	53
Kriek Mk1 494cc Motorcycle	(SA/Japan)		35

TABLE IX continued

Weapon/System	Manufacture	Note	Refs.
TRUCKS			
Unimog 2.5	SA(FRG)		
Magirus Deutz	FRG		
Bedford 4000kg & 8000kg	UK		
Samil 20, 50 & 100 (numerous types)	SA(FRG/Jap)		10/11
COMMUNICATIONS SYSTEMS			
Ebbehout SADF C3 network	SA(various)		31
Netor SA Army C3 network	SA(various)		41
Marnet Area Defence network	SA(various)		41
Civil Defence network	SA(various)		41
RADIOS			
TR250 Series (Grinel)	SA(UK/Neth)	48	16/28/56
TR178 (Grinel)	SA(various)	49	54
Tricom/Gemini/Trident HF Series (Grinel)		49	16
TR450 Centaur Delta Series (Grinel)			16
400 & 500 Series for Armoured Vehicles (Grinel)			15/47
TR15H/TR32/TR48/TR61H/TR62/T96 (Grinel)			47
B25/B25H/B26 (Fuchs/Tactel)	SA(Fr)	50	21/29
A53/A55/A72/B56/B75/C28 (Fuchs/Tactel)			21/26/28/30
MISCELLANEOUS COMMUNICATIONS EQUIPMENT			
Tropospheric Scatter & Microwave Systems	SA(UK)	51	31/44/65
DT170/Milcom KY500 Data Entry Terminal (Grinel)			27/46
Mobile PABX system (Grinel)			46
SU165 Secure Voice Adaptor (Grinel)			47
TM16 Telephone Threat Recorder (Grinel)			27
RX/TX/TG Series of Communications shelters			31
OPTICS			
E5010 Laser Rangefinder			3
Gogga Image Intensifying rifle sight			3/37
Armson OEG Binocular gunsight			52
E2030 Night Driver's periscope			45/55

Source: World Campaign Against Military and Nuclear Collaboration with South Africa, Oslo, Norway.

Notes:

1. Franchise for marketing obtained by Armscor's Musgrave.
2. Manufactured under licence from FN since the 1960s.
3. Appeared on Armscor's available-for-export list in 1984.
4. In service with SA Police.
5. Based on Czechoslovakian Model 25. Manufactured by Dan Pienaar Enterprise.
6. FN FAL manufactured under licence from FN since 1960s.
7. R2 is the South African designation for the German G3. Many reached South Africa via the defeated Portuguese colonial forces in Angola and Mozambique.
8. Heavy-barrelled version of the R1.
9. SA version of the Israeli Galil.
10. Short-barrelled version of the R4 used by the SA Air Force and for urban operations.
11. Commercial version of the R5 being sold to farmers and other 'qualified' civilians.
12. Stocks held for use by special and surrogate forces.
13. Standard infantry platoon weapon, replacing the BREN.
14. SA modification of the Browning, 30 M1919 A4.
15. SA version of an obsolete Mecar grenade.
16. SA copy of the American M26 and the British L2A1.
17. SA development based on the M79.
18. Introduced by Armscor in 1984. Fires baton rounds, tear gas, etc.
19. A wide range of shotguns are used both by the police for riot control as well as by the army for COIN patrolling.
20. Manufactured under licence from Hotchkiss-Brandt since 1964.
21. Hotchkiss-Brandt MO-81-61.
22. Hotchkiss-Brandt MO-120-60.
23. Delivered from Israel in the late 1970s, mounted on American Motor Corporation jeeps.
24. The SADF reportedly used a 68mm rocket launcher. The French SARPAC is the only weapon of this calibre on the market.
25. The International Institute for Strategic Studies *Military Balance 1981/2* listed the Milan ATGW – but this entry has been dropped from subsequent editions.
26. Centurions modified using an Israeli package.
27. According to Adams [1984], Israeli sources claim a substantial number Merkavas are to be supplied to SA.
28. One thousand six hundred Eland 60s and 90s were manufactured under French licence from the early 1960s.
29. A New version of the Eland mounted with a 20mm cannon is currently under development.
30. The Ratel was reportedly developed by the Belgian company Sibmas, most probably on the basis of South African finance. Sibmas has produced its own APC which is virtually identical to the Ratel.
31. Two hundred and fifty were delivered in the 1950s and had become obsolete until a modification programme was begun in the early 1980s.
32. Armoured body mounted on a Merceded Benz Unimog.
33. Armoured versions of the Samil 20 manufactured by Magnis.
34. Armoured vehicles used by the police manufactured by TFM.

TABLE IX continued

35. Manufactured by TFM.
36. The barrel is a direct copy of the British ROFL7.
37. Mounted on Ratel 90 and Eland 90.
38. Mounted on Ratel 20 and Eland 20.
39. The history of the development of the G5 and G6 has been widely documented. The G6 has a Magirus Deutz engine. On the G5, the sight is a metricated version of the British No.9 dial sight, the breach mechanism is similar to the US 155mm M198 Howitzer, the APU engine is from Magirus Deutz and the cam plate resembles the US M109 howitzer.
40. Delivered to SA during the 1975/76 invasion of Angola.
41. Developed in France with 70% South African finance.
42. Modification of old British 5.5in.
43. Modification of French F-1 DEFA D921.
44. Similar to the Israeli David system. Most of the computer components are of US origin.
45. Exact copy of M18A1 Claymore.
46. Similar to Belgian PRB ammunition. The M572 point detonating fuse used on the High Explosive, High Explosive Base Bleed and White Phosphorous shells is of US origin.
47. Developed from the Land Rover and Land Cruiser.
48. Grinel products originate from Racal equipment (Grinel took over Racal in the 1970s). According to the British journal, *Defence*, 'The TR250 series bears an uncanny resemblance to the 150 series of HF radios produced by MILCOM Electronics SA of Antwerp.'
49. According to the *International Defence Review*, most of the components in the TR178 are of foreign origin.
50. SA versions of the French Thomson CSF TRC 300.
51. The original tropospheric scatter systems delivered to SA were supplied by Marconi, and it is likely that Marconi SA has continued to supply systems. Marconi SA has publicly advertised microwave systems.

References:
1. *Journal of the Royal Artillery*, Vol. CX, No.2, Sept. 1983, pp.124-9.
2. *Defence & Armament*, Nov. 1983.
3. *Jane's Defence Weekly*, 25.2.84, pp.290-5; *Strategy & Defence*, Aug. 1984, pp.59-60.
4. *Flight International*, 4.2.84, p.337.
5. *Jane's Defence Weekly*, 2.6.84, pp.875–80.
6. *Jane's Defence Weekly*, 16.6.84.
7. *Jane's Armour and Artillery*, 1983–4.
8. *Jane's Infantry Weapons*, 1983–4.
9. *Jane's Defence Review*, Vol.4,No.4/No.7, 1983.
10. *Jane's Military Vehicles and Ground Support Equipment*, 1983–4.
11. *Jane's Defence Review*, Vol.4, No.4,1983.
12. *International Defence Review*,11/1984,p.1758.
13. *Jane's Defence Weekly*, 9.6.84, pp.922–4.
14. *Armed Forces (SA)*, May,1984, pp.18–20.
15. *Miltech*, 8/82, pp.50–8.
16. *International Defence Review*,12/1982, pp.1729–32.

17. *Jane's Defence Review*, Vol.4, No.1, 1983.
18. *NATO's Fifteen Nations*, Oct/Nov, 1982.
19. *Miltech*, 1/1983, pp.10–17.
20. *Jane's Defence Weekly*, 25.8.84.
21. *Jane's Military Communications*, 1983–4.
22. *Armed Forces (SA)*, July 1984.
23. *Armed Forces (SA)*, Aug. 1983.
24. *Armed Forces (SA)*, Sept. 1983.
25. *Armed Forces (SA)*, Mar. 1984.
26. *Armed Forces (SA)*, Oct. 1983.
27. *Armed Forces (SA)*, Mar. 1983.
28. *Armed Forces (SA)*, July 1983.
29. *Armed Forces (SA)*, June 1983.
30. *Armed Forces (SA)*, May 1983.
31. *Uniform*, 30.7.84.
32. *Armed Forces (SA)*, Apr. 1983.
33. Badcock, [1981].
34. *Armed Forces (SA)*, Sept. 1982.
35. *CT*, 16.5.83.
36. *SA Man*, Oct. 1981.
37. *SA Digest*, 9.3.84.
38. *Daily Mail*, 11.4.84.
39. *SA Man*, Jan. 1982.
40. *CT*, 15.10.83.
41. *Paratus*, March 1979.
42. *Jane's Weapon Systems*, 1982–3.
43. Heitman [1985].
44. *International Defence Review*, 3/1983, pp.268–71.
45. *Eagle*, Aug. 1983.
46. *Jane's Defence Review*, 3/1983, pp.268–71.
47. *Armed Forces*, Nov. 1983.
48. *Defence*, Jan. 1984, pp.23–6.
49. *Jane's Military Review*, 1983–4, pp.128–40.
50. *Defence Update*, No.52, pp.44–52.
51. *Strategy & Defence*, Aug. 1984, pp.59–65.
52. *Soldier of Fortune*, July 1984.
53. *Soldier of Fortune*, Dec. 1983, pp.84–90.
54. *International Defence Review*, 10/1984, pp.1499–501.
55. *International Defence Review*, 10/1984, pp.1494–5.
56. *Defence*, Dec. 1984, pp.678–80.
57. *RDM*, 8.9.84.
58. IISS *Military Balance*, 1984–5.
59. IISS *Military Balance*, 1988/4.
60. IISS *Military Balance*, 1981/2.
61. Adams [1984]
62. Armscor Supplement to *Paratus*, Nov. 1982.
63. Stockwell [1978].
64. *Jane's Armour and Artillery*, 1981–2.
65. *Armour Action*, 1981, p.9.

TABLE X: SA Navy Vessels in Service

1   *Daphne* Submarines
1   *President* (ex-British *Whitby*) frigate with 1 *Wasp* helicopter
8   Israeli *MOD (Minister of Defence) Reshef*-type fast attack
    craft with 6 *Skerpioen* (*Gabriel*-type) surface-to-surface
    missiles
3   Israeli fast attack craft with 2 *Skerpioen* surface-to-surface
    missiles
4   British *Ford*, 2 *Ton* large patrol craft
6   British *Ton* minesweepers, 2 *Ton* minehunters
1   Fleet replenishment ship
30 *Namacurra* armed harbour patrol craft
1   Ocean, 1 inshore hydrographic ships
    (On order: 4 *MOD*, 3 *Dvora*-type fast attack craft

Source: IISS *Military Balance*, 1984–5.

TABLE XI: SA Air Force Squadrons

Squadron	Location	Aircraft	Role
1 Squadron	Hoedspruit	Mirage F1AZ	Ground Attack/Day Fighter
2 Squadron	Hoedspruit	Mirage IIICZ	Day Fighter/Ground Attack
3 Squadron	Waterkloof	Mirage F1CZ	All-Weather Fighter/Ground Attack
4 Squadron	Lanseria	Impala II	Ground Attack
5 Squadron	Durban	Impala II	Ground Attack
6 Squadron	Port Elizabeth	Impala II	Ground Attack
7 Squadron	Cape Town	Impala II	Ground Attack
8 Squadron	Bloemspruit	Impala II	Ground Attack
11 Squadron	Potchefstroom	Cessna 185	Liaison/Battlefield Recce/Utility
12 Squadron	Waterkloof	Canberra	Photo Recce/Medium and High level Bombing
15 Squadron	Swartkops	Super Frelon	Troop and Equipment Transport/Navy Support/Search and Rescue Support
16 Squadron	Port Elizabeth	Alouette III	Battlefield Support/Counter-insurgency/Search and Rescue
17 Squadron	Bloemfontein	Alouette III	Battlefield Support/Counter-insurgency/Search and Rescue
19 Squadron	Swartkops	Puma	Troop Transport/Casevac/Search and Rescue
21 Squadron	Waterkloof	HS 125 Mercurius Swearingen Merlin Viscount	VIP Transport
22 Squadron	Ysterplaat	Alouette III/Wasp	Anti-Submarine Warfare/Search and Rescue
24 Squadron	Waterkloof	Buccaneer	Naval Strike/Interdiction
25 Squadron	Ysterplaat	Dakota	Short-Range Tactical Battlefield Support/Air Support
27 Squadron	Ysterplaat	Piaggio 166S Albatross	Inshore Maritime Patrol/Air-Sea Rescue
28 Squadron	Waterkloof	C-130 Hercules/C-160 Transall	Support/Search and Rescue
30 Squadron	Ysterplaat	Puma/Super Frelon	Transport/Search and Rescue/Casevac
31 Squadron	Hoedspruit	Alouette III/Puma	Battlefield Support/Counter-insurgency/Troop Transport/Casevac/Search and Rescue
40 Squadron	Dunnottar	Impala II	Ground Attack
41 Squadron	Lanseria	Kudu	Light Battlefield Support
42 Squadron	Potchefstroom	Bosbok	Battlefield Recce
44 Squadron	Swartkops	Dakota/DC-4	Passenger Transport

Source: Heitman [1985]

TABLE XII: Aircraft in SA Air Force Service

Type	Role	Estimated Maximum Number	Country of Origin
LANDWARD AIR DEFENCE/ATTACK			
Mirage F.1AZ	Ground attack fighter	32	Fr./SA
Mirage F.1CZ III CZ	Interceptor	15	Fr./SA
Mirage III RZ and D2Z	Two-seater trainer	15	Fr.
Mirage III RZ and R2Z	Tactical reconnaissance	8	Fr.
Mirage III EZ	Ground Attack fighter bomber	16	Fr./SA
BAC Canberra	Strike-reconnaissance	9	UK
Impala MB 326M Mb1	Two-seater basic trainer	216	Italy/SA
Impala MB 326K Mk2	Ground attack	122	Italy/SA
MARITIME			
Buccaneer S Mk50	Maritime strike/reconnaissance	6	UK
P.166 S Albatross	Coastal patrol/light transport	20	Italy
TRANSPORT			
Lockheed C-130B Hercules	Heavy transport	7	US
Lockheed L-100	Heavy transport	15	US
Transall C-160	Heavy transport	9	Fr./FRG
Douglas C-47 Dakota	Medium transport	45	US
Douglas DC4	Medium transport	7	US
HS 125	Light transport	4	UK
Swearingen	Light transport	6	US
UTILITY/LIAISON			
Cessna CE-185 and Skywagon	Light transport and reconnaissance	30+	US
AM.3CM Bosbok	Forward air control/tactical reconnaissance/light transport/casualty evacuation	40+	Italy/SA
Atlas C3M Kudu	Forward air control/tactical reconnaissance/light transport/casualty evacuation	25+	SA
HELICOPTERS			
Alouette II and III (SE-313 and SE-316)	Light air support	97	Fr.
SA-330 Puma	Air Support	60+	Fr.
SA-321L Super Frelon	Medium transport	14	Fr.
Westland Wasp	Light maritime support	8	UK

Also: 12 CL-13B Sabre Mk 6 trainers; 30 HS Vampire trainers; 74 Rockwell; T-6 Havard trainers; 1 BAC Viscount transport. There have been allegations that the SAAF also has the following: Agusta Bell 205A Iroquois helicopters, Kfir C2; Phantom RF-4E.
Sources: Flight International, 30.11.85; IISS *Military Balance,* 1984/5, pp.82–3.

TABLE XIII: Major Armaments Producers in South Africa

Company	Plant Location	Activity
A. ARMSCOR SUBSIDIARIES		
Atlas Aircraft corporation	Kempton Park	Aircraft manufacture and maintenance
– Telcast	Kempton Park	High technology alloys
Kentron	Pretoria, Irene	Guided Weapon Systems
– Eloptro	Kempton Park	Optical equipment
Lyttleton Engineering Works	Verwoerdburg	Small arms and guns
Naschem	Lenz, Potchefstroom	Heavy calibre ammunition and bombs
Pretoria Metal Pressings	Pretoria West, Elandsfontein	Small calibre and quick-fire ammunition
Somchem	Somerset West, Wellington	Propellants, explosives and rockets
Swartklip Products	Cape Flats	Pyrotechnics, grenades and commercial ammo
Musgrave	Bloemfontein	Commercial rifles, shotguns & handguns
Infoplan	Pretoria	Computer services
B. PRIVATE SECTOR		
Sandock Austral	Boksburg	Armoured vehicles
	Durban	Naval vessels
	Rosslyn	Military vehicles
Magnis Truck Corporation	Jo'burg, East London	Police vehicles
TFM	Boksburg	Electronic components and telecommunications
Allied Technologies (Altech)[1]	Pretoria	Communication systems
Grinaker Electronics[2]	various subsidiaries	Electronic components and communications (Reutech)[3]
Reunert Technology systems	Wadeville	Various electronic systems
Marconi[5]	Pretoria	Electronic components and telecoms
Siemens[4]	Cape Town	Various electronic systems
Plessey[6]		

Sources: Defence and Armament, Nov. 1983; various published advertisements and articles in South Africa.

Notes:
1. Altech's subsidiaries include African Capacitors, Scottish Cables, Telecommunications Technology and MSN Products.
2. Subsidiaries include Grinel, Grinton Commercial Systems and Grinaker Data Systems.
3. Subsidiaries definitely involved in Armscor contracts are: Aserma, OMC Engineering, Fuchs Electronics (Tactel), Barcom, and ESD.
4. Subsidiary of Marconi (UK).
5. Subsidiary of Siemens (FRG).
6. Subsidiary of Plessey (UK).

TABLE XIV: Military and Police Headquarters and Bases in South Africa

Location	Military HQs	Police HQs	Army and Police Bases	Air Force and Naval Bases
TRANSVAAL				
Amsterdam				
Bourke's Luck				
Devon	Northern Air Defence			
Dunnottar			111 Battalion SADF Dog School	Air Force Base (AFB) Dunnottar
Giyani		Gazankulu Police		
Hammanskraal			SAP African Training College Signals School	
Heidelberg				
Hoedspruit				AFB Hoedspruit
Johannesburg	Witwatersrand Command	Witwatersrand Division W Rand Division		
Krugersdorp				
Lebowakgomo		Lebowa Police		
Lenz			21 Battalion	
Louis Trichardt				AFB Louis Trichardt
Maleoskop			SAP Counter-Insurgency Training School	
Middelburg	Eastern Tvl Command	E Tvl Division	4 SA Infantry Btn	
Mmbatho	Bophuthatswana Defence Force	Bophuthatswana Police	1 BDF Battalion	
Nelspruit				
Phalaborwa			7 SA Infantry Btn 113 Btn 3 & 5 Recconaissance Regiments	
Pietersburg	Far Northern Tvl Command	Far Northern Tvl Division		AFB Pietersburg
Potchefstroom	North West Command	Western Tvl Division	3 SA Infantry Btn Artillery School 4 & 14 Field Regiments Equestrian Centre	AFB Potchefstroom
Pretoria	SADF HQ SA Army HQ SAAF HQ SAN HQ Special Forces HQ N Tvl Command Airspace Control Command Air Logistics Command	SAP HQ N Tvl Division	SADF College SA Army College Personnel Services School School of Ordnance Technical Services Training Centre Provost Training Centre State President's Guard SAP College	AFB Swartkops AFB Waterkloof AFS Voortrekkerhoogte AFS Snake Valley SAAF Gymnasium SAAF College SAAF School for Technical Training
Sibasa	Venda Defence Force	Venda Police		

Location	Command	Division	Units	Air Force Base / Naval Base
Bethlehem **Bloemfontein**	OFS Command	OFS Division	2 Field Engineer Reg 1 SA Infantry Btn 1 Parachute Btn School of Armour 1 Special Service Btn School of Engineers	AFB Bloemspruit
Kroonstad **Welkom**		N OFS Division		
NATAL				
Dukuduku **Durban**	Natal Command Naval Command Natal	Port Natal Division	121 Btn 1 Reconnaissance Reg SAP Indian Training College 5 SA Infantry Btn	AFB Durban Salisbury Island Naval Base
Ladysmith **Newcastle** **Pietermaritzburg** **Ulundi**		Northern Natal Div Natal Division KwaZulu Police		
CAPE				
Cape Town	Western Province Command Southern Air Command Naval Operations Command Naval Logistics Command Naval Command Cape	Western Cape Division	SA Cape Corps School 1 SA Cape Corps Anti-Aircraft Artillery Defence School SAP Coloured Training College Ammunition School	AFB DF Malan AFB Ysterplaat Simonstown Naval Base
De Aar **East London** **George** **Grahamstown** **Kimberley**		Border Division N Cape Division	SA Army Women's College 6 SA Infantry Btn Danie Theron Combat school 1 Maintenance Unit Army Battle School Infantry School	AFB Kimberley
Lohatla **Oudtshoorn** **Paarl** **Port Elizabeth** **Saldanha**	S Cape Command EP Command	SW Districts Division Boland Division EP Division	Military Academy 4 Reconaissance Reg	AFB Port Elizabeth AFB Langebaanweg Naval Gymnasium 1 Marine Brigade
Umtata **Upington** **Zwelitsha**	Transkei Defence Force Ciskei Defence Force	Transkei Police Ciskei Police	1 TDF Btn 8 SA Infantry Btn	

TABLE XV: Occupation Forces in Namibia

SA DEFENCE FORCE

Standard Counter-Insurgency Forces	Mainly infantry units based at camps in the Operational Areas.
Reaction Forces	Highly trained, mobile units which can be helicoptered in to back up the standard forces.
Specialised Forces	Highly trained professional forces with specialised training and equipment, often secret.
Conventional Forces	Six brigades of mainly National Servicemen, each 7,000 strong, based in South Africa and deployed for attacks on Angola.
Walvis Bay Force	Navy, Air Force, Armour & Artillery Unit, Infantry battalion & National Service training facility.
Air Force	Reconnaissance, attack and helicopter squadrons.
Logistics & Administration	Back-up and supply structure covering the entire country.
Command	SADF officers and staff based in Windhoek and at sector HQs in the Operational Areas.

SWA TERRITORY FORCE

Standard Counter-Insurgency Forces	Six bantustan-related infantry battalions and one 'multi-ethnic' battalion, supplemented by Namibian National Servicemen.
Conventional Forces	White Citizen Force members based mainly in Windhoek. Trained for conventional war, but used mainly for Counter-Insurgency duties.
Area Defence Forces	More than 30 part-time mainly white Commando units based around the territory.
Air Force	Private light aircraft flown part-time by owners.
Logistics Administration & Command	Based south of the Operational Areas.

TABLE XV continued

SA POLICE

Police Counter-Insurgency Forces	Sent from SA to about 40 bases in the Operational Areas.
Uniformed & Security Police	Serving at police stations throughout the territory.
Railway Police	Administered by SA Railways.

SWA POLICE

Uniformed & Security Police	Work in parallel with SA Police. Also sent to the Operational Areas.
Special Constables	Bantustan-related units used in Counter-Insurgency work in the war zone.
Koevoet (COIN unit)	Special, highly mobile, counter-insurgency unit.
Special Task Force	Windhoek-based élite Counter-Insurgency unit.
Municipal Police	Armed police used in traffic control etc., also to suppress urban dissent.
Company Police	Established by private companies to protect installations.

Source: Resister, No.27, Aug./Sept. 1983.

TABLE XVI: Official SADF Figures on PLAN Operations in Namibia

	1977	1978	1979	1980	1981	1982	1983	1984
Contacts and ambushes	260	180	324	644	545	297	299	307
Mine incidents	211	190	245	327	349	311	188	169
Sabotage	0	30	59	84	37	46	41	96

Source: ISSUP *Strategic Review*, June 1985.

TABLE XVII: Area Defence Mobilisation by December 1985

Registration	Commando	Magisterial Districts
Feb 1983	Northern Natal	Paulpietersburg, Utrecht, Vryheid
July 1983	Piet Retief	Piet Retief
	Carolina	Carolina
	Nelspruit	Nelspruit, Witrivier, Waterval Boven
	Barberton	Barberton
Nov 1983	Soutpansberg	Soutpansberg, Messina, part of Pietersburg
Jan 1984	Ermelo	Ermelo
	Zeerust	Marico
	Potgietersrus	Potgietersrus
May 1984	Northam	Northern part of Rustenberg
	Thabazimbi	Thabazimbi
	Magol	Part of Waterberg (Ellisras)
	Pongola	Part of Piet Retief (Pongola), Ngotshe, Ubombo
	Phalaborwa	Part of Letaba
	Lydenberg	Lydenberg, Pilgrim's Rest
Sept 1984	Aliwal North	Aliwal North, Lady Grey, Wodehouse
	Bethlehem	Bethlehem
	Amatola	King Williams Town, Stutterheim, Komga
	Barkly East	Barkly East, Elliot, Maclear, Indwe
	Caledon river	Marquard, Clocolan
	Dundee & District	Dundee, Glencoe, part of Nqutu
	Ficksburg	Ficksburg
	Fouriesburg	Fouriesburg
	Harrismith	Harrismith
	Ladybrand	Ladybrand
	Midlands	Albany, Bathhurst, Alexandria
	Queenstown	Queenstown, Sterkstroom, Tarkastad, Cathcart
	Wepener	Wepener
	Winterberg	Adelaide, Bedford, Fort Beaufort
	Zastron	Zastron
April 1985	Letaba	Part of Letaba
	Pietersburg	Pietersburg
	Waterberg	Part of Waterberg
	Warmbad	Warmbad
	Stellenbosch	Stellenbosch, Strand, Somerset West (postponed in May 1985)
May 1985	Kimberley	Kimberley
	Klerksdorp	Klerksdorp
	Gatsrand	Oberholzer
	Potchefstroom	Potchefstroom
	Rustenberg	Rustenberg
	Stellaland/Kalahari	Vryburg
	Belfast	Belfast, Waterval Boven
	Loskop	Groblersdal
	Middelburg	Middelburg (Tvl)
	Standerton	Standerton
	Volksrust	Volksrust
	Wakkerstroom	Wakkerstroom, Amersfoort
	Witbank	Witbank
	Cradock	Cradock
	Humansdorp	Hankey, Humansdorp
	Kirkwood	Kirkwood
	Somerset East	Somerset East
	Umkhombe	Part of Lower Umfolozi, Hlabisa
	Pongola	Umbombo, Umqwawuma
Nov 1985	Brits	Brits
	Bronkhorstspruit	Bronkhorstspruit

Sources: Government Gazettes.

BIBLIOGRAPHY

Newspapers, Periodicals and Press Agencies

AA News	*Anti-Apartheid News*, Anti-Apartheid Movement, London
Africa-Asia	*Africa-Asia*, Paris
Africa News	*Africa News*, Durham, North Carolina
AIM	*Agencecia de Informacao de Mocambique*, Maputo
ANGOP	*Angencia Angola Press*, London
Annual Estimates	*Estimate of the Expenditure to be Defrayed From the State Revenue Account*, Pretoria
Argus	*Argus*, Cape Town
Armed Forces	*Armed Forces*, Johannesburg
Armed Forces (UK)	*Armed Forces*, London
BBC	*Survey of World Broadcasts*, British Broadcasting Corporation, London
BD	*Business Day*, Johannesburg
Burger	*Burger*, Cape Town
CCN Information	*CCN Information*, Council of Churches in Namibia, Windhoek
CH	*Cape Herald*, Cape Town
Cit	*Citizen*, Johannesburg
Combatant	*Combatant*, People's Liberation Army of Namibia, Lubango, Angola
CT	*Cape Times*, Cape Town
DD	*Daily Despatch*, East London
Debates	*House of Assembly Debates (Hansard)*, Cape Town/Pretoria
Defence Africa	*Defence Africa*, Winchester, Kent
Defence and Armament	*Defence and Armament*
DMS Market Intelligence	*DMS Market Intelligence Reports*, Greenwich, Connecticut
DN	*Daily News*, Durban
Economist	*Economist*, London
EPH	*Eastern Province Herald*, Port Elizabeth
Financial Gazette	*Financial Gazette*, Johannesburg
Flight International	*Flight International*, Sutton, Surrey
FM	*Financial Mail*, Johannesburg
FOCUS	*Focus on Political Repression in Southern Africa*, IDAF, London
FT	*Financial Times*, London
GG	*Government Gazette*, Pretoria
GN	*Guardian*, London
Grassroots	*Grassroots*, Cape Town
Hansard	*Parliamentary Debates*, House of Commons, London
Intercontinental Press	*Intercontinental Press*
International Defence Review	*International Defence Review*, Geneva
ISSUP Strategic Review	*Strategic Review*, Institute for Strategic Studies, University of Pretoria, Pretoria
Jane's Defence Review	*Jane's Defence Review*, London

Jane's Weapons Systems	*Jane's Weapons Systems*, London
LWI	*Lutheran World Information*, Geneva
Mail on Sunday	*Mail on Sunday*, London
Moto	*Moto*, Gweru, Zimbabwe
MS	*Morning Star*, London
Nam	*Namibian*, Windhoek
Namibia News Briefing	*Namibia News Briefing*, Namibia Support Committee, London
NCC	*Namibia Communications Centre*, London
New African	*New African*, London
New Statesman	*New Statesman*, London
NY Herald Tribune	*New York Herald Tribune*, New York
NYT	*New York Times*, New York
Obs	*Observer*, London
Paratus	*Paratus*, South African Defence Force, Pretoria
Post	*Post*, Johannesburg
RDM	*Rand Daily Mail*, Johannesburg
Resister	*Resister*, Committee on South African War Resistance, London
S	*Sowetan*, Johannesburg
SA Digest	*SA Digest*, Bureau for Information, Pretoria
SASPU National	*SASPU National*, South African Students' Press Union, Johannesburg
Sechaba	*Sechaba*, African National Congress, London
Servamus	*Servamus*, South African Police, Pretoria
SEx	*Sunday Express*, Johannesburg
SNS	Solidarity News Service, Gaberone
Soldier of Fortune	*Soldier of Fortune*, Boulder, Colorado
Southern Africa Record	*Southern Africa Record*, South African Institute of International Affairs, Johannesburg
SRC News	*SRC News*, Students Representative Council, University of Natal, Durban
S Star	*Sunday Star*, Johannesburg
ST	*Sunday Times*, Johannesburg
Star	*Star*, Johannesburg
State of the Nation	*State of the Nation*, South African Students' Press Union, Johannesburg
S Tel	*Sunday Telegraph*, London
Strategy and Defence	*Strategy and Defence*, Dublin
S Trib	*Sunday Tribune*, Durban
T	*Times*, London
Tel	*Daily Telegraph*, London
WA	*Windhoek Advertiser*, Windhoek
War Machine	*War Machine*, London
Weekend Argus	*Weekend Argus*, Cape Town
WIP	*Work in Progress*, Johannesburg
Wits Student	*Wits Student*, University of the Witwatersrand, Johannesburg
WM	*Weekly Mail*, Johannesburg
WO	*Windhoek Observer*, Windhoek
Yorkshire Post	*Yorkshire Post*, Leeds
Zambia Daily Mail	*Zambia Daily Mail*, Lusaka

Books and Articles

ADAMS, J., 1984, *The Unnatural Alliance: Israel and South Africa*, Quartet, London.

AFRICAN NATIONAL CONGRESS, 1980, *Fuelling Apartheid*, Notes & Documents No.13/1980, United Nations, New York.

AFRICAN NATIONAL CONGRESS, 1984, *Apartheid Destablisation*, ANC, Lusaka.

ANTI-APARTHEID MOVEMENT, 1981, *Plessey Arms Apartheid*, Anti-Apartheid Movement, London.

ANTI-APARTHEID MOVEMENT, 1984, *South African Aggression*, Seminar to Consider South Africa's Policies of Aggression and Destabilisation, London, 29.2.84

ANTI-APARTHEID MOVEMENT, 1985, *How Britain Arms Apartheid*, Anti-Apartheid Movement, London.

BADCOCK, P., 1981 *Images of War*, Graham, Durban.

BAILEY, M., 1980, *Oil Sanctions: South Africa's Weak Link*, Notes & Documents No.15/81, United Nations, New York.

BAILEY, M. 1981a, *Sasol: Financing of South Africa's Oil-from-coal Programme*, Notes & Documents No.8/1981, United Nations, New York.

BAILEY, M. 1981b, *Western Europe and the South African Oil Embargo*, Notes & Documents 9/81, United Nations, New York.

BAKER, P.H., 1976, *South Africa's Strategic Vulnerabilities: The 'Citadel Assumption' Reconsidered*, Paper presented at the Nineteenth Annual Meeting of the African Studies Association, Boston 3-6 November.

BARBER, J., 1973, *South Africa's Foreign Policy 1945-70*, Oxford University Press, London.

BROOKS, A. & BRICKHILL, J., 1980, *Whirlwind Before the Storm*, IDAF, London.

BUELL, J. & HORNER, D., 1985, *Weapons Implications of US-South African Uranium Trade*, Nuclear Control Institute, Washington.

CACHALIA, F., 1983, 'The State: Crisis and Restructuring 1970-80', *Africa Perspective* No.23.

CAMPBELL, R.K., 1984, *Sea Power and South Africa*, Institute for Strategic Studies, Pretoria.

CARD, [undated], *An Analysis of the Training Centre for Coloured Cadets Act No.46 of 1967, The Regulations Issued Thereunder and the System in Practice*, Campaign Against Racial Discrimination.

CCSA, 1981, *Arms For Apartheid*, Christian Concern for Southern Africa, London.

CENTRE OF AFRICAN STUDIES, 1982, *South Africa's Policy on Swaziland*, Centre of African Studies, Eduardo Mondlane University, Maputo.

CHARNEY, C., 1982, 'Business and Politics', *Management*, Oct.

CIIR & PAX CHRISTI, 1982, *War and Conscience: The Churches and Conscientious Objection in South Africa*, Catholic Institute of International Relations/Pax Christi, London.

COCKRAM, B., 1971, 'A Strategy for South Africa', *S.A. Journal of African Affairs*, Vol.1.

COETZEE, General P.J., 1983, *Urban Terror and Counter-Measures*, Conference Paper: Revolutionary Warfare and Counter Insurgency.

COMMISSIONER OF SAP, *Annual Report of the Commissioner of the South African Police*, Department of Law and Order, Republic of South Africa, Pretoria. (Various years).

COSAWR, 1982, *Some Aspects of South Africa's Military Occupation of Namibia*, Seminar on the Military Situation in and Relating to Namibia, UN Council for Namibia, Vienna.

COSAWR, 1984a, *State of War: Apartheid South Africa's Decade of Militarism*, Committee on South African War Resistance, London.

COSAWR, 1984b, *The South African Military–Industrial Complex: The Myth of Self-Sufficiency*, Committee of South African War Resistance, London. (unpublished paper)

COSAWR, 1984c, *The Apartheid Military Build Up*, International Hearing on South African Aggression Against the Neighbouring States, Oslo, 22-24 March 1984, Committee of South African War Resistance, London.

COSAWR–N, [undated], *The Militarisation of the Apartheid State*, Fact Paper No.1, Committee of South African War Resistance, Amsterdam.

CROCKER, C.A., 1980, *The South African Security Apparatus and the Regional Balance*, Paper prepared for the Foreign Policy Study Foundation.

DAVIES, R.H. & O'MEARA, D., 1982, *The State of Analysis of The Southern African Region: Issues Raised by South African Strategy*, Experts meeting on Problems and Priorities in Social Science Training in Southern Africa, Centre of African Studies, Eduardo Mondlane University, Maputo.

DAVIES, R & O'MEARA, D., 1983, *South Africa's Strategy in the Southern African Region: A Preliminary Analysis*, Centre of African Studies, Eduardo Mondlane University, Maputo.

DAVIES, D., O'MEARA, D. & DLAMINI, S., 1984, *The Struggle for South Africa: A Reference Guide to Movements, Organisations and Institutions*, Zed Books, London.

DEFENCE WHITE PAPER, *White Paper on Defence and Armaments Supply*, Department of Defence, Republic of South Africa, Pretoria (various years)

DSG/SARS, 1982, *Homeland Tragedy*, Southern Africa Research Services, Johannesburg.

DUTTON, General J., 1978, 'Military Aspects of National Security', Louw, H.H. (ed.) *National Security: A Modern Approach*, Institute for Strategic Studies, University of Pretoria,1978.

FAUVET, P., 1984a, *South Africa's War Against Mozambique*, International Hearing on South African Aggression Against Neighbouring States, Oslo.

FAUVET, P., 1984b, *Roots of Counter-Revolution: The MNR*, Review of African Political Economy, No.29, July 1984.

FOURIE, D., 1975, *Strategic Consequences for SA of Events in Southern Africa*, Natal Branch, South African Institute of International Affairs, 25.3.75 (mimeographed speech).

FRANKEL, P., 1980, 'Race and Counter-Revolution: South Africa's Total Strategy', *Journal of Commonwealth and Comparative Politics*, Vol.18, No.3, Oct. 1980.

FRANKEL, P., 1984, *Pretoria's Praetorians: Civil–Military Relations in South Africa*, Cambridge University Press.

FULLERTON, J., 1979, 'South Africa: Day of the Generals', *Now!* 5.10.79.

GANN, L.H. & DUIGAN, P., 1981, *Why South Africa Will Survive*, Croom Helm, London.

GELDENHUYS, D., 1978, *South Africa's Search for Security Since the Second World War*, South African Institute of International Affairs, Johannesburg.

GELDENHUYS, D., 1980, 'Some Strategic Implications of Regional Economic Relationships for the Republic of South Africa', *Strategic Review*, January.

GELDENHUYS, D., 1981, *Some Foreign Policy Implications of SA's 'Total National Strategy' with Particular Reference to the '12 Point Plan'*, South African Institute of International Affairs, Johannesburg.

GELDENHUYS, D., 1982, *The Destabilisation Controversy: An Analysis of a High Risk Foreign Policy Option for SA*.

GELDENHUYS, D., 1983, 'Recrossing the Matola Threshold: the "Terrorist Factor" in SA's Regional Relations', *SA International*, Vol.13, No.3, January.

GELDENHUYS, D., 1984, *The Diplomacy of Isolation: South Africa's Foreign Policy Making*, Macmillan, Johannesburg.

GELDENHUYS, D & KOTZE, H., 1983, 'Aspects of Political Decision Making in South Africa', *Politikon*, Vol.10, No.1, June.

GRAY, M., 1985, *Press Under Pressure: Militarization and Propaganda in South Africa*, Commonwealth Secretariat, London.

GRUNDY, K.W., 1978, *Defence Legislation and Communal Politics: The Evolution of a White South African Nation as Reflected in the Controversy over the Assignment of Armed Forces Abroad, 1912-1976'*, Ohio University Centre for International Studies Africa Programme.

GRUNDY, K.W., 1983a, *Soldiers Without Politics: Blacks in the South African Armed Forces*, University of California Press, Berkeley, California.

GRUNDY, K.W., 1983b, *The Rise of the South African Security Establishment*, Bradlow Paper No.1, SA Institute of International Affairs, Johannesburg.

GUTTERIDGE, W., *SA: Strategy for Survival?* Institute for the Study of Conflict.

GUTTERIDGE, W., 1980, *SA's Defence Posture*, The World Today, January.

HANLON, J., 1984, *Mozambique — The Revolution Under Fire*, Zed Books, London.

HAYSOM, N., 1983, *Ruling with the Whip*, Centre for Applied Legal Studies, University of the Witwatersrand, Johannesburg.

HEITMAN, H.R. 1985, *The South African War Machine*, Galago Publishing, Bromley, Kent.

HOLNESS, M., 1983, *Apartheid's War Against Angola*, UN Centre Against Apartheid/World Campaign Against Military and Nuclear Collaboration with South Africa, London.

HOUGH, M., 1980, 'The Political Implications of the Possession of Nuclear Weapons For South Africa' *ISSUP Strategic Review*, May.

IDAF, 1974, *Rhodesia: South Africa's Sixth Province*, IDAF, London.

IDAF, 1980a, *Nelson Mandela: The Struggle is My Life*, IDAF, London.

IDAF, 1980b, *The Apartheid War Machine: The Strength and Deployment of the South African Armed Forces*, Fact Paper on Southern Africa, No.8, IDAF, London.

IDAF, 1980c, *Namibia: The Facts*, IDAF, London.

IDAF, 1981a, *Namibia: The Constitutional Fraud*, Briefing Paper No.2, IDAF, London.

IDAF, 1981b, *South Africa: Entrenchment of White Domination*, Briefing Paper No.3, IDAF, London.

IDAF, 1982a, *Apartheid's Army in Namibia: South Africa's Illegal Military Occupation*, Fact Paper on Southern Africa No.10, IDAF, London.

IDAF, 1982b, *Apartheid in Namibia Today*, Briefing paper No.4, IDAF, London.

IDAF, 1982c, *Namibia: The Elusive Settlement*, Briefing Paper No.6, IDAF, London.

IDAF, 1983a, *Apartheid The Facts*, IDAF, London.

IDAF, 1983b, 'Chronology of South African Aggression Against Frontline and Neighbouring States, 1982', *Documentation Set for Public Hearing on South African Aggression*, Netherlands Anti-Apartheid Movement, Amsterdam.

IDAF, 1983c, *South African Aggression*, Briefing Paper No.7, IDAF, London.

IDAF, 1983d, *Fighting for Namibia*, Briefing Paper No.8, IDAF, London.

IDAF, 1984a, *Repression and Resistance in South Africa*, Briefing Paper No.11, IDAF, London.

IDAF, 1984b, *Namibia: Settlement Negotiations*, Briefing Paper No.12, IDAF, London.

IDAF, 1984c, *Repression and Resistance in Namibia*, Briefing Paper No.14, IDAF, London.

IDAF, 1985a, *Repression and Resistance in South Africa*, Briefing Paper No.15, IDAF, London.

IDAF, 1985b, *Reshaping the Constitution of Apartheid*, Briefing Paper No.16, IDAF, London.

IDAF, 1985c, *South African Attack on Botswana*, Briefing Paper No.18, IDAF, London.

IDAF, 1985d, *State of Emergency*, Briefing Paper No.19, IDAF, London.

IDAF, 1985e, *Massacre at Maseru: South African Aggression Against Lesotho*, Fact Paper No.12, IDAF, London.

IISS MILITARY BALANCE, *The Military Balance*, International Institute for Strategic Studies, London. (Various years).

JASTER, R.S., 1980, *South Africa's Narrowing Security Options*, Adelphi Papers No.159, International Institute for Strategic Studies, London.

JASTER, R.S., 1983, *A Regional Security Role for Africa's Front Line States: Experience and Prospects*, Adelphi Papers No.180, International Institute for Strategic Studies, London.

KINGDOM OF LESOTHO, 1983, *Destabilisation: A Brief to the Lesotho Parliament by the Prime Minister, the Rt. Hon. Dr. Leaubua Jonathan, on South Africa's Activities against Lesotho*,, Prime Minister's Press Office, Maseru.

KLINGVIEW, A.J., 1980, *The Angolan War: A Study in Soviet Policy in the Third World*, Westview Press, Boulder, Colorado.

KONIG, B., 1983, *Namibia, The Ravages of War*, IDAF, London.

KUHNE, W., 1984, *Sudafrika in den 80er Jahren: Militarisierung Einer Gesellschaft und Einer Region*, Stiftung Wissenschaft und Politik, Ebenhausen, January.

LEONARD, R., 1983, *South Africa at War: White Power and the Crisis in Southern Africa*, Lawrence Hill & Co., Westport, Connecticut.

LIPTON, M., 1970, 'British Arms for South Africa', *The World Today*, October.

LLOYD, C.J., 1979, *The Importance of Rural Development in the Defence Strategy of South Africa and the Need for Private Sector Involvement*, Urban Foundation Workshop, Durban, 10.8.79.

LOBSTEIN, T., (ed.), 1984, *Namibia: Reclaiming the People's Health*, Namibia Support Committee, London.

LODGE, T., 1984, 'The African National Congress in South Africa 1976–83: Guerilla War and Armed Propaganda', *Journal of Contemporary African Studies*, Vol.3,No.1/2, Oct.1983–Apr. 1984.

LOMBARD, J.A., 1978, 'The Economic Aspects of National Security', Louw, H.H. (ed.) *National Security: A Modern Approach*, Institute for Strategic Studies, University of Pretoria.

LOUW, H.H., 1978a, 'Introduction to the National Security Concept', Louw, H.H., (ed.) *National Security: A Modern Approach*, Institute for Strategic Studies, University of Pretoria.

LOUW, H.H., 1978b, 'The Nature of National Security in the Modern Age', Louw, H.H., (ed.) *National Security: A Modern Approach*, Institute for Strategic Studies, University of Pretoria.

LOUW, H.H., 1978c (ed.), *National Security: A Modern Approach*, Institute for Strategic Studies, University of Pretoria.

LOWIN, D.R., 1977, *Causes and Aspects of the Growth of the SADF and the Military Industrial Complex 1960–77*, MA Dissertation, University of York Centre for Southern African Studies.

MALAN, Gen. M.A., 1983, *Address to the Industrialists' Association*, Kempton Park, 16.6.83.

MATTELART, A., 1978, 'Notes on the Ideology of the Military State'. *Communication & Class Struggle Vol.1*, Mattelart, A. & Slelgelaub, S., (ed.), International General, New York & International Mass Media Research Centre, Bagnolet, France.

MINTY, A.S., 1969, *South Africa's Defence Strategy*, Anti-Apartheid Movement, London.

MINTY, A.S., 1985, *Oil as a Strategic Commodity*, Conference of Maritime Trade Unions, London.

MOORCRAFT, P.L., 1977, *Towards the Garrison State*, Symposium of International Pressures and Political Change, University of Natal, 26.8.77.

MOORCRAFT, P.L. — MCLAUGHLIN, P., 1982, *Chimurenga! The War in Rhodesia 1965-1980*, Sygma Books, Johannesburg.

MOSS, G., 1980, 'Total Strategy', *Work in Progress* No.11.

MOZAMBIQUE ANGOLA COMMITTEE, 1984, *South Africa's Undeclared War Against Mozambique*, Mozambique Angola Committee, London.

NARMIC, 1982, *Automating Apartheid: US Computer Exports to South Africa and the Arms Embargo*, American Friends Service Committee, Philadelphia.

NARMIC, 1984, *Military Exports to South Africa*, American Friends Service Committee, Phildelphia.

NETHERLANDS AAM, 1980, *The Philips Connection*, Netherlands Anti-Apartheid Movement, Amsterdam.

NETHERLANDS AAM, 1984, *Report of the Proceedings of the Public Hearing on South African Aggression in Southern Africa*, Netherlands Anti-Apartheid Movement, Amsterdam.

NUSAS, 1982, *Total War in South Africa: Militarisation and the Apartheid State*, National Union of South African Students, Cape Town.

NUSAS, 1983, *South Africa's Bantustans: The Pillars of Apartheid*, National Union of South African Students, Cape Town.

NUSAS, 1984, *In Whose Defence?*, National Union of South African Students, Cape Town.

O'MEARA, D., 1982, *Muldergate and the Politics of Afrikaner Nationalism*,

Supplement to *Work in Progress* No.22, April 1982, Johannesburg.

OVENDALE, R., 1983, 'The South African Policy of the British Labour Government 1947-51', *International Affairs*.

PARSONS, N., 1982, *A New History of Southern Africa*, Macmillan, London.

PEOPLE'S REPUBLIC OF ANGOLA, 1983, *White Paper on Acts of Agression by the Racist South African Regime Against the People's Republic of Angola, 1975–1982*, Ministry of External Relations, Luanda.

PUTTER, Rear-Admiral A.P., 1982, 'South African Maritime Policy' *Contemporary Maritime Strategy*, Institute for Strategic Studies, Pretoria.

REED, J., 1982, 'Defending the South Atlantic – A Quandry for the West?', *Armed Forces* (UK), July.

ROGERS, B., 1980, '*Divide and Rule': South Africa's Bantustans*, IDAF, London.

ROHERTY, J.M., 1984, 'Managing the Security Base in South Africa', *South Africa International*, Vol.15, No.2, October, South Africa Foundation.

ROTBERG, R.I., 1983, *The Process of Decision Making in Contemporary South Africa*, African Studies Programme, Georgetown University Centre for Strategic and International Studies, No.22.

SAIRR SURVEY, *Survey of Race Relations in South Africa*, South African Institute of Race Relations, Johannesburg. (Various years).

SEFALI, Dr. M., 1983, *Address to the Public Hearing on South African Aggression in Southern Africa*, Netherlands Anti-Apartheid Movement, 1983.

SEILER, J., 1980, 'SA's Regional Role', *Southern Africa Since the Portuguese Coup*, (ed.), Seiler, J., Westview Press, Boulder, Colorado.

SEILER, J., [undated], *The South African State Security System*, School of International Studies, US Army John F. Kennedy Special Warfare Centre.

SIMONS, J & SIMONS, R., 1983, *Class and Colour in South Africa, 1850–1950*, IDAF, London.

SIPRI, 1976, *Southern Africa: The Escalation of a Conflict*, Almquvist & Wiksell, Stockholm.

SIPRI YEARBOOK, *World Armaments and Disarmament Yearbook*, SIPRI (various years).

SMITH, D., 1980 *South Africa's Nuclear Capability*, World Campaign Against Military and Nuclear Collaboration with South Africa, Oslo.

SOLIDARITY NEWS SERVICE, 1984, *South Africa – The Militarisation of a Society*, International Hearing on South African Aggression Against the Neighbouring States, Oslo, 22.24 March 1984.

SOUTH AFRICA (REPUBLIC OF) 1970, *Report of the Commission of Inquiry into Matters Relating to the Security of the State* (abridged), Government Printer, Pretoria.

SOUTH AFRICA (REPUBLIC OF) 1982, *Report of the Commission of Inquiry into Security Legislation*, Government Printer, Pretoria.

SOUTHERN AFRICAN CATHOLIC BISHOP'S CONFERENCE, 1982, *Report on Namibia*, Southern African Catholic Bishop's Conference, Pretoria.

SOUTHERN AFRICAN CATHOLIC BISHOP'S CONFERENCE, 1984, *Report on Police Conduct During Township Protests*, SACBC and Catholic Institute for International Affairs, London.

STEENKAMP, Major-General E.M.A., 1984, *Press Briefing for Accredited Foreign Correspondents on the History, Aims, Activities and the Level of Threat Posed by the ANC'*, Cape Town, 8.2.84.

STEENKAMP, W., 1983, 'The SADF – Rogue Elephant, Slave of Circumstance or

Cyclops in the Land of the Blind?', *Leadership SA*, Vol.2, No.4.

STOCKWELL, J., 1978, *In Search of Enemies: A CIA Story*, Andre Deutsch, London.

SUTER, K.D., 1980, *The Laws of Armed Conflicts and Apartheid*, Notes and Documents 24/80, United Nations, New York.

SWAPO, 1981, *To be Born a Nation: The Liberation Struggle for Namibia*, Zed Press, London.

THORNHILL, C., 1983, 'Administrative Arrangements for Change', in van Vuuren D.J., Wiehahn N.E., Lombard J.A., Rhoodie N.J., *Change in South Africa*, Butterworths, Durban.

TOMASELLI, K., 1984, 'Adapt or Die: Militarisation and the Mass Media', *Reality*, Jan/1984, p.9.

TRAINOR, L., 1975, *South African Foreign Policy: The Immediate Impact of the Portuguese Coup*, SA Institute of International Affairs, 10.4.75.

UNITED NATIONS, 1981, *South Africa's Plan and Capability in the Nuclear Field*, Doc. A/35/402, United Nations, New York.

UN COUNCIL FOR NAMIBIA, 1983, *The Military Situation in and Relating to Namibia*, United Nations General Assembly, New York.

UN UNIT ON APARTHEID, 1967, *Military and Police Forces in the Republic of South Africa*, United Nations, New York.

UN UNIT ON APARTHEID, 1970, *Security Council Resolutions on Apartheid*, UN, New York.

VENTER, D., 1976, 'South Africa as an African Power', *Bulletin of the Africa Institute of SA*, No's. 5 & 6.

VISSER, J.A., [undated], *The South African Defence Force's Contribution to the Development of South West Africa*, Military Information Bureau, SADF.

WASHINGTON OFFICE ON AFRICA, 1982, *Stop the Apartheid Bomb*, Washington Office on Africa, Washington.

WASHINGTON OFFICE ON AFRICA EDUCATION FUND, 1985, *The September 22, 1979, Mystery Flash: Did South Africa Detonate a Nuclear Bomb?*, Washington Office on Africa Education Fund, Washington.

WEAVER, T., 1983, 'Caught in the Crossfire: The War in Namibia', *Work in Progress*, No.29, October.

WOLFERS, M. & BERGEROL, J., 1983, *Angola in the Frontline*, Zed Press, London.

WOOD, B., 1984, 'The Militarisation of Namibia's Economy', *Review of African Political Economy*, No.29, July.

WORLD CAMPAIGN AGAINST MILITARY AND NUCLEAR COLLABORATION WITH SOUTH AFRICA, 1984, *Statements by Major-General J.N. Garba and A.S. Minty Before the Security Council Committee*, World Campaign, Oslo.

References

1: Rule of the Gun

1. Grundy [1983a], p.34.
2. Frankel [1984].
3. Grundy [1978], p.11; Frankel [1984], p.27
4. *Cavalry Journal*, date unknown, probably 1909, pp.188–9.
5. Frankel [1984], p.14.
6. Simons & Simons [1983], pp.156–61.
7. Simons & Simons [1983], pp.167–9.
8. Simons & Simons [1983], p.177; Grundy [1978], pp.15–20.
9. Grundy [1983a], pp.51–8.
10. Simons & Simons [1983], pp.252–3/303.
11. Simons & Simons [1983], pp.286–96.
12. *Star*, 9.2.80.
13. *Paratus*, July 1982, p.36.
14. *Senate Debates* 1940–41, cols. 13–14.
15. Grundy [1978], p.30; *Paratus*, July 1982, p.37.
16. Grundy [1983a], pp.63–80.
17. Grundy [1983a], pp.70–82.
18. Simons & Simons [1983], p.554.
19. Simons & Simons [1983], p.557.
20. Jaster [1980], p.6.
21. Ovendale [1983], pp.44–6.
22. Jaster [1980], pp.49–50.
23. *Paratus*, July 1978, p.16; November 1979, pp.12–15.
24. Jaster [1980], p.7.
25. Commissioner of SAP [1974], p.20.
26. Jaster [1980], p.5.
27. *Paratus*, July 1982, p.37.
28. *Kommando*, May 1960, pp.5–6.
30. IDAF [1980a], p.10.
30. SAIRR *1959–60 Survey*, pp.52–61.
31. SAIRR *1959–60 Survey*, p.73.
32. SAIRR *1959–60 Survey*, pp.63–4.
33. *Kommando* [May 1980], p4.
34. SAIRR *1959–60 Survey*, pp.64–8; *Kommando*, May 1980, pp.4–13.
35. SAIRR *1961 Survey*, p.52.
36. SAIRR *1959–60 Survey*, p.41.
37. SAIRR *1961 Survey*, p.47.
38. IDAF [1980a], pp.153–4.
39. Jaster [1980], p.12.
40. UN Unit on Apartheid [1967], p.1.
41. Minty [1969], pp.2–3.
42. *RDM*, 22.10.68.
43. Smith [1980], pp.8–9.
44. Jaster [1980], p.19.
45. Jaster [1983], p.4.
46. *BBC*, 18.6.79; IDAF [1980b], p.65; Moorcraft & McLaughlin, [1982], pp.167–8.
47. IDAF [1980b], p.65; *FT* 4.8.79.
48. Jaster [1983], p.19.
49. SWAPO [1981], p.174.
50. SWAPO [1981], p.176.
51. SWAPO [1981], p.177.
52. SWAPO [1981], p.177.
53. SWAPO [1981], p.178.
54. IDAF [1980b], p.53.
55. IDAF [1980b], p.54.; SWAPO [1981], pp.188–203.
56. IDAF [1983], p.73; Minty [1969], p.13.
57. Jaster [1980], p.18; Minty [1969], pp.13–14.
58. Jaster [1980], p.19.
59. Jaster [1980], pp.19–20; Minty [1969], pp.19–21.
60. *Debates* 26.4.72; *Star* 25.11.72.
61. *ST* 2.9.73.

62. Jaster [1980], p.20; IDAF [1980b], p.41.
63. IDAF [1980b], p.35.
64. *1973 Defence White Paper*, pp.6–13.
65. *RDM*, 25.1.71.
66. *1973 Defence White Paper*, p.5.
67. *1973 Defence White Paper*, p.4.
68. *1973 Defence White Paper*, p.2.

2: The Apartheid Security Strategy

1. Trainor [1975], p.1.
2. Jaster [1980], p.22.
3. *1977 Defence White Paper*, p.11.
4. *Hansard* 22.4.75, Col. 4551.
5. Trainor [1975], p.2.
6. IDAF [1980b], pp.54–61; Wolfers & Bergerol [1983], pp.2–44.
7. Grundy [1983b], pp.28–9.
8. IDAF [1982a], pp.12–14.
9. Brooks & Brickhill [1980], pp.256–60.
10. Seiler [undated], p.1.
11. Davies, O'Meara and Dlamini [1984], pp.30–8; Cachalia [1983], pp.13–16; Charney [1982]; Davies & O'Meara [1982]; Moss [1980].
12. South Africa (Republic of) [1970], p.34.
13. *1975 Defence White Paper*, p.4.
14. O'Meara [1982].
15. *1975 Defence White Paper*, pp.3–4.
16. Seiler [undated], pp.2–3.
17. Leonard [1983], p.199; *FM*, 2.4.82; *Christian Science Monitor*, 19.12.80.
18. *Resister*, No. 30, Feb.–Mar. 1984, pp.12–13.
19. *Southern Africa Record*, No.40, Oct.1985, p.8.
20. Frankel [1984], p.11.
21. Frankel [1984], p.46.
22. Frankel [1984], pp.46–52; *Star* 29.1.82.
23. *Southern Africa Record*, No.40, Oct.1985, pp.6–7.
24. *1977 Defence White Paper*, p.1.
25. *1977 Defence White Paper*, p.4.
26. *1977 Defence White Paper*, p.5.
27. Louw [1978c].
28. Dutton [1978], p.105.
29. Dutton [1978], p.114.
30. Dutton [1978], p.113.
31. Moss [1980], p.7.
32. Geldenhuys & Kotze [1983], p.36–7.
33. *Star*, 5.8.79.
34. Geldenhuys & Kotze [1983], p.36; Thornhill [1983], p.83.
35. COSAWR [1984], p.7; Grundy [1983b], p.10.
36. IDAF [1985b], pp.1–3.
37. *1977 Defence White Paper*, pp.1,5.
38. *Debates* 29.4.80, col.5087.
39. Geldenhuys [1981], pp.26–7.
40. Geldenhuys [1984], p.90.
41. Frankel [1984], p.44; Geldenhuys [1984], p.90.
42. Leonard [1983], pp.202–3.
43. Charney [1982], p.27.
44. Lombard [1978], pp.92–3.
45. Lombard [1978], p.95.
46. Lombard [1978], p.92.
47. Cachalia [1983], p.20; O'Meara [1982], p.16.
48. Geldenhuys & Kotze [1983], p.35.
49. Geldenhuys [1984], p.92.
50. Frankel [1980], p.277.
51. Geldenhuys & Kotze [1983], p.40.
52. *CT*, 23.1.82.
53. Grundy [1983b], p.15.
54. *Resister*, No.15, Aug./Sept. 1981, p.15.
55. Grundy [1983b], p.15.
56. Geldenhuys & Kotze [1983], p.40.
57. Rotberg [1983], p.6.
58. Seiler [undated], p.6.
59. Rotberg [1983], p.5.

60. Geldenhuys & Kotze [1983], p.41.
61. Grundy [1983b], p.16.; Rotberg [1983], p.5.
62. Seiler [undated], p.12; Geldenhuys & Kotze [1983], p.41; Geldenhuys [1984], p.93.
63. Seiler [undated], p.12.
64. *ST*, 11.7.82.
65. Grundy, [1983b], p.12.
66. Geldenhuys [1984], p.147.
67. *Obs*, 13.1.80; Fullerton [1979].
68. *Obs*, 13.1.80.
69. Fullerton [1979].
70. *T*, 16.1.80.
71. *DD*, 15.1.80.
72. *RDM*, 15.1.80.
73. *S*, 9.2.82; *Obs*, 13.1.80.
74. *S*, 9.2.82; *Star*, 5.10.82.
75. *ST*. 24.5.81.
76. Grundy [1983b], p.13; Geldenhuys [1984], p.149.
77. Roherty [1984], p.62.
78. *SEx*, 14.2.82.
79. *GN*, 18.5.82.
80. *SEx*, 14.2.82; *FM*, 4.6.82.
81. *FM*, 4.6.82.
82. *FM*, 4.6.82.
83. Roherty, [1984], p.62.
84. *ST*, 4.9.83.

3: Mobilising for War

1. *CT*, 25.4.75.
2. *T*, 11.12.80.
3. *Paratus*, March 1982, pp.16–20.
4. *Paratus*, April 1982, p.34.
5. *Paratus*, June 1983.
6. *S Post*, 30.3.80.
7. *SEx*, 20.4.80.
8. NUSAS [1982], p.52.
9. *Burger*, 2.2.80
10. Unpublished interview with SADF deserter, COSAWR (N), 1981.
11. *Resister*, No.33 Aug./Sept. 1984, p.17.
12. *Resister*, No. 33 Aug./Sept. 1984, p.17.
13. COSAWR [1984], p.16.
14. *Argus*, 26.10.79.
15. *Star*, 5.9.85.
16. *Resister*, No.34, Oct./Nov. 1984, pp.18–19.
17. Personal interviews by COSAWR.
18. SATIS Press Release, London, 27.9.84
19. *Star*, 22.3.85.
20. *CT*, 24.3.80.
21. *RDM*, 25.3.80.
22. *CT*, 26.3.80.
23. *RDM*, 25.4.80.
24. *ST*, 29.6.80; *SEx* 6.7.80.
25. *RDM*, 2.11.81.
26. Tomaselli [1984], p.9.
27. *ST*, 7.5.78.
28. *S Trib*, 7.5.78
29. Solidarity News Service [1984], p.10.
29. *Resister* No.28 Oct./Nov. 1983, p.8.
30. *Uniform*, Jan.84.
31. *The Journalist*, Nov. 1981.
32. Gray [1985], p.11.
33. *New African*, Aug.1980, p.50.
34. *Resister*, No.28, Oct./Nov. 1983, p.8; *GN* 17.11.84.
35. Solidarity News Service, [1984], p.9.
36. *Resister*, No.28, Oct./Nov. 1983, p.8.
37. Gray [1984], p.11.
38. *SEx*, 30.12.79.
39. *CT*, 6.12.79.
40. *BBC*, 16.4.90.
41. Gray [1984], pp.9–10.
42. *Star*, 14.9.84.
43. GN, 28.9.81
44. *RDM* 2.11.81.
45. *Cit/BBC*, 30.8.85; *DD*, 31.8.85; *CT*, 5/18.10.85; *S Trib* 3.11.85.
46. Tomaselli [1984], p.9.
47. *SEx*, 30.3.80
48. *RDM*, 21.8.84.
49. *Paratus*, Feb. 1981, p.49.
50. *CT*, 26.1.76.
51. *ST*, 18.1.76, 14.3.76.
52. *RDM*, 6.2.76.

53. *Paratus*, Nov. 1981, p.51.
54. *1982 Defence White Paper.*
55. Objects shown to COSAWR by National Servicemen; *CT* 15.8.78.
56. *Paratus* Supplement, June 1978.
57. See, for example, *Paratus*, Nov. 1979, p.49.
58. *Paratus*, Nov. 1979.
59. *CT*, 10.1.78.
60. *Resister*, No.25, Apr./May 1983.
61. *Cit*, 18.8.78; *SEx*, 20.1.80.
62. *CT*, 8.12.83.
63. *ST*, 15.10.78.
64. *Paratus*, Jan. 1980; *Star* 3.2.79.
65. *Paratus*, Dec. 1980, p.39.
66. *Paratus*, Jan. 1981, p.19.
67. *Paratus*, Aug. 1980.
68. *RDM*, 21.7.82.
69. *Star*, 14.2.81.
70. For example, *Welcome Home*, supplement to *DN*, 24.6.80.
71. *ST*, 6.9.81.
72. IDAF [1983], p.28.
73. *RDM*, 11.3.78.
74. NUSAS [1982], p.58.
75. *RDM*, 14.10.76.
76. *Paratus*, Sept. 1978, p.30.
77. *Armed Forces*, May 1983, p.18; *Paratus*, Sept. 1978, p.30.
78. *Debates*, 19.3.85.
79. NUSAS [1982], pp.62–3.
80. *SA Digest*, 6.6.80, p.28.
81. *CT*, 10.9.83.
82. NUSAS [1982], p.63.
83. *CT*, 7.6.78.
84. *ST*, 14.2.78.
85. *Cit*, 18.5.78.
86. *CT*, 7.6.78.
87 *Debates*, 17.8.83
88. *Grassroots*, 4.3.82.
89. *Grassroots*, 4.3.82.
90. *Debates*, 19.3.85.
91. *Paratus* Mar. 1981, Aug. 1979; *Star*, 8.5.78.
92. *Wits Student*, 15.5.79, pp.8–9.
93. *Wits Student*, 15.5.79.
94. NUSAS [1982], p.66.
95. *Wits Student*, 15.5.79, p.9.
96. *S Star*, 4.8.85.
97. *SEx*, 16.9.79.
98. *Paratus* [1985], p.52.
99. *Resister*, No.24, Feb./Mar. 1983, p.8.
100. *Resister*, No.24, Feb./Mar. 1983, p.8.
101. NUSAS [1982], p.72.
102. *SRC News*, University of Natal, Durban, Sept. 1981.
103. *FM*, 15.10.76.
104. *ST*, 24.10.76.
105. *RDM*, 11.10.76.
106. *ST*, 30.1.77.
107. *SEx* 16.5.81.
108. *ST*, 27.11.83.
109. *DN*, 5.12.84
110. *S Star*, 1.12.85.
111. *Resister*, No.25, Apr./May 1983, p.20.

4: Conscription and Recruitment

1. *1982 Defence Amendment Act.*
2. Barber [1973], p.195.
3. SIPRI [1976], p.121.
4. *Resister*, No.19, Apr./May 1982, p.15.
5. *Resister*, No.19, Apr./May 1982, p.14.
6. *FM*, 15.1.82.
7. *Debates*, 25.3.85.
8. *SA Digest*, 7.6.74; *Debates*, 22.4.77.
9. *Star*, 25.3.82 – the total then given was 3,000.
10. *1984 Defence White Paper*, p.13.
11. *Resister*, No.34, Oct./Nov. 1984, p.9.
12. *1982 Defence White Paper.*
13. *Debates*, 12.3.85.
14. *Debates*, 15.2.63, Col.1576.
15. *Debates*, 31.8.70.
16. *Star*, 15.6.74.
17. IDAF [1980b], p.40.

18. *Defence Act, No.44 of 1957,* Sec.2.
19. Grundy [1983a], pp.158–9.
20. Grundy [1983a], p.163.
21. *Training centres for Coloured Cadets Act, No.46 of 1967.*
22. *Burger*, 8.3.67; CARD [undated], p.6.
23. *Post*, 29.11.70.
24. SAIRR *1967 Survey*, pp.218–9.
25. CARD [undated], p.3; Grundy, [1983b], p.181.
26. CARD [undated], p.8; *CT*, 9.8.72.
27. *RDM*, 10.5.69.
28. See Chapter 3.
29. *CT*, 15.7.72, 12.8.72.
30. *Argus*, 18.11.76; *Star*, 28.8.76.
31. Grundy [1983a], p.167, estimates 4,900 Coloureds in service in 1982.
32. *ST*, 30.11.75.
33. *RDM*, 28.11.80.
34. *Cit*, 5.12.84.
35 NUSAS [1984], p.45.
36. Grundy [1983a], p.171.
37. *S*, 27.3.85.
38. *GN*, 23.12.80.
39. *Debates*, 12.3.85
40. *CT*, 24.8.82.
41. *ST*, 16.6.74.
42. *Star*, 15.6.74.
43. *ST*, 16.6.74.
44. *RDM*, 21.2.76.
45. *SEx*, 22.1.78.
46. *RDM*, 26.5.78.
47. *Paratus*, May 1978, pp.10–11.
48. *New York Times*, 16.9.79; Grundy [1983a], p.200–1.
49. *Paratus*, June 1985, p.53.
50. *Paratus*, June 1985, p.54.
51. Grundy [1983a], p.203.
52. *RDM*, 27.5.80.
53. *RDM*, 3.12.83 (see Chapter 9).
54. *CT*, 12.9.83.
55. *Obs*, 26.4.81.
56. *White Paper on Defence, 1982.*
57. *BBC*, 7.1.85.
58. *WA*, 31.10.84; *Star*, 13.12.84.
59. CIIR & Pax Christi [1982], pp.26–7.
60 CIIR & Pax Christi [1982], p.78.
61. *Section 121 (c) of the Defence Act of 1957* as amended.
62. *Debates*, 17.2.78.
63. *CT*, 5.12.79.
64. CIIR & Pax Christi [1982], pp.54–7.
65. See issues of *Resister* for this period.
66. *Resister*, No.25, Apr./May 1983, pp.2–3.
67. Solidarity News Service, No.20/ 1984.
68. *S Trib*, 21.10.84.
69. *S Trib*, 28.10.84.
70. Issues of *Resister*, 1984–85.
71. Supplement to *Paratus*, Sept. 1984.
72. *Star*, 20.10.84; *SEx*, 14.10.84.
73. *FOCUS*, Special Issue No.2, Apr. 1981, p.7.
74. *GN*, 29.1.81.
75. *GN*, 29.1.81.
76. *GN*, 23.3.81.
77. *ST*, 22.11.81.
78. *FOCUS*, Special Issue No.2, Apr. 1981, p.7; BBC, 7.2.81
79. *S.Tel. Magazine*, 27.2.83.
80. *Soldier of Fortune*, Oct. 1984, p.66.
81. *S.Tel.*, 15.6.80.
82. *Anti-Apartheid News*, May 1983.
83. *Soldier of Fortune*, June 1983.
84. *S. Tel.*, 27.4.80.
85. *New African*, June 1981.
86. *SEx*, 1.6.80.
87. *S Tel*, 27.4.80; *SEx*, 1.6.80; *T*, 19.9.80.
88. *Resister*, No.13, Apr./May 1983, p.9.
89. *Star*, 23.6.81.
90. *DD*, 30.5.81
91. *RDM*, 8.3.83.
92. *Star*, 28.11.81; *Sowetan*, 27.11.81.
93. *New African*, Jan. 1982; *SEx*, 21.3.82; *Star*, 30.3.82.

94. *Debates*, 12.2.82; 19.2.82.
95. *Resister*, Apr./May 1983, pp.8–9.

5: Arming Apartheid – Towards a War Economy

1. *1984 Defence White Paper*, p.18.
2. *1983 SIPRI Yearbook*, pp.195–212.
3. *Resister*, No.32, June/July 1984, p.18.
4. *Resister*, No.32, June/July 1984, p.18.
5. *Business Day*, 19.3.85.
6. *FM*, 29.7.83.
7. *RDM*, 6.10.84.
8. *FM*, 6.10.78.
9. *Debates*, 22.4.75; *1977 Defence White Paper*.
10. *GN*, 29.3.84.
11. Lombard [1978], pp.98–9.
12. *Star*, 17.1.76.
13. *RDM*, 17.4.74; *FM*, 27.1.84.
14. *ST*, 18.11.79.
15. *ST*, 26.8.84.
16. *1973 Defence White Paper*, p.7.
17. *Africa Now*, June 1981; *FT*, 24.20.81.
18. *FM*, 17.8.79.
19. *1982 Defence White Paper*, p.16.
20. *Paratus*, Jan. 1984, Author's translations.
21. *Cit*, 18.5.84.
22. *S Trib*, 23.9.84; *Cit*, 24.9.84.
23. *Resister*, No.28, Oct./Nov. 1983 p.12.
24. *Civil Defence Act*, 1966.
25. *Resister*, No.28, Oct./Nov. 1983, p.17.
26. *National Key Points Act, 1980*.
27. *ST*, 19.10.80.
28. SAIRR *Survey, 1980*, p.215.
29. General Motors (SA) Pty. Ltd. Inter-office Memo, 20.6.77.
30. *FM*, 15.7.83, Supplement 'Security: A Survey'.

31. *ST*, 17.2.80
32. *Paratus*, Dec. 1985, p.46.
33. *S Trib*, 7.10.84.
34. *Paratus*, Dec. 1985, pp.46–8.
35. *Resister*, No.24, June/July 1983, p.19.
36. *RDM*, 25.1.85; ANC, [1980], p.3.
37. Bailey [1981a], p.2.
38. Bailey [1980], p.18.
39. Bailey [1981a], p.2.
40. Bailey [1981a], p.4; Crocker [1980], p.98.
41. ANC [1980], p.5.
42. ANC [1980], p.7.
43 Crocker [1980], p.92.
44. Bailey [1981b], p.2.
45. ANC [1980], pp.7–8.
46. ANC [1980], p.6.
47. *Obs*, 3.6.84.
48. Minty [1985], p.5.
49. ANC [1980], pp.9–10.
50. *FT*, 23.6.79; *Government Gazette*, 22.6.79.
51. *FM*, 22.3.85; BBC, 9.8.85.
52. *FM*, 25.5.79.
53. *Sechaba*, July 1980, p.28.
54. Security Council Document S/5386.
55. UN Unit on Apartheid [1970], p.5.
56. Minty [1969], pp.4–7; CCSA [1981].
57. Minty [1969], pp.4–7; CCSA [1981].
58. Lipton [1970], pp.427–34.
59. *Air International*, May 1976.
60. IDAF [1980b], p.13.
61. *1985 SIPRI Yearbook*, p.302.
62. *1978 SIPRI Yearbook*, p.233.
63. IDAF [1980b], p.33.
64. *GN*, 10.6.75.
65. *ST*, 21.10.73.
66. CCSA [1981], p.32.
67. CCSA [1981], pp.32.
68. *GN*, 10.6.75; IDAF [1980b], p.33.
69. *T*, 30.4.76.
70. CCSA [1981], p.30; *Intercontinental Press*, 15.3.76.

71. *Star*, 14.12.74.
72. *GN*, 19/20/21.11.80.
73. *Mail on Sunday*, 20.11.83;
    ST(UK), 20.11.83; *Tel*,
    30.12.83; *Obs*, 17.6.84.
74. *Hansard* (UK), 12.4.82, col.462;
    Anti-Apartheid Movement
    [1985], p.29.
75. *New African*, April 1977.
76. *Economist*, 15.11.77; *Armed
    Forces* (UK), Oct. 1982; IISS
    Military Balance, 1984–5.
77. *Defence and Armament*, Nov.
    1983.
78. *Armed Forces* (UK), Oct. 1982;
    IISS *Military Balance* 1984–85.
79. *FM*, 19.12.80; *DMS Market
    Intelligence Reports*, 1981, p.11.
80. *Star*, 9.11.82; *FM*, 12.11.82.
81. *Adams* [1984], p.93.
82. *ST*, 20.11.83.
83. *New African*, Aug. 1983.
84. *Armed Forces* (UK), Oct. 1982;
    IISS *Military Balance* 1984–95.
85. *International Defence Review*,
    No.12, 1982.
86. Adams [1984], p.93, pp.108/117;
    Middle East No.5, 1983.
87. *Congressional Research Report*
    No.81–17AF, 30.7.81, p.8;
    Adams [1984], p.117.
88. *BBC*, 18.11.85; *BD*, 3.7.85/
    4.9.85: *DD*, 25.1.85.
89. 'South Africa's Bombshell',
    World in Action (ITV),
    21.10.80.
90. *Paratus*, Feb. 1982, pp.12,13,78;
    ST, 28.3.82; *GN*, 29.3.82; *BBC*,
    30.3.82.
91. *GN*, 18.11.82; *Cit*, 13.9.82.
92. *ST*, 24.10.82; *T*, 14.5.81; *Obs*, 8/
    15.4.84; *Hansard* (UK),
    13.4.84.
93. Anti-Apartheid Movement,
    [1985], p.13.
94. *Anti-Apartheid News*, June
    1984.
95. World Campaign Against
    Military and Nuclear
    Collaboration with South
    Africa, 20.5.83.
96. *BBC*, 2.3.84.
97. NARMIC [1982]; Anti-
    Apartheid Movement, [1978].
98. NARMIC [1984], p.2.
99. NARMIC [1984], p.4.
100. NARMIC [1984], p.1,170.
101. NARMIC [1984], Appendix V.
102. World Campaign Against
     Military and Nuclear
     Collaboration with South Africa
     [1984], pp.3–8
103. *Debates*, 14.2.74, col. 911.
104. *Annual Estimates*, 1977.
105. *Annual Estimates*.
106. SAIRR, *Annual Survey* 1980,
     p.213.
107. *RDM*, 22.3.84.
108. Anti-Apartheid Movement
     [1985], p.19.
109. Minty [1969], pp.4–7.
110. *RDM*, 1.3.68.
111. *Financial Gazette*, 15.7.77.
112. *Debates*, col. 4868, 1968.
113. *National Supplies Procurement
     Act No.89 of 1970.*
114. *FM*, 26.11.76.
115. *ST*, 5.5.68.
116. Leonard [1983], pp.140–1;
     Debates, 25.2.65, col. 1775;
     Lowin, [1977], p.57.
117. *Star*, 15.9.73.
118. *EP*, 9.10.68.
119. *RDM*, 7.8.68.
120. *RDM*, 20.9.69.
121. *RDM*, 12.2.70.
122. *Strategy and Defence*, Aug.
     1984, pp.59–60.
123. SIPRI [1976], p.145.
124. *DN*, 11.4.84.
125. *1977 Defence White Paper*,
     p.27.
126. Resolution 418, [1977].
127. *FM Top Companies
     Supplement*, 4.5.84.
128. *S Star*, 30.12.84; *International
     Defence Review*, 10/84; *GN*,
     18.11.82.
129. *1982 Defence White Paper*;
     COSAWR [1984]; *FM*, 11.9.81.

130. *FM*, 11.9.81.
131. *FM*, 11.9.81.
132. *FM*, 11.9.81.
133. *GN*, 18.11.82; *FM*, 26.11.76; *DN*, 16.11.83.
134. *GN*, 18.11.82.
135. *DD*, 22.3.84; *CT*, 21.3.84; *ST*, 25.3.84.
136. Steenkamp [1983], p.60.
137. Steenkamp [1983], p.62; *S Star*, 28.7.85.
138. *Jane's Weapon Systems*, 1982–83.
139. *Strategy and Defence*, Aug. 1984, pp.59–60.
140. *RDM*, 11.12.82.
141. *Jane's Weapons Systems*, 1982–83; *CT*, 10.2.78.
142. Steenkamp [1984].
143. COSAWR [1984].
144. *RDM*, 21.3.79.
145. COSAWR [1984].
146. *FM*, 15.11.85.
147. *Jane's Defence Review*, Vol.4, No.9, 1983.
148. *ST*, 28.3.82
149. *ST*, 28.3.82; *FM*, 16.10.81.
150. *ST*, 28.3.82.
151. *ST*, 7.7.85.
152. Netherlands Anti-Apartheid Movement [1980].
153. *Jane's Defence Review*, Vol.4 No.9, 1983.
154. *International and Defence Review*, No.10, 1984, p.1500.
155. *FM*, 14.12.79.
156. *Star*, 18.11.84.
157. *FM*, 21.10.83; *Resister*, No.29, 1983/84, p.15.
158. *ST*, 10.10.82.
159. *ST*, 18.11.84.
160. *FM*, 27.2.81.
161. *Star*, 10.7.82.
162. *ST*, 11.7.82.
163. *International Defence Review* 3, 1983, p.269.
164. *S Trib*, 30.12.84; *Cit*, 31.12.84.
165. *International Defence Review*, No.3, 1983, p.269.
166. *FT*, 14.9.82; *FM*, 17.9.82; *Flight International* 22/29.12.84.
167. *Star*, 31.10.83.
168. *FM*, 12.11.82.
169. *Cit*, 3.3.84.
170. *International Defence Review*, No.3, 1983, p.269.
171. *International Defence Review*, No.3, 1983, p.269.
172. *International Defence Review*, No.3, 1983, p.269.
173. *GN*, 18.4.84.
174. Anti-Apartheid Movement [1985], pp.25–6; *GN*, 15.12.84.
175. *FT*, 14.9.82; *FM*, 17.9.82; *Flight International* 22/29.12.84.
176. Washington Office on Africa Education Fund [1985], pp.1/25.
177. Washington Office on Africa Education Fund [1985], pp.1–2.
178. Washington Office on Africa Education Fund [1985], pp.1–17; *GN*, 31.1.80; *New York Times* 16.10.79.
179. Smith [1980], p.9.
180. Washington Office on Africa Education Fund [1985], p.4.
181. United Nations [1981].
182. United Nations [1981], p.4.
183. Washington Office on Africa [1982], p.5.
184. United Nations [1981], pp.8–12.
185. United Nations [1981], pp.11–12; *FT*, 28.7.85; *S Star*, 19.5.85.
186. United Nations [1981], pp.11–12.
187. Washington Office on Africa [1982], p.2; Buell & Horner [1985], p.6.
188. Buell & Horner [1985], p.6.
189. Washington Office on Africa Education Fund [1985], pp.23–4; *RDM*, 18.3.83.
190. BBC *Monitor*, 16.3.82; *CT*, 1.3.84.
191. UN [1981], pp.20–1.
192. UN [1981], pp.22–3.
193. UN [1981], p.17.
194. Washington Office on Africa

Education Fund [1985], pp.1–2.
195. UN [1981], p.27.
196. Hough [1980], p.10.
197. COSAWR [1984a], p.11.
198. *Resister*, No.31, Apr./May 1984, p.16.
199. Minty [1969], p.7.
200. *NY Herald Tribune*, reporting on comments made by Prof. L J le Roux, vice-president of CSIR, 8.11.63.
201. *Africa Now*, Sept. 1981.
202. Communiqué issued by the Ministry of Defence of the PRA, 20.12.81.
203. ANGOP Communiqué, 4.1.84.
204. Netherlands Anti-Apartheid Movement [1984], p.7.
205. *Africa Now*, Sept. 1981.
206. *WA*, 5.6.85.

6: Structure of the Apartheid War Machine

1. IDAF [1980b], p.19.
2. *RDM*, 16.8.83; *Uniform*, Jan. 1982.
3. *1979 Defence White Paper*, p.17.
4. *1979 Defence White Paper*, p.17.
5. *Defence Africa*, Jan. 1984, pp.16–17 (see Tables XI and XII).
6. IDAF [1980b].
7. *Flight International*, 19.1.85.
8. IDAF [1980b], pp.26–7; *War Machine*, Nov. 1983.
9. IDAF [1980b], pp.26–7; *War Machine*, Nov. 1983.
10. IDAF [1980b], p.27; Steenkamp [1983], p.60.
11. IDAF [1980b], p.27; *War Machine*, Nov. 1983.
12. *1984 Defence White Paper*, p.7.
13. Heitman [1985], p.60.
14. *1984 Defence White Paper*, p.6.
15. *Defence Africa*, Jan. 1984, p.17.
16. IDAF [1980b], p.332.
17. Putter [1982], p.41.
18. Heitman [1985], pp.79–81.
19. *Star*, 14.12.74; Campbell [1984], pp.9–10.
20. Heitman [1985], p.82.
21. *RDM*, 22.4.78.
22. Putter [1982], p.5.
23. IISS *Military Balance* 1983–84, p.73.
24. IISS *Military Balance* 1983–84, p.73.
25. Campbell [1984], p.24; Steenkamp [1984], p.60.
26. *1984 Defence White Paper*, p.9.
27. *1984 Defence White Paper*, p.9.
28. *1977 Defence White Paper*.
29. *Uniform*, Jan. 1982.
30. IDAF [1980b], p.20.
31. IDAF [1980b], p.20.
32. *Debates*, 16.2.79; *FM*, 16.4.82.
33. *Sechaba*, July 1982, p.27.
34. *1975 Defence White Paper*, p.10.
35. *RDM*, 10.9.84.
36. *1984 Defence White Paper*, p.5.
37. *Resister*, No.21 Aug./Sept. 1982, p.14.
38. *Strategic Review*, June 1983, pp.2–8.
39. IISS *Military Balance*, 1983–84, pp.67–81.
40. *1977 Defence White Paper*, p.8.
41. *Defence Amendment Act 1982*.
42. *Uniform*, Sept. 1982.
43. *Resister*, No.26 June/July 1983, p.14.
44. *Paratus* May 1984.
45. *SEx*, 23.12.84.
46. *Soldier of Fortune*, Oct. 1984, p.66.
47. COSAWR [1984c], p.8; *Paratus*, May 1985, p.30; *WA*, 20.6.85; *BBC*, 30.5.85.
48. COSAWR [1984c], p.8.
49. *Paratus*, May 1985, p.31; Heitman [1985], pp.99–101; *ST*, 26.5.85.
50. *Paratus*, May 1985, p.30.
51. *FOCUS* No.51, Mar.–Apr. 1983, p.12.
52. *BBC*, 30.5.85.
53. *S*, 3.6.85.

54. COSAWR [1984c], p.8.
55. COSAWR [1984c], p.5; *Soldier of Fortune*, Oct./1984, p.69 (see Chapter 4).
56. *CT*, 28.1.80; *SEx*, 31.5.81.
57. *ST*, 6.12.81; *WO*, 5.12.81; *CT*, 7.12.81.
58. *Armed Forces*, April 1985, pp.25–9.
59. *WA*, 27.2.81.
60. Weaver [1983], p.5; *Armed Forces*, Dec./Jan. 1984, p.7.
61. *New Statesman*, 18.11.83; *WO*, 18.7.81.
62. *New Statesman*, 18.11.83.
63. *WA*, 26.9.83; *WO*, 8.10.83.
64. *RDM*, 24.2.84.
65. *DN*, 16.1.84.
66. *Armed Forces*, Dec./Jan. 1984, p.7.
67. *Armed Forces*, Dec./Jan. 1984, p.7.
68. *Armed Forces*, Dec./Jan. 1984, p.7; Weaver [1983], p.5.
69. Weaver [1983], p.5.
70. *WA*, 21.8.85.
71. *Armed Forces*, Dec./Jan. 1984, p.7.
72. *WO*, 28.8.82.
73. IDAF [1982a],; *Paratus*, July 1979; *WO*, 18.12.82; *Uniform*, 24.4.84; Heitman [1985], pp.108–10.
74. Heitman [1985], p.116.
75. Rogers [1980], p.10.
76. Grundy [1983a], p.231.
77. Grundy [1983a], p.233; *Armed Forces*, August 1984, p.7.
78. Grundy [1983a], p.233; *Armed Forces*, August 1984, p.7.
79. DSG/SARS [1982], p.14.
80. Grundy [1983a], pp.234–5.
81. Grundy [1983a], p.235.
82. Grundy [1983a], p.236.
83. *Armed Forces* Aug./1984, pp.7–8.
84. *Armed Forces*, Aug./1984, pp.7–8; *ST*, 7.11.82.
85. *Armed Forces* Aug./1984, p.8.
86. DSG/SARS [1982], p.15.
87. *DD*, 4.8.81.
88. *Armed Forces* Oct./1981, p.18, Sept./1984, pp.18–20.
89. *S Trib*, 30.10.85; DSG/SARS [1982].
90. *Resister* No.20, June/July 1982, p.8.
91. *Resister* No.20, June/July 1982, p.8.
92. *Paratus*, Jan./1985, p.37.
93. Grundy [1983a], p.240.
94. *RDM*, 3.8.79.
95. *Uniform*, Dec./Jan. 1985.
96. *DD*, 28.9.83.
97. *RDM*, 17.6.80; *FOCUS*, No.53, July/Aug. 1984, p.4.
98. DSG/SARS [1982], p.16.
99. *Resister*, No.19, April/May 1982, pp.8–9.
100. *GN*, 20.7.83.
101. *DD Supplement*, 2.12.83; Heitman [1985], p.119.
102. *ST*, 14.11.82.
103. *DD*, 18.7.83.
104. *DD Supplement*, 2.12.83.
105. *DD*, 12.9.80.
106. Haysom [1983], pp.44–7.
107. *DD*, 26.2.80.
108. *Resister*, No.18, Feb./Mar. 1982, p.15.
109. *DD*, 22.1.85.
110. *FM*, 31.5.85.
111. DSG/SARS [1982], p.130.
112. *DN*, 29.5.84.
113. *Paratus*, July 1985, p.12.
114. Weaver [1983], p.5.
115. Weaver [1983]. pp.6–7. Personal interviews by COSAWR with South African National Servicemen.
116. IDAF [1982a], p.40.
117. *Debates*, 6.6.77.
118. IDAF [1980b], p.43.
119. *Cit*, 17.10.84.
120. *Servamus*, June 1983, p.4.
121. *Resister*, No.35, Dec./Jan. 1985, pp.14–15.
122. IDAF [1980b], p.44.
123. *GN*, 15.9.81; *Tel*, 21.9.81.
124. *Servamus*, Jan. 1985 p.21.

125. *Debates*, 21.2.85.
126. *DD*, 14.3.85.
127. *FM Supplement*, 31.5.85.
128. *S*, 24.10.84; BBC, 21.1.85.
129. *Star*, 16.5.85.
130. *RDM*, 22.1.85.
131. *Resister* No. 35, Dec./Jan. 1985, pp.15–16; Commissioner of SAP, 1979 and 1983.
132. South Africa (Republic of) [1970], p.8.
133. *Debates*, 6.6.77; *Resister*, No.36, Feb./Mar. 1985, pp.20–22.
134. *Debates*, 28.2.77.
135. *Servamus*, Nov. 1984.
136. *Seramus*, Aug. 1984, p.24.
137. *Resister*, No.37, April–May 1985, p.22.
138. *Servamus*, May 1983, p.8.
139. *Star/Argus*, 7.9.84.
140. *Resister*, No.27, Aug./Sept. 1983, p.7.
141. *1973 Defence White Paper*.
142. *RDM*, 31.1.79.
143. *Star*, 12.1.80, 10.7.82.
144. *DD*, 12.4.84.
145. *Cit*, 14.2.85
146. *BBC*, 21.12.85.
147. *Resister*, No.27, Aug./Sept. 1983, p.10.
148. *BBC*, 2.3.83.

7: Regional Aggression

1. Parsons [1982], pp.305–7.
2. IDAF [1983c], p.2.
3. Davies & O'Meara [1983], pp.3–4.
4. Jaster [1983], p.3.
5. ANC [1984], p.1.
6. *RDM*, 14.3.79.
7. *ST*, 7.1.80.
8. Geldenhuys [1981], p.20.
9. *RDM*, 2.2.83.
10. IDAF [1983], pp.1–3.
11. *Star*, 12.11.85; *Obs*, 12.1.86; *GN*, 15.1.86; *T*, 21.1.86.
12. Anti-Apartheid Movement [1984b].
13. Mozambique Angola Committee [1984], p.26.
14. *GN*, 6.3.85; Wolfers & Bergerol [1983], p.193–5.
15. Wolfers & Bergerol [1983], p.197.
16. Wolfers & Bergerol [1983], pp.6–7.
17. Stockwell [1978], p.187.
18. Wolfers & Bergerol [1983], p.8.
19. Klingview [1980], p.45.
20. Klingview [1983], p.44.
21. IDAF [1980b], p.57.
22. Klingview [1980], p.44.
23. Wolfers & Bergerol [1983], p.15.
24. Wolfers & Bergerol [1983], pp.17–19.
25. IDAF [1980b], p.57.
26. Wolfers & Bergerol [1983], p.24.
27. Wolfers & Bergerol [1983], p.19; People's Republic of Angola [1983], p.10.
28. IDAF [1980b], pp.58–60.
29. IDAF [1980b], p.58.
30. Klingview [1980], p.44.
31. Wolfers & Bergerol [1983], p.56; IDAF [1980b], p.60; People's Republic of Angola [1983], pp.11–12.
32. IDAF [1980b], p.60.
33. Grundy [1983b], pp.28–9.
34. IDAF [1980b], p.61.
35. *Resister*, No.36, Feb./March 1985, pp.16–17.
36. Geldenhuys [1982], pp.28–29.
37. People's Republic of Angola [1983], p.15.
38. People's Republic of Angola [1983], p.16; *BBC*, 28.2.79, 1.3.79.
39. *Tel*, 27.2.79.
40. People's Republic of Angola [1983], pp.19–20.
41. People's Republic of Angola [1983], pp.23–4; Angolan Ministry of Defence

Communiqué, 26.6.80.
42 Holness [1983], p.17.
43. *GN*, 29.1.81; *FOCUS Special Issue*, No.2. p.7.
44. Leonard [1984], p.250.
45. *Tel*, 13.3.81.
46. *T*, 5.12.81; *FT*, 2.12.81.
47. Holness [1983], p.18.
48. People's Republic of Angola [1983], pp.27–8.
49. *Resister*, No.16, Oct./Nov. 1981. pp.8–9
50. *FOCUS*, No.81, Nov./Dec. 1981, p.9.
51. Angolan Ministry of Defence Communiqué, 20.12.81.
52. BBC, 31.8.81.
53. *WO*, 11.7.81.
54. *BBC*, 12.9.81.
55. People's Republic of Angola [1983], pp.29–30; *GN*, 2.12.81; BBC, 1.12.81.
56. IDAF [1983b], p.C60.
57. *Strategic Review*, June 1983, pp.2–8.
58. *ANGOP*, 21/26.10.82; *RDM*, 7.4.82; *WA*, 6.4.82.
59. *Resister*, No.36, Feb./March 1985, pp.16–17.
60   *WO*, 30.7.83.
61. *WA*, 17.3.82.
62. *ANGOP*, 19.3.82.
63. *Washington Post*, 19.8.82.
64. *Jornal de Angola*, 7.8.82.
65. *WA*, 27.8.82; *BBC*, 18.9.82.
66. Beeld, 23.8.82; *GN*, 2.9.82; *Star*, 6.8.82.
67. *Jornal de Angola*, 22.1.83.
68. *ANGOP*, 31.3.83.
69. *Jornal de Angola*, 29.3.83.
70. Press Conference by Lt. Col. Ngongo, Deputy Chief of Staff of FAPLA, Luanda, 24.8.83.
71. *Resister*, No.36, Feb./March 1984, pp.6–8.
72. Press Conference by Lt. Col. Ngongo, Deputy Chief of Staff of FAPLA, Luanda, 24.8.83.
73. *ANGOP*, 20.10.83.
74. *GN*, 11.11.83.

75. *FOCUS*, No.51, Mar./April 1984, p.12.
76. *FOCUS*, No.51, Mar./April 1984, p.12; *ANGOP*, 4.11.83, 18/22/24/30.12.83; BBC, 2/10.1.84.
77. *FOCUS*, No.51, Mar./April 1981, p.12.
78. *ANGOP*, 22.2.84.
79. *ANGOP*, 22.2.84.
80. *ANGOP*, 9.3.83.
81. *ANGOP*, 21.2.84.
82. *ANGOP*, 22.2.84.
83. *ANGOP*, 21.2.84.
84. *FM*, 6.7.84.
85. *GN*, 10.4.84.
86. *Tr*, 21.3.84.
87. *GN*, 27.4.84.
88. *GN*, 2.4.84.
89. *FOCUS*, No.54, Sept./Oct. 1984, p.12.
90. *GN*, 26.5.84.
91. *ANGOP*, 16.6.84.
92. *ANGOP*, 14.10.84.
93. *Africa–Asia* Special Report, Jan/1985, pp.75–6.
94. *ANGOP*, 4.1.85.
95. *ANGOP*, 11.1.85.
96. *ANGOP*, 23.10.84, 4/13.1.85; *BBC*, 7.1.85.
97. *ANGOP*, 13.1.85.
98. *ANGOP*, 13.12.84.
99. *ANGOP*, 6.1.85.
100. *ANGOP*, 10.10.84.
101. *Africa–Asia Special Report*, January 1985, pp.56–7.
102. *Obs*, 26.5.85.
103. *FOCUS*, No.60, Sept./Oct 1985, p.11.
104. *GN*, 19.9.85; *ST*, 15.9.85; *DD*, 23.9.85.
105. *GN*, 24.9.85; *Tel*, 20.9.85; *MS*, 19.9.85.
106. *BBC*, 14.1.85; *DD*, 24.12.85; 13.1.86.
107. *Africa News*, 16.12.85; *T/GN*, 24.9.85; BBC, 25.9.85.
108. Hanlon [1984], pp.24–41.
109   Hanlon [1984], p.45.
110. Hanlon [1984], pp.45–51.

111. *Southern Africa*, Dec. 1982, pp.5–10; Fauvet [1984a, 1984b], pp.109–15.
112. *Star*, 29.8.81; Fauvet [1984b], pp.109–15; Southern Africa, Dec. 1982, pp.5–10.
113. *Star*, 29.8.81; Fauvet [1984b], p.116.
114. *New African* Jan. 1982; Fauvet [1984b], p.116.
115. Fauvet [1984b], p.117; *SEx*, 3.1.82; *Obs*, 20.6.82.
116. *FT/T/GN*, 31.1.81; *RDM/S/T*, 19.3.81.
117. *CT*, 25.8.82
118. BBC, 25.4.83; *AIM*, 24.4.83
119. *Star/CT*, 3.5.83.
120. *MS*, 14.9.82; *NYT/GN/Tel*, 18.8.82; *S*, 20.8.82;
121. *Star/NYT*, 23.5.83; *NYT/CT/ANC Press Statement/FT/MS*, 24.5.85; *Star*, 28.5.85.
122. Fauvet [1984a], p.6.
123. Fauvet [1984a], p.9; Hanlon [1984], p.226.
124. *Economist*, 30.9.82; Hanlon [1984], pp.226–7.
125. BBC, 16/17.2.83; *AIM*, 20.1.84.
126. Hanlon [1984], pp.226–7; *Resister*, No.37, April/May 1985, p.1.; *Noticias*, 10.5.83; 9.9.83; 29.11.83, 8.9.84.
127. Hanlon [1984], pp.252–3.
128. *GN*, 22.5.84.
129. *Sechaba*, May 1984.
130. Arusha Communiqué, 29.4.84.
131. *GN*, 3.4.85; *AIM*, 30.9.85.
132. *GN*, 18.5.84.
133. *GN*, 4.7.84.
134. *SA Digest*, 12.10.84.
135. *AIM*, 3.10.84.
136 *SA Digest*, 12.10.84.
137. *AIM*, 1.10.85.
138. *GN*, 18.3.85.
139. *AIM Bulletin*, March 1985.
140. *AIM*, 30.9.85; 1.10.85.
141. *S Star*, 15.9.85; *ST(UK)*, 22.9.85; *BBC*, 21.9.85.
142. *AIM*, 8.11.85.
143. Sefali [1983].
144. *GN*, 10.12.79.
145. *Star*, 4.12.82.
146. *Star*, 27.11.82, 4.12.82.
147. Kingdom of Lesotho [1983].
148. *Resister*, No.35, Dec. 1984/Jan. 1985, p.23.
149. *Star*, 15.8.83.
150. IDAF [1985e], pp.14–17.
151. *BBC*, 29.8.85.
152. *Cit*, 5.10.81.
153. *MS*, 28.10.80; *GN*, 24.10.80
154. *GN*, 24.10.80; *Resister*, No.12, Feb./March 1981, p.22.
155. *RDM*, 24.6.81; *S*, 14.10.81; *FOCUS*, No.41, July/Aug. 1982.
156. *Tel*, 7.10.80.
157. *Yorkshire Post*, 26.8.80.
158. *GN*, 30.3.82.
159. *GN*, 30.4.84.
160. *GN*, 30.4.84, p.12.
161. *GN*, 8.3.84, 30.4.84.
162. *GN*, 30.4.84.
163. *GN*, 1.8.84.
164. *GN*, 24.8.82.
165. *GN*, 21.12.81.
166. *Flight International*, 11.4.84; *Weekend Argus*, 11.9.82.
167. *RDM*, 31.12.82; *Star*, 18.12.82
168. *Star*, 26.3.84.
169. *Obs*, 12.12.82; *T*, 10.12.82.
170. *GN*, 11.12.82; Kingdom of Lesotho [1983]; IDAF [1985c].
171. IDAF [1985c], pp.1–4.
172. IDAF [1985c], p.4.
173. *GN*, 2.8.81
174. IDAF [1983b], p.65.
175. *GN*, 22.11.83.
176. *RDM*, 11.12.82.
177. *RDM*, 9.7.82; T, 14.8.82.
178. *T*, 14.8.82; *RDM*, 30.7.82.
179. *Star*, 24.9.85; *BBC*, 9/11.10.85; *GN/Cit*, 21.12.85.
180. *FT*, 29.9.82.
181. IDAF [1985c], p.1.
182. *FT*, 29.9.82.
183. *S*, 13.7.83.
184. *ST*, 1.7.84.
185. *Resister*, No.12, Feb./March

186. *RDM*, 19.3.79; BBC, 18/ 20.9.79, 24/29.10.79.
187. *FOCUS*, No.28, May/June 1980, p.9.
188. *New African*, April 1981; *MS* 7.7.80.
189. *FOCUS*, No.28, May/June 1980, p.9.
190. *Zambia Daily Mail*, 3.4.81.
191. *Tel*, 20.3.82.
192. *BBC*, 29.8.85.
193. *BBC*, 8.1.80.
194. *GN*, 21.2.80.
195. *MS*, 3.1.83.
196. *GN*, 9.12.85
197. *T*, 1.8.81.
198. *RDM*, 12/26.3.82.
199. *DD*, 16.1.81.
200. *Tel*, 20.3.81; *GN*, 20.3.81; *Resister*, No.35, Dec./Jan. 1985, p.21.
201. *FT*, 29.9.82.
202. *FM*, 5.8.82.
203. BBC, 25.10.85, 8/9.1.86.
204. *GN*, 28.12.85; *Star*, 27.12.85.

8: Namibia: Occupation and Liberation War

1. Calculation by Prof. R Green, *CT*, 4.1.85.
2. *New Statesman*, 22.8.80; *WO*, 23.8.80.
3. *FM*, 29.10.82.
4. *GN*, 19.6.85.
5. *S Tel*, 22.3.81; UN Council for Namibia [1983].
6. Konig [1983], p.5.
7 *GN*, 19.6.85; *CT*, 21.12.84.
8. *WA*, 5.10.84.
9. *CT*, 31.1.76.
10. IDAF [1982a], pp.43–4.
11. *CT*, 4.1.85.
12. Konig [1983], p.54; *Resister*, No.27 Aug./Sept. 1983, p.13.
13. Weaver [1983], p.9.
14. Southern African Catholic Bishops' Conference, [1982].
15. IDAF [1982a], pp.5-6.
16. *ST*, 19.12.65; IDAF [1982], pp.6–8.
17. IDAF [1980a], p.10.
18. SWAPO [1981a], p.210.
19. IDAF [1980c], pp.59-60.
20. Konig [1983], p.19; SWAPO [1981], pp.223-6.
21. IDAF [1980c], pp.60–61.
22. IDAF [1980c], pp.61-2; SWAPO [1980], pp.232-6.
23. IDAF, [1981a], p.2.
24. IDAF [1980c] pp.62–3.
25. SWAPO [1981], pp.229–62.
26. IDAF [1980b], p.61; *GN*, 28.6.73; SWAPO [1981], pp.221–3.
27. *GN*, 1.9.76.
28. *WA*, 8.7.76.
29. Konig [1983], pp.12–13.
30. *WA*, 17.6.76; *Star*, 17.7.76.
31. SWAPO [1981], p.232.
32. *CT*, 26.10.77.
33. Konig [1983], p.20.
34. IDAF [1982a], p.45.
35. *Debates* 9.3.79.
36. *WO*, 3.3.79.
37. IDAF [1982a], p.46; *ST*, 10.2.80.
38. IDAF [1982a], p.46.
39. *WO*, 17.5.80
40. *Resister*, No.12, Feb./March 1981, p.12; *FOCUS Special Issue No.2*, April 1981, p.10.
41. IDAF [1981a] pp.2–3.
42. IDAF [1981a], p.4.
43. IDAF [1982c].
44. IDAF [1982a] p.47.
45. *Resister*, No.16, Oct–Nov 1981, pp.2–9.
46. *WO*, 12.4.79.
47. IDAF [1984b], pp.2–3; IDAF [1982c], pp.2–3.
48. IDAF [1982c], pp.2–3.
49. *WO*, 1.4.81.
50. *WO*, 4.4.81.
51. *WO*, 9.5.81.
52. *MS*, 18.7.81.
53. *RDM*, 21.9.81.
54. Konig [1983], p.14.

55. *GN*, 14.6.80.
56. *Tel*, 30.7.81; *WO*, 5.12.81.
57. *WO*, 2.5/27.6/31.10.81.
58. *ST*, 27.9.81.
59. *T*, 24.3.82.
60. *Resister*, No.20, June/July 1982, pp.12–17.
61. *WO*, 15.5.82.
62. SWAPO War Communiqué, 12.8.82.
63. *WA*, 11.8.82.
64. *WO*, 14.8.82; *Resister*, No.22 Oct./Nov. 1982, p.16.
65. WA, 30.12.82.
66. *WA*, 28.2.83.
67. *Star*, 5.3.83.
68. *WA*, 7.2.83.
69. *WA*, 11/19.2.83.
70. FM, 4.3.83.
71. SWAPO War Communiqué, London, 9.3.83.
72. *WO*, 19.3.83.
73. *CT*, 22.3.83.
74. *WO*, 30.4.83; *RDM*, 26.4.83.
75. *WA*, 29.4.83.
76. *WA*, 5.8.83.
77. IDAF [1984c], pp.1–2.
78. *BBC*, 9.5.83.
79. IDAF [1984c], p.4.
80. *RDM*, 14.9.83.
81. *WA*, 19.8.83.
82. *WA*, 12.4.84.
83. *T*, 17.2.84; *BBC*, 24.2.84.
84. *T*, 11.3.84.
85. *WO*, 7.4.84; IDAF [1984b], p.3.
86. *WO*, 12.5.84; BBC, 14.5.84; *T*, 11.5.84.
87. *WA*, 20.1.84; *RDM*, 2.3.84.
88. *WA*, 6.3.84.
89. *CT*, 6.3.84.
90. *RDM*, 10.3.84.
91. *WA*, 18.1.84; *BBC*, 21.1.84; *RDM*, 3.3.84.
92. *LWI*, 13/14/29.3.84; *CT*, 23.3.84; *WO*, 31.3.84.
93. *WO*, 19.4.84.
94. *FOCUS*, No.54, Sept./Oct. 1984, p.2; *FOCUS*, No.56, Jan./Feb. 1985.
95. *RDM*,2.3.84.
96. IDAF [1984a].
97. *The Combatant*, Aug. 1984, p.22.
98. *Obs*, 9.9.84.
99. *Resister*, No.34. Oct./Nov. 1984, p.18.
100. *WA*, 21.12.84.
101. *CT*, 21.12.84.
102. *BBC*, 28.8.82; *GN*, 30.11.84.
103. *FOCUS* No.58, May/June 1985, p.1.
104. *WO*, 19.1.85, 27.4.85; *DD*, 8/19/25.6.85, *Nam*, 20.12.85.
105. *Nam*, 20.12.85.
106. *FOCUS* No.59. July/Aug. 1985, p.10.
107. *FOCUS* No.60, Sept/Oct. 1985; Namibian Communications Centre 20.6.85.
108. *FM Supplement*, 22.7.83; *WA*, 10.5.85.
109. *Armed Forces* (London), Feb. 1984, p.60.
110. Some reports suggest that Kaokoland is not part of the Operational Area – for example, *Armed Forces* (London), Feb. 1984, p.60.
111. *FM Supplement*, 22.7.83, p.38.
112. Interviews with ex-SADF troops conducted by COSAWR.
113. Personal interviews with COSAWR; *Armed Forces* (London), Feb. 1984, p.60; COSAWR [1982], p.2.
114. *Armed Forces* (London), Feb. 1984, p.60.
115. COSAWR [1982], p.3; IDAF [1982a], p.25.
116. *Armed Forces*, London, Feb. 1984, p.60.
117. *Star*, 19.8.83.
118. *Paratus*, Apr. 1983, p.5.
119. *WO*, 26.3.83; *Paratus*, Oct.1983, pp.56–7.
120. IDAF [1982], p.35.
121. *Paratus*, Oct. 1983, pp.56–7.
122. Wood [1984], p.140; *GN*, 29.5.82.

123. IDAF [1982a], pp.25–6; Konig [1983], pp.39–40.
124. IDAF [1982a], p.19.
125. IDAF [1982a], p.19.
126. *WA*, 26.11.82.
127. *T*, 20.5.67; *RDM*, 2.6.72; *ST*, 26.3.72.
128. IDAF [1982a], p.30; *T*, 9.2.81.
129. IDAF [1982a], pp.30–1.
130. IDAF [1982a], pp.31–2.
131. Before 1976 the Special Police were called 'Tribal Police'.
132. *CT*, 31.5.82.
133. *DN*, 2.2.81.
134. *Armed Forces*, Feb. 1985, pp.12–13.
135. *WA*, 29.4.80.
136. *Cit*, 1.7.80; IDAF [1982a], p.34.
137. *Armed Forces*, Sept. 1980.
138. *Resister* No.29, Dec./Jan. 1984, p.5.
139. IDAF [1982a], p.35.
140. *RDM*, 13.9.82.
141. *CT*, 2.4.81.
142. *Star*, 19.4.85.
143. *CT*, 18.1.84.
144. *WA*, 21.8.85.
145. *RDM*, 18.10.79.
146. *WO*, 25.10.80.
147. *WA*, 21.8.80.
148. *WO*, 29.11.80; *WA*, 21.11.80.
149. IDAF [1982a], pp.38–9; *WO*, 13.12.80.
150. *WO*, 13.12.80.
151. *RDM*, 15.12.80.
152. *WA*, 20.1.81.
153. *LWI* 3/81.
154. IDAF [1982a], p.39.
155. *ST*, 5.4.81.
156. *RDM*, 2.4.81; *Paratus*, May 1981, pp.34–6.
157. IDAF [1982a], p.39.
158. SWAPO interview, *Anti-Apartheid News*, July/Aug. 1981.
159. *WA*, 13.7.81.
160. *CCN Information*, Aug. 1981, pp.1–3.
161. *Resister*, No.13, April/May 1981, p.3.
162. *WA*, 27.1.82; 9.3.82.
163. *WA*, 8.6.83.
164. *FOCUS*, Sept./Oct. 1983.
165. *FOCUS*, Sept./Oct. 1984, pp.2–3.
166. *WA*, 24.3.82.
167. *WA*, 31.10.84.
168. *Namibian News Briefings*, Dec./Jan. 1985.
169. *WA*, 13.11.84.
170. *WA*, 31.10.84.
171. *WA*, 1.11.84.
172. *MS*, 20.11.84.
173. *BBC*, 20.11.84.
174. *Star*, 13.12.84.
175. *Southern Africa Record*, No.40, Oct./1985. p.4.
176. *WA*, 14.11.84.
177. *Namibia News Briefing*, Dec./Jan., 1985.
178. *Resister*, No. 30. Feb./Mar. 1984, p.13.
179. Grundy [1983a], p.254; *WA*, 2.12.85.
180. *Post*, 14.4.78.
181. IDAF [1982a], p.51.
182. *T*, 9.2.81.
183. *Star*, 4.12.82; *DN*, 21.10.80.
184. *Moto*, 6.12.80; *T*, 9.2.81; *WO*, 2.6.84.
185. *WA*, 18.1.80.
186. *WA*, 2.12.85.
187. *Uniform*, 24.4.84.
188. *Southern Africa Record*, No.40, Oct./1985, pp.10–11.
189. *DD*, 14.5.79.
190. *WA*, 20.7.82.
191. *Nam*, 13.12.85, 24.1.86.
192. IDAF [1984c], pp.1–2.
193. *Resister No.30*, Feb./March 1984, p.15.
194. *WA*, 1.9.78.
195. *Paratus*, Feb. 1981, pp.28–9.
196. *WA*, 3.10.77.
197. *RDM*, 23.3.78.
198. *CT*, 28.1.85.
199. *Nam*, 30.8.85.
200. *Nam*, 13.12.85.
201. Visser [undated], p.15.

202. *FT*, 12.2.81.
203. *Nam*, 30.8.85; *RDM*, 23.3.78.
204. IDAF [1982b], p.4.
205. IDAF [1982b], p.2.
206. IDAF [1982b], p.2.
207. *FOCUS*, March/April 1984, p.4.
208. Konig [1983], p.32.
209. *WO*, 19.3.83
210. Konig [1983], p.36; *WO*, 29.11.80; *Star*, 27.12.80.
211. *FOCUS*, No.50, Jan./Feb. 1984, p.10; Weaver [1983], pp.7–8.
212. *RDM*, 12.9.83; Weaver [1983], p.8.
213. *WA*, 17.10.83; Lobstein [1984], p.12.
214. *WA*, 28.4.83
215. Weaver [1983], p.8.
216. *WA*, 12.10.83.
217. *WA*, 21.8.85.
218. *WA*, 30.6/1.7.82.
219. CT, 23.7.83.
220. *WA*,4.12.83, 14.1.85.
221. *WO*, 8/17.10.83.
222. *WA*, 19.6.82.
223. *CT*, 10.10.83.
224. *WO*, 28.8.82.
225. *FOCUS*, No.55, Nov./Dec. 1984, p.8.
226. Weaver [1983], p.8.
227. *FOCUS*, No.59, July/Aug. 1985, p.9.
228. *WA*, 21.10/9.11.83.
229. *WA*, 29.11.83.
230. *WA*, 26/29.9.83, 8.10.83.
231. *WA*, 19.2.82; *FOCUS*, No.40, May/June 1982, p.11.
232. Southern African Catholic Bishop's Conference [1982], pp.20–21.
233. *RDM*, 20.2.85; *GN*, 21.10.84; *RDM*, 5.2.83.
234. *FOCUS*, No.58, May/June 1985, p.3.
235. *RDM*, 5.3.84.
236. *WA*, 15.3.82.
237. *ST*, 30.5.82; *T* 2.6.82.
238. *FOCUS*, No.42, Sept./Oct. 1982.
239. *WO*, 11.12.82; *CT*, 9.12.82.
240. *WA*, 16.9.83; *WO*, 9.6.84.
241. *FOCUS*, No.54, Sept./Oct. 1984, pp.1,4.
242. *FOCUS*, No.36, Sept./Oct. 1981; *WO*, 16.1.81; *RDM*, 2.2.83.
243. Weaver [1983], p.8.
244. Konig [1983], p.46.
245. *Resister*, No.11, Dec./1980, pp.15–16.
246. *FOCUS*, No.32, Jan./Feb. 1981, p.3.
247. *Star*, 18.8.81.
248. Southern African Catholic Bishop's Conference, [1982].

9: Battle for South Africa

1. *ST (UK)*, 25.8.85.
2. Steenkamp [1984], p.23.
3. *RDM*, 17.1.85; *DD*, 12.1.86.
4. *WM*, 5.7.85.
5. *DD*, 12.1.86.
6. Davies, O'Meara & Dlamini [1984], Vol.1, p.35.
7. Steenkamp [1984], p.23.
8. IDAF [1983b], pp.98–100.
9. Lodge 1984], pp.153–4.
10. *AA News*, Sept. 1985; *BBC*, 9.8.85.
11. *Africa News*, 15.7.85.
12. Crocker [1980].
13. *RDM*, 25.9.84.
14. Crocker [1980], p.110a.
15. Coetzee [1983], p.13.
16. Steenkamp [1984]
17. South Africa (Republic of), [1982], p.137.
18. South Africa (Republic of), [1982], p.85.
19. South Africa (Republic of), [1982], pp.137–201.
20. Suter [1980], p.12.
21. *1982 Defence White Paper*, p.5.
22. *Paratus*, June 1982.
23. Dutton [1978], p.107

24. Seiler [undated], p.107.
25. *Debates*, 22.6.76.
26. *RDM*, 3.3.79.
27. *RDM*, 21.6.84; *Resister*, No.7, Feb./Mar. 1980
28. *Star*, 21.7.79.
29. *FM*, 9.3.79.
30. *Act No.87 of 1979*.
31. *Debates*, 4.6.79.
32. *SEx*, 30.5.82.
33. *S Trib*, 9.1.83.
34. *RDM*,5.5.83.
35. *S Star*, 22.12.85.
36. *SEx*, 23.12.84.
37. *CT*, 26.5.80.
38. *Debates*, 10.2.84, col.847; *RDM*, 28.10.81.
39. *Uniform*, Dec. 1985.
40. *ST*, 22.12.85; *GN*, 13.1.86.
41. *RDM*, 1.6.68.
42. *1973 Defence White Paper*, p.8.
43. *1973 Defence White Paper*, p.9.
44. *Star*, 6.4.74.
45. *1975 Defence White Paper*, p.11.
46. *Star*, 19.10.81; *RDM*, 16.10.81.
47. *Debates*, 7.6.82, col. 8444.
48. *FM*, 15.1.82.
49. *RDM*, 15.8.81; *DN*,26.2.82.
50. *RDM*, 24.3.82; 25.3.82.
51. *FM*, 18.2.83.
52. *ST*, 28.3.82.
53. *Cit*, 26.4.83.
54. *RDM*, 24.3.82.
55. *Resister* No.26, June/July 1983, p.15; *RDM*, 24.3.82.
56. *Defence Amendment Act 1982*.
57. *Debates*, 12.3.85.
58. *Resister*, No.26, June/July 1983.
59. *ST*, 22.1.75.
60. *Star*, 22.9.83.
61. *DD*, 11.5.83.
62. *Star*, 15.8.84; *Paratus*, June 1985.
63. *Star*, 13.8.85; *1984 Defence White Paper*,p.6.
64. *Jane's Defence Review*, Vo.4 No.9, 1983.
65. *RDM*, 21.6.82; *Cit*, 9.2.84.
66. For example, *RDM*, 17.12.82.
67. *RDM*, 20.12.83.
68. *Star*, 20.2.84.
69. *S*, 15.8.84.
70. *Pretoria News*, 18.10.83.
71. NUSAS [1983], p.25.
72. *RDM*, 15.3.84.
73. *1982 Defence White Paper*.
74. DSG/SARS [1982], p.15; *Sechaba*, Sept. 1983, p.19.
75. Haysom [1983], pp.35–40.
76. Haysom [1983], pp.68–70.
77. *RDM*, 14.9.83.
78. *S Trib*, 25.10.81.
79. *RDM*, 21.2.85.
80. *RDM*, 14.9.83.
81. Lloyd [1979].
82. *WIP* No.28, Aug. 1983, p.27.
83. *Star*, 27.1.73.
84. *SEx*, 27.4.75.
85. *ST*, 14.7.74.
86. *Paratus*, July 1978, p.10.
87. *Cit*, 25.5.78; *RDM*, 25.5.78.
88. *Paratus*, June 1980.
89. *Paratus*, June 1980, p.44.
90. *RDM*, 4.1.78.
91. *RDM*, 15.1.81.
92. *WIP* No.29, Sept. 1983; p.24 – the total in September 1982 was given as 178.
93. COSAWR-N [undated], p.21; *Paratus* Oct. 1978, p.5.
94. *RDM*, 12.3.83.
95. Letter from Brigadier Lloyd to New Republic Party MP, Vause Raw, 25.10.79.
96. *WIP*, No.29, Sept. 1983, p.21.
97. *WIP* No.29, Sept. 1983, p.21.
98. *WIP* No.29, Sept. 1983, p.21.
99. *State of the Nation*, Feb./Mar. 1985.
100. *WIP* No.29, Sept. 1983, p.21.
101. *Post*, 29.10.79.
102. *WIP* No.29, Sept 1985, p.27.
103. *WIP* No.29, Sept. 1983, pp.28–30.
104. *WIP* No.29, Sept. 1985, p.30.
105. *WIP* No.29, Sept. 1983, p.21.
106. *WIP* No.29, Sept. 1983, p.21.
107. SAIRR *1959–60 Survey*, pp.63–4.

108. Brooks & Brickhill [1980], pp.268–9.
109. Brooks & Brickhill [1980], p.267.
110. *RDM*, 1.4.78.
111. *RDM*, 16.6.78; *CT*, 16.6.78.
112. *ST*, 31.5.81; *RDM*, 29.5.81.
113. *S*, 4.6.81.
114. *RDM*, 4.6.81; *S*, 5.6.81.
115. *Debates*, 5.8.81
116. *SASPU National*, Dec, 1984; *SNS*,20.12.84.
117. *MS*, 6.9.84.
118. *SEx*, 7.10.84.
119. *DD*, 8.10.84; *BBC*, 9.10.84; *ST*, 14.10.84.
120. *S*, 11.10.80.
121. BBC, 11.10.84.
122. *SASPU National*, 1984; *FT*, 24.10.84; *S*, 23.10.84.
123. *SASPU National*, Dec. 1984.
124. *FT*, 24.10.84; *S*, 23.10.84.
125. *SASPU National*, Dec./1984; *GN*, 25.10.84; *RDM*, 25.10.84.
126. *S*, 1.11.84.
127. *SNS*, 21/84, 9.11.84.
128. *SASPU National*, Dec./1984.
129. *SASPU National*, Dec./1984.
130. *DN*, 8.11.84; *DD*, 8.11.84.
131. *DN*, 8.11.84.
132. *RDM*, 24.11.84.
133. *CT*, 22.11.84.
134. Southern African Catholic Bishops' Conference [1984], p.5.
135. *FOCUS* No.59, July/Aug. 1985, p.1.
136. *RDM*, 19.4.85; *GN*, 3.4.85.
137. *BBC*, 25.3.85; *SNS*, 14/29.1.85; *S*, 26.2.85.
138. *BBC*, 28.5.85; *Star*, 3.7.85; *CT*/*S*, 4.7.85; *DN*, 25.6.85.
139. *BBC*, 1.5.85; WM, 11.7.85; *Star*, 19.6.85.
140. IDAF [1985d], p.2; *GG*, 21.7.85.
141. *GG*, 21.7.85, 8/15.8.85; IDAF [1985d], p.2.
142. IDAF [1985d], pp.1–2.
143. *BD*, 23.12.85.
144. See Chapter 2.
145. *DD*, 23.11.85.
146. *Paratus*, Aug./1985, p.41.
147. *Paratus*, Aug./1985, pp.31,41.
148. BBC, 2.12.85; *FT*, 30.11.85.
149. *Resister* No.41 Dec. 1984–Jan, pp.15–16; IDAF [1985d], p.3.
150. *Nam*, 1.11.85.
151. *CT*, 5.4.85; *City Press*, 18.8.85; *DN*, 26.8.85, 12.9.85; *DD*, 11.9.85.
152. *DD*, 21/22.11.85.
153. *CT*, 16.12.85.
154. *BD*, 21.10.85, 6.11.85.
155. *Star*, 28.1.85, 16.5.85; *BD*, 27.8.85; *S*, 24.10.85.
156. *DN*, 25.6.85; *CT*, 25.6.85; *Star*, 23.8.85.
157. *S*, 23.5.85, 21.8.85; *CT*, 21.8.85, 4.9.85; *Star*, 23.4.85.
158. *ST*, 4.8.85; *S*, 15.8.85; *T*, 18.9.85.
159. *GN/T*, 18.9.85; *S*, 5.9.85; *Star*, 6.8.85; *S*, 14/15.8.85.
160. *DN/CT*, 30.8.85; IDAF [1985d], p.4.
161. *Uniform*, 22.4.85; *CT*, 11.4.85; *Star*, 11.8.85.
162. *CT*, 11.4.85.
163. See *FOCUS* No.55 Nov./Dec. 1984 to *FOCUS*, No.62 Jan./Feb. 1985.
164. *FOCUS* No.61, Nov.–Dec./1985, pp.1,6; *State of the Nation* [undated], pp.1–11; *CT*, 22.10.85.
165. *S*, 9/11.9.85; *Star*, 4.8.85; *CT*, 27.7.85, 18.10.85.
166. *S Trib*, 8.9.85.
167. *Tel*, 4.4.85; *CT*, 10.4.85; BBC 13.4.85.
168. BBC, 25.11.85; *DD*, 21.11.85.
169. *CT*, 15.8.85, 22.10.85; *DN*, 13.9.85; *ISSUP Strategic Review*, Oct./1985, p.11.
170. *CT*, 15.8.85, 22.10.85; *DN*, 13.9.85; ISSUP *Strategic Review*, Oct./1985, p.11.
171. *Servamus*, Sept./1985, p.31.
172. ISSUP *Strategic Review*,

Oct.,1985, p.11.
173. *WM*, 8.11.85.
174. *BBC*, 10.9.85.
175. *WM*, 5.7.85; *FM*, 15.11.85; *Star*, 15.8.85; *DD*, 30.8.85.
176. *BBC*, 14.12.86.
177. Press Release, South African Embassy, London, 31.1.86.
178. ANC Press Release, Lusaka, 8.1.86.

Index

*Acts of parliament are all indexed under
legislation*

1 SA Corps 24, 117-18

African National Congress [ANC] 12,
13, 20, 22, 140, 141, 164, 165, 216-17
 anti-propaganda 42, 43
 armed struggle 216-18, 249, 255
  Umkhonto we Sizwe 15-16, 17-18,
  85-6, 87, 218
 banned 14, 15
 calls for a 'peoples war' ['85] 218, 255
 and Geneva Conventions 222
 members, assassinated 142, 163, 172,
 173
 National Executive Conference ['86],
  Oliver Tambo's address 256
 premises [outside SA], attacked 142
 support for 217
Africans:
 21 Battalion 70-1, 125, 237, Table XIV
 conscription 62, 66-7, 69-72, Table VIII
 employment, increase of during
  WWII 10
 in occupation army in Namibia 182,
  193-4, 198-9, 202-4
  see also bantustan forces
 serve in WWI & II 8, 9-10
Air Force *see* South African Air
 Force [SAAF]
ANC *see* African National Congress
Angola 140, 144-59
 civilian suffering 77, 158
 destabilisation 141, 142, 143, 148-50,
  183-4
  see also SADF operations *below*
 independence, effect of 140, 147, 149
 liberation struggle 17, 20, 22, 144-7
 SA intervention 24-5
 SA 'security' agreement with 142
 SADF operations/occupation 131, 141,
  142, 144, 149-50, 176, 194; ['75–6]
  24-5, 139, 144-8; ['81] 150-2, 183; ['82]
  152-3; ['83] 153-5; ['84] 158;
  ['85] 159
 withdrawal 155-7, 158-9, 189, 190
 see also FNLA; MPLA; UNITA;
  Lusaka Untertaking
'Area Defence' 3, 5, 64, 119-21, 228-33,
 Table XVII
 see also Commandos
Area Force Units [AFUs] 132, 194, 197

armaments:
 chemical 109-10, 154
 conventional 89, 91, 93, 94, 100-1, 103,
  113-14, 117, Tables IX, X, XI, XIII
 nuclear 105-6
 acquisitions 12, 16, 89, 90-1, 93
 embargo 4, 16, 90, 93-4, 99, 105
  effect of 89, 103, 115, 196
  circumventions/violations 90-2, 93-7
 self-sufficiency 16, 89, 98-104
Armscor [Armaments Development and
 Production Corporation] 16, 65, 94,
 97-100, 104, 112, Table XIII
 board of directors 99-100
 exports 104-5
 subsidiaries 99, Table XIII
  African Explosives and Chemical
   Industries Plant 98
  Atlas Aircraft Corporation 98, 100
  Kentron 98
  Musgrave & Sons 98
army:
 'joint' operations 8, 14, 133, 223-5, 234,
  241-6, 247, 250, 251-6
 personnel strength Tables V, VI
 reorganisation 24
 structure and administration 111, 117-19
 weapons and equipment 101, Table IX

Bantustans/bantustan system 125, 180,
 181
 bantustan forces 70-1, 113, 125-31, 134,
  182, 199-200, 234-6, 251
  21 Battalion and 70, 71, 125, 237
  personnel strength Tables VI & VIII
  'regional' units 71, 130
 in Namibia: leaders, under SADF
  protection 186, 199
  'Special Police'/'Home Guards' 132,
   185, 198, 199-200
  northern, sealed off 192
  repression 234-5
  see also under individual names
Barnard, Lukas Daniel 39, 40
 quoted 109
Beaufre, Andre 28-9, 42
Belgium, and arms supplies 16, 91
Binga, Eric, contests call-up orders 203
Black Local Authorities 134
 'community police' 134
 councillors, under police
  protection 251
 elections to, boycott of 219
 resistance to 247
 Town council police 251
Bophutatswana bantustan:

of mercenaries 77, 78-80
End Conscription Campaign [ECC]
  75-6
  and deployment in townships 76, 244
extension of 62-4, 85, 119, 182, 194, 229
and manpower 83-4
in Namibia 19, 72-3, 132, 182, 193-4,
  198-204
resistance to 62, 73-6, 203, 240
in WWI & II 8, 9
conscription *see* Citizen Force;
  Commandos; National Servicemen
'constellation of states' 33, 34, 138-40
Council of Churches in Namibia;
  and Commission of Inquiry into
    security legislation 214
  condemns conscription 202, 204
Council for Scientific & Industrial
  Research [CSIR] 59, 96
counter-insurgency warfare 28-9, 113,
  116, 119, 220-1
  in bantustans 235
  in border areas 227-9
  SA Navy and 116-17
  SAP and 225
  urban 123, 241-55
  see also Koevoet
Crocker, Chester 155, 220
Cuba: military presence in Angola 147,
  184, 189

Defence Advisory Council 84
defence expenditure *see* military
  expenditure
Democratic Turnhalle Alliance [DTA]
  181, 184-5, 201
Department of Military Intelligence
  [DMI] *see* Military Intelligence,
  Department of
Department of National Security
  see DONS
destabilisation campaign 3, 39, 122-3,
  140-3, 168
  in Angola 144-59, 183-4
  in Botswana 169, 172, 175
  in Lesotho 37, 168, 172, 174-5
  in Mozambique 160-8, 171-2
  in Zambia 169, 173-4
  in Zimbabwe 169-71, 172, 174
  border incidents and airspace
    violations 173-5
  objectives 140
  raids and assassinations 171-3
  Regional Strategy 138-9, 219
  strategy 141-3

use of surrogate forces [other than
  UNITA and MNR] 142, 168-9
  see also UNITA; MNR
Development Boards 134
  police controlled by 251
DMI *see* Military Intelligence,
  Department of
DONS [Department of National
  Security] [*previously* BOSS *later*
  National Intelligence Service] 39
Dreyer, *Brigadier* Hans 124
du Toit, *Captain* Wynand 122, 159
Dutton, *Lt-General* J R 30-1, 70
  quoted 223, 225

Economy 26, 83, 85
  see also military expenditure
education system: police/aims 55
  see also schools
Edwards, Trevor 77, 150
electronics industry [military] 101-2
  British subsidaries 90
End Conscription Campaign [ECC]
  see under conscription
ESCOM [South African Electricity
  Supply Commission]:
  and nuclear industry 107
  security measures 233
ex-service organisations:
  resistance by 10
  and sanctions 54
  support for SADF 53

FAPLA *see under* MPLA
farmers:
  in border areas: absentee landlords
    226-7
  armed 197, 227-8
  in Commandos 227, 232
  intelligence gathering 197, 232
  SOS system [MARNET] 232-3
  in Namibia 197
  stock thefts 235-6
Federal Republic of Germany [FRG]: aid
  with nuclear industry 106-7, 108
firearms:
  increase in sales of 59-61
  per head of population 59
First, Ruth assassinated 163
FNLA 24, 124, 144-7, 148, 157
France:
  aid with nuclear industry 107, 108
  and arms supplies 16, 89, 91
Frelimo 17, 24, 144, 160
Front Line States grouping 140, 143, 166
  see also under individual countries

elections 181
Emergency legislation 182-3
emigration [White], resulting from 186
martial law 19-20, 183
SAP deployment 134-5, 179-80, 199, 201, 225, Table XV
phases of war 193-4
social and economic conditions, deterioration in 208-10, 215
withdrawal 215
SADF/SWATF 131-2, 186, 200-1, Table XV
  atrocities/torture 20, 190, 210-12
  'kill ratios' 178, 187, 191-2
  media reporting, control of 187
  military zones 198
  'Operational Area' 194-6
  operations 19-20, 185-9, 190-1, 194-6
  personnel strength 25, 178, 181, 183, 229
Namibian Bar Council 213, 214
National Key Points 83, 85-6
  private security bodies [Namibia] 197-8
National Intelligence Service [NIS] 39, 40
National Security Department see DONS
National Security doctrine 29-30, 223-5
National Security Management System 32, 35-8, 40
  expenditure 82
  Interdepartmental Committees [IDCs] 37
  Joint Management Centres 37-8
  Twelve Point Plan 33
National Service:
  increases in 13, 21, 63-4, 85
  overall pattern of 62, 63-4
National Servicemen 13, 113, 121
  aggression perpetrated by 61
  'area bound' system 232
  as back-up to Commandos 228, 230
  Civic Action tasks 57-8, 206-7, 237, 238, 239
  deployed: in Namibia 131, 132, 179, 182, 206-7, 208
    in townships 241, 244, 251
  disaffection among 45-6, 74
  personnel strength 16, Tables V, VI
  in Special Forces 121, 125
  units 117, 119
  voluntary 132, Table V
  wages and salaries 84
  see also conscientous objectors
Nationalist government 10-11
  conflict within 27
  'detente' 24
  international position 12, 18, 22, 219

and military, tension between 25-6
'nationalisation' process 11, 13, 111
overall strategic approach ['85] 220-1
policies: defence 13-14
  education 55-6
  search for alliances 11-12, 18, 20-1, 25, 93
NATO: SA participation in 11, 12, 21, 92
Naude commission recommendations 75
Navy see South African Navy [SAN]
NIS see National Intelligence Service
Nkadimeng, Vernon, assassinated 173
Nkomati Accord 142, 155, 165-8
North Atlantic Treaty Organisation see NATO
nuclear industry/weapons 17, 39, 105-9
  foreign collaboration 17, 105, 106-7, 108
  research 197-8
  sabotage attacks 217
  tests 105, 108
  uranium supplies 106, 107
Nzima, Petrus and Jabu, assassinated 172

Oil 87-9
  embargo 88-9
    effect of 53, 103
  see also Sasol plants
Ovambo bantustan:
  Civic Action programme 207-8
  defoliants used in 188
  elections 180
  Etango 208
  forced removals 190
  health service, SADF takeover 209-10
  leaders, under SADF protection 199
  military units 131, 199
  in 'Operational Area' 194
  sealed off 192
  school pupils, on strike 207
  war conditions 185

Pan-Africanist Congress [PAC] 14, 217
  banned 14, 15
Parachute ['parabat'] Battalions 121
Pathfinder Company, 77, 79, 123
Permanent Force 6, 9, 13, 15, 16, 21, 64, 79-80, 111, 113, 117, 121
  Coloured men in 68
  lingua franca 111
  personnel strength Tables V & VI
  in Special Forces 125, 132
  women in 65
Plessey 95, 104, 114, Table XIII
police [SAP] 43, 132-5

limited 219
independent African states press for 25
SAP *see* police
Sasol plants 88
  capacity 88
  sabotage attacks 85-6, 217
  strikes 246
Savimbi, Jonas 144, 147, 150, 153
schools:
  boycotts 243, 247, 249, 252
  cadet training schemes 55-7
  closures 209, 252
  SADF and: personnel as teachers 57,
    206-7, 237, 238, 239
    raids and occupations 252
  youth camps, students recruited for
    57-8, 239
  Youth Preparedness programmes 55
Schoon, Jeanette, assassinated 173
security:
  in Namibia 197-8
  of rural installations 233
  security industry 86-7
Security Branch [SB] [*previously* Special
  Branch] 16, 38, 39, 134, 222
Seiler, John, *quoted* 27, 220
Selous Scouts 78, 122, 124, 169, 210
Seychelles, attempted coup in 40, 79
Silvermine surveillance centre 91-2, 100,
  115, 233
Simonstown agreement ['55] 12, 90
  termination of 25, 115
Simonstown base 9, 115
South African Air Force [SAAF] 8-9, 10,
  14, 15, 112-15, 128
  command structures 113
  weapons and equipment 91, 100,
    112-113, Tables XI, XII
South African Council of Churches
  [SACC] 43
  and conscription 73
  delegation to Namibia, findings of 212
South African Indian Council [SAIC] 69
South African Navy [SAN] 9, 10, 115-17
  Marine units 116-17
  SAS Jalsena 68-9, 237
  strategic shift 115-16
  weapons/equipment 90, 100-1, 115,
    116, Table X
    and arms embargo, effect of 115
South African Police [SAP] *see* police
South Atlantic Treaty Organisation
  [SATO] 21
South West Africa Peoples Organisation
  see SWAPO
Southern African Catholic Bishops'

Conference 208, 245, 247
Southern African Development
  Co-ordination Conference [SADCC]
  140
Southern Cross Fund 52-3
Soweto uprisings ['76] 23, 25
  deaths 254
  effects of 56, 60, 139
Space Research Corporation [SRC] 94
Special Forces *see Reconnaissance
  Commandos*
SSC *see* State Security Council
State of Emergency:
  ['60] 14
  ['85-6] 135, 219, 223, 249-55
    Civic Action programme during
      240-1
    deaths 255
    detentions 255
    media restrictions 50-51, 250
    powers conferred by 249
    resistance to 240
    and stability of manpower 85
State Security Council [SSC] 27, 29-30,
  32, 35-7, 38, 40, 111, 250, Table I
Steele, Richard 74
Steenkamp, *Major General* Frans 39, 217,
  221
Steenkamp, *Captain* Willem 48
  quoted 236, 241
Steyn Commissions 49-50
support groups 52-5
  fundraising schemes 52-3
  'Ride Safe'/'Sleep Safe' system 53-4
'SWA Air Force' 197, Table XV
SWA Police [SWAP] 19, 124-5, 132, 183,
  198, 201, Table XV
  atrocities/torture 210-12
  joint operations 196
  personnel strength Table VI
  Koevoet 123-5, 131, 132, 190, 193, 196,
    200, 201, 210-12, 251, Table XV
  Municipal Police 198
  Railways Police 198
  Reserves 198
  Security Police 198, 201
  Special Constables 124, 192, 200
    Table XV
  Special Police 132, 185, 198, 200, 210
  Special Task Force 123
  SWA Specialists 125
SWA Police Counter-Insurgency Unit
  [COIN] *See* Koevoet
SWA Specialists [SWASpes] 125
SWA Territory Force [SWATF] 113, 131,
  132, 178, 183, 186, 193, 194, 199, 200-1,